Charles D. Harvey

Finding Morality in the Diaspora?

Beihefte zur Zeitschrift für die alttestamentliche Wissenschaft

Herausgegeben von
Otto Kaiser

Band 328

Walter de Gruyter · Berlin · New York

2003

Charles D. Harvey

Finding Morality in the Diaspora?

Moral Ambiguity and Transformed Morality
in the Books of Esther

W
DE
G

Walter de Gruyter · Berlin · New York
2003

♾ Printed on acid-free paper which falls within the guidelines of the ANSI
to ensure permanence and durability.

ISBN 3-11-017743-9

Bibliographic information published by Die Deutsche Bibliothek

Die Deutsche Bibliothek lists this publication in the Deutsche Nationalbibliografie; detailed
bibliographic data is available in the Internet at <http://dnb.ddb.de>.

Foreword

This project is a revised and updated version of my Ph.D. thesis of the same title (University of Edinburgh, 2000). Its appearance in the series "Beihefte zur Zeitschrift für die Alttestamentliche Wissenschaft" is indeed an honour and I am grateful to all those who have made this possible. I would like to thank Prof. Dr. Otto Kaiser, editor of the series BZAW, for showing interest in the project and recommending it for publication with Walter de Gruyter. The commissioning editor at de Gruyter, Dr. Albrecht Döhnert, deserves many thanks for his kind and generous assistance throughout the publication process. I have greatly valued the ongoing friendship and personal interest of Prof. A. Graeme Auld and Prof. Iain W. Provan throughout the life of this project. Their encouragement throughout has been steadfast and upbuilding. I would also like to express my appreciation to Dr. David J. Reimer, Dr. Timothy H. Lim, and Dr. Alison Salvesen for the time they invested in earlier stages of the project. Many others have ventured with me at different points throughout this process and have offered much in the way of friendship, advice, and encouragement. I wish to express my gratitude to Brian Aucker, Iain Duguid, Paul House, John Lewellen, Troy Miller, Jeffrey Privette, Ka Leung Wong, and my colleagues at Taylor University. These broad and various contributions have not gone unnoticed; they are much appreciated and have brought clarity to this project in many ways. The love and support of my family has been a consistent source of blessing all through my life in intangible and tangible ways. I thank you all for your care and prayers. I would like to highlight several who have been especially close to this work. Henry and Julia Harvey, my parents, have been unwavering in their support for me. In a wonderful way, this is what they do, and I am among the beneficiaries of their love and kindness. My three children, Hannah, Fiona, and Pavel, are ever generous with their affection and cause me often to (re)adjust my perspective. And most significantly, my heartfelt appreciation goes to Meribeth, my wife of almost ten years now. For more than half of that time, Esther has been in our midst. For your patience, good humour, care, and especially your love, I am deeply grateful. None is this could have happened without you.

C.D.H.
4 Lent 2003

Contents

Part I: Approximations & Anticipations

Part II: Elucidations & Evaluations

Abbreviations

Periodicals, Serials, and Reference Works

AB	Anchor Bible
ABD	D.N. Freedman (ed.), *Anchor Bible Dictionary*
ABR	*Australian Biblical Review*
AJSL	*American Journal of Semitic Languages and Literature*
ASTI	*Annual of the Swedish Theological Institute*
ATD	Das Alte Testament Deutsch Series
ATDA	Das Alte Testament Deutsch Apokryphen Series
AUSS	*Andrews University Seminary Studies*
BA	*The Biblical Archaeologist*
BAGD	Bauer, Arndt, Gingrich, Danker, *A Greek-English Lexicon of the New Testament and Other Early Christian Literature*, 2nd ed.
BBR	*Bulletin for Biblical Research*
BDB	*The Brown-Driver-Briggs Hebrew and English Lexicon*
BibInt	*Biblical Interpretation*
BibLeb	*Bibel und Leben*
BIOSCS	*Bulletin of the International Organization for Septuagint and Cognate Studies*
BJS	Brown Judaic Studies
BKAT	Biblischer Kommentar Altes Testament
BN	*Biblische Notizen*
BR	*Biblical Research*
BibRev	*Biblical Review*
BibSac	*Bibliotheca Sacra*
BS	*Biblische Studien*
BTB	*Biblical Theology Bulletin*
CBQ	*Catholic Biblical Quarterly*
CHALOT	W.L. Holladay, *A Concise Hebrew and Aramaic Lexicon of the OT.*
CJ	*Concordia Journal*
CJAS	Christianity and Judaism in Antiquity Series

CRINT	Compendia Rerum Iudaicarum ad Novum Testamentum
DCH	D.J.A. Clines (ed.), *The Dictionary of Classical Hebrew.*
DSB	The Daily Study Bible
DSD	*Dead Sea Discoveries*
EJT	*European Journal of Theology*
EncJud	*Encyclopaedia Judaica*
ER	*The Ecumenical Review*
ExpT	*Expository Times*
FCB	The Feminist Companion to the Bible
FOTL	The Forms of Old Testament Literature
GKC	E. Kautzsch (trans. A.E. Cowley), *Gesenius' Hebrew Grammar.*
HAR	*Hebrew Annual Review*
HAT	Handbuch zum Alten Testament
HDR	Harvard Dissertations in Religion
HS	*Hebrew Studies*
HSCPRT	Heythrop Studies in Contemporary Philosophy, Religion and Theology
HSM	Harvard Semitic Monographs
HTR	*Harvard Theological Review*
HUCA	*Hebrew Union College Annual*
ICC	International Critical Commentary
ITC	International Theological Commentary
JANES	*Journal of the Ancient Near Eastern Society*
JBL	*Journal of Biblical Literature*
JBQ	*Jewish Bible Quarterly*
JBS	Jerusalem Biblical Studies
JES	*Journal of Ecumenical Studies*
JETS	*Journal of the Evangelical Theological Society*
JNES	*Journal of Near Eastern Studies*
JQR	*The Jewish Quarterly Review*
JRAS	*Journal of the Royal Asiatic Society of Great Britain and Ireland*
JRS	*Journal of Religious Studies*
JSOT	*Journal for the Study of the Old Testament*
JSOTSup	Journal for the Study of the Old Testament Supplement Series
JSNTSup	Journal for the Study of the New Testament Supplement Series
JSPSup	Journal for the Study of the Pseudepigrapha Supplement Series
JSS	*Journal of Semitic Studies*
JTS	*Journal of Theological Studies*

KAT	Kommentar zum Alten Testament
LS	Liddell and Scott, *An Intermediate Greek-English Lexicon.*
MQ	*Mankind Quarterly*
NCBC	The New Century Biblical Commentary
NEB	Die Neue Echter Bibel
NIBC	New International Biblical Commentary
NIVAC	New International Version Application Commentary
OTG	Old Testament Guides
OTL	Old Testament Library
OTM	Old Testament Message
OTS	Old Testament Studies
PAAJR	*Proceedings of the American Academy for Jewish Research*
PTR	*Princeton Theological Review*
RB	*Revue Biblique*
ResQ	*Restoration Quarterly*
RHA	*Revue Hittite et Asianique*
RQ	*Revue de Qumran*
RTR	*The Reformed Theological Review*
SBL	Society of Biblical Literature
SBLDS	Society of Biblical Literature Dissertation Series
SBLMS	Society of Biblical Literature Monograph Series
SBLSCSS	Society of Biblical Literature Septuagint and Cognate Studies Series
SBLSS	Society of Biblical Literature Semeia Series
SBM	Stuttgarter Biblische Monographien
SBT	Studies in Biblical Theology
SEÅ	*Svensk Exegetisk Årsbok*
SFSHJ	South Florida Studies in the History of Judaism
SJT	*Southwestern Journal of Theology*
SOTSMS	Society of Old Testament Studies Monograph Series
SR	*Studies in Religion/Sciences religieuses*
TB	*Tyndale Bulletin*
TDOT	*Theological Dictionary of the Old Testament*
TEH	Theologische Existenz Heute
ThEv	*Theologia Evangelica*
TOTC	Tyndale Old Testament Commentaries
TWOT	R. Harris, *et. al.* (eds), *Theological Wordbook of the OT.*
TZ	*Theologische Zeitschrift*
USQR	*Union Seminary Quarterly Review*
VT	*Vetus Testamentum*

WBC   Word Biblical Commentary
WUNT   Wissenschaftliche Untersuchungen zum Neuen Testament
WZKM   *Wiener Zeitschrift für die Kunde des Morgenlandes*
ZAW   *Zeitschrift für die Alttestamentliche Wissenschaft*
ZB   Zürcher Bibelkommentare

Texts and Versions

AT   Alpha-Text
BHS   Biblia Hebraica Stuttgartensia, 4th ed.
CB   The Century Bible
LXX   Septuagint
MT   Masoretic Text
OT   Old Testament

Miscellaneous

ed.   editor
eds   editors
LBH   Late Biblical Hebrew
MH   Mishnaic Hebrew
pl   plural
SBH   Standard Biblical Hebrew
sg.   singular

Part I
Approximations & Anticipations

1 Introduction

1.0 Context

Perhaps mirroring the troubles faced by Jews in the perilous Diaspora of the Esther story and beyond, the way travelled by the book of Esther has been fraught with difficulties and misunderstandings. As a work of literature, it has always been pleasing; its moral content, however, has often been suspect.

> Virtually from the time of its composition, the book of Esther has posed many problems for its readers, who have been disturbed by its place in the canon and consequently by its presumed sacred character. *In modern times, readers have been troubled primarily, though not exclusively, by moral issues.*[1]

Actually, to say that moral issues in the book have been troubling to readers is to put it mildly in some cases. Consider the verdict of Lewis B. Paton concerning the moral teaching of the book: "Morally Est. falls *far below* the general level of the OT., and even the Apocrypha."[2] Bernhard W. Anderson begins an article which seriously questions the place of Esther in Christian Scripture in the following manner: "Like Saul among the prophets, the Book of Esther seems strangely out of place in the Christian Bible."[3] It should be said that perceived moral deficiencies greatly contribute to his displeasure and ultimate discontentment with the canonical inclusion of the book. In broadening the scope of these less than positive evaluations, Robert H. Pfeiffer makes the following assertion unreservedly: "From the moral point of view the book has little to commend it to civilized persons enjoying the benefits of peace and freedom, whatever their race."[4]

Why have so many readers been troubled, especially more recently, by moral issues in the book of Esther? What has prompted this discomfort? Is

---

1   R. Gordis, "Religion, Wisdom and History in the Book of Esther: A New Solution to an Ancient Crux," *JBL* 100 (1981), 359 (*emphasis added*).
2   L.B. Paton, *The Book of Esther* (ICC; Edinburgh: T & T Clark, 1908), 96 (*emphasis added*).
3   B.W. Anderson, "The Place of the Book of Esther in the Christian Bible," *JR* 30 (1950), 32.
4   R.H. Pfeiffer, *Introduction to the Old Testament* (London: A & C Black, 1952), 747.

this anxiety justified? Or is a measure of moral uneasiness to be expected as one engages the Esther story?

Approaching the issue from a slight different angle: Has the reception always been thus? Have readers found difficulties with moral issues in the book of Esther from the very beginning? If so, how did early readers approach and/or handle the ethical problems that they perceived?

One way to deal with such problematic issues would be by *avoidance*. Readers might avoid the book altogether on account of its questionable and perhaps contentious moral content. In other words, if the moral content of a narrative is deemed unacceptable by a certain community, it might not be included as acceptable reading material in that community. It is possible that such concerns played a part in the reason(s) why the book of Esther has not been found at Qumran.[5] Strictly speaking, Esther is the only book of the Hebrew Bible that has not been found among the fragments and scrolls of the Qumran caves.[6] This is no secret, and it is most likely not an accident that the book was not included in the Qumran collection, for the story appears to have been well-known at the time.[7] Yet mystery persists concerning its lack of inclusion. Was it passed over for ideological reasons? Could it have been the case because of calendrical issues? Was is not accepted because Purim was not accepted?[8] What role did theological concerns play, if any? Did the moral complexion of the story ruin its chances of inclusion? To be sure, many of these matters are interrelated, and it might have been that a combination of factors (some of these and/or others not suggested here) resulted in Esther's lack of inclusion.[9]

Another, and it should be said, more common, way of handling troublesome moral issues in the story would be *transformation*. That is, as moral difficulties, ambiguities, or gaps are perceived in a given text, and when

---

5   This possibility is suggested, albeit in a general way, by A. LaCocque, *The Feminine Unconventional: Four Subversive Figures in Israel's Tradition* (Minneapolis: Fortress Press, 1990), 68.

6   This is true only if one assumes that the book of Nehemiah was already joined to the book of Ezra at that time, for no fragment of Nehemiah has been found either (S. Talmon, "Was the Book of Esther Known at Qumran?," *DSD* 2 (1995), 249 n. 2).

7   Talmon, "Was the Book of Esther Known at Qumran?," 266. See also S. White Crawford, "Has *Esther* Been Found at Qumran? *4Qproto-Esther* and the *Esther* Corpus," *RQ* 17 (1996).

8   Both the calendrical and Purim issues are set out in a helpful way in Adele Berlin's recent commentary (*Esther* (The JPS Bible Commentary; Philadelphia: The Jewish Publication Society, 2001), xliv-xlv).

9   See the concise discussion of R. Beckwith concerning the issue at hand ("Formation of the Hebrew Bible," in M.J. Mulder (ed.), *Mikra: Text, Translation, Reading and Interpretation of the Hebrew Bible in Ancient Judaism and Early Christianity* (CRINT 2.1; Assen/Philadelphia: Van Gorcum/Fortress Press, 1988), 76f.

confusion or discomfort arises on account of this, readers (reading communities) might seek to transform the material so as to ease, if not eradicate altogether, any perceived moral tension. This interpretative transformation might be achieved *via* clarification or definition, expansion or amplification, or even alteration.[10] Perhaps this is the manner in which the moral content found in earlier stories of Esther has been handled by the two primary Greek versions of the book.

1.1 Delimitation of Texts

In what follows, we shall investigate the moral content found within three distinct versions of the Esther story – the Hebrew Masoretic Text (MT); the Greek text found in the Septuagint (LXX); and the Greek Alpha-Text (AT). These are the versions which have been considered "primary"[11] in recent Esther studies, and we have chosen to limit the scope of our present inquiry to these three. To be sure, we do not wish to imply by our delimitation that subsequent translations and paraphrases of the Esther story such as those found in the Peshitta, the Old Latin (OL), the Vulgate, Josephus,[12] Targum Rishon and Targum Sheni[13] are unimportant as texts or ones that could not contribute to serious endeavours of moral inquiry; they most certainly have own their places in any such investigation and scrutiny. However, given the scope of this work, and given the depth in which we seek to delve into the three primary versions of the Esther story, we shall not formally engage the later translations and paraphrases mentioned above.

---

10 See the general discussion of G. Vermes in his essay "Bible and Midrash: Early Old Testament Exegesis," in *The Cambridge History of the Bible* (vol. 1 – From the Beginnings to Jerome; Cambridge: Cambridge University Press, 1970), 203f.

11 L. Day, *Three Faces of a Queen* (JSOTSup 186; Sheffield: Sheffield Academic Press, 1995), 26. Indeed, the three versions are commonly being grouped and addressed together in recent works. E.g., see the section entitled "The Three Esthers" in the recent commentary of T.K. Beal (*Esther,* in T. Linafelt and *idem, Ruth and Esther* (Berit Olam; Collegeville, MN: The Liturgical Press, 1999), xvii-xix.

12 Josephus' paraphrase of the Esther story is found in his *Jewish Antiquities* 11.184-296.

13 Translations of these two Targums (complete with apparatus and notes) can be found in B. Grossfeld, *The Two Targums of Esther* (The Aramaic Bible 18; Edinburgh: T & T Clark, 1991).

1.2 A Brief Description of the Esther Texts to be Studied[14]

1.2.1 The Hebrew Masoretic Text (MT)

This Hebrew witness to the Esther story has survived well-preserved in the
Codex Leningradensis.[15] This is fortunate, according to Frederic W. Bush,
because of the limited nature of the evidence for the text of the book of
Esther among the ancient (non-Hebrew) versions.[16] However, despite this
early scarcity of Esther texts, later Hebrew manuscripts of the book "are more
numerous than of any other portion of the Old Testament."[17] This is due, at
least in part, to the immense popularity of the deliverance story and its jovial
festival, Purim, among Jews. To be sure, the book of Esther has been held in
high esteem by many.[18] The most famous statement concerning the renown
of the book is the one by Simeon ben Lakish (c. 300 C.E.) who related that
although all other Scriptures should pass away at the coming of the Messiah,
the Law and the scroll of Esther would endure.[19]

Due to linguistic and other internal evidence, many scholars date the composition of the Hebrew book within the late Persian period or the early Hellenistic period (4th-3rd c. B.C.E.).[20] Yet others prefer a later date and see the

---

14 For a more expansive presentation of the Esther texts, see the textual study of K. De
Troyer, *The End of the Alpha Text of Esther: Translation and Narrative Technique in
MT 8:1-17, LXX 8:1-17, and AT 7:14-41* (trans. B. Doyle; revised and updated;
SBLSCSS 48; Atlanta: SBL, 2000), 2-15.
15 For more information see W. Harrelson, "Textual and Translation Problems in the Book
of Esther," *Perspectives in Religious Studies* 17 (1990), 197. For even more depth into
the subject, see Paton (*The Book of Esther*, 5-10).
16 F.W. Bush, *Ruth, Esther* (WBC 9; Dallas: Word Books, 1996), 278.
17 Paton, *The Book of Esther*, 5.
18 On the great popularity of the Scroll of Esther, see R.D. Aus, *Barabbas and Esther and
Other Studies in the Judaic Illumination of Earliest Christianity* (SFSHJ 54; Atlanta:
Scholars Press, 1992), 4-5.
19 Cited in E. J. Bickerman, *Four Strange Books of the Bible: Jonah, Daniel, Koheleth,
Esther* (NY: Schocken, 1967), 211.
20 Many commentators believe that the events and outlook of the book suggest a date in the
Persian period as opposed to a Maccabean, or even later date. T.K. Beal proffers a date
in the fifth century B.C.E. (*The Book of Hiding: Gender, Ethnicity, Annihilation, and
Esther* (London: Routledge, 1997), 112). For a recent discussion which explores and favours an earlier date, see Bush (*Ruth, Esther*, 295-6). Coupled with that, though, is the
linguistic evidence recently submitted by R.L. Bergey that supports the above scope. See
his in-depth study entitled "The Book of Esther – Its Place in the Linguistic Milieu of
Post-exilic Biblical Hebrew Prose: A Study in Late Biblical Hebrew" (Ph.D. Diss.;
Dropsie College, 1983); and subsequent articles, "Late Linguistic Features in Esther,"
JQR 75 (1984), 66-78; and "Post-exilic Hebrew Linguistic Developments in Esther: A
Diachronic Approach," *JETS* 31 (1988), 161-68. For a slightly different view on the
LBH of Esther, see R. Polzin, *Late Biblical Hebrew: Toward an Historical Typology of
Biblical Hebrew Prose* (HSM 12; Missoula, MT: Scholars Press, 1976), in which he

book having been occasioned by an analogous historical situation of difficulty that faced the Jewish people.[21] The dating of the Hebrew book of Esther
is far from a simple matter in light of the silence that surrounds it between the
reign of Xerxes I (486-465 B.C.E.) and the LXX translation of the book in the
second or first century B.C.E. If this particular dating of the LXX is not followed, one must wait until the first century C.E. for the narrative's first official mentioning in the paraphrase of Josephus (ca. 90 C.E). The Hebrew story
of Esther has been placed historically within the מגלות – "Megilloth" –
scrolls read in association with certain Jewish festivals.[22] Yet, often times,
Hebrew Esther is simply referred to as המגלה – "the Scroll" – i.e., the scroll
par excellence.[23]

1.2.2 The Greek text found in the Septuagint (LXX)[24]

The longest form of the Esther story that we shall study is the one located in
the Septuagint. By either a comparative word-for-word count[25] or a count of
syntactic units,[26] the LXX contains far more material than is found in either
the MT or the Greek Alpha-Text. The canonical portions[27] of this text have
been described as reading in a manner which is "somewhat free and para-

---

concludes that even though the book of Esther contains "deliberate archaisms" so as to
appear classical, the elements of LBH are still quite evident.

21 E.g., during the time of the Maccabean revolt and the persecutions of Antiochus Epi-
phanes (see Pfeiffer, *Introduction,* 740-42; more recently in favour of a later date – in the
context of a discussion of the Jewish novel in the ancient world – see L.M. Wills, *The
Jewish Novel in the Ancient World* (Ithaca: Cornell University Press, 1995), 98f.). A
good summary of the range of proposed dates for the book can be seen in E.M. Yamauchi, *Persia and the Bible* (Grand Rapids: Baker Book House, 1990), 226-28; and C.A.
Moore, *Esther* (AB 7B; Garden City, NY: Doubleday & Co., Inc, 1971), lvii-lx.

22 Paton claims that this arrangement first occurred in the Middle Ages (*The Book of
Esther,* 2). See further Editorial Staff, "Scrolls, The Five," *EncJud* (Jerusalem: Keter,
1971), 14:1058.

23 Paton, *The Book of Esther,* 119; M.V. Fox, *Character and Ideology in the Book of
Esther* (Columbia: University of South Carolina Press, 1991), 2 n. 5.

24 Sometimes designated by the Greek numeral indicator for 70 – 'o'' (see R. Hanhart
(ed.), *Esther* (Septuaginta. Vetus Testamentum Graecum Auctoritate Academiae Scientiarum Gottingensis editum, VIII, 3; Göttingen: Vandenhoeck & Ruprecht, 1983²); C.V.
Dorothy, *The Books of Esther: Structure, Genre and Textual Integrity* (JSOTSup 187;
Sheffield: Sheffield Academic Press, 1997), 27-28).

25 Dorothy, *The Books of Esther,* 13-16. Dorothy's counts find 3,044 words in the MT,
4,761 words in the AT (including its so-called Additions), and 5,837 words in the LXX
(including its so-called Additions).

26 Concerning this approach, see K.H. Jobes, *The Alpha-Text of Esther: Its Character and
Relationship to the Masoretic Text* (SBLDS 153; Atlanta: Scholars Press, 1996), 147-48.

27 For the purposes of clarity, we are using the term 'canonical portions' to refer to those
portions of text which correspond to what is found in the MT version.

phrastic"[28] – even "idiomatic"[29] – yet it is most likely the case that these portions are essentially a translation of the MT.[30]

In comparison with the MT, this gap is even more pronounced when additional Greek Esther material is taken into account (six further sections of text
commonly labelled A-F).[31] There is ongoing scholarly debate concerning
whether these texts were first attached to the LXX or the AT.[32] At the very
least, what is clear is that they are not carbon copies of one another. Yet historically in the Western church, these so-called 'Additions' have been sepa-
rated from the canonical portions, following their placement at the end of the
book by Jerome in his Latin [now Vulgate] translation (4th c. C.E.),[33] and further isolated in the Apocrypha since the time of the Protestant Reformation.[34]
More recently, however, in the quest for coherent reading and holistic study,
the additional material has been read along with the canonical text in the

---

28 D.J.A. Clines, *The Esther Scroll: The Story of the Story* (JSOTSup 30; Sheffield: JSOT
   Press, 1984), 69. See also the relevant comments of E. Tov concerning LXX translation
   technique and exegesis ("The Septuagint," in M.J. Mulder (ed.), *Mikra: Text, Translation, Reading and Interpretation of the Hebrew Bible in Ancient Judaism and Early
   Christianity* (CRINT 2.1; Assen/Philadelphia: Van Gorcum/Fortress Press, 1988), 173).
29 Bickerman, *Four Strange Books of the Bible,* 218. Bickerman states that the LXX "does
   not read like a translation" (218).
30 Clines, *The Esther Scroll,* 69. This is current consensus among Esther scholars and is
   against the contention of C.C. Torrey who held that "the Greek Esther is a translation,
   but it was not made from any Hebrew text." Torrey's position is that the two Greek versions were from Aramaic originals ("The Older Book of Esther," *HTR* 37 (1944), 2, 5).
31 It is important to note that the LXX also contains what might be termed minor additions
   within its translation/interpretation of its source text. For the moment, though, we are focusing on the six major so-called Additions, which greatly expand the story in the LXX.
32 C.A. Moore states that "it is probable that the AT borrowed all of its Additions from the
   LXX rather than the reverse" (*Daniel, Esther, and Jeremiah: The Additions* (AB 44;
   Garden City, NY: Doubleday & Co., Inc, 1977), 165). Clines takes a similar position
   (*The Esther Scroll,* 140), as does M.V. Fox (*The Redaction of the Books of Esther: On
   Reading Composite Texts* (SBLMS 40; Atlanta: Scholars Press, 1991), 9,16) and I. Kott-
   sieper (*Zusätze zu Ester* in O.H. Steck, R.G. Kratz and I. Kottsieper, *Das Buch Baruch,
   Der Brief des Jeremia, Zusätze zu Ester und Daniel* (ATDA 5; Göttingen: Vandenhoeck
   & Ruprecht, 1998), 121-28). Conversely, Jobes suggests that there is "mounting evi-
   dence that the AT preserves the older form of additions A, B, C, E and F" (*The Alpha-
   Text of Esther,* 193,232). On this latter view, cf. De Troyer, *The End of the Alpha Text of
   Esther,* 74-75; 351-93 (focusing primarily on Add E, but including an introductory sec-
   tion reviewing the history of research into the Adds (351-63)).
33 See the comments concerning Jerome's treatment of this additional material in G.W.E.
   Nickelsburg, "The Bible Rewritten and Expanded," in M.E. Stone (ed.), *Jewish Writings
   of the Second Temple Period* (CRINT 2.2; Assen/Philadelphia: Van Gorcum/Fortress
   Press, 1984), 135. Clines notes that the contents of the Additions were transported from
   their "logical places" in the Greek Esther story to the end of the book when Jerome made
   his Latin version. Jerome made this decision because the Additions had no counterpart in
   the Hebrew book (*The Esther Scroll,* 69).
34 G.M. Tucker, "Esther, The Book of," in B.M. Metzger and M.D. Coogan (eds), *The
   Oxford Companion to the Bible* (NY: Oxford University Press, 1993), 200.

Greek versions.[35] There has even been a move to scrap the label 'Addition' altogether in light of the reality that these Greek texts have served many Jewish and Christian communities as whole narratives.[36] Care is now being given to matters of natural and original placement in the quest for fuller and truer understanding.[37] It must be admitted, nevertheless, that neither Greek version (LXX or AT), in the form we now possess, reads as if these additional sections have been "systematically integrated."[38]

Scholarly consensus holds that the colophon[39] of the book (F.11) dates the original production of the version around the second or first century B.C.E.[40] As the majority Greek text, the LXX survives in thirty-six manuscripts. The oldest testimony to the LXX is found in the second/third century C.E. It is here, in the text of the Chester Beatty papyrus no. 967, that we find the most ancient preservation of what can be called an "extensive fragment" of the Esther Scroll.[41] Not too much later, though, we can find the oldest complete

---

35 This is the way in which the story has been and continues to be read in Eastern Orthodox and Roman Catholic tradition (see Tov, "The Septuagint," 163). See also the treatments of the additions in reference to the canonical text in Moore, *Daniel, Esther and Jeremiah: The Additions;* J.D. Levenson, *Esther* (OTL; SCM Press, Ltd., 1997); NEB; NRSV.

36 Concerning the influence of the LXX among Hellenistic Jews and the Christian church in the East, see H.B. Swete, *An Introduction to the Old Testament in Greek* (Cambridge: Cambridge University Press, 1900), 28. For a broader discussion, see Dorothy, *The Books of Esther,* 16. This matter will be addressed further below (§ 1.4.1).

37 This would apply to the AT as well (see E. Tov, "The "Lucianic" Text of the Canonical and the Apocryphal Sections of Esther: A Rewritten Biblical Book," *Textus* 10 (1982), 10).

38 Clines, *The Esther Scroll,* 105-106.

39 This colophon (i.e. a tailprint in a book giving information about that book), according to Moore is the most important verse in the LXX of Esther. He thinks that it provides us with the date and place of the translation as well as the name and antecedents of the translator. For more details, see his article, "On the Origins of the LXX Additions to the Book of Esther," *JBL* 92 (1973), 382. Also see E.J. Bickerman, "The Colophon of the Greek Book of Esther," *JBL* 63 (1944), 339-62; and B. Jacob, "Das Buch Ester bei den LXX," *ZAW* 10 (1890), 278-79.

40 Recently, Jobes has affirmed either 114 or 78 B.C.E. as possible dates for the arrival of the "letter of Phrourai" [ἐπιστολὴν τῶν Φρουραι] in Egypt (*The Alpha-Text of Esther,* 226). For the foundation, further support and explanation of these dates see H.B. Swete (*An Introduction to the Old Testament in Greek,* 25), R.K. Harrison (*Introduction to the Old Testament* (Grand Rapids: Eerdmans, 1969), 1101-1102) and Moore (*Esther,* 112). Levenson, however, is a bit sceptical concerning a firm date for the colophon, and thus, the *terminus ad quem* for this early version of the Esther story. Levenson sees problems concerning the identification of both the particular Ptolemy and Cleopatra mentioned, and to which form of the Greek Esther the ἐπιστολὴν τῶν Φρουραι was originally appended (*Esther,* 136). Even so, it is still most likely this Greek version of the Esther story was in circulation before the turn of the era.

41 For proposed evidence that suggests that the story of Esther and Mordecai was known at the time that most of the Dead Sea Scrolls were penned, see J. Finkel, "The Author of the Genesis Apocryphon Knew the Book of Esther," in Y. Yadin and C. Rabin (eds), *Es-*

text of the LXX in the great uncials of the fourth century C.E.[42] It is thought
that most Jews read the LXX version of the Esther story in the first five centuries C.E.[43] The influence of this Greek version of the book of Esther has
indeed been broad.

1.2.3 The Greek Alpha-Text (AT)[44]

This cannot be said, however, with reference to the Greek Alpha-Text. Its
witness can only be found in four medieval manuscripts.[45] Yet the first public
knowledge of the AT came as a result of the publication of the two distinct
Greek versions (LXX and AT) by J. Usher in 1655.[46] Despite this, little significant attention was paid to this rare Greek text until P. de Lagarde published a critical edition of the two texts in 1883.[47] This text was then printed
after the LXX version in the Brooke-McLean Cambridge Septuagint with the
title "ESQHR A."[48] Following this designation, scholars have conveniently
utilised the label 'Alpha-Text' for this distinctive Greek version of the Esther
story.

It was also at this point that de Lagarde pushed forward the view that the
AT was a Lucianic recension of the LXX – a view that has been commonly
presumed in the study and discussion of the text.[49] Yet this notion has become much less popular as a result of the 1965 doctoral thesis of Cary A.

---

says on the Dead Sea Scrolls in Memory of E.L. Sukenik (Jerusalem: Hekhal Ha-Sefer,
1962), 163-82 (Hebrew); J.T. Milik, "Les Modèles araméens du livre d'Esther dans la
grotte 4 de Qumran," *RevQ* 15 (1992), 321-99 + pls. I-VII; and esp., S. Talmon, "Was
the Book of Esther Known at Qumran?," 249-67.

42 Jobes, *The Alpha-Text of Esther*, 2.
43 T.C.G. Thornton, "The Crucifixion of Haman and the Scandal of the Cross," *JTS* 37
(1986), 420.
44 The AT is sometimes designated 'L' (e.g., Hanhart, *Esther*; see Dorothy, *The Books of
Esther*, 27-28).
45 Jobes, *The Alpha-Text of Esther*, 2, Appendix 2. The four mss. are as follows: 1) ms. 19
– Chigi R. vi. 38, 12th c., Vatican Library, Rome; 2) ms. 93 – Royal I. D. 2, 13th c.,
British Library, London; 3) ms. 108, Vat. Gr. 330, 13th c., Vatican Library, Rome; 4)
ms. 319 – Vatop. 600, 1021 AD, Mt. Athos, Greece.
46 J. Usher, *De Graeca Septuaginta interpretum versione syntagma: cum libri Estherae
editione Origenica, et vetere Graeca altera, ex Arundelliana bibliotheca nunc primum in
lucem producta* (London: J. Crook, 1655). Fox notes that the AT manuscript printed by
Usher here was Ms 93 (*Redaction*, 10).
47 P. de Lagarde, *Librorum Veteris Testamenti Canonicorum Pars Prior Graece* (Göttingen: Arnold Hoyer, 1883).
48 Fox, *Redaction*, 10.
49 In reference to the Lucianic recension in general, see the helpful summary by Swete, *An
Introduction to the Old Testament in Greek*, 80-86.

Moore[50] and the subsequent scholarly attention given to the study of the AT.[51] One recent Esther scholar has even remarked: "Once freed from the name of Lucian, the L text could derive from an earlier, perhaps a much earlier, period."[52] According to many developmental histories of the book of Esther, this is likely the case.[53] Indeed, a recent study of the AT assigns its origins to the early Hellenistic period.[54] It should be noted, however, that evidence between its early development and the time of its oldest surviving eleventh century manuscript is scant.[55]

Scholarly opinion varies regarding the proposed development of AT Esther as questions continue to remain concerning how it fits into the textual history of the Esther story.[56] At the risk of oversimplification, it could be generalised that two scholarly opinions exist on the question: (1) those who posit that the core of the AT (i.e., without Additions, and at least up to 8.17) is a translation of a Semitic *Vorlage* different from the MT (to varying degrees); (2) those who hold that the AT is not an independent translation of a Semitic *Vorlage*, but a recension or revision of the LXX.

Following the initial impressions of Charles C. Torrey[57] and the more penetrating doctoral dissertation of Cary A. Moore,[58] many scholars were beginning to be persuaded by the possibility that AT represents a Greek translation of Esther story from a Semitic *Vorlage* different from the MT. This thesis then takes more extensive shape in the 1984 monograph of David J.A. Clines, *The Esther Scroll: The Story of the Story*. There, and in the midst of a presentation of the literary-redactional history of the Esther story as a whole, Clines posits that the "essential core" of the AT (i.e., proto-AT – up to

---

50 C.A. Moore, "The Greek Text of Esther," (Ph.D. Diss.; Johns Hopkins University, 1965).

51 Against designating the AT Lucianic, see Hanhart, *Esther*, 92f.

52 Dorothy, *The Books of Esther*, 19.

53 Concerning the place of the AT as early in the developmental history of the Esther story, see especially the work of Clines, *The Esther Scroll*; Fox, *Redaction*; Dorothy, *The Books of Esther*; and Jobes, *The Alpha-Text of Esther*.

54 Jobes, *The Alpha-Text of Esther*, 232.

55 There is little to be said concerning the circulation of the AT between the 3rd and 11th centuries C.E. due to the fact that 'neither Christian nor Jewish literature mentions or quotes the AT of Esther' (Jobes, *The Alpha-Text of Esther*, 233). Neither the NT, nor the Targums or Talmud, nor the Church Fathers preserve any clear quote of or reference to the AT. Because of this, many question marks are present in any theory of its origins and development (233).

56 For a more in-depth presentation and critical evaluation of the textual history and development of the AT, see De Troyer, *The End of the Alpha Text of Esther*, 25-70.

57 Torrey, "The Older Book of Esther."

58 Moore, "The Greek Text of Esther." See also his subsequent article of interest on this subject: "A Greek Witness to a Different Text of Esther," *ZAW* 79 (1967), 351-58.

AT 7.17,[59] and without the Additions) is indeed a translation of a Semitic original substantially different from, but a direct ancestor of, the MT.[60] Karen H. Jobes encapsulates Clines' position concerning the AT thus: "For Clines, the AT provides a snapshot of an earlier literary stage of the MT and thus provides direct evidence for the redactional history of the MT."[61] This line of thought concerning the AT is confirmed, altered somewhat and taken forward by the work of Michael V. Fox. In his 1991 monograph, *The Redaction of the Books of Esther*,[62] Fox agrees with Clines that the proto-AT (i.e., without the Additions, but whose ending is found in 7.18-21, 33-38)[63] descends from a Semitic *Vorlage* different from the MT, but that it is not a *source* of the MT but rather a *collateral version* of the Esther story.[64] In his view, these two texts – AT and MT – have in common a hypothetical proto-Esther source, but develop independently[65] – a view similar to the one earlier (though independently) proposed by Charles V. Dorothy in 1989.[66] This brings us to the most recent proponent of this first view concerning the development of the AT of Esther, K.H. Jobes. With the publication of her doctoral thesis, *The Alpha-Text of Esther: Its Character and Relationship to the Masoretic Text*, scholarship on the AT has been taken forward once again. Jobes contends that the AT (excluding its six major Additions) is a translation of a Hebrew *Vorlage* "quite similar" to the extant MT in both "content and extent" – indeed, it is its direct ancestor. This first Greek translation was "almost certainly" made

---

59 8.17 in Clines' numeration.

60 Clines, *The Esther Scroll*, 71-92.

61 Jobes, *The Alpha-Text of Esther*, 219.

62 See also the more condensed version of his thesis: "The Alpha Text of the Greek Esther," *Textus* 15 (1990), 27-54.

63 viii.18-21, 33-38 in Fox's numeration. The reference system of Fox follows the Brooke-McLean edition and is explained on page seven of *Redaction*.

64 Fox, *Redaction*, 96.

65 See Fox's diagram "The History of the Esther Texts" (*Redaction*, 9). As for the development of the AT, Fox describes it in the following way: "The AT arose in two distinct stages: first the original composition of the proto-AT, unrelated to the LXX, and second a redaction that drew upon the LXX as its source or donor text, working some of its material into the proto-AT, the receptor text" (34).

66 C.V. Dorothy, "The Books of Esther: Structure, Genre and Textual Integrity," (Ph.D. Diss., Claremont Graduate School, 1989). A revised version of this work has been posthumously published in the JSOTSup under the same title in 1997. The heuristic graphic on page 332 shows Dorothy's proposed development of the books of Esther. Similar to the suggestion of Fox, the AT of Dorothy has at its source a hypothetical Semitic *Uresther*, from which the Hebrew book also developed – although independently. But in slight distinction from Fox, Dorothy suggests that the proto-AT (which he calls 'proto-L') ended at 7.41 or 7.52 and did not include any sections that were not in the MT. (Dorothy, *The Books of Esther*, 348).

prior to the MT at an "earlier literary stage."[67] Thus, and necessary to their respective hypotheses, the proponents of this first view suggest that the origins of the AT are early in the textual development of the book of Esther.

Advocates of the second view see matters differently, and concentrate (for the most part) on later stages of development. They propose that the LXX is the (primary) source of the AT version of the story, *not* a hypothetical or reconstructed Semitic *Vorlage*. But within this view, two distinctive variations on the overall position exist. The first of these can be found in the 1982 *Textus* article written by Emanuel Tov.[68] In short, Tov holds that the AT (which he calls "L") is a recension of the LXX that corrects it back towards a Hebrew (or Aramaic) "midrash-type rewriting" of a the biblical Esther story – a rewriting that had previously embellished, omitted and revised the story freely and often extensively.[69] The other variation of this second overall view posits no such hypothetical Hebrew or Aramaic source – midrash-type or otherwise – being involved at all. It suggests that the AT retells, revises or reworks the LXX story. In 1966 Robert Hanhart put forth the proposal that the AT (which he calls the '*L*-Text') is not a *Rezension* of the LXX [i.e., towards some Hebrew text], but rather a re-shaping (*Neugestaltung*) of the Greek based in strong measure upon the LXX.[70] Hanhart's hypothesis is supported and furthered in the 1997 work of Kristin De Troyer – *Het einde van de Alpha-tekst van Ester*.[71] Her view sees the AT as "some kind of revision from the LXX"[72] that has been adapted with a particular historical context in mind – i.e., the AT is a "new vision" of the LXX.[73] André LaCocque holds a similar view in which the translator/author, writing in Greek, altered the text

---

67 For a fuller account of Jobes's view, see *The Alpha-Text of Esther*, esp. 219-33. For a condensed presentation of her thesis, see "The Alpha-Text of Esther: Its Character and Relationship to the Masoretic Text," in B.A. Taylor (ed.), *IX Congress of the International Organization for Septuagint and Cognate Studies* (SBLSCSS 45; Atlanta: Scholars Press, 1997), 369-79.
68 Tov, "The 'Lucianic' Text."
69 Tov, "The 'Lucianic' Text," 17-25.
70 Hanhart, *Esther*, 87 (NB: the first edition was published in 1966 and the position appears to be the same in the second edition of 1983). Cf. the comments of Dorothy, which point out how "cautious" he believes Hanhart's language is in this case. He submits that Hanhart's statement "does not of itself address all necessary issues nor the issue of rewriting" (*The Books of Esther*, 289). This is a matter that De Troyer takes up in her work.
71 K. De Troyer, *Het einde van de Alpha-tekst van Ester: Vertaal- en verhaaltechniek van MT 8,1-17, LXX 8,1-17 en AT 7,14-41* (Leuven: Uitgeverij Peeters, 1997). This study has been revised and updated in K. De Troyer, *The End of the Alpha Text of Esther*.
72 De Troyer, *Het einde van de Alpha-tekst van Ester*, 359-60. For a more recent statement of her conclusions on this issue, see De Troyer, *The End of the Alpha Text of Esther*, 396-97.
73 K. De Troyer, email correspondence. I am grateful to Dr De Troyer for clarifications concerning her understanding of the technical terms 'recension' and 'revision'.

(i.e., the AT) for specific, apologetic purposes – deliberately diverging from the LXX text.[74] This second view, in both variations, sees the LXX as the source text of the AT – a position which necessarily places the AT later in the textual development of the book of Esther.

It is quite clear that just where and how to situate and handle the AT within the history of development of the book of Esther has provided and continues to provide many challenges.

1.3 Versification

Concerning versification for the Hebrew story, we shall follow the sequence found in the fourth, revised edition of *BHS*. This text begins at 1.1 with the introduction of the king and a description of the extent of his empire, and culminates at 10.3 with the prominence of Mordecai – both in the court of the king and among his people, the Jews. For the Greek texts, we shall observe the versification found in the 1983 edition of the Göttingen Septuaginta edited by Robert Hanhart.[75] The text of the LXX begins at A.1 with the ἐνύπνιον of Mardochaios, and completes the story with the colophon at F.11.[76] The AT also begins at A.1 with the ἐνύπνιον of Mardochaios, but the narrative ends at 7.59 with the call for Israel's perpetual and glad observance of 14th and 15th Adar – the days of Φουραια (7.49).[77]

---

74 A. LaCocque, "The Different Versions of Esther," *BibInt* 7 (1999), 316-21.
75 Hanhart, *Esther*.
76 The LXX material is enumerated as follows: A.1-17 – 1.1-22 – 2.1-23 – 3.1-13 – B.1-7 – 3.14-15 – 4.1-17 – C.1-30 – D.1-16 – 5.3-14 – 6.1-14 – 7.1-10 – 8.1-12 – E.1-24 – 8.13-17 – 9.1-31 – 10.1-3 – F.1-11.
77 The AT material is enumerated as follows: A.1-18 – 1.1-21 – 2.1-18 – 3.1-19 [14-19 // B.1-7] – 4.1-29 [12b-29 // C.1-30] – 5.1-24 [// D.1-5.14] – 6.1-23 – 7.1-59 [22-32 // E.1-24; 53-59 // F.1-10].

1.4 Explanation of Procedure

1.4.1 Approach to the Esther texts

Following the recent position of Charles V. Dorothy concerning the study of Esther texts, this project intends to investigate the three aforementioned books of Esther in their entirety.[78] With Dorothy, we seek to treat the MT, LXX and AT as "whole documents which may witness to variant but venerable traditions in several faithful Jewish and Christian communities."[79] This particular approach bears most significantly on the study of the Greek texts (LXX and AT). Concerning those narratives, the 'Additions' will be read as they appear within the plot development of their respective texts. To be sure, this approach does not necessarily minimise or downplay the dynamics of the textual history of these texts, nor does it ignore the importance of the possible redactional processes and endeavours that have produced the texts we now possess.[80] Yet, presently, we shall leave most of those formal concerns to the side and concentrate primarily on the ends of the various means and stages. Following the recent textual approach of De Troyer, we shall examine the moral character of the three Esther stories using "only existing texts, and not reconstructed ones."[81]

In short, we shall strive to treat each of these witnesses as an entire work, within its own (full) context, and in its own right.[82] Thus, we shall analyse the MT Esther narrative as presented in the fourth, revised edition of *BHS,* and the LXX and AT narratives as they appear in the 1983 edition of Hanhart's *Esther* in the Göttingen Septuaginta. These particular documents are the current accepted scholarly texts of Esther and represent the authoritative Esther stories of many and various Jewish and Christian communities through the years. Each of the three texts has its own particular context, interest and design, and "each deserves to be attended to on its own."[83] Reading them finally

---

78 Day chooses to work with the "final form" versions of the texts as well, but does not elaborate on her choice to do so (*Three Faces of a Queen,* 18). See M.E. Mills concerning the necessity to view the "overall literary context," especially when studying passages with specific ethical content (*Biblical Morality: Moral Perspectives in Old Testament Narratives* (HSCPRT; Aldershot/Burlington/Singapore: Ashgate, 2001), 74, 243.

79 Dorothy, *The Books of Esther,* 16.

80 We desire to make it clear at this point that we are *not* stating that these latest stages of textual development in any given text are necessarily the only valid objects of literary study (see the section concerning "The literary significance of redaction" in Fox, *Redaction,* 142-48). Neither do we hold that we find 'perfection' in the latest forms of the texts we here intend to study (see this subject addressed in *Redaction,* 148 n. 18).

81 De Troyer, *Het einde van de Alpha-tekst van Ester,* 359.

82 Dorothy, *The Books of Esther,* 18.

83 Beal, *Esther,* xix.

as hybrid texts would not do justice to the narratives.[84] Furthermore, it has even become apparent that studying these texts as "completely separate literary works" is the "ideal solution" in one's approach to current Esther studies.[85] For each of them has, in the forms to be studied here, a "fundamental coherence."[86]

1.4.2 Textual selectivity

In her insightful study, *Three Faces of a Queen*, Linda Day suggests that certain portions of the narrative are "more illuminating" than others when it comes to a characterisation of Esther.[87] She focuses only upon those portions of the narratives that serve her thesis. In the present study, we shall follow a similarly selective approach. This entails that we shall focus only upon those sections of text that inform and serve our project, thus leaving some of the narrative and many of its concerns and emphases to the side. In these selective decisions, however, in which we shall focus upon those texts that we deem most relevant to our investigation, we hope neither to exclude germane portions nor include superfluous ones. But, of course, the relevance of these textual choices will be tested as the reader proceeds through chapters two through four. Finally, because the three primary narratives of our study are distinctive, the sections of text receiving attention in each will not necessarily correspond one to another, even when they are (roughly) parallel. This will be easily observed as one comes to the material in chapters two, three and four.

---

84 Dorothy, *The Books of Esther*, 360. Here, Dorothy is following the conclusions of S.D. Walters concerning the relationship between the Hanna and Anna stories ("The Translator and the Text: Which Text Do We Translate?" (SBL paper, Boston, 1987); "Hanna and Anna: The Greek and Hebrew Texts of 1 Samuel 1," *JBL* 107 (1988), 385-412). By reading the *books* of Esther, Dorothy hopes that they "will go on living" (360).
85 S.W. Crawford, Review of J.D. Levenson, *Esther* (*JBL* 118 (1999), 135). See further the comments of C. Boyd-Taylor in support of reading the LXX in its redacted form, thus recognising "its own integrity as a literary composition" ("Esther's Great Adventure: Reading the LXX version of the Book of Esther in light of its assimilation to the conventions of the Greek romantic novel," *BIOSCS* 30 (1997), 88-89). He goes on to state (even more strongly) that "it is methodologically unsound to persist in treating the additions independently of the redactive *Tendenz* of the LXX text. Even if it was reshaped by many hands before reaching its extant form, this composition is more than the sum of its interpolations" (112). We have taken the liberty to expand the scope of the comments of both Crawford and Boyd-Taylor to include the study of the AT as well, for this would not seem to compromise the respective general points made.
86 A phrase borrowed from Boyd-Taylor in his discussion of LXX-Esther ("Esther's Great Adventure," 112).
87 Day, *Three Faces of a Queen*, 25.

1.4.3 Describing moral character

In his book entitled *The Moral Vision of the New Testament,* Richard B. Hays sets out what he terms "The Fourfold Task of New Testament Ethics." The four parts of this overall task are as follows: 1) the *descriptive* task: reading the text carefully; 2) the *synthetic* task: placing the text in canonical context; 3) the *hermeneutical* task: relating the text to our situation; and 4) the *pragmatic* task: living the text.[88] It is with the first of these that we shall be primarily concerned throughout this study. Concerning this initial, descriptive task, Hays makes the point that it is "fundamentally exegetical in character."[89] Thus, *via* exegetical labour, Hays contends that the first order of business for an interpreter endeavouring in the area of New Testament ethics is to describe carefully the content or message of a passage or text. The investigator of Old Testament ethics could utilise this starting point as well, even if the particular project is only considered prolegomena (as this one is).

Whereas the methodology of Hays proceeds through the descriptive to synthetic, hermeneutical and pragmatic tasks, this study will concentrate primarily upon the description of relevant moral content in the three primary versions of the Esther story. We shall employ the term 'moral character' in our descriptive efforts as we investigate the Esther stories found in the MT (chapter two), the LXX (chapter three) and the AT (chapter four).

1.4.4 Towards an assessment of moral character

Following the exegetical/descriptive efforts of chapters two through four, we shall approach the tasks of assessing and concluding in chapter five. In terms of moral character, the Hebrew version of the story leaves much unsaid, many ambiguities, and, for some, much to be desired. It appears that the two Greek versions of Esther – LXX and AT – have, in many ways and often to a great extent, transformed the moral character of the story as they have modified it for specific contexts and needs.

---

88 R.B. Hays, *The Moral Vision of the New Testament* (Edinburgh: T & T Clark, 1996), 3f.
89 Hays, *The Moral Vision of the New Testament,* 3.

Part II
Elucidations & Evaluations

2 Moral Character in the MT

2.0 Introduction

When a perceptive reader engages the Hebrew book of Esther, an interpretative weight necessarily falls heavily upon his or her shoulders. A masterfully told story though it is,[1] one cannot escape facing the reading decisions that exist as a result of what the author says, alludes to, or does not say in the pages of the narrative. Interestingly enough, gaps in understanding abide in all three of these situations.

> Biblical narratives are notorious for their sparsity of detail.... And the resultant gaps have been left open precisely at key points, central to the discourse as a dramatic progression as well as a structure of meaning and value. Hence their filling in here is not automatic but requires considerable attention to the nuances of the text, both at the level of the represented events and at the level of language; far from a luxury or option, closure becomes a necessity for any reader trying to understand the story even in the simplest terms of what happens and why.[2]

This narrative situation and resultant interpretative task lies before us as we approach and engage ambiguous aspects of morality in the Scroll of Esther. Since the book was not composed as an ethical treatise, much of its moral vision is unspoken, not addressed specifically, or implied at best. With the exception of Haman, in whose character little ambiguity is found,[3] the motives and (in)actions of the main actors in the narrative exhibit intriguing 'moral gaps' that have been open historically to varied and wide-ranging interpretation. It must be said, however, that not all of this past explication has been equally satisfying.

In this chapter we shall seek primarily to focus in on these lacunae *via* exegetical analysis, and, when possible, attempt cautiously to suggest some ways in which this material might be understood within its various contexts –

---

1 "Indeed, the narrative art of the book is grudgingly admired by its worst enemies" (R. Bauckham, *The Bible in Politics: How to Read the Bible Politically* (Louisville: WJKP, 1989), 119).

2 M. Sternberg, *The Poetics of Biblical Narrative* (Bloomington: University of Indiana Press, 1985), 191-92.

3 Mills comments that "Haman...is open to the reader" (*Biblical Morality,* 80).

both near and far. To be sure, we shall neither be able to clear up all of the
moral ambiguities of the narrative, nor do we intend to fill in completely all
of the gaps pointed out in these episodes; Sternberg's closure is not always
achieved easily, and it might not always be possible or even advisable.[4]
Rather, a more descriptive and interrogative process will follow – one with a
view to an interaction with and a fresh look at the moral complexion of the
book of Esther in its MT form.

2.1 Vashti

2.1.1 Refusal to appear when summoned (1.10-12)

Queen Vashti has declined the request of the king![5] Little could anyone know
how monumental this simply reported 'No' would be. For a character who
remains almost exclusively in the background of a small portion of the narrative, it is intriguing that the refusal of Vashti threatens to turn the kingdom
upside-down (at least in the eyes of some men[6]). Indeed, the queen's snub
sends shock waves of influence throughout both the story and the far-
reaching history of interpretation that has been fascinated by her and her decision. Yet precisely *why* Vashti refuses is not stated.[7]

Concerning her character, the text is parsimonious in terms of description
and explanation. It informs the reader tersely that when the summons of the
king arrives, the queen refuses to come [וַתְּמָאֵן הַמַּלְכָּה וַשְׁתִּי לָבוֹא] (1.12).
What could have motivated this behaviour? The text reports that the merry
king is noticeably affected by drinking at the time of his request
[כְּטוֹב לֵב־הַמֶּלֶךְ בַּיָּיִן] (1.10). The choice of words here suggests both that the

---

4   Cf. C.S. Rodd's (general) warning about superficial resolutions to problematic ethical
     "stances," which lead easily "to a distortion of the Old Testament morality itself"
     (*Glimpses of a Strange Land* (OTS; Edinburgh: T & T Clark, 2001), 2).
5   See T.S. Laniak for a discussion of the weighty implications that the refusal of Vashti
     had on the honour (status) of the king in this context. "The simplest test of a superior's
     status is the obedience of the vassal, client, wife, child or slave who is under authority.
     The hierarchy which is celebrated through ceremony is easily subverted simply by the
     refusal of one of the king's subordinates to comply with his demands" (*Shame and
     Honor in the Book of Esther* (SBLDS 165; Atlanta: Scholars Press, 1998), 40).
6   Cf. K. Butting's exploration of the "social background" involved here, especially as it
     touches the issue of sexism ("Esther: A New Interpretation of the Joseph Story in the
     Fight Against Anti-Semitism and Sexism," in A. Brenner (ed.), *Ruth and Esther: A
     Feminist Companion to the Bible* (FCB second series 3; Sheffield: Sheffield Academic
     Press, 1999), 241-42).
7   Bickerman conjectures some interesting explanations, all of which are unverifiable
     (*Four Strange Books of the Bible*, 185-86).

mood of the king is good and that (or because) he was intoxicated to some measure at his party.[8] These descriptions are likely related and may have sketched a negative picture of the king's present state in the mind of the queen. The likelihood of impaired judgement may have sent off warning signals to Vashti because of the desire of the king to show-off[9] [לְהַרְאוֹת] the beauty [יָפְיָהּ] of his queen to the people.[10] Undoubtedly, for a woman, pretentiousness and inebriation are not a comforting combination in a man.

But it is not entirely clear that the probable instability of the king has anything to do with the decision of Vashti not to appear at the beckoning of the eunuchs. Indeed, there is no steady inference to be drawn in that manner. Neither can one firmly decide from the text that the queen refuses the call of the king as a matter of dignified principle; information on the thought processes of Vashti are simply not given.[11] Despite the argument of Paton that the author takes the actions of the queen to be whimsical because no good reason for her refusal can be found,[12] it appears that the unknown motivations of Vashti are neither of great consequence to the narrator nor of much concern to the other characters who were present at the revelrous seven-day banquet.[13] The story moves quickly on to the question of how the court should now *handle* the insubordinate queen, spending little time on the components that relate the act of disobedience itself. Because of this, it is the reader alone who is left to wrestle with the ambiguity (unclarity) surrounding the inaction of the queen, for a satisfying appraisal of her moral character on the basis of the text does not appear to be forthcoming.

It has been suggested that for the author, the silence of the narrative concerning Vashti's grounds for refusal "effects a sort of closure, limiting the attention the reader will give this character."[14] Yet whatever the possible in-

---

8   According to D. Daube, the power of wine is a prominent feature in the book of Esther and serves to tie it structurally to 1 Esdras 3f. (*Esther* (Yarnton, Oxford: The Oxford Centre for Postgraduate Hebrew Studies, 1995), 36-37). One cannot say for sure that the influence of wine was the reason for the refusal of Vashti (*contra* the later suggestion of Daube (55)), but it is undeniable that wine figures quite prominently in the book, especially in this opening chapter.

9   Cf. 1.4 and note the previous intention of the king to show-off "the glory of his wealth." Showing-off Vashti at the culmination of the celebration would be highlighting his "greatest status symbol" (Laniak, *Shame and Honor,* 41).

10   Levenson, *Esther,* 47.

11   The common suppositions offered are textually unfounded (e.g., see D.C. Rudavsky, "In Defense of Tradition: Haftarat Zachor in the Light of Purim," *Judaism* 47 (1998), 84).

12   Paton, *The Book of Esther,* 149-50.

13   Fox, *Character and Ideology,* 165-66.

14   Fox, *Character and Ideology,* 167. But we should not think, according to Beal, that this is the extent of the function of Vashti in the story. Indeed, although she is "written out" of the narrative, the implications of her presence and inaction will continue to reverberate throughout the story in many ways (*The Book of Hiding,* ch. 1; *Esther,* 1f).

tentions of the author, the fascination of subsequent readers with the motives of the queen has been far from contained. Indeed, Vashti's silence has led to interpreters' verbosity; depending on his or her mindset and contexts, the ethical verdicts on the behaviour of Vashti have been (and will likely continue to be) widely varied.[15] At the very least, the brief presence of Vashti in the story serves to heighten narrative tension,[16] and to set up a literary comparison with a later queen who would manage her behaviour and office in a quite different fashion.[17] In this light, the behaviour of Vashti could be viewed 'positively' even though no particular moral assessment is attainable. But, to be sure, this explanation is a practical one.[18]

2.2 Esther

2.2.1 Concealment of Jewishness (2.10, 20)

The act of concealing one's identity is not uncommon in the Old Testament. A few examples include the account of Jacob dressing in kids' skins and wearing the clothes of Esau in order to obtain the blessing of Isaac (Gen 27.1-29), and the story of Tamar disguising herself as a prostitute to fool Judah (Gen 38.11-26). Perhaps even more analogous to the Esther account are the stories that relate Abraham (on two occasions!) and Isaac instructing their beautiful wives to pose as their sisters so that the patriarchs might avoid what they feared to be certain death at the hands of foreign kings (Gen 12.10-20; 20.1-18; 26.7-11). Whereas these texts display an *active* concealment that could be characterised as deception, the information related in Esther, though not altogether dissimilar, is more ambiguous. In the Esther account, *inaction*

---

15 In rabbinic literature, Vashti receives a disparaging portrait. This could be in order to distinguish her from Esther, the true heroine of the book (L.L. Bronner, "Esther Revisited: An Aggadic Approach," 188; see also in this regard, K.P. Darr, *Far More Precious than Jewels: Perspectives on Biblical Women* (Louisville: Westminster/John Knox Press, 1991), 169). This trend continues into the medieval period (see B.D. Walfish, *Esther in Medieval Garb: Jewish Interpretation of the Book of Esther in the Middle Ages* (Albany: SUNY Press, 1993), 195-96). Yet in more contemporary thought, the image of the deposed queen has been resurrected. She has even been deemed "a moral exemplar of the highest order" (J.M. Cohen, "Vashti – An Unsung Heroine," *JBQ* 24 (1996), 106). Moreover, Laniak mentions that in current feminist scholarship, "Vashti usually receives more praise [than Esther] for what she did *not* do" (*Shame and Honor*, 6-7 (*emphasis original*)).

16 J.G. Baldwin, *Esther* (TOTC; Leicester: Inter-Varsity Press, 1984), 60.

17 That is, she would better fulfil royal "expectations," unlike her predecessor, Vashti (Laniak, *Shame and Honor*, 52, 58).

18 Fox, *Character and Ideology*, 169. Cf. Berlin, *Esther*, lvi, 3.

circumscribes the heroine's behaviour – "Esther *did not make known*[19] her people or her descent" [לֹא־הִגִּ֣ידָה אֶסְתֵּ֔ר אֶת־עַמָּ֖הּ וְאֶת־מֽוֹלַדְתָּ֑הּ] (2.10) – as she carried out the unexplained wishes of Mordecai in her new palace environment.

It should be noted that the reason(s) for the request of Mordecai are not stated (neither for the reader, nor for her), but it is not likely that the author *merely* desires to show Mordecai's patriarchal dominance over Esther at this and other points.[20] Further, there is no hint of prejudice or selectivity in the general call for the empire's women of marriageable age (2.2). As it reads, we simply do not know from the text that Esther would have been disqualified because she was Jewish,[21] although some sort of apprehension seems to be in place.[22] It could be assumed that the Jews are in servitude to some degree in Persia during this time causing the social class of Esther to preclude her, but this assumption would not be based on any firm evidence. In the face of all the possible scenarios and suppositions, the narrative remains silent.

The initial instruction for concealment in 2.10 frames the front end of a chiastic inclusio that finds its reversed counterpart in 2.20[23] – a fuller instruc-

---

19 Beal notes that this sense of "not revealing" carries the basic meaning of the verb *ngd* (*Esther*, 31).

20 *Pace* B. Wyler who believes that the main purpose of the concealment theme is to indicate that Esther was subordinate both when she was under the care of Mordecai *and* after she became queen ("Esther: The Incomplete Emancipation of a Queen," in A. Brenner (ed.), *A Feminist Companion to Esther, Judith and Susanna* (FCB 7; Sheffield: Sheffield Academic Press, 1995), 114).

21 *Pace* Paton, who claims that Esther knew that she would be the subject of ill treatment if she disclosed her race. The beliefs of Paton stem from his understanding of a general notion of anti-Semitism that follows the Jews wherever they have lived because of "their pride and exclusive habits" (*The Book of Esther*, 175). For a similarly pessimistic reading of the standing of the Jews in foreign contexts, see P. Cassell, *An Explanatory Commentary on Esther* (trans. A. Bernstein; Edinburgh: T & T Clark, 1888), 63-66. Fox, in a more nuanced reading, also holds that fear of anti-Semitic treatment lay behind the events of the concealment of Esther. Yet the view of Fox does not envision an ubiquitous anti-Semitic hostility as that of Paton does; instead, he posits that the danger faced is "a manifestation of an ever-present – but not universal – hostility, for which one must always be prepared" (*Character and Ideology*, 32). For Fox, a kingdom-wide anti-Semitism is not consonant with the text; instead, the ambiguously identified group, "enemies of the Jews," are the constant threat (33). While the suggestion of Fox is plausible concerning the text as a whole, it is still unclear that Esther would have been aware of this unpredictable threat. And even if Mordecai was so aware, he might not have informed Esther. The silence of the text gives the reader no particular guidance here.

22 M.V. Fox, *The Redaction of the Books of Esther: On Reading Composite Texts* (SBLMS 40; Atlanta: Scholars Press, 1991), 113.

23 Whereas 2.10 reads "her people or her descent" [אֶת־עַמָּ֖הּ וְאֶת־מֽוֹלַדְתָּ֑הּ], 2.20 reads "her descent or her people" [מֽוֹלַדְתָּ֑הּ וְאֶת־עַמָּ֖הּ]. In the midst of these bracketing statements lies the detailed account of the preparations and triumph of Esther in the kingdom-wide beauty pageant. This instance of a chiastic pattern that points to an inclusio of Esther's

tion that also underlines the fact of the compliance of Esther to the will of
Mordecai even after she becomes queen. According to Jon D. Levenson, the
point here is clear: Esther does not "break faith" with Mordecai even after she
had surpassed him in all aspects of civic rank. Even though it is questionable
how the queen managed not to reveal her nationality, the main plot of the
story (i.e., the genocidal plot of Haman) is dependant upon the fact that she
did just that.[24] Questions concerning the *manner* in which Esther went about
her concealment appear not to be a great point of interest for the author. Similar to the handling of the Vashti account, the narrative leaves many details to
the curiosity and imagination of the reader. What seems clear, nevertheless, is
that in the midst of the obedience of Esther, "secrecy"[25] or concealment is
certain, though deception is not necessarily implied. In the end, it seems that
readers need not know *why* or even *how* Esther manages not to reveal her
people and descent, just that she *does* conceal them, and very well.

2.2.2 Winning the favour and love of the king (2.17a)

In the cover of the concealment plan Esther is gathered along with a vast
group of eligible young women and placed under the care of Hegai (2.8). It is
clear from the narrative that her presence in the court brings about extremely
positive feelings from all persons with whom she comes in contact, especially
the king (2.15). Yet it is interesting to note that these sentiments of favour
are, at least to some extent, the result of an *active* manner on the part of the
young Jewess. In other words, Esther appears to take it upon herself to ensure
that she is well pleasing before Hegai, and consequently, the king. But the
actual extent of Esther's activity is unknown. The different ways in which the
author chooses to relate the favour that Esther receives within the book testifies to a clear distinction in the posture of the young woman in different
situations.

The normal biblical Hebrew idiom used to relate the favour or acceptance
of one in the presence of another is מצא חן בעיני. This phrase, which describes one's finding of favour in the eyes of another, is found over fifty

---

crisis is noted by Moore (*Esther*, 22) who follows the stylistic analysis of W. Dommershausen (*Die Estherrolle* (SBM 6; Stuttgart: Verlag Katholisches Bibelwerk, 1968), 44-
55). For a more general treatment of chiasm in the book of Esther, see Y.T. Radday,
"Chiasm in Joshua, Judges and Others," *Linguistica Biblica* 3 (1973), 9-11.

24 Levenson, *Esther*, 61. "It stretches credibility to imagine that Esther could keep her
ethnic identity a secret, but it is vital to the plot and really no more unrealistic than many
other aspects of this fictive story" (Berlin, *Esther*, 27).

25 A term employed by LaCocque in this context (*The Feminine Unconventional*, 50).

times in the Hebrew Bible.[26] Three of these instances occur in the book of Esther (5.8; 7.3; 8.5). In these particular cases, the queen prefaces her requests with a conditional clause that includes this form of the idiom and carries along with it a more passive sense.[27] Esther places herself in the presence of the king and conditions her petition upon his acceptance of her person and her standing. The queen makes no noticeable *active* effort to persuade His Majesty of her worth or attributes at this point; she instead bases her requests upon the hope that the king is presently well-disposed towards her and that he has been pleased with her previously.

This more passive sense is in contrast with the more active idiom found in 2.9, 15, 17 and 5.2.[28] In these four verses, the distinctive form of the idiom is נשׂא חסד/חן. This phrase is a hapax legomenon in the Hebrew Bible but is found at Qumran as well as in rabbinic literature.[29] It could be argued that, at the very least, this form of the idiom should not be thought as synonymous with the regular idiom, מצא חן. However, it is the view of some scholars that נשׂא חסד/חן connotes a more active Esther in the sense that she wins or earns favour in these particular cases.[30] Applying this understanding presently, Esther appears to do something *active* to deserve the favour that she re-

---

26 B. Grossfeld, "מצא חן בעיני – 'Finding Favor in Someone's Eyes': The Treatment of this Biblical Hebrew Idiom in the Ancient Aramaic Versions," in K.J. Cathcart and M. Maher (eds), *Targumic and Cognate Studies: Essays in Honour of Martin McNamara* (JSOTSup 230; Sheffield: Sheffield Academic Press, 1996), 52.

27 E.g., אִם־מָצָאתִי חֵן בְּעֵינֵי הַמֶּלֶךְ (5.8).

28 See the comments of Beal concerning this idiom in the context of 2.9. He notes that Esther gained or lifted "loyalty" in the eyes of Hegai [Beal: Heggai]. Beal understands this as Esther causing Hegai "to look loyally" upon her. He continues and suggests that "she might possess a kind of unexpected agency in relation to the male subject" (*The Book of Hiding,* 35). Among other things, it is clear here that Beal does not rule out some sort of activity on the part of Esther at this point.

29 S. Talmon, "Was the Book of Esther Known at Qumran?," 263-64. Talmon cites 1QS 2.3-4 as well as the rabbinic sources B. Meg. 13a and Sifre Num 41 as containing the phrase in question. These sources do not necessarily support the fact that this later usage is characteristically active. In B. Meg. 13a and in Sifre Num 41, the citations are "verbatim quotations from the biblical book in reference to Esther." The 1QS 2.3-4 reference is a paraphrase of the priestly blessing of Num 6.24-26 and is not a verbatim quote from the Esther text. Yet Talmon argues that because the phrase נשׂא חסד/חן did not have a "general currency in post-biblical (rabbinic) Hebrew," the probability that the book of Esther was known at the time is high. However, the possible linguistic connections are of main interest here.

30 H. Bardtke first suggested this understanding: "Gegenüber *māṣāʾ* hat *nāśāʾ* die Bedeutung eines aktiven Gewinnens der Huld" (*Das Buch Esther* (KAT; Gütersloh: Gütersloher Verlagshaus Gerd Mohn, 1963), 303). This sense has been followed by Moore (*Esther,* 21); S.A. White, "Esther: A Feminine Model for Jewish Diaspora," in P.L. Day (ed.), *Gender and Difference in Ancient Israel* (Minneapolis: Augsburg Fortress, 1989), 167; L.M. Wills, *The Jewish Novel in the Ancient World* (Ithaca: Cornell University Press, 1995), 94; and Bush (*Ruth, Esther,* 364).

ceives.[31] Literally, the maiden lifts up/obtains חסד before Hegai in 2.9, she is one lifting up/obtaining חן in the eyes of everyone who sees her in 2.15, Esther lifts up/obtains both חן *and* חסד before the king in 2.17,[32] and the queen lifts up/obtains חן in the eyes of the king in 5.2.[33]

That Esther is somehow active in these instances might be further supported by the aforementioned reference to נשא חסד/חן in the Qumran literature. In 1QS 2.3-4, the priestly blessing of Num 6.24-26 is paraphrased and contains the phrase וישא פני חסדיו – "May he [God] lift up his merciful countenance."[34] Both of these texts appear to be portraying an active subject. Moreover, a common utilisation of the idiom in the LBH of Esther and a like use in the text of a Qumran scroll would not be a farfetched proposition.[35]

Yet if Esther can be said to be active in these four cases, might this then raise the curiosity of the reader concerning the *nature* of her actions at these times? If it is possible that Esther is not a passive, helpless damsel in the hands of a power hungry, manipulative king in 2.17a, what kind of portrait are we to have of the young woman who successfully realises a victory in the kingdom-wide beauty pageant?[36] It is most likely that Esther is to some degree aware of the nature of the situation in which she finds herself, and that she actively seeks to be the one whom the king finally comes to choose and love.[37] To be clear, the argument here is not for an exclusively (or even

---

31 Moore, *Esther*, 21.
32 According to Grossfeld this combinatory doublet occurs in biblical Hebrew only in this verse ("מצא חן בעיני – 'Finding Favor'," 58).
33 Laniak states that Esther "actively acquires the benevolence of her male superiors. She literally 'takes' (נשא) or, better, 'elicits' or 'wins' kindness (חסד) and favor (חן)" (*Shame and Honor*, 64).
34 Talmon's rendering ("Was the Book of Esther Known at Qumran?," 264).
35 For comment on the characterisation of Esther as LBH, see the recent work of Bergey: "The Book of Esther; 'Late Linguistic Features in Esther," 66-78; and "Post-exilic Hebrew Linguistic Developments in Esther," 161-68. For a different view of the LBH of Esther, see Polzin, *Late Biblical Hebrew*.
36 The opinion that Esther displays any activity whatsoever in this scene argues against the proposition of Fox who pictures Esther as *exclusively* passive, even docile, at this point in the narrative (*Character and Ideology*, 37, 197-98). Interestingly, Fox believes that "[A]lmost every word stresses Esther's passivity in all this" (37). It would appear that K.M. Craig, Jr. would follow Fox in this judgement (*Reading Esther: A Case for the Literary Carnivalesque* (Westminster/John Knox Press, 1995), 94). Day also characterises Esther as "more passive in attaining her favored status," yet she does acknowledge that Esther "actively attains the favor" of Hegai. Concerning her time with king, however, Day only comments on the "emotional response" of the king "over which she [Esther] would not have had much control" that decides the recipient of the queenly crown (*Three Faces of a Queen*, 45).
37 Even if it is "as stroke of good luck" that Esther was chosen in the search, as Moore suggests (*Daniel, Esther, and Jeremiah: The Additions*, 186), it does not appear as if she would sit back and wait for more good fortune to fall in her lap.

mostly) active Esther whose passivity is nowhere to be found in this scene. Instead, only the likelihood of Esther's activity in connection with the hapax legomenon idiom נשא חסד/חן is being pursued – i.e., a hint of activity in the midst of a generally passive portrayal of the young woman.[38] Exactly what this activity entails *behaviourally* is not stated in the text, but it is plausible that Esther acts persuasively in some way during her encounters with the king[39] – the fruits of which appear to encourage, if not bring about, his love for her.

2.2.3 Apprehension about transgressing the law (4.11)

At this point in the narrative Esther is the reigning queen and the genocidal plot of Haman is firmly in place. This brings about confusion in Shushan (3.15) and prompts Mordecai to cry out bitterly in sackcloth and ashes (4.1) – a fact that causes Esther the deepest distress[40] even though she is not aware initially of the reasons for the posture of Mordecai.[41] Esther's severe reaction

---

38 Again, the distinction that Bardtke sees between the passivity and activity of Esther is supportive here as he comments concerning 2.17: "Die Wendung *nāśāʾ ḥen* weist darauf hin, daß Esther sich diese Gunst errang dank ihrer persönlichen Vorzüge" (*Das Buch Esther*, 306).

39 L.L. Bronner supports our claim by stating that Esther is "overtly cooperative and compliant" in the early portions of the narrative. Interestingly, she qualifies her statement when she states that Esther is overtly cooperative and compliant "to an approved degree" ("Reclaiming Esther: From Sex Object to Sage," *JBQ* 26 (1998), 5). What Bronner means exactly is not clear. Perhaps since there is no explicit comment by the narrator (negatively or positively) in the story, Bronner assumes that whatever it was that Esther did was categorically approved.

40 Moore suggests translating the hapax legomenon hithpalpel form of חיל as "perplexed" since the LXX translates the verb ἐταράχθη (*Esther*, 48). However, the decision of Moore tends to soften the excruciating emotional content of the queen's reaction. G. Gerleman points to the Akkadian and Ugaritic parallels of חיל and argues for a stronger expression here, one likened to "das schmerzliche Stöhnen und Schreien der gebärenden Frau" (*Esther* (BKAT 21; Neukirchen-Vluyn: Neukirchener Verlag, 1982²), 105). In a similar vein, Bush refers to the hithpolel forms of חול/חיל that occur in Job 15.20 and Jer 23.19 and connote an active physical reaction "occasioned by the shock of calamity or pain" (cf. *BDB*, which notes the following active rendering: "*and she writhed* in anxiety" (297)). In this verse, however, a more figurative sense of the verb is preferred – "to be deeply distressed" (*Ruth, Esther*, 390). Yet it should be kept in mind that this figurative sense still incorporates the intense force of the root. Cf. Mills concerning Esther's "mental state of distress" (*Biblical Morality*, 79).

41 In 4.4 the text reads that when the eunuchs come and relate the posture of Mordecai, "the queen becomes deeply distressed" (following the suggestion of Bush for the rendering of וַתִּתְחַלְחַל הַמַּלְכָּה מְאֹד (*Ruth, Esther*, 390)) and sends him clothes. It is not until the next verse that Esther actually sends Hatach to inquire as to the reason why Morde-

to his state of being gives rise to a measure of bewilderment, for the force of
the hithpalpel verb, תתחלחל, would not appear to fit with the extent of her
present awareness of the overall situation.[42] Only in 4.8-9 does Esther find
out the reason for the grief of Mordecai after Hatach brings back to her a
copy of the edict of Haman. Interestingly, no further reaction of distress from
the queen is recorded upon hearing *this* news. One supposes that the deep
anguish of 4.4 would be exacerbated by the clarification of the plight of Mordecai and the Jews, yet the text displays no such increase of emotion.

It is also the case in verses 8-9 that Mordecai charges the queen to go to
the king and seek with regard to her people. It is here that we encounter the
apprehensive response of Esther – a response that is possibly shaped by the
reality of her high position in the court and her disconnected proximity to the
Jewish problem of that time. The queen diplomatically relates a message
back to Mordecai informing him that the decree of the king prohibits her
from entering into his presence unless she is summoned; and she has not been
called for thirty days. To do so unbidden would spell certain death, that is,
unless the king extends his golden rod (4.11). At this juncture, the queen
seems uninterested in jeopardising either her life or her lofty position for
anyone, and it even appears possible that she does not even count herself
among the threatened Jews here. In a long, round-about way, she is saying
'No' to Mordecai.[43]

The apprehension of Esther in this scene could be attributed to a convenient commitment to decrees of the king. It is doubtful that the queen possesses a firm conviction that the laws of the king are infallible and altogether
insuperable in light of both the golden rod loophole[44] and her later decision to
enter into his presence uncalled (4.16-5.1). Instead, it is more likely that this

---

cai has assumed such a position (she asks: מַה־זֶּה וְעַל־מַה־זֶּה – "what-ever and why-
ever?").

42 Many commentators agree that at this point in the narrative Esther could not have
known why Mordecai had begun the rites of mourning. At a loss for a better answer,
Bush posits that the reaction of the queen was occasioned by her actions of her relative
and people (4.3) – i.e., a serious reaction for a serious posture of mourning. At best,
Bush supposes, Esther is aware that something serious has occurred (*Ruth, Esther*, 394).
Yet it is difficult to imagine that the physical appearance of Mordecai could have caused
such distress in the queen. If, as Baldwin suggests, she merely was embarrassed and desired to clothe her relative so that he might enter the court complex and meet with her
(*Esther*, 77), such a painful recoil seems out of place. But if the author wanted to use her
embarrassment in order to distance effectively Mordecai the Jew from Esther the Gentile
queen, the author has succeeded for the moment (Levenson, *Esther*, 79). Beal presents
the ambiguity well in this scene and does not attempt to clear it up (*Esther*, 60).
43 See Beal, *The Book of Hiding*, 71.
44 Craig recognises that "[S]ome Persian laws have built-in escape clauses" (*Reading
Esther*, 57). Berlin suggests that Esther is already here hinting at her strategy by producing this new, golden rod, information to Mordecai (*Esther*, 47).

uneasiness emanates from her feeling of disconnectedness from the larger Jewish community.[45] In other words, Esther might consider herself safe from the threat of the edict of Haman at this point and thus not desire to risk her life and position unnecessarily.[46] To be sure, these emotions are humanly possible and should be able to be understood at least, even if not supported. But the lack of an explicit reaction at the news of the genocidal plot, when it had only taken a mentioning that Mordecai was in sackcloth and ashes to bring about deep distress, heightens our curiosity concerning the thoughts and motivations of Esther as she dwells comfortably in the Persian court. For the fact of the queen's apprehension is clear, even though a perceptible rationalisation of it is not expressly stated. Tacitly, though, her misgivings come into clearer view – misgivings that she must face in the upcoming message exchanges with Mordecai.

2.2.4 An unoptimistic submission (4.16)

What is encountered in the material between 4.11 and the end of the chapter is certainly remarkable, yet it is probably not quite as exceptional as many readers suppose. The persuasive rhetorical techniques of the Esther's father-figure, Mordecai, should not go unnoticed, for they are undoubtedly effective. Yet as far as the words of Mordecai go in prompting Esther forward in the cause for her condemned people, the queen likely remains somewhat unoptimistic concerning her chances before the king. Whereas traditionally,

---

45 Day recognises the changes that Esther goes through in her relationship with the Jewish people. She submits that in the MT, "her persona shifts from being very Jewish to being very much the Persian queen." This is the queen we are witnessing at present – "her status within the Jewish community is no longer as important to her" (*Three Faces of a Queen*, 182). However, note the overall picture of the transformation of Esther from a "self-styled Persian to a reconnected Jew" given by Levenson concerning chapter four (*Esther*, 80). Yet this reconnection, it will be suggested, is not fully made in this scene. Indeed, J.A. Berman argues that Esther's "evolution" carries on through to the end of the narrative ("*Hadassah bat Abihail*: The Evolution From Object to Subject in the Character of Esther," *JBL* 120 (2001), 647-69).

46 This understanding is supported by Fox who calls the motives of Esther in this verse "self-centered, although she has been informed of the massive danger facing the people" (*Character and Ideology*, 61) *Pace* Gerleman, who holds that the hesitancy of Esther should be likened to the stalling actions of Moses in taking on God's task in Ex 3.11; 4.10, 13; 6.12, 30 (*Esther*, 105-6), Fox believes that the behaviour of the queen in this case attests that her concern for her own personal well-being (*Character and Ideology*, 61-62). D.J.A. Clines might be correct not to attribute the hesitancy of Esther to cowardice in this case, but it is most likely that some less than heroic personality trait is driving the character of Esther at this particular point (*Ezra, Nehemiah, Esther*, (NCBC; Grand Rapids: Eerdmans, 1984), 301).

readers have imagined a brave, confident and unwavering Esther at the close of chapter four, the text leaves the door open for, and seems to suggest, a slightly different portrait of the queen. In other words, the change in the attitude of the queen from 4.11 to 4.16 might *not* be a complete about-face.

Integral to a fuller understanding of the mindset of Esther in 4.16 is an informed reading of the oft-commented upon 4.14a; for depending on how 4.14a is rendered, the possibility of at least two scenarios emerges for the queen to face in 4.16. In short, the translation of 4.14a is key in determining just what kind of decision confronts Esther in the pivotal sixteenth verse. In the past, the first portion of 4.14 has been seen as "a conditional statement, with one protasis and two apodoses,"[47] usually translated as follows: "For if you certainly keep silent at this time, (then) relief and deliverance will arise for the Jews from another place, and [then] you and the house of your father will be destroyed."[48] J.M. Wiebe notes the interpretative consequences of such a translation:

> Taken in this way, this text seems to affirm that if Esther does not take action to help save the Jews, they would still be delivered by some other unnamed agent. Moreover, her reluctance to act would result in the elimination not only of herself, but of her entire family as well.[49]

This conventional rendering of the Hebrew is not without its problems. Wiebe points out two of the most glaring in question form: 1) How is the mysterious phrase ממקום אחר to be handled? and 2) How might one explain the condemned fate of Esther and her family if she does not act, leaving the destiny of the Jews to the uncertainty of an unnamed deliverer?[50]

Concerning the first difficulty, it is not likely that the narrator utilises מקום as a surrogate reference to God, even though this is a common veiling technique in later Jewish literature.[51] If surrogacy were the case, one would have to account for the inclusion of אחר in the phrase, which produces the theologically problematic translation – "from *another* place [i.e., *another* god]." Thus, concerning the implications of this thinking, Peter R. Ackroyd contends that salvation for the Jews must arise from "some other source" and not

---

47   J.M. Wiebe, "Esther 4.14: 'Will Relief and Deliverance Arise for the Jews from Another Place?'," *CBQ* 53 (1991), 410.
48   Following the translation of Wiebe, "Esther 4.14," 410.
49   Wiebe, "Esther 4.14," 410.
50   Wiebe, "Esther 4.14," 410-12.
51   Gordis, "Religion, Wisdom and History in the Book of Esther," 360 n. 6.

directly from God at all.[52] Suggestions vary as to what this other source might be. Could it be another high ranking Jew? Perhaps deliverance would come as a result of a popular revolt of the Jews or even *via* sympathetic Persians.[53] Maybe the other source is an outside political power that will rescue the Jews and is not mentioned in the story at all?[54] Despite these suggestions, however, Wiebe remarks that the text "nowhere even hints at the source of such a hope."[55] Thus, the difficulty in understanding the phrase מִמָּקוֹם אַחֵר is in no real way eased; the verse leaves large gaps in the understanding of the reader and important questions as to its meaning and reference. Yet it could well be that these gaps and questions are necessary and purposive techniques of the often subtle narrative.

The second difficulty that Wiebe points out issues from the first. If the traditional translation and interpretation of 4.14a is followed, the second apodosis presents a problem – Esther and her family are doomed to destruction if she does not act and the unnamed agent delivers the Jews. Yet the reasons for this fate are not clear. Clines supposes that God himself would punish the queen and her family in judgement if she does not act.[56] Yet the proposal of Clines envisions God explicitly entering a story in which God is, at most, only implicitly present and working. Fitting in better with the human-focused action of the narrative, other scholars imagine that Esther and her family would not be spared because the Jews would look upon them as perfidious and act in retribution.[57] In the end, however, the proposed solutions to the two problems are unsatisfying enough to encourage another rendering of 4.14a. For this, we shall continue with the work of Wiebe.

His proposal centres on the rendering of the first apodosis, which he believes to be "an *interrogative apodosis*."[58] Read in this way, the suggestion is

---

52 P.R. Ackroyd, "Two Hebrew Notes," *ASTI* 5 (1967), 82. The conclusions of Ackroyd are followed by Fox who supposes "another human as a source of deliverance" (*Character and Ideology*, 63).
53 See Clines, *Ezra, Nehemiah, Esther*, 302; *The Esther Scroll*, 42-43.
54 For this proposal, note the work of Paton (*Esther*, 223), Moore (*Esther*, 50), and other sources listed by Wiebe ("Esther 4.14," 412 n. 14).
55 Wiebe, 'Esther 4.14', 412.
56 Clines, *Ezra, Nehemiah, Esther*, 302; *The Esther Scroll*, 35-36. Cf. Fox, *Character and Ideology*, 62, and Wiebe, "Esther 4.14," 412 n. 15 for other like sources.
57 Concerning this position, Wiebe ("Esther 4.14," 412 n. 16) notes the work of L.H. Brockington, *Ezra, Nehemiah and Esther* (CB; London: Thomas Nelson & Sons, 1969), 235, Moore, *Esther*, 53, and S.B. Berg, *The Book of Esther: Motifs, Themes and Structure* (SBLDS 44; Missoula, MT: Scholars Press, 1979) 76, 90 n. 71.
58 Wiebe, "Esther 4.14," 413 (*emphasis original*). Though the normal, SBH, construction used to introduce an interrogative apodosis in a conditional clause includes an interrogative ה (413 n. 19), it is not necessarily the case that the normal construction be present in these kinds of clauses. Some interrogative clauses in SBH do not show forth this normal

that this interrogative apodosis asks a rhetorical question that expects a negative response.[59] Thus, Wiebe's translation reads as follows: "For if you certainly keep silent at this time, *will* relief and deliverance arise for the Jews
from another place? then you and the house of your father will be destroyed."[60] On this reading, Mordecai states pointedly that Esther is the *only*
possible hope for her people; indeed, there is no mystery deliverance
ממקום אחר at all.[61] His strategy, then, is to motivate the queen to appear before the king not out of threat, but out of a sense of family and national loyalty. If she does not act, the elimination of all of the Jews, including Esther
and her family, would result from the genocidal edict of Haman. Upon this
rendering, Wiebe submits that the aforementioned problems that arise from
the traditional translation and interpretation vanish,[62] allowing 4.14a to fit
much better into the overall context of the present scene, and subsequently,
the book as a whole.[63]

If 4.14a is taken traditionally, the scenario that faces the queen in 4.16 pre-
supposes a choice with two options. Esther either can choose to go before the
king herself and take her chances, or she can attempt to remove herself from
the situation altogether hoping that liberation would indeed come from some
other source. Yet if she prefers to put her faith in another deliverer, the
chances for survival, oddly enough, look slim according to the second apodosis.[64] However, if the rendering of Wiebe is followed, the scenario that confronts Esther still presents a choice, although there seems to be only one vi-
able option in view. The interrogative apodosis limits the realm of possible
deliverers to one, the queen herself. This is all part of the persuasive technique of Mordecai.

In light of the translation/interpretation discussion above, the dilemma of
the queen in 4.16 comes into clearer view. The suggestions of Wiebe concerning 4.14a slightly alter the portrait of Esther in her greatest narrative
moment thus far – the instance when the queen assumes the leadership of the

---

interrogative ה pattern, and this linguistic phenomenon is all the more common when we
move into LBH and MH (414 n. 20, 21).
59 On positive rhetorical questions that make negative statements, see G.R. Driver, "Affirmation by Exclamatory Negation," *JANES* 5 (1973), 107-13; and esp. R.T. Hyman,
"Questions and the Book of Ruth," *HS* 24 (1983), 17-25.
60 Wiebe, "Esther 4.14," 413 (*emphasis original*).
61 *Pace* J.G. McConville who states that "the Jews will be saved whether or not she meets
the call of the moment" (*Ezra, Nehemiah & Esther* (DSB; Edinburgh: The Saint Andrew
Press, 1985), 171).
62 Wiebe, "Esther 4.14," 413.
63 Wiebe, "Esther 4.14," 415.
64 Cf. the words of Mordecai in 4.13: "Do not imagine, of all the Jews, to escape the house
of the king with your life" [אַל־תְּדַמִּי בְנַפְשֵׁךְ לְהִמָּלֵט בֵּית־הַמֶּלֶךְ מִכָּל־הַיְּהוּדִים].

Jewish cause and resolves to place the survival of her people over the decree
of the king. Soon Esther would go into the presence of the king, doing that
which is not according to the law [לֹא־כַדָּת], and risking (laying down?) her
life for her kindred.[65]

Despite an undeniable display of courage and loyalty,[66] the resolve of the
queen is likely underlined by an unoptimistic submission to her task.[67] In her
most famous words, "and when I perish, I perish" [וְכַאֲשֶׁר אָבַדְתִּי אָבָדְתִּי],
Esther submits to the likelihood that her life would not continue. Yet since
she is the only hope for her people, perhaps her efforts would go some way to
expose how heinous (that is, in Jewish eyes) the edict sealed by the king
really is – so vile that, at the very least, he stands to lose his beloved queen if
something is not done.

The keys to this interpretation lie in the adopted reading of 4.14a and the
understanding of כאשר in the famous phrase of brave submission seen above.
Against the traditional rendering, the interpretation suggested here understands the challenge of Mordecai in 4.14a to be singularly focused – Esther
presently stands as the only hope for the Jewish people. His rhetorical interrogative, "*will* relief and deliverance arise for the Jews from another place?,"
demands a negative response as he lays on the line the desperate need for the
advocacy of Esther. Beginning to move towards her people, the queen calls
on all the Jews of Shushan to fast for three days while she and her maidens
do likewise (4.16a). The seriousness of the time is evidenced by these actions, for the survival of the Jewish people is hanging in the balance. Then, in
a moment of high dramatic tension, the queen decides to relinquish her life
for her people by breaking the civil law – an offence punishable by immediate death.

---

65 Interestingly, M. Bar-Ilan doubts that Esther ever risked her life. He admits that 4.11
    presents "such an allusion" however (*Some Jewish Women in Antiquity* (BJS 317; At-
    lanta: Scholars Press, 1998), 8). It will be suggested below that the unoptimistic submis-
    sion of Esther was more than just an allusion.

66 Laniak highlights the loyalty of Esther at this juncture to be the issue that was most
    important to the ancient reader: "She is a model of loyalty to her people" (*Shame and
    Honor*, 96; see further 111). While not necessarily in disagreement with this general ob-
    servation, this project is seeking also to explore the *dynamics* of Esther's loyalty at this
    point and from now on in the story.

67 *Pace* F.W. Bush that Esther "resolutely" heeded the call of Mordecai to save her people
    ("The Book of Esther: *Opus non gratum* in the Christian Canon," *BBR* 8 (1998), 49).
    Berman's view seems closer to the mark: "The notion that inner processes of struggle
    are resolved in Esther instantaneously is open to serious challenge. Such sanguine as-
    sessments are incongruent with intonations found in Esther's own statement at the end
    of 4:16" ("*Hadassah bat Abihail*," 655).

The usual translation given for the phrase וכאשר אבדתי אבדתי renders the
conjunction כאשר "if."[68] Translated thus, the reader might be misled because
the likely sense conveyed in the translation of כאשר is conditional. Yet it is
doubtful that the author wishes to communicate such an impression at this
point. If this were the case, it would seem that the context would have been
more suiting and the narrative would have been more likely to press into service either the particles כי or אם.[69] It is more probable that a temporal clause
is being employed here, which is seen more clearly in the translation – "and
when I perish, I perish." In Hebrew, generally speaking, the translation
"when" can be expressed by "כַּאֲשֶׁר with a finite verb (or nominal cl.)" in a
temporal clause.[70] This appears to be the usage in the present phrase; the simultaneously temporal, not the conditional, nature of the action is being exhibited.[71]

In light of all this, the well-known declaration of the queen is neither one
of carelessness[72] nor one of unwavering confidence; instead, it is one of cognisant[73] and perhaps pained submission[74] to the foreboding plight staring
down at her.[75] Indeed, she alone is in a position to undertake the challenge of

---

68 E.g., "and if I perish, I perish" (NRSV); "Wenn ich zugrunde gehe, gehe ich zugrunde"
    (A. Meinhold, *Das Buch Esther* (ZB; Zürich: Theologischer Verlag, 1983), 51).
69 See J.C.L. Gibson, *Davidson's Introductory Hebrew Grammar – Syntax* (Edinburgh: T
    & T Clark, 1994[4]), § 120.
70 Gibson, *Syntax,* § 124a; P. Joüon, *A Grammar of Biblical Hebrew* (2 vols.; trans. and
    rev. T. Muraoka; Rome: Editrice Pontificio Istituto Biblico, 1993), § 166n.
71 See Joüon, *GBH,* § 166l. Specifically to the Esther text, Day supports the reading that
    sees כאשר carrying a temporal sense in this instance. In her view, the temporal use best
    fits the context of the scene (*Three Faces of a Queen,* 57-58).
72 Levenson is not sure whether Esther has merely resigned to death at this point or will-
    ingly accepted her role as the hope of the Jews. What he does admit, however, is that
    there is a sense of reluctance present as he compares the plight of Esther to that of Jacob
    in Gen. 43.14 (*Esther,* 82). Venturing further, Clines posits a "courageous determina-
    tion" involved in both the Esther and Jacob instances (*Ezra, Nehemiah, Esther,* 303).
73 Craig suggests that "Esther is portrayed as a contemplative, one who considers her ac-
    tions' possible consequences before she acts" (*Reading Esther,* 146). If this is an accu-
    rate statement, it is nowhere better illustrated than in this case as the queen encounters
    her most difficult decision.
74 Esther is clearly aware of the danger that lies before her (4.11, 13-14), and she likely
    possesses "eine verzweifelte Entschlossenheit" in the face of it (H. Ringgren, *Das Buch
    Esther,* (ATD 16/2; Göttingen: Vandenhoeck & Ruprecht, 1981[3]), 407; see also Bardtke,
    Das Buch Esther, 335). With this in mind, my view of Esther's submission is in contrast
    with the sense of "passive resignation" that Day supposes (*Three Faces of a Queen,* 57).
    Instead, it comes closer to the idea of "self-sacrifice" offered by Dorothy (*The Books of
    Esther,* 245), and the notion of W. Dommershausen concerning Esther's "Opfers des
    Gehorsams und der Liebe" (*Ester* (NEB; Stuttgart: Echter Verlag, 1995[3]), 26; see also
    his *Die Estherrolle,* 74).
75 This understanding is supported by the reading *BDB* offers, which likens the expression
    in 4.16b to the similar one found in Gen. 43.14 – "when I am bereaved, I am bereaved"

the uninviting court of the king; there is no other potential deliverer waiting in the wings (4.14a). It is to this task that she ultimately submits,[76] likely with hope, but, at best, with uncertainty concerning even the chances of her own survival.[77] In light of all this, it would be fair to suppose that the apprehension of the queen so evident in 4.11 has not been *fully* reversed in 4.16.[78]

2.2.5 Tact at the second banquet (7.1-8)

When Esther comes to terms with her unique role in the fight for Jewish deliverance (4.16), and after she successfully negotiates her first approach before the king (5.1-2), the resolve of the queen seems to strengthen and her skills as a shrewd negotiator are increasingly on display. Once she is given a voice (5.4),[79] Esther requests one banquet (5.6) at which she successfully asks for the presence of the king and Haman at a further one (5.8). The rhetorical

---

[כַּאֲשֶׁר שָׁכֹלְתִּי שָׁכָלְתִּי] – displaying an "expression of resignation" (455). GKC similarly submits that this is "an expression of despairing resignation" (§ 1060). See also *CHALOT*, 149.

76 This is submission not necessarily to the wishes of Mordecai, but to the task that lies before her. In light of this, it can be said that Esther displays a measure of initiative independent of Mordecai and is not solely acting out of fear or respect of her father-figure (*contra* the view of Bar-Ilan who believes that Esther "became the deliverer of her people purely by chance, and only through the encouragement of Mordechai" (*Some Jewish Women in Antiquity*, 8). Esther is a genuine heroine in her own right, even morphologically – a fact that shines through especially in § 2.2.5 (*pace* E. Fuchs, "Status and Role of Female Heroines in the Biblical Narrative," *MQ* 23 (1982), 154).

77 Paton, Berg, and Day believe that Esther possesses little hope, if any, as she prepares to go into the king. Paton likens the anticipation of the queen to one who is submitting to an operation "because there is a chance of escaping death in that way" (*The Book of Esther*, 226). Berg believes that the decision of the queen is made "in spite of the utter helplessness of the situation and the presumed futility of her actions" (*The Book of Esther*, 120 n. 55; cf. Berman, "*Hadassah bat Abihail*," 655). Day states that "[I]t appears here that Esther already accepts her death as a foregone conclusion to her decision to go in to the king. She appears even less hopeful of escaping death than Paton suggests" (*Three Faces of a Queen*, 58). These opinions are in contrast with those of Fox, who is not sure that Esther believes that death would accompany her refusal to go in to the king. Rather, Fox sees the queen as one who is "coming to grips" with the danger of the situation; one who realises that she might fail, but "expresses the hope – though not certainty – of success" (*Character and Ideology*, 64). In terms of the extent of Esther's hope in the present situation, the view suggested presently is closest to that of Fox.

78 Although a measure of narrative suspense has resulted from the delay of Esther in complying with the directives of Mordecai, I hope to have shown that her hesitation has not merely been the product of a literary move to heighten dramatic suspense (*pace* A. Meinhold, "Die Gattung der Josephsgeschichte und des Estherbuches: Diasporanovelle, II," *ZAW* 88 (1976), 82).

79 For an interesting exploration of this moment, see Berman, "*Hadassah bat Abihail*," 659.

skill of Esther in these petitions is evident, and her plan is being flawlessly executed. It is clear that we are no longer dealing here with the young woman under the hovering care of Mordecai. Now it is Queen Esther who was active, keen and conscientiously determined in her efforts to save her people.

We come at this time to the crucial scene of the second banquet – a show-case of the queen's craft *par excellence* (7.1-8). Indeed, her courage, ingenuity and initiative are in full view here as she achieves her desired result.[80] This episode clearly displays a unity of composition, but for the purposes of presentation, it will be analysed in two parts – vss 1-4 and 5-8. In the leading section, the observant reader will notice the cunning tact and rhetorical gifts[81] of the queen at their finest; in the latter division, the fruits of Esther's labour are gathered as she puts the finishing touches on Haman's demise.

With verses 1-2 comes a brief scene-setting in which the king and Haman sit down to drink with the queen at her second banquet in a quick succession of events (6.14-7.2). At this point the king reiterates his longing to know the wish (request) of Esther [מַה־שְּׁאֵלָתֵךְ] and her desire [מַה־בַּקָּשָׁתֵךְ]. Apparently the timing is now right for the Jewess to put her plan into action as she exclaims:

תִּנָּתֶן־לִי נַפְשִׁי בִּשְׁאֵלָתִי וְעַמִּי בְּבַקָּשָׁתִי

Let my life be given to me as my wish and my people as my desire (7.3b).

The curiosity of the king would certainly have been heightened at these words, and one might suppose an uneasy sweat beginning to moisten the back of Haman's neck. But Esther does not stop there. In the words that follow, the queen tactfully constructs a brilliant line of reasoning that carries with it the Jews' greatest hope for survival. Everything hangs upon the persuasive techniques of Esther at this moment.

Likely playing upon her knowledge of the offered blood money promised in exchange for the annihilation of the Jews (3.9), Esther explains to the king that she and her people have been "sold…to be exterminated, killed and destroyed" [כִּי נִמְכַּרְנוּ…לְהַשְׁמִיד לַהֲרוֹג וּלְאַבֵּד].[82] On account of this impending doom, the present leader of the Jewish people resolves to act and inform the

---

80 Craig, *Reading Esther*, 26. Paton would likely not have agreed, stating generally that "[S]he [Esther] wins her victories not by skill or by character, but by her beauty" (*The Book of Esther*, 96). Interestingly, the beauty of Esther does not explicitly come into the frame in this episode; Esther negotiates her victories by other means, through other techniques (see L. Day, "Power, Otherness, and Gender in the Biblical Short Stories," *HBT* 20 (1998), 113).

81 Clines, *The Esther Scroll*, 18.

82 Baldwin, *Esther*, 92.

king. Yet while the reader might suppose that this information would be
enough to compel the king to react and do something to save his beloved
queen and her people, Esther pre-empts any reaction of the king with a further inducement:

וְאִלּוּ לַעֲבָדִים וְלִשְׁפָחוֹת נִמְכַּרְנוּ הֶחֱרַשְׁתִּי כִּי אֵין הַצָּר שֹׁוֶה בְּנֵזֶק הַמֶּלֶךְ

If we had been sold for male and female slaves I would have kept silent, for the calamity is not comparable with the annoyance to the king[83] (7.4b).

With this, the queen successfully (and purposely) whets the appetite of the
king to know who has caused all of this trouble.[84] The answer is close at
hand.

---

83   While the general gist of the statement of Esther is clear, the specific nature of the last
clause is unclear, and thus, disputed. *Pace* Paton (*The Book of Esther,* 258) and Moore,
(*Esther,* 70), some sense can be made of the MT as it stands. By translating הַצָּר "the
adversary" (cf. Zech 8.10) and not "the adversity" (cf. Ps 4.2), and looking forward to
the use of צָר in the designation of Haman [אִישׁ צַר וְאוֹיֵב הָמָן הָרָע הַזֶּה] (7.6), Levenson
proposes the following translation: "for then the adversary would not have been worth
the king's loss." Upon this, he suggests that Esther would not ruin the vizier of the king
if only the sale of her people into slavery were in view. Yet since the threat of annihilation is present, a greater loss than the merely financial is threatened (*Esther,* 100 n. a). In
other words, Esther *must* bring this before the king, no matter who might get hurt by its
uncovering – physically or financially – because she is saving him from a greater loss.
See also the comments of Daube concerning political/economic factors that might weigh
in the consideration here, especially his political interpretation of נזק (*Esther,* 3f.)
Daube's appeal to an economical argument is followed by LaCocque, *The Feminine
Unconventional,* 54. Baldwin also favours this rendering and calls the technique of
Esther here "good psychology" (*Esther,* 92). Bush, on the other hand, translates the
clause thus: "for the trouble would not be commensurate with the annoyance to the
king," taking צר in the sense of "calamity, difficulty" and נזק in sense of "trouble, annoyance." Bush elucidates his translation by explaining that the צר (the Jews being sold
into slavery) would not "be worth/justify" the נזק (which she is presently causing) to the
king (see *Ruth, Esther,* 427-28 for a full discussion; note that the rendering of Beal (*The
Book of Hiding,* 135 (following Haupt)) is quite similar to that of Bush). (Positions also
worth noting are R. Gordis, "Studies in the Esther Narrative," *JBL* 95 (1976), 56; Clines,
Ezra, Nehemiah, Esther, 311; Day, *Three Faces of a Queen,* 123-24; Laniak, *Shame and
Honor,* 113; and Berlin, *Esther,* 67-68.) Thus, in the rendering of Bush, there is neither a
financial element explicitly present (*pace* Fox, *Character and Ideology,* 84-85, 282), nor
is there any allusion to Haman as the adversary. For the latter, the reader must wait until
7.6. Although I have followed Bush in my translation, the reading of Levenson is
equally as satisfying contextually; it all comes down to how one deals with the textual
ambiguity caused by the uncertain meanings of a few words. Nevertheless, and most
importantly, even though there are differences of opinions concerning the rendering of
this portion of text, commentators are united in their opinion that the skilful diplomacy
of Esther is on full display here.

84   Fox (*Character and Ideology,* 85) and Craig (*Reading Esther,* 83) both point to the
tactics of Esther in her rhetoric and choice of approach here, although from slightly different angles.

Her plan unfolds quickly in the heightened suspense of verses 5-8. Because of the skill of Esther in the presentation of the dilemma of the Jews, the agitated king has trouble even formulating a coherent question as he now seeks to know who is responsible for the threat against his wife's people.[85] His desire comes across clearly enough, however, and the queen is quick and ready to oblige him by calling out: "a man, an enemy and a foe – this evil Haman!" [אִישׁ צַר וְאוֹיֵב הָמָן הָרָע הַזֶּה] (7.6a).[86]

This disturbing news affects the two men in the room in quite different ways. The king is clearly enraged, but finds himself at a loss for words, and storms from the banquet into the garden to ponder what actions he might take (7.7).[87] The reaction of Haman to this pronouncement is one of terror [נִבְעַת],[88] and he remains in the presence of the queen when the king departs to the garden so that he might plead for his life. The vizier senses that the anger of the king is directed towards him, and it is likely only a matter of time before His Majesty would return to execute his judgement (7.7).[89]

Upon the king's return, it is not known whether or not the fate of Haman has been decided. Yet if he had not made up his mind as he strode in the garden, the newly assumed posture of his vizier greatly assists his decision-

---

85   Literally: "who [is] he, this (one)? and where [is] this he who has filled his heart to do thus?" [מִי הוּא זֶה וְאֵי־זֶה הוּא אֲשֶׁר־מְלָאוֹ לִבּוֹ לַעֲשׂוֹת כֵּן] (7.5b). Here, "form and content unite with dramatic effect" as the king's "highly charged feelings" of rage are expressed with staccato syllables. For a literary discussion of this (purposefully?) awkward syntax, consult Bush (*Ruth, Esther*, 426), Fox (*Character and Ideology*, 86), Dommershausen (*Die Estherrolle*, 95) and Berlin (*Esther*, 68).

86   Possibly for political or psychological reasons, Esther leaves aside the culpability of the king in the edict condemning the Jews (3.10) (Berg, *The Book of Esther*, 92; see also Beal, *The Book of Hiding*, 98). However, see § 2.6.3.

87   Bush notes a dramatic ellipsis here in that the reader is not sure why the king bolts from the room, or to whom is rage is directed. The latter question is actually answered before the former one in that the actions of Haman hint against whom the king is furious. Concerning the former question, Bush supposes that the king "was at a loss to know what to do" and needed some time to decide (*Ruth, Esther*, 423, 430). A bit more certain about the matter is Clines who submits that the king stormed into the garden to decide between his publicly promoted vizier and his beautiful queen (*The Esther Scroll*, 15). However, the text leaves the reader to use his or her imagination.

88   Moore supposes that instead of being afraid, Haman "was dumbfounded" or "taken by surprise" by this proclamation. He bases his rendering on the use of בעת in Dan 8.17 and 1 Chr 21.30 (*Esther*, 71). If the fact that the queen was Jewish dumbfounded Haman, then the rendering of Moore carries some weight. Yet, contextually, the translation "was terrified" fits better because of Haman's ensuing fearful grovelling before the queen in the subsequent verse. In both cases the vizier knows exactly what the situation is and he acts quickly out of fear (cf. *BDB*, 130; *TWOT*, 1:122; and Day, *Three Faces of a Queen*, 127). This reading is widely supported in commentaries. Further, and ironically, Haman is now exhibiting the same response he wants others to show to him (Laniak, *Shame and Honor*, 109 n. 21).

89   Paton, *The Book of Esther*, 263. Concerning king's judgement on Haman, see § 2.6.4.

making process. By his *appearance* Haman signs his own death-warrant.[90] What exactly he is doing as he falls upon the couch of the queen is uncertain,[91] and for all narrative purposes it does not matter.[92] Yet although Esther is the central character of this episode and is active throughout it, the narrative is silent concerning what part she plays in the present scene other than to mention, in passing, that she is upon her couch (7.8).[93] It is likely, however, that between the quick judgement of the returning king and the self-destructive appearance (or action) of his vizier, no further persuasive work is needed.

2.2.6 The vengeful queen (9.13)

Although most readerly attention in regard to vengefulness centres around the behaviour of an anonymous group of Jews in the book of Esther,[94] there is sufficient reason to take a brief look at the queen herself concerning this subject. At best, the ethical complexion of Esther is questionable in her dealings with her enemies. But can she fairly be called "a sophisticated Jael?"[95] In what follows, we shall look specifically at the sole relevant textual example in which Esther directly speaks. By limiting ourselves to this occasion, we shall hopefully avoid the risk of attributing to Esther more attention that she deserves concerning the matter of vengeance.

Ever since 8.9, Mordecai returns as the lead actor of the two Jewish heroes in the book. He is the one who apparently commands and has written the counter decree (8.9-10). Mordecai alone proceeds from the house of the king in royal attire [בִּלְבוּשׁ מַלְכוּת] to the delight of the citadel of Shushan (8.15). It is he who is reckoned great [גָּדוֹל] in the house of the king, the figure whom many people now fear (9.3), the one whose fame spreads throughout the land as he grows more and more powerful (9.4), and the Jew who will

---

90 Laniak makes a similar observation (*Shame and Honor,* 111).
91 Beal, *The Book of Hiding,* 99. Berlin suggests that Haman actually assumes the pose of a supplicant, which is intentionally misunderstood by the king as he re-enters the room, "casting the supplicant as a seducer" (*Esther,* 70).
92 See further on the unfortunate appearance of Haman before the queen (§ 2.4.4).
93 Laniak suggests that Esther set up a "sting" for Haman at the very least (*Shame and Honor,* 151 n. 68).
94 See § 2.5.
95 Moore notes that this designation, referring to Judg 4.17-22, has come from scholars because of the *in*action of Esther in 7.9 to come to the aid of Haman when wrongly accused, and because of her requests in 9.13. He comments, however, that this kind of conclusion takes the acts of Esther in isolation with disregard to "her inner motives" and "without full knowledge of the external circumstances" (*Esther,* 88).

occupy the stage solely at the end of the story (10.2-3). Yet, however small it
is, Esther is not entirely without a voice in the latter portions of the narrative.

On 13 Adar, after the Jews have completed their first day of battle with
their enemies, the word concerning the casualties in Shushan comes in before
the king (9.11). After receiving this information, the king turns to his queen
and relates that 500 men and the ten sons of Haman have died that day. He
then inquires of her what the Jews have done in the rest of the provinces,
formulaically restating that her wishes and requests would be done (9.12).
But instead of answering the question of the king concerning the activities of
the Jews in the wider kingdom, Esther skips right to her requests as she
speaks these words:

אִם־עַל־הַמֶּלֶךְ טוֹב יִנָּתֵן גַּם־מָחָר גַּם־מָחָר לַיְּהוּדִים אֲשֶׁר בְּשׁוּשָׁן לַעֲשׂוֹת כְּדָת הַיּוֹם וְאֵת עֲשֶׂרֶת בְּנֵי־
הָמָן יִתְלוּ עַל־הָעֵץ

If unto the king it is pleasing, let it be granted also tomorrow to the Jews who [are] in
Shushan to do according to the law (decree) of today – and the ten sons of Haman, let
them hang upon the tree (9.13).

One should notice in this particular text that the queen carefully keeps all of
her petitions for action within the realm of the law [דָּת].[96] Yet we would do
well to keep in mind that *lawfulness* does not necessarily entail *morality*.[97]
Her first request is that the king approves the decree of 13 Adar for the Jews
in Shushan the next day. The reason for this particular request for a punishing
massacre is unknown, and hence, puzzling. Could it be that the enemies of
the Jews are still a threat in Shushan?[98] According to the edict that only gave
them a mandate to attack on 13 Adar, they should not have been. In light of
this probability, the suspicion concerning the motives of Esther is perhaps
heightened a bit. Further, it seems clear that the victory of the Jews on 13
Adar is nothing short of comprehensive.[99]

In a comment that goes beyond suspicion to conclusion, Paton calls the
request of the queen "horrible" and sees only a "malignant spirit of revenge"

---

96 This Jewish conscientiousness concerning the law is noteworthy in view of the earlier
    accusation of Haman in 3.8 (Craig, *Reading Esther*, 130 (cited in Laniak, *Shame and
    Honor*, 136 n. 27)).
97 *Pace* A.M. Rodriguez who stresses the law-abiding nature of the Jews over against
    accusations of vindictiveness (*Esther: A Theological Approach* (Berrien Springs, MI:
    Andrews University Press, 1995), 15).
98 A reality supposed by J. Magonet, "The Liberal and the Lady: Esther Revisited," *Juda-
    ism* 29 (1980), 174; followed by Rodriguez, *Esther: A Theological Approach*, 15.
99 *Pace* H. Gevaryahu who submits that Esther calls the second day of battle in Shushan
    because "there was not a clear victory for either side" ("Esther is a Story of Jewish De-
    fense not a Story of Jewish Revenge" (trans. G.J. Gevaryahu), *JBQ* 21 (1993), 9).

present in it.[100] But is the picture different if the petition of the queen at this point is "punitive and precautionary" so as to eliminate further threat as Fox has suggested?[101] Along these same lines, can we assume that because there had been an intended threat against the Jews, the intentions of Esther here are justified?[102] Is the request of Esther excusable, necessary, or even laudatory in its context? To be sure, the text does not appear to entertain our questions; it reports only the ensuing results of the altercations on 14 Adar (9.15).

The second request of Esther is for the public humiliation of the sons of Haman who had already been killed in 9.10. Following the majority of commentators, this petition is not a repeated call for the death of the sons of Haman – thus, evidence for other source material.[103] This practice, likely for the purposes of public disgrace, is attested both in biblical and non-biblical sources.[104] But unlike the similar hanging cases of the king of Ai and the five kings of the Amorites (Josh 8.29; 10.26), חרם does not appear to be governing the book of Esther; God neither explicitly commands nor actively directs this battle[105] (even if we are to assume God's hand behind these events).[106] Although some contend that Esther is using this public spectacle as a deterrent against further enemy action, the text neither explicitly indicates this nor leans towards it in a strong way.[107]

It would be difficult to comment conclusively concerning the words of Esther in relation to the enemies of the Jews. Yet it is clear that the text depicts Esther as the impetus behind the call for more bloodshed on 14 Adar.[108]

---

100 Paton, *The Book of Esther*, 287.
101 Fox, *Character and Ideology*, 112. Clines comments that although the first request of Esther "lacks any narrative motivation," it could have been in the service of promoting "Jewish supremacy at the heart of the Persian empire" (*The Esther Scroll*, 48; *Ezra, Nehemiah, Esther*, 324).
102 Note the position and rationale of Laniak concerning the "intention" of the enemies and Jewish response under the governing notions of just recompense, retribution, vindication and reversal (*Shame and Honor*, 140f).
103 E.g., see Paton (*The Book of Esther*, 287); Fox (*Character and Ideology*, 112); Levenson (*Esther*, 122); and Baldwin (*Esther*, 106).
104 Cf. Josh 8.29; 10.26; 1 Sam 31.10; on the practice of hanging/impalement in particular, see Herodotus, *The Histories* (Rev. ed.; trans. A. de Sélincourt; London: Penguin Books, 1996), 3.125 and 6.30.
105 See further Craig, *Reading Esther*, 126.
106 See Laniak, *Shame and Honor*, 134 n. 22.
107 This "deterrent" view is held by Rodriguez (*Esther: A Theological Approach*, 15).
108 *Contra* the developed explanation of Magonet that the paranoid king is the real power and impetus behind the call for more bloodshed. Magonet reasons that the king is fearful of further Hamanic factions being left over after the 13th, and since His Majesty had been suspecting a *coup d'état* from Haman since his inclusion in Esther's small and exclusive guest list for her banquet (contrast the invitees of 5.4 and 5.8), he desired that any lingering conspirators be eliminated. Thus, in the thinking of Magonet, the request of Esther for a second day of fighting "is as much a bowing to a political necessity

In the words of Fox, "Esther seems vindictive" at this point in light of the fact that "the Jews are in no present danger...they have massacred their enemies.... Even if Esther's request is for a precautionary massacre, it is, literally, overkill."[109] However, in the view of Fox, the underlying seriousness of the actions of Esther is lessened somewhat by literary-cultic explanations concerning the celebration days of Purim.[110] Yet the gravity of the narrative's words might not be so easily undercut or explained away.[111] It might well be appropriate that the moral overtones of the petition of Esther in 9.13 override, or at least rival in seriousness, the establishment or explanation of the festival schedule.[112] Thus, to suggest that Esther resembles "a sophisticated Jael"

---

forced upon her by the king" than any "bloodthirstiness" that she herself shows. He summarises: "The violence that she displays is only a reflection of the violence implicit in the system into which she has been cast" ("The Liberal and the Lady: Esther Revisited," 174). Attempting to stop short of suggesting a total exoneration of Esther, Magonet merely desires to "locate the source of violence outside the will of Esther or Mordecai" and to position it "in the nature of the regime, of their society itself" (175). It is doubtful, however, that the narrative totally supports his notions; Esther and Mordecai both work successfully within and against the regime (see the work of D.G. Firth, "The book of Esther: A neglected paradigm for dealing with the state," *Old Testament Essays* 10 (1997), 20-26).

109 Fox, *Character and Ideology*, 203.

110 Fox, *Character and Ideology*, 203. To be fair in my use of Fox at this point, I must also include his views on chapter 9 (MT) as a whole. He is not sure that this vindictive picture of Esther is intended. He writes: "According to my theory of the book's development...all of Esther 9 is an expansion of a few sentences in an earlier version of the Esther story. Literary values are here less important than liturgical purposes. The request of Esther for a second day of fighting results more from the need to explain an existing practice than any literary conception of her personality." Meinhold concurs with the literary explanation and states on that basis that "ist eine moralische Entrüstung unangebracht" (*Das Buch Esther*, 86; see also Berlin's comments on the etiological function and carnivalesque nature of chapter nine (*Esther*, 81f.); cf. Dommershausen, *Ester*, 45; and Moore, *Esther*, 91).

111 Fox continues: "Yet whatever the author's intentions, the effect of 9.13 is to introduce a note of harshness and even bellicosity into the picture" (*Character and Ideology*, 203). This is the uncomfortable textual reality that has prompted our comments in this section. *Pace* B.W. Jones, one does not have to be a literalist or act as if he/she were to raise serious questions concerning the moral actions in the book of Esther. Even if one regards the book as fiction and realises the obvious comic intent underlying much of the narrative, that does not necessarily imply that all moral inquiry is abandoned. Humour can carry along with it serious messages and implications ("Two Misconceptions About the Book of Esther," *CBQ* 39 (1977), 180-81). For comment on the relationship of the comic to irony and ethics, see S. Goldman, "Narrative and Ethical Ironies in Esther," *JSOT* 47 (1990), 30 n. 18.

112 The claim of Goldman is that the "ironic exploration of Jewish-Gentile relationships" is foremost in the mind of the author here and not "an explanation for a minor Jewish holiday." He also believes that the request of Esther in 9.13 is "a literary device" operative in a 'deliberately overdrawn revenge scene' which sets forth the Jews' "tragically ironic expansion of vengeance" ("Narrative and Ethical Ironies," 23). At this point, however, we are only concentrating on the possibilities of the queen's vengeance and shall address the behaviour of the Jews as an anonymous group in § 2.5 below.

might not be so wide of the mark after all.[113] In the heat of the battle, she might well have lost her ability to critique herself.[114] As a result she appears helpless to be anything but "determined and inflexible."[115]

2.3 Mordecai

2.3.1 A joint policing operation (2.21-23)

Aside from his introduction in 2.5-7 and a further descriptive mention (2.10-11), the first substantive encounter that we have with the character of Mordecai finds him exhibiting the traits of a loyal official and subject of the king (2.21-23).[116] For present purposes, knowledge of the exact nature of his official role within the court of the king is not primary;[117] instead, our focus will be on the reality of the upstanding and conscientious 'legal' actions of Mordecai in the service of the king. It is here that we observe the initial Jewish interaction with the whimsically unsystematic, and curiously unalterable, Persian law.

---

113 Knowing what we can about the character of Esther and the circumstances of the Hebrew Esther story, it might be unfair *not* to admit that the appearance of the queen in the book is less than wholly upright. Perhaps the character traits suggested in this section attest to an aspect of the *true* moral complexion of the Hebrew Esther, one whose apprehension demands a reader's imagination and willingness to have an open mind.

114 Firth suggests that Esther is too "caught up within the system" at this point and has become "too enmeshed in the context" to critically work within the state at this point. He submits that she has done well to use the Persian system throughout the entire narrative, but appears to slip up in 9.11-15 ("The book of Esther: A neglected paradigm for dealing with the state," 25-26).

115 J.F. Craghan, "Esther, Judith, and Ruth: Paradigms for Human Liberation," *BTB* 12 (1982), 13.

116 The loyalty that the character of Mordecai exhibits is thought to progress in line with one of the main purposes of the book – i.e., that Jews can and should work well within foreign environments (B.W. Jones, "The So-Called Appendix to the Book of Esther," *Semitics* 6 (1978), 38). This loyalty is not without some qualification however (see § 2.3.2).

117 That Mordecai holds some sort of official capacity by nature of his "sitting in (at) the gate of the king" [יֹשֵׁב בְּשַׁעַר־הַמֶּלֶךְ] is a commonly held view. The precise nature of that capacity is not fully known, although cf. Berlin for the view that Mordecai perhaps was a "member of the king's secret police" – the "eyes" and "ears" of the king (*Esther,* 31). For some more detailed general and specific studies, consult the following: O. Loretz, "*šʿr hmlk* – 'Das Tor des Königs'," *Die Welt des Orients* 4 (1967), 104-108; H.P. Rüger, "'Das Tor des Königs' – der königliche Hof," *Biblica* 50 (1969), 247-50; H. Wehr, "Das Tor des Königs in Buche Esther und verwandte Ausdrücke," *Der Islam* 39 (1964), 247-60; D.J.A. Clines, "In Quest of the Historical Mordecai," *VT* 41 (1991), 129-36; E.M. Yamauchi, "Mordecai, the Persepolis Tablets, and the Susa Excavations," *VT* 42 (1992), 272-75.

As has been observed previously in the actions of Esther's neglect of the decree of the king that forbade an unbidden entrance into his presence (4.16-5.1), the attitude of the Jews concerning the civil law is not entirely consistent. Whereas Persian legal inconsistencies are likely the result of a sense of personal interest and insecurity, Jewish behaviour regarding the Persian law appears ultimately to be governed by a sense of national interest and security.

The episode in focus is introduced by the temporally vague phrase "in those days" [בַּיָּמִים הָהֵם], giving the reader the impression that the exact time and circumstances surrounding the event are not of first importance. Of primary interest, though, is the careful response of Mordecai to the assassination plot that has become known to him [וַיִּוָּדַע הַדָּבָר לְמָרְדֳּכַי] as he occupies his place in the gate of the king. The machination of the eunuchs, Bigthan and Teresh, who guard the threshold of the king, prompts Mordecai to perform his public duty and report the conspirators to a higher authority. In this case, Mordecai reports the evil scheme to his cousin, who also happens to be the queen. Esther subsequently informs the king of the plot of the eunuchs in the name of Mordecai [בְּשֵׁם מָרְדֳּכָי] (2.22). Then, in what appears to be a quick (and possibly impromptu) inquisition, Bigthan and Teresh are sentenced to death. Finally, and for future reference, these events are recorded in the court annals in the presence of the king (2.23).

In this instance, the actions of Mordecai are publicly commendable in theory even if they do not result in any immediate public distinction.[118] He conducts himself in a manner that is both for the good of the kingdom, as he proceeds through the appropriate and necessary judicial channels, and eventually positive for his own person. Because of this, the court of the king is stabilised and the standing of the Jews in the kingdom is not at all hindered. In the wider narrative scope, the Jewish cause is greatly aided by the loyal behaviour of Mordecai and his joint policing operation with Esther.[119] At this point

---

118 That the king does not immediately reward Mordecai is puzzling (see Fox, *Character and Ideology*, 40). While in the greater narrative framework, more sense can be made (see 6.1-11), the reader still would have expected Mordecai to be recognised. The failure of the king to do so points, in the view of Firth, to the fact that the Persian government has "lost touch with the people it purports to govern" ("The book of Esther: A neglected paradigm for dealing with the state," 21-22).

119 It is interesting to notice the relational solidarity between Mordecai and Esther shown in the teamwork they exhibit in order to bring the conspirators to justice in 2.21-23 (Clines, *The Esther Scroll*, 105; Day, *Three Faces of a Queen*, 187-89). This collaboration for the Jewish community is evident throughout the narrative, even if at certain points the actions of one hero are emphasised over the other. In this vein, Fox comments on the possibility of the co-operative efforts of the two Jews in the service of promoting the "importance" of Esther within the court (*Character and Ideology*, 40). In a narrative link, Levenson notices the foreshadowing that this partnership provides for their joint

in the story, the loyalty of Mordecai to the king is unquestionable, but, as yet, unchallenged.

2.3.2 Refusal to bow before Haman (3.1-4)

The inner struggles of the character of Mordecai leave much to the imagination of the reader. Even the narrative descriptions of him fall short of a total portrait of the man who stands alongside the king in greatness at the close of the narrative (10.1-3). But is the picture of Mordecai seen in the previous section an adequate or final one? According to Fox, "Mordecai is an ideal figure, a repository of virtues, a shining example of how a Jew of the diaspora should behave."[120] The text of 3.1-4 put this lofty description to the test. The stance of Mordecai in this episode calls into question the nature of his virtue, if not the depth of it. At the very least, an understanding of the motivations of his inaction is desired.

The initial words of 3.1, "After these things" [אַחַר הַדְּבָרִים הָאֵלֶּה], do not tightly follow the ending of chapter two (2.21-23). This perplexing beginning leaves us to ponder the future of Mordecai in the court of the king after he has prevented the assassination plot of the two door guards. One would expect to read on and find Mordecai being promoted within the royal government at this time. Instead, what we observe is the inexplicable elevation of Haman, son of Hammedatha, the Agagite, to a high position in the kingdom. What is clear, however, is that this literary scenario nicely sets up the next episode in the story and moves the plot of the narrative forward quickly.

Yet regardless of the issue of an unexplainable time sequence,[121] the more pressing (and more perplexing) issue of the elevation of Haman in the Persian court persists. The reason for this lofty distinction is certainly left unspecified in the text, and the story does not pause for much consideration on this point. Verse two moves right along to the fact that everyone is bowing down and doing obeisance [כֹּרְעִים וּמִשְׁתַּחֲוִים] to the new vizier at the command of the

---

foiling of "an infinitely larger assassination plot – Haman's attempted genocide of the Jewish people" (*Esther*, 64).

120 Fox, *Character and Ideology*, 185.

121 The common biblical idiom, אחר הדברים האלה, does not even have to have a temporal element. It can also "join loosely together different episodes in a story (e.g., Gen. 15.1)" (S.P. Re'emi, 'The Faithfulness of God: A Commentary on the Book of Esther', in *Israel Among the Nations: A Commentary on the Books of Nahum, Obadiah, Esther* (ITC; Grand Rapids: Eerdmans, 1985), 121. See also Laniak for suggestions concerning the effect(s) of the transition between chapters two and three (*Shame and Honor*, 70).

king – that is, all except Mordecai.[122] This unyielding disobedience[123] and inaction presents a problem in the narrative – a *huge* problem considering that the whole Jewish race is condemned to death on account of the refusal of Mordecai to bow and do obeisance to his court superior (3.6-13). Interestingly enough, the servants of the king anticipate our next question as they ask the unyielding Mordecai: "Why [are] you violating the command of the king?" [מַדּוּעַ אַתָּה עוֹבֵר אֵת מִצְוַת הַמֶּלֶךְ] (3.3b). Even though the servants are long-suffering,[124] the text reports that the reluctance of Mordecai is nevertheless brought to the attention of Haman (3.4). The narrative goes on to add that this is done in order to see if the reason that Mordecai gave for not bowing down to the king would exempt him – "for he told them that he [was] a Jew" [כִּי־הִגִּיד לָהֶם אֲשֶׁר־הוּא יְהוּדִי] (3.4b). Yet even though the reason for refusal has been given, it is somewhat cryptic, and the matter is in no way resolved.

Having given this terse rationale behind the unwillingness of Mordecai to do obeisance to Haman, it appears that the writer feels no further need to explain or excuse the Jew.[125] Literarily, the unknown motivations of Mordecai are not of prime importance since the stage of the conflict has been set and the provocation of Haman has been achieved.[126] Nevertheless, the curious interpreter throughout the years has not been able to leave the matter so easily.[127] For without a better and more contextual attempt at an explanation, the accusation of Paton that Mordecai exhibited an "inexplicable" and "unreasonable" arrogance before Haman stands perhaps as firmly as any other.[128] But upon closer inspection of the text here and heretofore, the reader's gap in understanding is diminished, if it does not vanish altogether. Perhaps a plau-

---

122 The text tells us explicitly about the refusal of Mordecai: "but Mordecai did not bow down and did not do obeisance" [וּמָרְדֳּכַי לֹא יִכְרַע וְלֹא יִשְׁתַּחֲוֶה].
123 E.L. Greenstein notices that the repetition of the negative לֹא in 3.2 highlights the disobedience of Mordecai ("A Jewish Reading of Esther," in J. Neusner, B.A. Levine and E.S. Frerichs (eds), *Judaic Perspectives on Ancient Israel* (Philadelphia: Fortress Press, 1987), 233.
124 This is seen in the editorial comment: "And it was in their saying to him daily – but he would not listen to them" [וַיְהִי בְּאָמְרָם אֵלָיו יוֹם וָיוֹם וְלֹא שָׁמַע אֲלֵיהֶם]. *Pace* B. Goodnick, the servants of the king do not appear to have become "resentful" of Mordecai and thus informed Haman ("The Book of Esther and its Motifs," *JBQ* 25 (1997), 102). Instead, their persistence [וַיְהִי בְּאָמְרָם אֵלָיו יוֹם וָיוֹם] suggests that they were seeking the welfare of Mordecai and his survival in the court.
125 Fox, *Character and Ideology*, 43.
126 Paton, *The Book of Esther*, 197.
127 For a good summary of the main suggestions, see Fox, *Character and Ideology*, 43-45.
128 Paton, *The Book of Esther*, 196-97, 213.

sible and reasonable explanation has been there in the text for the perceptive reader all along.[129]

It is likely that the non-compliance of Mordecai is linked to the long-standing ethnic animosity between the Israelites and the Amalekites.[130] The genealogical lines provided for Mordecai (2.5) and Haman (3.1) undoubtedly link them to the warring kings of 1 Sam 15.[131] It is these patronymics that would tip off alert readers of the Hebrew text. For the keen and circumspect reader, it might possibly be suggested that the explanation of Mordecai – כִּי־הִגִּיד לָהֶם אֲשֶׁר־הוּא יְהוּדִי – provides ample if not overabundant rationalisation concerning his refusal to bow to his ancestral and tribal arch-enemy, Haman, *the Agagite*.[132]

A better understanding of the reasoning of Mordecai and the convictions behind his resistance to follow the decree of the king could complicate the moral question in this case. If, as some have suggested, his inaction here is due to hubris, then we are perhaps faced with a moral problem of personal selfishness – one that would cast a shadow over the "shining example" of behaviour that Fox claims for his "ideal figure" and "repository of virtues." Yet if, as others have posited, the inaction of Mordecai is tied to a commitment to Jewish solidarity and a conviction to place the interests of his community over above any loyalties he has to the civil government (or persons of authority therein), then the question of the disobedience is not so cut-and-

---

129 Clines, *The Esther Scroll*, 14. According to Daube, the perceptive reader would have connected the refusal of Mordecai to a similar account related in Herodotus of unyielding obeisance involving Spartan nobles being ordered to prostrate themselves before Xerxes I by his guards. The Spartans refused and surprisingly are not condemned (*The Histories*, 7.133f.). Daube claims that "anyone coming upon Esther was bound to associate Haman with the savage guards" (*Esther*, 15). Perhaps.

130 Cf. Gen 36.12 (?); Exod 17.8-16; Num 24.7; Deut 25.17-19; 1 Sam 15. Interesting also is the apparent conclusion of the Israel-Amalekite struggle in 1 Chr 4.42-43 in the days of Hezekiah. Fox notes that the Amalekites as a nation appear not to exist past this point, yet the possibility of an Amalekite Diaspora is not out of the question (*Character and Ideology*, 42, 43-46). For support of this link see Bardtke, *Das Buch Esther*, 316-17; A.B. Ehrlich, *Ranglossen zur hebräischen Bibel: Textkritisches, Sprachliches, und Sachliches* (vol. XII; Hildesheim: Georg Olms, 1968), 115; Moore, *Esther*, 36; Berg, *The Book of Esther*, 67-68; Meinhold, *Das Buch Esther*, 42-43; Dommershausen, *Ester*, 20; Clines, *Ezra, Nehemiah, Esther*, 294; D.F. Morgan, *Between Text & Community: The 'Writings' in Canonical Interpretation* (Minneapolis: Fortress Press, 1990), 69; Craig, *Reading Esther*, 114; Bush, *Ruth, Esther*, 385; Levenson, *Esther*, 66-67; Laniak, *Shame and Honor*, 70 n. 7, 73-75; Rudavsky, "In Defense of Tradition," *passim*; Berlin, *Esther*, 33-34.

131 A. LaCocque, "Haman in the Book of Esther," *HAR* 11 (1987), 216.

132 The comments of Laniak concerning linear genealogies and corporate personality are informative here. To be sure, Mordecai and Haman are "royal representatives of rival groups" (*Shame and Honor*, 76-78). See also the helpful comments of Berlin on this link (*Esther*, xxxviii, 33-34).

dried.[133] Though perhaps characterised by gaucheness,[134] Mordecai displays a weighed allegiance, and it is evident that similar persuasions can be seen in the resolve and actions of Esther in 4.16-5.1 (§ 2.2.4). To be sure, the assimilation of these Jews into the foreign culture and court is not without certain difficulties and reservations.

2.3.3 Refusal to transgress court regulations (4.2)

The selective nature of Mordecai's civil obedience evidences itself once again after the genocidal edict of Haman is published (3.12-15). Upon the refusal of Mordecai to bow down and do obeisance to him, Haman approaches the king with a diplomatic proposition in order to rid the kingdom of an unassimilated[135] and unlawful people (3.8; § 2.4.1). To this plan, the king complicitously acquiesces (3.10-11; § 2.6.3). The result of this signet ring endorsement is confusion in the city of Shushan [וְהָעִיר שׁוּשָׁן נָבוֹכָה] (3.15), and utter despair, bitter crying and mourning in sackcloth and ashes among Mordecai and the Jews (4.1-3).[136] Nevertheless, in the midst of this crisis of Jewish existence, it is interesting to note that Mordecai carefully upholds the civil law in every respect.

It is in the text of 4.2 that we find these words:

וַיָּבוֹא עַד לִפְנֵי שַׁעַר־הַמֶּלֶךְ כִּי אֵין לָבוֹא אֶל־שַׁעַר הַמֶּלֶךְ בִּלְבוּשׁ שָׂק

> he [Mordecai] went as far as the face of the gate of the king, for no one [was] to go into the gate of the king in clothes of sackcloth.

---

133 Especially helpful is Berg's discussion concerning the theme of loyalty to the Jewish community that is manifested in the book of Esther (*The Book of Esther*, 98-103).

134 D.J.A. Clines, "Reading Esther From Left to Right: Contemporary Strategies for Reading a Biblical Text," in *idem*, S.E. Fowl, and S.E. Porter (eds), *The Bible in Three Dimensions* (JSOTSup 87; Sheffield: Sheffield Academic Press, 1990), 44.

135 See Fox (*Character and Ideology*, 279-80), who is followed by Bush (*Ruth, Esther*, 381), for the idea that the Pual of פרד (here the ptc – מְפֹרָד) carries the sense of "being isolated, unassimilated" religiously, culturally, etc. This plays into the argument of Haman well in that there would be no reason to deny his request once the otherness of this one people is established, and it is realised that they are not integral to the kingdom (Moore, *Esther*, 39).

136 The Jewish reaction appears to be a typical one *in the wake of* calamitous circumstances. Here, however, we are witnessing mourning and fasting in hope *for the prevention of* disaster. See further Laniak, *Shame and Honor*, 91 n. 76, 77.

Whether the troubled Jew is attempting to gain the attention of Esther by his actions,[137] or whether he is merely bitterly protesting the plight of his people in the public presence of the king,[138] or both or other options, it is not clear. It cannot even be said with any historical certainty that Persian law prohibited persons from going into the gate of the king in sackcloth.[139] Yet it appears, judging by his restraint, that Mordecai is quite conscientious about observing proper public conduct at this juncture.[140] On either side of his famous and controversial episode of civil disobedience, Mordecai shows the colours of an ideal and law-abiding subject (§ 2.3.1).

2.3.4 A joint or unilateral counter-edict? (8.8-10)

The events that follow the tactful second banqueting episode (7.1-8) mark only success for the Jews. Yet aside from the queen's questionable moment of planned vengeance (9.13) and the confirming 'second letter of Purim' (9.29-32),[141] Mordecai figures almost exclusively as the leading Jew in the

---

137 This interpretation is offered by Paton (*The Book of Esther*, 214), and Ringgren (*Das Buch Esther*, 406), among others.

138 See the discussions of Clines, *Ezra, Nehemiah, Esther*, 299; Bush, *Ruth, Esther*, 394; and Craig, *Reading Esther*, 96-97, which are all helpful here.

139 Clines, *Ezra, Nehemiah, Esther*, 299. Berg asserts that the explanation of Esth 4.2 suggests that the prohibition is "a Persian, not Jewish, custom" (*The Book of Esther*, 75, 89 n. 66). There is little to support this practice save the possible references in Herodotus, *The Histories*, 8.99 and 9.24. Mordecai's acts of mourning appear to be in line with the conventional Jewish rites of mourning commonly seen in the Hebrew Bible (e.g., Gen 37.29; 2 Sam 13.19; 2 Kgs 18.37; Job 2.8, 7.5; Dan 9.3; *et. al*). That this kind of posture and appearance was not allowed in certain areas of the Persian court is not entirely surprising (cf. the dubious reference in Herodotus, *The Histories*, 3.117). But *pace* Cassel, the "historical originality" of the book of Esther cannot be established by "this casual remark" (*An Explanatory Commentary on Esther*, 145).

140 Craig suggests that even the approach of Mordecai to the gate of the king would have been seen as "provocative and possibly dangerous" (*Reading Esther*, 122). However, neither Craig nor the story offers any reasons why this action of restraint might be considered so. If it were considered to be provocative, so as to call attention to himself, it still appears that the action was done within the confines of proper civil conduct. Here, Mordecai was neither careless nor reckless concerning the civil law.

141 For a discussion of the syntactic and interpretative issues in these verses, see S.E. Loewenstamm, "Esther 9.29-32: The Genesis of a Late Addition," *HUCA* 42 (1971); the excursus of Bush, which surveys past interpretation and outlines the three main difficulties (*Ruth, Esther*, 469-71); the comprehensive treatment of Fox, *Character and Ideology*, 123-28; and the comment by Levenson, *Esther*, 125, 129-32. It could be that 9.29-32 is attempting to fill in the gap of prominence and attention concerning the Jewish heroine in the latter parts of the narrative, but this is a narrative supposition. Whether 9.29-32 is a late addition is a live question. For an argument for the book's unity placing great importance on 9.20-10.3, see Jones, "The So-Called Appendix," 36-43.

last portions of the narrative.[142] In an intriguing and puzzling manner, Esther
all but disappears in the waning segments of the story as the (royal?) status of
Mordecai both in the court of the king and in the Jewish community is described by various forms of גדל (8.15; 9.4; 10.2-3). This prominence plays
out, among other examples, in the description of the counter-decree to the
genocidal edict of Haman – most notably in the singular authority of Mordecai behind it (8.8-12). The (seemingly) unilateral nature of the counter-edict
raises some textual and interpretative questions.

In speaking to both Esther the queen and Mordecai the Jew in 8.8, the king
specifically declares: "*you* [pl.] yourselves write with regard to[143] the Jews as
is good *in your* [pl.] *eyes*" [וְאַתֶּם כִּתְבוּ עַל־הַיְּהוּדִים כַּטּוֹב בְּעֵינֵיכֶם]. It is expressly implied[144] that what *they* – Esther and Mordecai – decide and write,
sealed in the name of the king, would act as if it were a royal decree.[145] To be
clear, however, it is unlikely that both of them would actually dictate the
counter-edict by taking turns speaking; one or the other would likely instruct
the scribe(s). Nevertheless, this singular voice should be communicating the
corroborative thoughts and plans of the Jewish leaders. As can be seen in the
subsequent narrative, this task of formulating clearly falls to Mordecai.[146]
However, it also appears at the level of the narrative that he is acting as the
sole authority behind the edict, for the role of the queen in the supposed joint
effort is not explicit, and doubtfully even implied.[147]

To illustrate this point, a few examples from the progression of the narrative from 8.9-10 will be highlighted. A relevant portion of the text of 8.9 relates that all that *Mordecai* commanded the scribes was written to all the
kingdom [וַיִּכָּתֵב כְּכָל־אֲשֶׁר־צִוָּה מָרְדֳּכַי]. 8.10 proceeds to inform the reader
further:

---

142 Clines supposes that Mordecai was "drawn into the king's reply" in 8.7 because he is the
     one who will draft the counter-decree (*Ezra, Nehemiah, Esther*, 315).
143 Following De Troyer's rendering (*The End of the Alpha Text of Esther*, 88). In the midst
     of a text critical focus, De Troyer suggests that the context of 8.9 retrospectively influ-
     ences the decision to render the sense "concerning" instead of "to" in this case (138f.).
144 Fox posits that "the *you* before the imperative is very emphatic, suggesting a contrast: *I*
     have done my part, now *you* go finish the job" (*Character and Ideology*, 95 (*emphasis
     original*)).
145 Cf. Baldwin, *Esther*, 96; Clines, *The Esther Scroll*, 18, 67; Day, *Three Faces of a
     Queen*, 145; De Troyer, *The End of the Alpha Text of Esther*, 136; Dommershausen, *Die
     Estherrolle*, 102-3; and Gerleman, *Esther*, 128.
146 Baldwin notices that Mordecai "took responsibility for drawing up the edict," but she
     does not comment on the implications of this (*Esther*, 96). Berlin notes that because
     Mordecai is in possession of the signet ring the task is his, not to mention the fact that it
     would have been highly irregular for a women to do such things (cf. 1 Kgs 21.8)
     (*Esther*, 76).
147 Beal makes a similar point (*Esther*, 96-97).

וַיִּכְתֹּב בְּשֵׁם הַמֶּלֶךְ אֲחַשְׁוֵרֹשׁ וַיַּחְתֹּם בְּטַבַּעַת הַמֶּלֶךְ וַיִּשְׁלַח סְפָרִים בְּיַד הָרָצִים...

and *he* wrote[148] in the name of King Ahashverosh and *he* sealed [it] with the signet ring of the king and *he* sent letters in the hand of the couriers...

The point being made here is not that the text should have been written so as to exhibit a joint effort in authority and composition in the counter-edict. Rather, these cases are cited only to point out the *apparent* singular influence of Mordecai in this process.[149] If anything, one would expect the person in higher authority to take the lead in the matter if the directives of the king for a joint effort are not followed.[150] Yet Mordecai dominates the narrative action from 8.9 on and emerges as the (apparently unilateral) authority figure for the Jewish community. Thus, most if not all of the responsibility for the actions that proceed from the counter-edict would fall upon his shoulders. *If* any moral blame can be measured out to the Jews because of their actions on 13 Adar, the narrative appears to hold Mordecai primarily if not solely accountable among the Jewish leaders.[151]

---

148 De Troyer submits that "[W]hile all three verbs in this verse are in the third person singular, the subject is not immediately evident." With this understanding, she chooses to render the third person singular expressing an undetermined subject – "it was written," suggesting, based on the end of 8.9, that it is the scribes who are responsible for writing the edict, and "not Mordecai himself" (*The End of the Alpha Text of Esther,* 142). Our translation obviously highlights Mordecai's explicit role in 8.10 over against De Troyer's rendering decision. However, even if her rendering were followed, it would seem that the overall thrust of our argument would remain intact, for it is commonly held that it is Mordecai who is the central (if not sole) influence behind the counter-edict here (cf. Fox, *Redaction,* 122; Loader, *Esther,* 117 (cited in De Troyer, 142-43)).

149 Believing there to be literary symmetry here, Fox holds that Mordecai composes and sends the counter-edict in order to provide a balance for Haman's composing and sending of his edict in 3.11-15. Although Esther has received joint authority here, it appears that she gives the reins over to the new vizier so that he can countermand the edict of the former vizier (*Character and Ideology,* 99; cf. Berlin, *Esther,* 76). While this explanation is plausible, the official status of Mordecai as vizier is only *implied* at this point in the narrative. While 8.15 adds further implication as to the vizierial role of Mordecai, it is really not until later that the reader can know that the king has elevated [גִּדְּלוֹ] Mordecai (10.2) and that he was "second to King Ahashverosh" [מִשְׁנֶה לַמֶּלֶךְ אֲחַשְׁוֵרֹשׁ] (10.3).

150 At this point in the story, the higher civil authority is Queen Esther. In 8.15, however, Mordecai emerges from the court dressed in royal attire. It is obvious from this point on that Mordecai carries more overall authority in the narrative, and possibly holds more civil authority within the empire (see 9.4; 10.2-3). However, in a literary move, the narrator might be returning to a more passive portrait of Esther like the one with which he began the narrative. These beginning and ending manifestations of passivity might form something of an inclusio around the active Esther of 4.16-8.6.

151 For a treatment of the behaviour of the Jews on 13 Adar, see § 2.5.1.

2.3.5 The wording of the counter-edict (8.11)

In the recent past, the wording of the counter-decree of Mordecai has been the subject of much suspicion concerning 'acceptable' moral conduct in the book of Esther. Specifically, questions have arisen in light of the traditional translation's inclusion of children and women in the number of those whom the Jews had authorisation to exterminate [לְהַשְׁמִיד], kill [לַהֲרֹג], and destroy [וּלְאַבֵּד] as they stood for their lives on 13 Adar. This, to be sure, is a modern "problem,"[152] and contemporary interpreters vary in their handling of the directives of Mordecai. According to Gordis, the moral uncertainties fade away if the verse is translated and understood in a different manner. Such a proposition warrants investigation. For the purposes of clarity and discussion, the Hebrew text of 8.11, the translation of Gordis, and a more traditional translation of the verse will be shown below. With these in view, we shall then proceed with a brief analysis of this important verse and some thoughts on what is at stake in its interpretation. The relevant portions of the counter-decree of Mordecai follow:

נָתַן הַמֶּלֶךְ לַיְּהוּדִים אֲשֶׁר בְּכָל־עִיר־וָעִיר לְהִקָּהֵל וְלַעֲמֹד עַל־נַפְשָׁם לְהַשְׁמִיד וְלַהֲרֹג
וּלְאַבֵּד אֶת־כָּל־חֵיל עַם וּמְדִינָה הַצָּרִים אֹתָם טַף וְנָשִׁים וּשְׁלָלָם לָבוֹז

the king permitted the Jews in every city to gather and defend themselves, to destroy, kill, and wipe out every armed force of a people or a province attacking "them, their children and their wives, with their goods as booty."[153]

the king was granting the Jews in every city the right to assemble and to fight for their lives – to destroy, slay, and annihilate the armed forces of any people or province that might attack them, women and children as well, and to take their property as plunder.[154]

That the counter-edict of Mordecai in 8.11 is modelled upon the initial writing of Haman in 3.13 is not really disputed by scholars. Instead, explanatory variances have arisen concerning the understanding of the syntax of the former when compared with the latter. Gordis claims that a "radical difference" exists between the two passages – a difference that in the end will clear the

---

152 Levenson relates that the killing of children and women is "offensive to any decent moral sensibility today" (*Esther*, 110; see also Berlin, *Esther*, 77). However, the ancient versions and Targums of the book fail to shy away from the fact that children and women were included in the scope of the Jews' "battle jurisdiction" on 13 Adar. Indeed, only Targum Sheni adds any element to the gist of 8.11 as it includes the slaves of enemies in the group (Grossfeld, *The Two Targums of Esther*, 185). This inclusion expresses the sense of total devastation that the Jews were to inflict on their enemies.
153 Gordis, "Studies in the Esther Narrative," 51-52.
154 Levenson, *Esther*, 109.

Jews of any hint of impropriety on 13 Adar.[155] In his reading, Gordis understands the final five words of the verse – אתם טף ונשים ושלל לבוז – to be a
citation[156] from the relevant portions of the edict of Haman:

3.13 וְנִשְׁלוֹחַ סְפָרִים בְּיַד הָרָצִים אֶל־כָּל־מְדִינוֹת הַמֶּלֶךְ לְהַשְׁמִיד לַהֲרֹג וּלְאַבֵּד אֶת־כָּל־
הַיְּהוּדִים מִנַּעַר וְעַד־זָקֵן טַף וְנָשִׁים בְּיוֹם אֶחָד בִּשְׁלוֹשָׁה עָשָׂר לְחֹדֶשׁ שְׁנֵים־עָשָׂר הוּא־חֹדֶשׁ
אֲדָר וּשְׁלָלָם לָבוֹז

This interpretative decision is based upon the belief that טף ונשים are the objects of הצרים rather than of להשמיד ולהרג ולאבד. In addition, Gordis suggests that the final clause, ושלל לבוז, is to be understood as co-ordinating
with the participle הצרים and not as a further infinitival clause related to the
previous infinitives – להשמיד ולהרג ולאבד. When viewed in this manner,
ושלל לבוז is seen as the behaviour expected of the Jews' *enemies* and not a
like permission given to the Jews themselves.[157] Hence, this interpretation
envisions *only* the Jews to be repelling an enemy force and not offensively
attacking children and women on 13 Adar. Moreover, the rendering also
harmonises better with the later decision of the Jews not to plunder their
enemies in battle (9.10, 15). For in the rendering of Gordis, the permission to
plunder was never given by the letter of Mordecai.

Although the work of Gordis here is seen as a "valiant effort to eliminate
the moral difficulty" that he perceives in the narrative, Fox claims that "this
rendering does not (regrettably) accord with the Hebrew."[158] In Fox's view,
for טף ונשים to be the direct objects of הצרים the repetition of 3ʳᵈ pl pro-
nominal suffixes would have to be present – i.e., אותם טפם ונשיהם.[159] To further this point, Bush adds that the direct object indicator את would also be
required to be in place.[160] These two scholars agree that the parallelism of
8.11 and 3.13 clearly shows that טף ונשים is "an appositional extension of the
dir. obj. clause כל חיל...הצרים אותם, exactly as it is an extension of

---

155 Gordis, "Studies in the Esther Narrative," 50.
156 De Troyer critiques this notion, stating that Gordis' suggestion that the final five words
    as a "quotation" (citation) is not an accurate description here (*The End of the Alpha Text
    of Esther*, 152).
157 My apprehension of Gordis' position is aided by the work of Bush (*Ruth, Esther*, 447).
    See also De Troyer's helpful discussion of Gordis' argument (*The End of the Alpha Text
    of Esther*, 150-51), and her critical examination of his position that follows (151f.).
158 Fox, *Character and Ideology*, 99-100.
159 Fox, *Character and Ideology*, 284. Cf. Paton, *The Book of Esther*, 274.
160 Bush, *Ruth, Esther*, 447.

זקן...כל היהודים, which is the dir. obj. of the same verbs, in 3:13."[161] This parallelism is shown below:[162]

3.13   וּלְאַבֵּד   אֶת־כָּל־הַיְּהוּדִים   מִנַּעַר וְעַד־זָקֵן   טַף וְנָשִׁים   וּשְׁלָלָם לָבוֹז

8.11   וּלְאַבֵּד   אֶת־כָּל־חֵיל עַם וּמְדִינָה   הַצָּרִים אֹתָם   טַף וְנָשִׁים   וּשְׁלָלָם לָבוֹז

The indefinite quality of the clauses טַף וְנָשִׁים and אֶת־כָּל־חֵיל עַם וּמְדִינָה serves to co-ordinate them. It is upon the parallelism platform also that the last clause – וּשְׁלָלָם לָבוֹז – is understood to be infinitival and not participial as it grammatically relates to וּלְאַבֵּד and not to הַצָּרִים.[163] Thus, the more traditional translation and understanding of the verse seems preferable in light of these rebuttals.

Yet even if the reasoning of Gordis were deemed correct, it is not at all clear from the narrative context that Mordecai *requires* to be exonerated for the wording of his counter-edict. Included in the letters of 3.13 and 8.11 is the rhetoric of battle in the ancient world. This is not necessarily to condone the intents found therein, but at least to contextualise them.[164] These fighting words are reminiscent of the rules of חרם that governed the conquests carried out by Israel in the time of Joshua, the Judges and the early part of the monarchy.[165] Yet, and importantly, we must note that differences exist between what Mordecai exhorted and what was authorised in the internal rules of חרם that serve to differentiate them from one another.[166]

For one thing, divine authorisation is *not* explicitly given for the battle in Esther, while the 'YHWH wars' of the earlier period were markedly theological in character and motive.[167] In addition, the 'earthly' decree of Mordecai sanctions a *defensive* effort in reaction to an enemy attack (cf. § 2.5.1),[168] while the battles governed by the rules of חרם advanced Israel's *offensive* conquest of the promised land under the 'heavenly' leadership of יהוה. Thus,

---

161 Fox, *Character and Ideology*, 285.
162 Following the chart provided by Bush, *Ruth, Esther*, 447.
163 Bush, *Ruth, Esther*, 447.
164 To aid this endeavour, consult the appendix concerning Ancient Near Eastern international law found in J. Barton, *Amos's Oracles against the Nations* (SOTSMS 6; Cambridge: Cambridge University Press, 1980), 51-61. Far from having in place the systemisation of the Geneva Convention, it appears that at least we are able to discern to some extent what might have been 'acceptable' and 'unacceptable' in ANE warfare.
165 Cf. Deut. 20.13-18 (cited in Fox, *Character and Ideology*, 100).
166 Fox concurs (*Character and Ideology*, 223).
167 See C.J.H. Wright, *Deuteronomy* (NIBC; Peabody, MA: Hendrickson, 1996), 229-31.
168 See Fox, *Character and Ideology*, 221-22.

what the Jews are licensed to do on 13 Adar cannot simply be equated to the חרם commission of the Israelites formerly.

In light of the above discussion, a facile assessment of moral responsibility of Mordecai in this instance is hard to make, if it can be made fairly at all. It is interesting to notice, nevertheless, that the narrator expresses no moral anxiety concerning either the sanctioning of the battle in 8.11 or in its carrying out in chapter nine. Even among the citizens of Shushan there is no confusion at *these* words (cf. 3.15). In its own context the wording of the counter-edict does not appear to be morally reprehensible. Further, even though we must deal with the inclusion of women and children in the scope of the counter-edict, we should keep in mind also that neither women nor children are mentioned in the later casualty reports of chapter nine.[169]

2.4 Haman

2.4.1 Calculating plans for genocide (3.5-8)

In his insightful chapter on the character of Haman in the MT Esther story, Fox leads with the following words:

> Devious though he is, Haman is allowed no mysteries. His motives, drives, and attitudes are transparent, his twisted soul laid bare to all. None of his motives are obscured, and little is left for the reader to wonder about. Evil, the author seems to say, is really quite simple and obvious, however sneaky the evil man may be and however subtle he may fancy himself. To demonstrate this, the author subjects Haman to special treatment: he exposes his thoughts to public view.[170]

Aside from his inexplicable elevation to vizier (3.1), the ins-and-outs of the character of Haman are in full view. This, of course, does not eclipse all of the craft and subtlety of Hebrew narrative, but it does provide the reader with at least one directly presented and less ambiguous character in the book of Esther. In addition, even though Haman is shown more straightforwardly, his blatant thoughts, emotions and actions serve to deepen and complicate the

---

169 Fox, *Character and Ideology,* 225.
170 Fox, *Character and Ideology,* 178. Taking his lead from the observations of R. Alter concerning the David story, Fox applies an understanding of "the interplay of opacity and transparency" to the Haman-Mordecai conflict. Whereas in the David story the thinking and emotions of Saul are on full display, those of David are hidden (R. Alter, *The Art of Biblical Narrative* (NY: Basic Books, 1981), 117-18). Similarly, but "with very different effects," the thoughts and passions of Haman are revealed, while those of Mordecai are all but concealed in the Esther story.

plot of the story. This observation is not without consequence for a study of moral character in the narrative.

We have suggested in § 2.3.2 that it is primarily for national and not merely personal reasons that Mordecai refuses to bow before and do obeisance to his ancestral antagonist, Haman. Yet the converse might not be so simply concluded. While tribal discord definitely contributes to the animosity of Haman towards the unyielding Jew, the text sets forth an equally prominent personal vendetta in the inner struggles of Haman's insecurity. The seemingly rootless existence of the Agagite leaves a chasm within – a void that he believes can only be filled by a complete mastery over all those who surround him. Indeed, his pride-filled quest for control will stop at nothing.[171]

Upon learning of Mordecai's unwilling posture (3.4), Haman makes a point to see it for himself [וַיַּרְא הָמָן כִּי־אֵין מָרְדֳּכַי כֹּרֵעַ וּמִשְׁתַּחֲוֶה לוֹ] (3.5). Then, in an interesting (yet explicable) development, he calculates in his own irritated mind that it would not be satisfying merely to punish Mordecai alone. Instead, when the servants of the king inform their new vizier of the race of the Jew, Haman then seeks to exterminate all of the Jews in the kingdom [וַיְבַקֵּשׁ הָמָן לְהַשְׁמִיד אֶת־כָּל־הַיְּהוּדִים אֲשֶׁר בְּכָל־מַלְכוּת] (3.6b). Fox suggests that on the side of Haman, the conflict between him and Mordecai is "essentially personal" while the "ancient tribal enmity...remains in the background." He reasons this way because the text does not inform the reader of the historical tribal conflict explicitly, but leaves it suggested within the genealogies of the Mordecai and Haman.[172] For Fox, then, the animosity is two-pronged, with issues of Haman's personal pride and insecurity being always primary, and any national resentment the Agagite feels deemed secondary at best.[173] While it is true that the personal rage of Haman and the national antipathy of the Agagite can both be seen clearly here, it is difficult (if not impossible) to distinguish between them from textual evidence. The description of events does not exhaustively inform the reader concerning the words, order of explanation, or precise timing in the disclosure of the servants.

A closer examination of the narrative bears this ambiguity out. For although we learn of the intentions of the servants to *inform* Haman that Mordecai was a Jew in 3.4, the text does not mention that the vizier *knows* of the race of Mordecai until 3.6b. In between, Haman observes the defiance of Mordecai first hand and becomes enraged [וַיִּמָּלֵא הָמָן חֵמָה] (3.5). In 3.6 we

---

171 For a helpful discussion of "Haman's Motives," see Fox, *Character and Ideology*, 179-82. Cf. Mills, *Biblical Morality*, 74.
172 Fox, *Character and Ideology*, 180.
173 Cf. Bickerman, *Four Strange Books of the Bible*, 196. Note that Bickerman views the conflict between Haman and Mordecai as a courtier struggle, and a source within itself.

are led to believe that because the Jews are the people of Mordecai, the Agagite cannot be satisfied to dispense his anger upon just one Jew; instead, the kingdom should be ridden of all of them.[174] But it is not at all clear whether Haman is enraged in a strictly personal way *before* he becomes informed about the race of Mordecai, or whether his personal and national antipathies are occasioned together, and always in some way co-existing. Because of this uncertainty, we are not prepared to say with Fox that

> Haman's hatred of the Jews is not the direct cause of his murderous scheme. In other words, it was not because of his spite for the Jews that Haman set out to eliminate them. Rather, he makes antisemitism an *instrument* for achieving perfect personal revenge. The tribal conflict is the context for a personal one.[175]

Neither are we willing to subsume all of Haman's emotions and actions under a simplistic explanation of ethnic animosity, for his inflated pride shows through even when the national conflict is not in view.[176] Yet in the scenes where the ancestral trouble is perceptible (beginning with this one), we would submit that at the very least the ethnic and personal feelings of hostility should be kept on the same level of importance and seriousness.

Within the context of the Hebrew Bible this latest scene in the age-old antagonism between Israelite and Amalekite deserves a fair focus.[177] The text insinuates that it is because the people of Mordecai are Jews that the Agagite seeks to eliminate them (3.6). The genocidal edict that proceeds from this desire is neither an accident, nor simply an instrument of a personal squabble. While it was true that Haman's side of the conflict *might* have begun solely with the personal affront of Mordecai (3.5), it certainly does not end there. The Agagite then goes on to great diplomatic lengths in order to malign the Jews before the king (3.8).

---

174 At the end of a section entitled "The 'Laws' of Challenge and Response," Laniak concludes that "Haman's disdain of Mordecai leads directly to the plot to slaughter his kin. His honor demands that he shame the one who shamed him" (*Shame and Honor,* 83). Even so, we must admit that the *extent* of the counter-shaming still stands out. However, Laniak responds that the extent of the action proposed by Haman fits in with "certain culturally-accepted rationale," and suggests further that because of this genocidal intention, the stakes are raised for the "just recompense" on the part of the Jews later in the narrative (84).

175 Fox, *Character and Ideology,* 181 (*emphasis original*).

176 E.g., see 6.6.

177 Indeed, LaCocque believes that the whole plot centres around the "religious historical-traditional background" of the conflict between Israel and Amalek – Mordecai and Haman ("Haman in the Book of Esther," 207-22).

Levenson rightly calls the proposal of Haman "a rhetorical masterpiece as subtle in construction as it is malevolent in intent."[178] Haman spitefully calls them "an insignificant people[179] scattered and unassimilated among the peoples" [עַם־אֶחָד מְפֻזָּר וּמְפֹרָד בֵּין הָעַמִּים] in the kingdom. Furthermore, the Jews are the ones whose laws are "differing from [those] of every people"[180] [שֹׁנוֹת מִכָּל־עָם], and (most importantly) they do not even obey the laws of the king.[181] Thus, they are a threat to the kingdom, and His Majesty should not leave them alone (3.8).[182] In this scene, ethnic tensions are certainly running as high as personal ones, while the breadth of Haman's hatred and subsequent threat leaves him in vast and troubled moral waters.

---

178 Levenson, *Esther*, 70. Levenson then cites Fox's analysis of the proposition of Haman: "He [Haman] begins with a truth stated in a way that makes the facts appear sinister, then slides into a half-lie, then into full lies" (*Character and Ideology*, 47-48). This progression is quite evident.

179 On this understanding of the overtones of the phrase עַם־אֶחָד, see Moore, *Esther*, 38 (followed by Clines, *Ezra, Nehemiah, Esther*, 295). Moore offers this interpretative option on the basis of the use in 2 Sam 18.10 and 1 Kgs 13.11 (following H.J. Flowers, *ExpT* 66 (1954-55), 273). See also the arguments of Fox along a similar line against a more narrow reading and understanding of the phrase given by Dommershausen (*Character and Ideology*, 48). Laniak suggests further that this very aspect of the Jews existence (i.e., distinctive, unnamed) might make them out to be even more threatening to the king in the presentation of Haman (*Shame and Honor*, 86). In a different line of argument altogether, Beal suggests that עַם־אֶחָד – "one people" – contrasts with the descriptions of these people as "scattered and divided." He summarises: "The manyness implied by 'scattered and divided' is reduced to a single divergence" (*The Book of Hiding*, 56).

180 This neutral phenomenon is cast in a negative light, especially in view of the following connotation that assumes that because the laws of the Jews are different, they do not then obey the decrees of the king. This could be a true accusation in reference to the stand of Mordecai, but it is thought that "given the variety and tolerance of the Persian empire, [it] would not have been damning in and of itself" (Moore, *Esther*, 39). This post-exilic negative appeal to the law of the Jews can also be seen in Dan 6.5 – a scene that has many similarities to this one.

181 Moore observes that the phrase "the king's decrees" [וְאֶת־דָּתֵי הַמֶּלֶךְ] is in a position of emphasis (*Esther*, 39). The purposed emphasis of Haman is to play upon the need of the king for significance and power here. It could be likened to the cunning and deferential approach of the chief ministers and satraps to King Darius in Dan 6.7. Concerning the verse as a whole, Baldwin surmises that the message Haman is craftily attempting to get across is that these unnamed people have their own laws and thus "ignore the laws of the Persian kingdom" (*Esther*, 73). For an interesting study concerning how the anti-Semitic libel of Haman has been interpreted in subsequent Jewish and Christian sources, see J. Berman, "Aggadah and Antisemitism: The Midrashim to Esther 3.8," *Judaism* 38 (1989), 185-96.

182 Haman argues that "for the king it is not suitable [satisfying] to give them rest" [וְלַמֶּלֶךְ אֵין־שֹׁוֶה לְהַנִּיחָם]. See Fox, *Character and Ideology*, 51, concerning the end of this proposal and how it foreshadows Jewish rest in the end of the narrative. Laniak concurs with this suggestion (*Shame and Honor*, 85 n. 50).

2.4.2 Self-controlled, boastful, yet with no satisfaction (5.9-13)

The quest of Haman for a feeling of self-worth and a grip on power reaches its highpoint in the present scene. With the genocidal edict in place (3.12-13), Mordecai challenges Esther to seek a higher authority (in this case, the king) in order to avert this national crisis somehow (4.8). To this task Esther hesitantly, but courageously, submits herself (4.16; § 2.2.4). After gaining a receptive audience with the king (5.1-2), Esther begins her effective scheme to save herself and her people. The queen's first move is to call upon the king and Haman to come to a series of banquets that she would prepare for them (5.4, 8). The resultant thoughts and reactions of the vizier in response to the second invitation will occupy our own considerations in the present section.

The news of his inclusion in the exclusive company of royalty delights Haman exceedingly. After the initial banqueting activity, we are explicitly told that he "went out on that day filled with joy and good of heart" [וַיֵּצֵא הָמָן בַּיּוֹם הַהוּא שָׂמֵחַ וְטוֹב לֵב] (5.9a). In round about way, the text alludes to the fact that even the inaction of Mordecai could not totally break the happy mood of the vizier. As Haman leaves the first banquet he passes through the gate of the king where he encounters the Jew. Yet instead of the anticipated refusal to bow down and do obeisance to his court superior, the narrative unexpectedly states that Mordecai does not rise or tremble[183] before him [וְלֹא־קָם וְלֹא־זָע מִמֶּנּוּ].[184] This, in turn, infuriates Haman in the same way as the refusal of Mordecai to do obeisance to him [וַיִּמָּלֵא הָמָן עַל־מָרְדֳּכַי חֵמָה] (5.9b).[185] But, showing extraordinary self-control, the vizier restrains himself [וַיִּתְאַפַּק הָמָן] and proceeds home;[186] not even Mordecai could *entirely* ruin his joyous day (5.10a). Even so, thoughts of the Jew seem always to be in the back of his mind.

Perhaps for a dual purpose, Haman then invites and receives[187] the family friends into his house.[188] In the presence of this affirming audience, he begins

---

183 On the translation and figurative rendering of זוע, see Bush, *Ruth, Esther,* 414.

184 Levenson submits that the non-compliant behaviour exhibited by Mordecai has escalated from simply not bowing to not moving at all (*Esther,* 92).

185 Cf. 3.5b where the same phrase is used to describe the reaction of Haman (minus עַל־מָרְדֳּכַי).

186 Paton suggests that the delay of Haman in taking vengeance on Mordecai is a literary move in order to keep the reader in suspense (*The Book of Esther,* 238).

187 Lit: "he sent and he brought" [וַיִּשְׁלַח וַיָּבֵא]. Bush notes that sending and bringing was the customary way of calling/escorting guests into one's presence (*Ruth, Esther,* 411).

188 Interestingly, Levenson sees Haman's gathering as a "comic inversion" to Esther's gathering of the Jewish people in the previous chapter (4.15-17). "Whereas Esther over-

to tell of his vast material wealth, his plenteous progeny,[189] and all of the distinction that the king and queen have conferred upon him (5.11-12). Indeed, to the boasting of Haman, there is no *self-imposed* limit. Yet it appears that the proud motives of the vizier in this case are not solely to relate to his close companions what they likely already know.[190] Haman is also in constant need of control and affirmation, either from himself or from others.[191] It seems that everyone is co-operating with him in this endeavour except Mordecai, and the Agagite cannot get the intractable Jew out of his mind. Everything positive that his friends provide for him, or he for himself, is soured by the constant presence of Mordecai, both physically and in his thoughts. All of his joy, riches and prestige matter not as long as Mordecai the Jew sits in the gate of the king; because of his presence Haman suffers an unsatisfying existence (5.13).[192] Indeed, "[O]ne wish ungratified poisons the whole cup of life for Haman."[193] Fox aptly summarises his state of being:

> Haman's domination must be absolute and it must be universally recognized, otherwise he cannot believe in it himself. Haman is devoured by this obsession with control. Such an obsession is a single, ineradicable notion that dominates the thoughts and feelings in spite of one's own will. Mordecai's refusal to show fear, indeed his very presence in the King's gate, proves to Haman that, whatever his might, he lacks control: he cannot govern the Jew's emotions; he cannot even prevent his current presence in the place of power. But ironically and appropriately, Haman's obsession with control in effect imposes Mordecai's presence upon all of his thoughts and gives Mordecai power over his mind, robbing him of all pleasure he might derive from the honor, wealth, and power in which he glories. Haman makes himself miserable.[194]

2.4.3 Adopted plans for personal satisfaction (5.14)

The despairing emotional predicament of Haman is, however, short-lived. Since he only makes himself miserable, outside help is welcomed. The

---

comes her self-regard and acts to avert a slaughter, Haman acts out of self-regard that has become egomaniacal and is told to arrange yet another slaughter (5.14)" (*Esther,* 92).
189 Paton cites Herodotus (1.136) in pointing out that it was those Persians who had the largest number of sons who were held in highest esteem (*The Book of Esther,* 238). Even though Haman was not by birth a Persian, he sought very much to achieve such honour in his adoptive society.
190 Levenson, *Esther,* 92.
191 Clines believes that common to the Persian manner advice is also being sought at this time (cf. 1.13-22; 2.2-4, 15; 6.6-10) (*Ezra, Nehemiah, Esther,* 306).
192 Berg, *The Book of Esther,* 79.
193 Paton, *The Book of Esther,* 239. Note also the analogy of Moore: "For just as a small coin held too closely to the eye can block out the entirety of the sun, so the preoccupation Haman had with revenge blocked out for him all his other blessings" (*Esther,* 60).

friends whom Haman had gathered around him in 5.10 now take on the role of advisors in 5.14.[195] Their counsel intends to put forth a suitable plan in order to rid their friend of his nagging problem, and to enable him to enjoy the privileges of his distinguished office. The initial part of this scheme advises Haman to construct an exorbitantly high gallows on which to hang his arch-enemy, Mordecai.[196] Though no trumped-up charge is mentioned in the text (cf. 3.8), Haman is then to proceed the following morning into the presence of the king to inform him [וּבַבֹּקֶר אֱמֹר לַמֶּלֶךְ] "so that *they* might impale Mordecai on it" [וְיִתְלוּ אֶת־מָרְדֳּכַי עָלָיו] (5.14b).

It is not clear who the subject "they" envisions in this last phrase. Grammatically, it is most likely that "they" refers to a group of anonymous executioners who would carry out the wishes of Haman, but this is only an educated guess since no such executioners appear in the text. It would be less grammatically satisfying, though more contextually logical, to posit the king and Haman as the subjects of the phrase since "they" are the only ones known to be present in the discussion. Either way, the point to be made is that the execution would have happened with the consent of the king, and it is interesting that the narrative alludes to his joint responsibility for this action against the Jews (see § 2.6.3).[197] Yet, as the story plays out, the activities of the next morning bring about a totally different set of circumstances.

With his Jewish 'problem' out of the picture, as the plot would have it, the vizier would be liberated to go and enjoy the second consecutive banquet to which he has been so prestigiously invited by the (Jewish) queen. This entire proposal delights Haman as he adopts it and sets phase one into action [וַיִּיטַב הַדָּבָר לִפְנֵי הָמָן וַיַּעַשׂ הָעֵץ] (5.14c). But in light of chapters six and seven, were the espoused intentions of Haman too little, too late? In what follows, it appears that the peaceful and satisfying night of sleep he likely enjoyed that evening was to be his last. The professional 'lot' of Haman, which had risen so unexpectedly and quickly (3.1), is reversed as it caves in

194 Fox, *Character and Ideology,* 180.
195 It is interesting to note the change that takes place concerning how these persons are described: friends in 5.10; friendly advisors in 5.14; wise men in 6.13. There appears to be a lessening of intimacy both in description and in narrative reality.
196 Most have deemed the height of the gallows humorously hyperbolic (e.g., Jones, "Two Misconceptions," 173). Yet even though she does not disagree with this sentiment, Berg believes that the high gallows could (and should) also be read in another way. Berg submits that the height of the gallows "could allude to Mordecai's importance and status in the narrator's eyes – an insignificant figure would not require a gallows of such impressive stature. Haman, then, unknowingly honors Mordecai with such a gallows." This is ironic judging by what follows in chapter six (*The Book of Esther,* 28 n. 85).
197 In this case, the king would have been responsible for his part in the move against one of the Jewish representatives. More on the accountability of the king can be seen in § 2.6.

on him just as rapidly and without warning (6.5-13a). Similarly, his personal 'lot', which once controlled the lives of his long-standing Jewish enemies, is reversed, and Haman cannot even save his own life (7.5-10).

2.4.4 Condemned for the appearance of evil (7.7-8)

The scene of his personal demise might have struck ancient (and some modern) readers as one of the more humorous in the Scroll. Queen Esther cunningly controls the occasion of her second banquet as she seeks to rescue her people (§ 2.2.5). Yet the nature of the role she plays in bringing Haman down is not spelled out in the narrative. While it is true that Esther points the vizier out in response to the demand of the king (7.6), judgement is not immediate for the Agagite. It could be that the enemy of the Jews is condemned on a technicality; that is, even though he certainly deserves to fall, his act of falling might have been royally misperceived.[198]

The text ambiguously states that Haman "was falling on the couch that Esther was upon" [וְהָמָן נֹפֵל עַל־הַמִּטָּה אֲשֶׁר אֶסְתֵּר עָלֶיהָ] (7.8), and this physical position escalates his downfall no matter his intentions. Even if Haman only violates the proper rules of court etiquette which forbid close proximity,[199] the *appearance* of an attempted improper sexual advance spoil the chances of the Prime Minister for any measure of pardoning grace.[200] As soon as His Majesty returns and accuses him of violating his wife and queen

198 Craig seems to be sure that a misperception has occurred (*Reading Esther,* 143), and Berlin suggests that "the king's understanding is intentional," giving him a way to punish Haman for his "real wrong" (his plot to kill the Jews), which was not circumscribed by any existing law (*Esther,* 70).

199 See Bardtke, *Das Buch Esther,* 358 n. 4, 359. Bardtke bases his understanding of the verb כבשׁ on its normal OT use – "to subdue, bring into subjection." And upon the Assyrian parallels concerning court etiquette between courtiers and women of the harem, he concludes that its use here can hardly carry the sense of assault. In contrast, Bush submits that there are no Persian parallels for this rule and believes that there is no doubt that Haman sought to deliberately assault the queen as he fell upon her couch. Bush supposes that the author would have used a different word than כבשׁ in this case if he wanted to merely cite a breach of court protocol. He envisions a stronger LBH meaning of the word – "to assault, violate" (*Ruth, Esther,* 430).

200 Many commentators believe that the comical nature of the narrative is in prime form in this instance where the thick-headed king mistakes the posture of Haman for an improper sexual advance (Levenson, *Esther,* 104; Fox, *Character and Ideology,* 87). However, Clines believes that there is no way that the king could have mistaken an entreaty by Haman as a sexual assault. He supposes that the reaction of the king is "decidedly theatrical," and it gives him the reason he needed to justify the end of Haman (*Ezra, Nehemiah, Esther,* 312; cf. Fox, *Character and Ideology,* 87). But, whatever the case, the

[הֲנַם לִכְבּוֹשׁ אֶת־הַמַּלְכָּה עִמִּי בַּבָּיִת], Haman's moment of doom descends upon him as his days are numbered (7.8b).[201] In this case, the old maxim might well be apropos: "Appearances *can* be deceiving."[202] Even though the perception of the enemy of the Jews could scarcely have gotten worse, the author chooses to leave his true motives to the imagination of the reader.

2.5 The Jews

2.5.1 13 Adar (9.1-10, 16)

In contradistinction to the "sharply etched individuality" and wilfulness of the community of Israel in most other biblical narratives, the Jews in the book of Esther appear "unified, undifferentiated, passive, and responsive."[203] Except for the trait of passivity, which is evident in other portions of the Scroll, a united, uniform and obediently active group can be seen unmistakably in the first half of chapter nine. Here the long-awaited events of the genocidal edict come to pass, but with very different result from ones sought by the (now deceased) Agagite.

Questions concerning the manner of the Jews toward their enemies [אֹיְבֵי הַיְּהוּדִים] and those who hated them [שֹׂנְאֵיהֶם] have historically been the hotbed of ethical discussion in the book of Esther.[204] Indeed, "[M]uch fault has been found with the temper displayed in the Book of Esther."[205] Many have turned a cold shoulder to the narrative as a whole and its importance within the OT because, in the oft-quoted words of B.W. Anderson (who likely has chapter nine in mind), "[T]he story unveils the dark passions of the

---

point of the narrative is that the end of Haman is at hand any way the scene is viewed – serious or comic.

201 The fall of Haman is predicted by his wife and wise men in 6.13. Indeed, the verb נפל appears three times in 6.13 as Haman's ultimate fall was foreshadowed. Here, in 7.8, although Haman is not falling before Mordecai, his fall (i.e., his demise) is surely coming to pass in the most ironic circumstances as he "was falling" [נֹפֵל] before Esther (Craig, *Reading Esther*, 124).

202 Laniak insightfully points out that it is Haman who was first guilty of misrepresentation in the story as he levelled false accusations against the (unnamed) Jews before the king. Poetic justice is now being served (*Shame and Honor*, 115 n. 33).

203 Fox, *Character and Ideology*, 212-13.

204 In fact, sometimes the entirety of one's ethical concern and discussion centres on the conflict described in chapter nine (see the section entitled "The Book's Moral Attitude" in Rodriguez, *Esther: A Theological Approach*, 12-15).

205 S.R. Driver, *An Introduction to the Literature of the Old Testament* (Edinburgh: T & T Clark, 1891), 456. It should be noted that Driver's remark is occasioned by the events of chapter nine.

human heart: envy, hatred, fear, anger, vindictiveness, pride, all of which are fused into an intense nationalism."[206] Other commentators attempt to downplay the seriousness of the actions of the Jews by citing the literary phenomena of satire,[207] irony,[208] humour,[209] and farce[210] as the best or only lens(es) through which to view the ethical questions that face the reader.[211] Yet although these features do have a place in the narrative, it is doubtful that all difficulties can simply be ameliorated by readings characterised by satire, irony, humour or farce.[212] Indeed, as Timothy K. Beal points out, inquiries are important concerning such things, "whether fictional or not, and no matter which side you are on."[213]

In this section we shall look specifically at the actions of the Jews on 13 Adar – the day in which the edict of Haman is to be enacted (3.13). We are provided with a concise summary of what happens on 13 Adar in 9.1. As the edict written in the name of the king becomes effective, the enemies [אֹיְבֵי] of the Jews wait (or hope) "to gain power (mastery)" [לִשְׁלוֹט] over them; but instead, it is the Jews who turn the tables and "gain power (mastery)" [יִשְׁלְטוּ] over those who hated them [שֹׂנְאֵיהֶם]. Because the fear [פַּחַד] of the Jews has fallen upon those seeking to harm them [מְבַקְשֵׁי רָעָתָם], and the fear of Mordecai [פַּחַד־מָרְדֳּכַי] has fallen upon the various officials of the land,[214] the triumph of the Jews is so comprehensive that no one can withstand[215] them

---

206 Anderson, "The Place of the Book of Esther in the Christian Bible," 39.

207 Dorothy, *The Books of Esther*, 354.

208 Goldman, "Narrative and Ethical Ironies," 14-31; M. J. Klaassen, "Persian/Jew/Jew/Persian: Levels of Irony in the Scroll of Esther," *Direction* 25 (1996), 25-26.

209 Jones, "Two Misconceptions," 171-81.

210 Wills, *The Jewish Novel in the Ancient World*, 98. See also Berlin's approach outlined in the introduction to her *Esther* commentary.

211 Note also the literary explanation that the ancient (implied) audience would have seen the reversed violence against the enemies of the Jews as a way of coping with fear and anxiety (C. McCarthy and W. Riley, "The Book of Esther: Banquet Tables Are Turned," in *The Old Testament Short Story: Explorations in Narrative Spirituality* (Wilmington: Michael Glazier, 1986), 86).

212 Fox supports the focus of this view. Speaking generally, he states that the "book's moral faults are not ameliorated by the fact that the book is deliberately hyperbolic or humorous" (*Character and Ideology*, 226 n. 25).

213 Beal, *Esther*, 102. Note that Beal makes his statement in the context of whether or not Mordecai's decree in 8.11 be considered defensive or preemptive. Nevertheless, his point is relevant in our present context as well.

214 Lit: "all the rulers (princes) of the provinces and satraps and governors and doers of the business that [was] to the king." Clines posits concerning the list order here that it is the leaders of ethnic groups who begin to assist the Jews before the government officials (cf. 8.9) (*Ezra, Nehemiah, Esther*, 322).

215 Following Bush in the understanding of the idiom עמד לפני (*Ruth, Esther*, 461).

[וְאִישׁ לֹא־עָמַד לִפְנֵיהֶם] (9.2-3). A graphic description of the day can be seen in 9.5:

וַיַּכּוּ הַיְּהוּדִים בְּכָל־אֹיְבֵיהֶם מַכַּת־חֶרֶב וְהֶרֶג וְאַבְדָן וַיַּעֲשׂוּ בְשֹׂנְאֵיהֶם כִּרְצוֹנָם

And the Jews struck dead all those who were hostile to them with a sword-blow and slaughter and destruction, and they did with those who hated them according to their will.

In Shushan, it is reported that 500 men are killed as a result of this clash (9.6). In addition to this, the ten sons of Haman, son of Hammedatha, "the enemy of the Jews" [צֹרֵר הַיְּהוּדִים], are also killed on 13 Adar (9.7-10). Yet the casualty numbers in the rest of the empire far exceed the number of those killed in the capital. The remainder [שְׁאָר] of the Jews who are dwelling in the provinces of king assemble[216] and make a stand for their lives[217] [נִקְהֲלוּ וְעָמֹד עַל־נַפְשָׁם] so that they might have rest from their enemies [וְנוֹחַ מֵאֹיְבֵיהֶם] (9.16). Moreover, none of the victorious Jews lay a hand on the plunder of their defeated foes even when the counter-edict of Mordecai has permitted it (9.10b, 15b, 16b).[218] The behaviour of the Jews on 13 Adar is decisive, comprehensive, conscientious, and most important of all, within the confines of the counter-edict.[219]

In attempting to comment thoughtfully on the nature of the actions of the Jews on this day, it would not be profitable to adopt an approach that does not deal with the material that we have before us.[220] C.C. Torrey, for exam-

---

216 Even though נִקְהֲלוּ is in the passive/reflexive niphal stem, semantically the verb is active, "describing something the Jews do, not something done to them" (Fox, *Character and Ideology*, 214 n. 2).

217 The phrase וְעָמֹד עַל־נַפְשָׁם, according to Fox, "shows that their lives were in danger." Hence, "the Jews are of necessity fighting defensively" (*Character and Ideology*, 222).

218 Fox likens this gesture to "a ratification of Saul's failing (1 Sam. 15)." The refusal of the Jews was "an assertion of dignity and self-sufficiency" in showing forth "a better way to conduct a war" (*Character and Ideology*, 216). Clines envisions a slightly different scenario which sees a possible "ethical motivation" behind the slaughter – it was not for "self-aggrandisement," but rather for "self-preservation" (*Ezra, Nehemiah, Esther*, 323). Similarly, W. McKane submits that this "diabolical purity of motive" supposedly saves the Jews from the gruesomeness of the scene ("A Note on Esther IX and 1 Samuel XV," *JTS* 12 (1961), 261).

219 Laniak, *Shame and Honor*, 138f.

220 A disappointing interpretative effort is found in the Targums. Targum Rishon attempts to justify the actions of the Jews by submitting that they *only* killed the descendants of Amalek on 13 and 14 Adar (9.6, 16-18), while in Targum Sheni Esther quotes Deut. 25.19 as she explains to the king the severity of the Jews' actions (9.25) (Grossfeld, *The Two Targums of Esther*, 84-86, 192-93). Unless the Targums are attributing a symbolic 'Amalekite status' to those who opposed the Jews on 13 and 14 Adar, this explanation seems to be a stretch. Moreover, the text in no way supports this notion.

ple, has proposed that the "note of revenge" concerning the Jews in the narrative is less a moral problem than it is a literary problem. Torrey eases the
final form issue of the violence of the Jews by positing that the revolting picture of revenge was not actually in the initial scheme of the book – he believes that it is introduced later for literary reasons. What these literary reasons might be Torrey does not state, but he does remark that this
understanding "relieves the author of the story of Esther of the charge of 'ferocity'."[221]

Yet it is arguable whether or not the charge of "ferocity" on 13 Adar even
needs to be relieved in the present text. The narrative has not pointed to a
ferocious group of Jews who actively seek out their foes. The reader is
graphically aware that they enact a serious and uneven slaughter on their
enemies, but the reported defensive nature of their actions does not appear to
step outside of the decree of the day.[222] As far as is possible to know, the
Jews have *lawfully* devastated those who hated them on 13 Adar.[223] Ferocity
need not have been a necessary component in that devastation, although justi-
fication should not be facilely given either. As the story is presented, much is
left to the imagination of the reader; indeed, some ambiguity (unclarity) remains.[224] We can only understand these events insofar as the author has chosen to present them,[225] but it is doubtful that we have been plunged as deeply
into an "ethical maelstrom" as some might suppose.[226]

---

221 Torrey, "The Older Book of Esther," 11. He later adds that the large numbers of casualties reported from the "imagined slaughter" reflects the purpose "to make the number of
   the slain high enough to comport with the greatness of Mordecai and Esther and the
   scale of the two-day celebration" (40).
222 Bush claims that "[T]he Jews' actions are strictly defensive....They do take offensive
   action, but such action would have been necessary against an enemy acting upon a decree that licensed their complete extermination" (*Ruth, Esther,* 464). Note also the vig-
   orous defence of the defensive actions of the Jews given by Fox (*Redaction,* 111). These
   opinions argue against the view of Clines whose strict literary and logic divisions between chs. 1-8 and 9-10 cause him to posit that ch. 9 presents "a Jewish massacre of
   anti-Semites rather than Jewish self-defence against an imperially sponsored pogrom"
   (*The Esther Scroll,* 40). Cf. the dissenting views of C. Montefiore and Driver who seriously doubt that the Jews have acted in self-defence (C. Montefiore, *The Bible for Home
   Reading,* 2:403 (cited in Craig, *Reading Esther,* 133); Driver, *Introduction,* 456).
223 Fox, *Character and Ideology,* 214-15. Counter to Haman's perception of them, Berlin
   notes that "[the Jews] would not undertake a battle unless it was legally authorized"
   (*Esther,* 86).
224 This point is stressed especially by Beal, *The Book of Hiding,* 105.
225 A similarly focused point is made by Craig (*Reading Esther,* 135).
226 Beal, *The Book of Hiding,* 105.

2.5.2 14 Adar (9.15)

The material that covers the events of 14 Adar might, however, not be so clearly judged. The questionable request of Esther for another day according to the law of 13 Adar in Shushan (9.13)[227] is quickly granted by the king in 9.14a – ויאמר המלך להעשות כן. Fox calls this massacre "a punishment executed by royal grant, not a battle."[228] It is important here to notice that the queen makes sure to proceed through acceptable legal measures in order to secure the approval of the state for Jewish actions. For as we have previously seen in the narrative, the word of the king is law. But, beyond this, the distinction that Fox provides is interesting in that it *seems* to envision that the actions of the Jews on 14 Adar are unprompted, and in contradistinction from those of 13 Adar – i.e., the Jews are executing a *further* slaughter upon their foes. Verse fifteen goes forward to report the results of the conflict on the morrow: the Jews assemble in Shushan on 14 Adar bear responsibility for killing 300 men.

Scholars have argued various reasons for the Jewish action on 14 Adar. Chief among these is the notion that this day is a literary construct to account for the extra day of Purim feasting in Shushan (9.18).[229] If this view is followed, many believe that the ethical problem is eased, if not altogether invalidated.[230] But if this outlook does not convince, the ethical question remains. We are not merely presented with a call for an extra day of feasting in the capital. If that were the case, there would be no ethical problem. This extra day of feasting is brought about *as a result of* the extra day of fighting on 14 Adar – a day in which the Jews kill an additional 300 men. This is not a day that has been awaited for the better part of a year as the 13th was. Instead, it appears to be a gratuitous day of overkill[231] that reflects badly onto the queen who has sought it[232] (§ 2.2.6), the king who has granted it (§ 2.6.9), and the Jews who have enacted it. The enemies of the Jews have no sanction

---

227 See § 2.2.6.
228 Fox, *Character and Ideology*, 215.
229 E.g., Moore, *Esther*, 91; Fox, *Character and Ideology*, 203; *Redaction*, 101; Levenson, *Esther*, 122. Cf. the contrasting view of Craig, *Reading Esther*, 131f.
230 See Torrey, "The Older Book of Esther," 11.
231 This is not necessarily presented as literary overkill resulting from a pattern of literary overstatement as Craig suggests (*Reading Esther*, 136; see also Berlin, *Esther*, 83). Though I would not deny that overstatement and hyperbole are employed literarily in the story, moral issues should not be lost in the literary fray. The story still might have something to say concerning moral character here, despite or perhaps in light of the literary presentation.
232 In Driver's understanding, the request of Esther cannot be excused (*Introduction*, 456).

to attack them on any day but 13 Adar.[233] In light of this, the actions of the
Jews on this day likely are without provocation and *appear* offensive. It
would seem that they have taken the initiative.[234] If this is the case, moral
questions have occasion to arise. It seems that the moral ground of the Jews
on 14 Adar has become "shakier."[235]

2.6 The King (אֲחַשְׁוֵרוֹשׁ)

2.6.1 Passive in the banishment of Vashti (1.16-22)

Among all the descriptions of the king, the appellations, "weak-willed, fickle,
and self-centred," seem to sum up his character adequately.[236] One can especially observe the weakness of the royal will in the episode of the banishment
of Vashti (§ 2.1.1). Even though the beautiful queen effectively ruins the self-
honouring extravagance of his seven-day banquet, the king finds himself void
of any recourse from within. With all of the power of the Persian empire at
his fingertips, the most powerful man in the kingdom appears politically and
mentally impotent when his party is crashed and his authority is challenged.[237] The formal responsibility for retribution in this case would have to
rest on the shoulders of someone else, for those of the king appear small and
weak.

From the very minute that the news of the refusal of Vashti arrives before
the king, he looks outside of himself to "the wise men" [חֲכָמִים] – "the ones
knowing the times"[238] [יֹדְעֵי הָעִתִּים], and his "close ones" [הַקָּרֹב אֵלָיו] – the
officials having pre-eminence and serving in the immediate presence of the

---

233 Clines, *The Esther Scroll*, 48.
234 J.R. Kriel, "Esther: The story of a girl or the story of her God?," *ThEv* 19 (1986), 9.
    Kriel explores the question of responsibility that the Jews might bear on account of their
    human initiative.
235 Fox, *Character and Ideology*, 225. Mills notes also that there is "a question mark over
    the violent revenge of the Jews" (*Biblical Morality*, 76).
236 Fox, *Character and Ideology*, 168.
237 Concerning the powerlessness of the king, see Day, "Power, Otherness, and Gender in
    the Biblical Short Stories," 112.
238 *Contra* the common primary connotation of astrology, Fox notes that the יֹדְעֵי הָעִתִּים
    were likely the "all-around experts" of the court who were comparable to the
    יוֹדְעֵי בִינָה לַעִתִּים of 1 Chr. 12.33 (*Character and Ideology*, 21). Looking at their identity
    from a functional angle, Beal suggests that these are ones who "know what is appropri-
    ate and when" (*The Book of Hiding*, 22).

king (1.13-14).[239] To these the king defers thought, decision and judgement.[240] But it is not as if a minor legal infraction has just taken place that
could be handled quickly and easily by the officials. Instead, the supreme
authority of the monarch is being haughtily questioned, and the honour of the
king is at stake. This is certainly no small matter; but then again, it might not
be as large as Memucan makes it out to be.

With all of his surrogate brains, wills and hands gathered closely around
him, the king asks the question: "According to the law, what should be done
with Queen Vashti?" [כְּדָת מַה־לַּעֲשׂוֹת בַּמַּלְכָּה וַשְׁתִּי] (1.15a). In other words,
are there any legal precedents that could guide the court in dealing with the
recalcitrant queen?[241] After this act of delegation the angered king is not
heard from in the scene again, that is, unless one counts the whooshing sound
of his head nodding affirmatively in 1.21. For all practical purposes, the role
of supreme legislator is taken on by Memucan,[242] one of his 'close' eunuchs,
while the king sits by passively.

In what follows, Memucan quickly escalates a private and domestic conflict into a national crisis. The eunuch effectively convinces the king that the
headstrong behaviour of Vashti threatens male dominance in the households
of the empire. If nothing is done in the first household, "the manner of the
queen will go out unto all women causing them to hate their husbands[243] in
their eyes" [כִּי־יֵצֵא דְבַר־הַמַּלְכָּה עַל־כָּל־הַנָּשִׁים לְהַבְזוֹת בַּעְלֵיהֶן בְּעֵינֵיהֶן]; these
women would act defiantly as Vashti[244] (1.17-18). Therefore, official letters
are sent out that limit the activities of women[245] by legislating that that all

---

239 Lit: "the ones seeing the face of the king; the ones sitting first in the kingdom"
    [רֹאֵי פְּנֵי הַמֶּלֶךְ הַיֹּשְׁבִים רִאשֹׁנָה בַּמַּלְכוּת].
240 Even though seeking counsel is "standard court procedure" (Bush, *Esther, Ruth,* 355),
    the king virtually disappears from all aspects of the decision in this case.
241 This is the understanding of the majority of commentators. It is not thought that there
    was a specific law in place that spoke directly to this situation (e.g., Levenson, *Esther,*
    51). It is interesting that the pragmatic advice of Memucan was the only 'law' offered
    (Clines, *Ezra, Nehemiah, Esther,* 281).
242 Bickerman submits that Memucan is a Zoroastrian name that means "good thought"
    (*Four Strange Books of the Bible,* 209). Even though an etymology is uncertain, it is in-
    teresting to note that however 'good' the thought of Memucan might turn out to be, he is
    indeed the one who is *thinking* for the king.
243 בַּעְלֵיהֶן gives the connotation of "master, lord" in its usage here (*CHALOT,* 42-43).
244 The rendering Bush gives for 1.18 (*Ruth, Esther,* 339) is the most textually satisfying as
    it best takes into account the ellipsis of the direct object of the verb תֹּאמַרְנָה (Bush is
    basing his decisions on the textual-philological notes of Fox, *Character and Ideology,*
    274-75; cf. GKC § 117*f*): "And this very day the noble ladies of Persia and Media who
    will have heard what the queen has said will say the same to the nobles of the king, and
    there will be no end to the disrespect and anger!"
245 Question: How much further could they be limited? Dorothy points out that "[T]he irony
    of an imperial highness having to legislate male dominance throughout the empire,

men should be the rulers of their own households[246] [כָּל־אִישׁ שֹׂרֵר בְּבֵיתוֹ]
(1.22). Through all of this, the king sits idly (and, for now, happily) by.

One commentator attributes the king's "need to seek advice in all situations and his alacrity in following it without discussion" to pure laziness.[247] Though it is true that the wisdom literature of the OT "praises the value of counsel," it does not envision that the one to whom counsel is provided would be utterly complacent.[248] The king is "a man not fond of thinking for himself.... Indeed, his most dangerous flaw is his failure to think."[249] This *passivity*, or perhaps indifference, paves the way for the *activity* of others in the story – an active role that they take gladly and often.[250] The following summary is apropos: "[t]he all-powerful Xerxes in practice abdicates responsibility and surrenders effective power to those who know how to press the right buttons."[251] Yet the choice of relinquishment, first witnessed here in the text, does not rid the king of (at least) some degree of moral responsibility in the resolutions that bear his seal. In the present case, the results of Memucan's plan are not known because nothing of this particular "royal word" [דְּבַר־מַלְכוּת] is heard of again in the narrative. However, the implications of a later decree will be more serious (see § 2.6.3). For the moment, though, the king likely second-guessed the passivity he showed concerning Vashti. And as his anger abates, the king remembers (sadly?) what Vashti had done and "that which had been decreed against her" [אֲשֶׁר־נִגְזַר עָלֶיהָ] (2.1). His chosen role in the matter had been minimal, and now he could do nothing about it.

2.6.2 A most passive judiciary role (2.23)

For the most part, the king continues to remain in the background of the narrative's movement as it proceeds. It is the young servants in his court who persuasively suggest that a kingdom-wide gathering of eligible young

---

within a culture already male-oriented, surely strikes a humorous note" (*The Books of Esther*, 238).

246 T.H. Gaster points out that the verb שׂרר in 1.22 "is couched in exactly the language which accredits governors to their provinces...[language] which is now carried over to the way husbands are to be the 'governors' of their homes" ("Esther 1:22," *JBL* 69 (1950), 381).

247 Fox, *Character and Ideology*, 173.

248 Cf. Prov 8.14, 11.14, 24.6, 19.20 (cited in Fox, *Character and Ideology*, 174 n. 2).

249 Fox, *Character and Ideology*, 173-74.

250 Here, Memucan; see also 2.1-4; 3.8-11; 8.3-8.

251 Fox, *Character and Ideology*, 173.

women[252] be made so that the king might choose a new queen in place of
Vashti (2.2-4). It is Hegai, the keeper of women [שֹׁמֵר הַנָּשִׁים], who distin-
guishes Esther and her maidens giving them an advantage[253] over all others in
the house of women as preparations are made for each to go into the king
(2.9). The account that follows only *describes* the king as it details the preparatory process and mainly focuses on the rise of Esther (2.12-16). Then,
with a flurry of *active* verbs, the treatment of the narrator changes slightly as
the king chooses Esther to be his queen. We observe that the king *loves*
Esther [וַיֶּאֱהַב הַמֶּלֶךְ אֶת־אֶסְתֵּר] (2.17a); he then *sets* the royal headband[254] on
her head [וַיָּשֶׂם כֶּתֶר־מַלְכוּת בְּרֹאשָׁהּ] (2.17b), and *causes her to reign* instead
of Vashti [וַיַּמְלִיכֶהָ תַּחַת וַשְׁתִּי] (2.17b); finally, the king *arranges* a great banquet [וַיַּעַשׂ הַמֶּלֶךְ מִשְׁתֶּה גָדוֹל] in honour of his new queen (2.18a). Soon
enough, however, we return to a more familiar role for the king as secondary
actor in the story.

While the king is indeed present in the scene of the 'arrest' of the conspiring eunuchs (§ 2.3.1), His Majesty is noticeably passive therein. Whereas in
most other cases the narrative at least describes the actions or decisions of the
king in reaction to the lead of others (e.g., 2.4), 2.23 appears not even to envision his rubber stamp being placed upon the important judiciary decision
that took place after the foiled assassination plot. The text merely states the
following:

וַיְבֻקַּשׁ הַדָּבָר וַיִּמָּצֵא וַיִּתָּלוּ שְׁנֵיהֶם עַל־עֵץ וַיִּכָּתֵב בְּסֵפֶר דִּבְרֵי הַיָּמִים לִפְנֵי הַמֶּלֶךְ

the matter was investigated and it was found [to be so]. The two of them were hanged
upon a tree, and all of this was recorded in the book of annals in the presence of the
king.[255]

The context lends to the possibility that since Esther tells the king of the matter at the end of 2.22, he is the one responsible for getting to the bottom of
the trouble in 2.23. Yet even if this is the case, the narrative chooses to describe the events in a way that keeps the king in the background – no verbs in
the verse have the king as their subject. At most, the reader gathers that the
king is aware of the judicial proceedings because they are recorded in his

252 Lit: "young women of marriageable age" [נְעָרוֹת בְּתוּלוֹת]. See G. J. Wenham, "*b*ᵉ*tûlāh*,
'A Girl of Marriageable Age'," *VT* 22 (1972), 326-48; also, M. Tsevat, "בתולה," *TDOT*,
2:341-43.
253 Following the understanding and rendering of Levenson (*Esther*, 60).
254 For a discussion of the etymology of כתר מלכות and the nature of this royal headgear,
see A. Salvesen, "כֶּתֶר (Esther 1.11, 2.17, 6.8): 'Something to Do with a Camel?'" *JSS*
44 (1999), 35-46.
255 Following the rendering of Levenson (*Esther*, 64).

presence [לִפְנֵי הַמֶּלֶךְ] (2.23b). But as is customary of his portrayal in the
book, His Majesty (at the most) reacts to what others do around him.[256] In this
particular case, the king again will have to react when the events of this day
are recalled to him on a sleepless night in the future (6.1-2). Not necessarily
ignoring the obvious literary connections between 2.21-23 and 6.1-3, might it
also be reasonable to suggest that the forgetfulness of the king and failure to
treat Mordecai with distinction for his life-saving service stems from the fact
that the king hardly appears to be involved in the plot uncovering and judicial
procedures in 2.21-23?[257] In other words, his apparent distance from the
events could help explain his negligence in remembering and rewarding
them. This idea might not be so far-fetched because there is another occasion
in which he does not appear to recall his knowledge of a major event in the
kingdom (7.4-7; cf. 3.8-11).

2.6.3 An accomplice in plans for genocide (3.10-11)

It has been said that the king is "all surface…[his] soul is exposed…[and] his
psychology is easily read" by the people both *inside* (i.e., the characters) and
outside (i.e., the readers) the story.[258] Yet even though this is true, not much is
gained in the way of really comprehending the inner workings of this intriguing character. This is certainly no fault of the author, for the story is told and
the characters are constructed in purposeful ways. But at the same time, one
cannot help but wonder concerning the extent of the knowledge and, subsequently, the level of accountability that can be exacted from the king – the
character through whom most (if not all) important decisions in the narrative
proceed.

The edict of genocide for the "people, scattered and unassimilated" having
been requested (3.8-9; § 2.4.1), the attention of the text now falls upon the
king to see what he would do. Initially, although he says nothing, his actions
speak as loudly as any words could. A people whose identity he does not
even know[259] is consigned to death by the seemingly unreflective transfer of
his signet ring to Haman, the son of Hammedatha, the Agagite, the enemy of

---

256 One curious exception is the unprompted elevation of Haman in 3.1.
257 See the educated guesses that Moore includes (*Esther*, 31-32). In the end, commentators
    attribute the delay to preparatory plot timing and requirement (see Clines, *Ezra, Nehe-
    miah, Esther*, 293; Bush, *Ruth, Esther*, 374). The matter is certainly not straightforward.
258 Fox, *Character and Ideology*, 171 (*emphasis original*).
259 That the king was convinced by the arguments of Haman and on that basis empowered
    him to rid the kingdom of such a dangerous bunch is unverifiable (see Baldwin, *Esther*,
    74). The extent of his care/interest in his vizier's problem and solution is questionable.

the Jews (3.10).[260] Though no authorial censure is present, it would seem that the moral character of the king suffers further. Concerning the ten thousand talents of silver offered by Haman to fund his plan (3.9),[261] the king utters these words: "[T]he silver is given to you; and the people, do with it as [is] good in your eyes" [הַכֶּסֶף נָתוּן לָךְ וְהָעָם לַעֲשׂוֹת בּוֹ כַּטּוֹב בְּעֵינֶיךָ] (3.11). At first glance it is not clear what the king desires Haman to do with the enormous sum. Even though Herodotus claims that this particular king has turned down larger sums than this in his life,[262] the text does not appear to suggest that he spurns the cash in this case.[263] It is more likely that with the words, הכסף נתון לך, the king sanctions the use of the money as the vizier sees fit.[264] This interpretation is supported at two further points in the narrative: 4.7 – Mordecai's communication of the edict (including the amount of the sum) to Esther; and 7.4 – Esther's claim that she and her people had been "sold."[265] Thus, the money is never absent from the picture.[266] Rather, in a customary way (likely known to ancient readers), the king is bargaining with the lives of people whose identity he does not know; he is condemning to destruction a people against whom he has no (known) animosity. In this technique of courteous refusal,[267] one could say that the king rolls "the responsibility entirely now on Haman. Haman must be the doer and decision maker."[268] But is the culpability not jointly held?

To this question the Hebrew story does not give an explicit answer. Thus, Fox submits the following observation:

> Neither the narrator nor the Jews in the story condemns Xerxes or even seems to resent his indifference to their existence. Xerxes is a lumpish, indifferent mass, not inherently vicious, not anti-Jewish, but erratic, childish, apathetic, and pliable.[269]

---

260 Re'emi submits that "the king...was pleased with the faithfulness and watchfulness of the vizier" and therefore gave his consent (*Esther*, 122). However, this is merely conjecture and does not resonate with the ostensible ignorance displayed by the king in 7.5f.
261 See Bush for a comprehensive comment on this enormous sum (*Ruth, Esther*, 381-82).
262 Herodotus, *The Histories*, 7.27-29 (cited in Moore, *Esther*, 40).
263 *Contra* a more literal understanding (e.g., see R.E. Murphy, "Esther," in *Wisdom Literature: Job, Proverbs, Ruth, Canticles, Ecclesiastes, and Esther* (FOTL, 13; Grand Rapids: Eerdmans, 1981), 161.
264 Clines calls this kind of rhetoric "a courtly way form of accepting the money" (*Ezra, Nehemiah, Esther*, 297). Berlin disagrees and sees the king here giving Haman the right to potential tribute collected (*Esther*, 42).
265 Bush, *Ruth, Esther*, 382.
266 Moore posits that the money was the king's motive for going along with the proposal of Haman (*Esther*, 43). This, however, is not clear from the narrative.
267 For comment on this on-going Near Eastern practice, see D. Daube, "The Last Chapter of Esther," *JQR* 37 (1946-47), 142-43.
268 Fox, *Character and Ideology*, 52.
269 Fox, *Character and Ideology*, 176.

If anything, the narrative implies that Haman is both *entirely* responsible and *totally* culpable for the decree that bears the seal of the king. For his complicitous role in the plot, the king is never implicated.[270] Yet, for the reader, moral assumptions and conclusions fill gaps left by the narrator.[271] For instance, in the opinion of one commentator:

> Xerxes is not particularly cruel, but he is nonetheless terrifying – such power, with so little thought invested in its employment. His foggy indifference to life is simply the capstone of this laziness. He had not even bothered to ask which people he is consigning to destruction. The offhand quality of his agreement is grotesque, as is his sitting down to feast with Haman right after the murderous decree is published and the capital thrown into dismay (3:15). So little impression does the extermination order make upon him that he does not even recall the incident only a few days after the edict was issued, for he asks Esther who had done such a thing, as if the engineering of genocide were a commonplace in his empire…One expects the force motivating a crime as horrendous as genocide to be a mammoth one…[but] the king has no such motives. His decision is driven not by hatred, but by indolence.[272]

Indolence, however, does not excuse facilitation; mere passivity and apparent lack of interest cannot clear him of all blame. After all, in the words of Hanna Arendt, "[W]ickedness may be caused by absence of thought."[273] In this sense, the king's complicity makes him an enemy of the Jews as well.[274]

2.6.4 Justice at the second banquet (7.8-10)

As we have discussed previously, the king does little on his own in the book of Esther. The narrator presents him as needing assistance in decision making at many points in the story. The general way that the narrative relates this phenomenon is threefold and can be witnessed in the following example from the episode in which a new queen is sought (2.1-4):

---

270 Cf. 3.12 – Haman had commanded the edict to be written; 4.7 – the silver was weighed out for the destruction of the Jews by Haman; 7.6 – Haman (alone) is accused by Esther; 7.8 – the king is flabbergasted at the thought that Haman would be responsible for the edict *and* attempt to violate his wife; 8.5, 7 – it was the intention of Haman to destroy the Jews and sent his hand against them; and 9.24-25 – Haman had devised the plan against the Jews for their destruction and should be impaled because of it.

271 E.g., D.F. Polish contends that the king's consent to Haman here is more correctly seen as an "injunction" ("Aspects of Esther: A Phenomenological Exploration of the *Megillah* of Esther and the Origins of Purim," *JSOT* 85 (1999), 92).

272 Fox, *Character and Ideology*, 175. Similarly, Clines questions whether the behaviour of the king should not have included him with Haman as an "enemy of the Jews" (*Ezra, Nehemiah, Esther*, 297). Cf. the comments of Daube concerning the involvement of the king here (*Esther*, 52).

273 H. Arendt, *Life of the Mind*, 13 (cited in Fox, *Character and Ideology*, 176).

274 Beal, *Esther*, 91.

1. *A problem is presented* – a calm and lonely king realises that he has no queen (2.1).
2. *Counsel and a proposal are given* – the young servants of the king propose a kingdom-wide search for a new queen to take the place of Vashti (2.2-4a).
3. *The king endorses the solution presented* – the plan of the servants is pleasing to the king and he endorses it into action (2.4b).

To be sure, not all of the various episodes of this type look exactly the same.[275] However, the general skeleton of the above structure is discernible in each. On several occasions, one or more of the steps is augmented, lacking or altered. For instance, a plus appears in the scene of the refusal of Vashti when the king actually seeks counsel before it is given (1.13-15). When Mordecai uncovers the assassination plot on the king, steps two and three are only implied (2.22-23). But for our immediate purposes, the episode of the demise of Haman will be highlighted so as to focus on the measure of justice that the king *himself* proposes (7.8-10).[276] Step three in this episode is altered and might prove to be significant in our assessment of the king's moral character.

In earlier sections we have observed the triumph of Esther (§ 2.2.5) and the downfall of Haman (§ 2.4.4) at the second banquet of the queen. Presently, then, we shall centre on the actions of the king in that scene – actions which are surprisingly not as passive and secondary as usual. The *problem* in the episode begins to develop in 7.4 as the queen relates the devastating details of her grief and the plight of her people: if nothing is done they are doomed to be exterminated [לְהַשְׁמִיד], killed [לַהֲרוֹג], and destroyed [וּלְאַבֵּד]. Upon learning of this plot, the *problem* develops further as the king demands to know (and is told) the identity of the person responsible for setting his heart to do such a thing (7.5-6). Enraged, the *problem* defines itself fully as the king storms out of the banquet only to return to witness the self-condemning posture of Haman before the queen (7.7-8). Thus, Haman is convicted, but the *problem* presented here concerns what now should be done with him.

In this particular case, very little *counsel* is given, but a subtle *proposal* arises quickly from Harbonah, one of the eunuchs of the king, in these words:

הִנֵּה־הָעֵץ אֲשֶׁר־עָשָׂה הָמָן לְמָרְדֳּכַי אֲשֶׁר דִּבֶּר־טוֹב עַל־הַמֶּלֶךְ עֹמֵד בְּבֵית הָמָן גָּבֹהַּ
חֲמִשִּׁים אַמָּה

---

275 E.g., 1.10-22; 2.21-23; 3.8-11; 6.1-11; 7.4-10; 8.3-8; 9.11-14.
276 This difference has also been noticed by Beal (*The Book of Hiding*, 99).

Behold, the tree that Haman had made for Mordecai who spoke good for the benefit of[277] the king is standing at the house of Haman fifty cubits high (7.9b).

Then, in a slight (but significant) contrast to the norm, the king plays a large part in determining how to act in the present situation. Whereas before he had customarily *endorsed* the solutions of those around him, in this instance he catches the shades of meaning in the words of his eunuch and commands that Haman be hanged on his very own gallows [וַיֹּאמֶר הַמֶּלֶךְ תְּלֻהוּ עָלָיו] (7.9b).[278] In short, although this is not an entirely independent *solution* on the part of the king, it is a long way from his usual passive resignation. This order is then followed by a description of the hanging event, a resolution that facilitates the subsequent abatement of his anger (7.10).

The significance of the activity of the king in this case might be thought to be minor (if noteworthy at all). However, in the broader view, it is interesting to notice that this kind of active behaviour can also be seen as the king is portrayed in the book of Esther. For the most part, he is passive, prone to be manipulated and generally indifferent to what has gone on around him.[279] But, in contrast, 7.9b depicts him to be active, decisive,[280] and interested in the welfare of his queen, her people, and the kingdom. This, of course, is not his normal posture, yet it is nevertheless a true and vital paint stroke in his overall portrait. Indeed, the king has never been presented to be morally neutral, and at this point his own words serve to aid us in assessing of his moral character. Here, it must be said, the king has emerged positively.

2.6.5 An accomplice in the vengeance of Esther (9.14)

The sentiments of the narrator appear similarly supporting when it comes to an appraisal of the role of the king in the call of Esther for another day of

---

277 Following P. Haupt ("Critical Notes on Esther," *AJSL* 24 (1907-8), 153), Bush renders the idiom דבר טוב על "to speak good *to the benefit of* someone" (*Ruth, Esther,* 424 (*emphasis original*).

278 Levenson suggests that Harbonah, being "a relatively lowly figure," wisely sets the king up to utter the imperative. That way, Harbonah would not be overstepping his court prerogatives (*Esther,* 105). Whether or not this is true, the point being stressed here is that the king in fact utters the imperative and acts in a way that differs from his usual manner (cf. Berlin, *Esther,* 71).

279 See especially the portrayals in § 2.6.1, 2.6.2 & 2.6.3.

280 Beal notes that the words of the king in this instance are particularly "terse" and "pointed" (*Esther,* 81 n. 6).

bloodshed in Shushan (see § 2.2.6). After the queen presents her *problem*[281] and *solution*, the king shows his approval by *endorsing* her wishes [וַיֹּאמֶר הַמֶּלֶךְ לְהֵעָשׂוֹת כֵּן] (9.14a). On the basis of his decree, the Jews undertake further killing in the capital on 14 Adar (9.15; § 2.5.2). It is not, of course, that the narrator explicitly praises the king for his authorisation. Rather, the lack of any voice of disapproval relays a condoning bent (if not an outright approval). Thus, and overall, the king is seen to be helplessly oscillating between what the narrator deems to be the forces of good (the Jews) and evil (Haman). He is rarely his own man; indeed, his defining moral character is that of a complaisant accomplice.

---

281 The exact nature of her problem is unknown in that it is not clear why Esther desires to have a second day of fighting in Shushan according to the law of 13 Adar. The reason why the queen wants to humiliate the bodies of the ten sons of Haman is, however, apprehensible (see § 2.2.6).

3 Moral Character in the LXX

3.0 Introduction

When compared with its MT counterpart, the LXX version of the book of Esther tells a differing story.[1] It would be somewhat misleading to say that the LXX is a *different* story, because foundationally and throughout the development of its plot it clearly manifests its Semitic predecessor.[2] To be more precise, then, we might say that the LXX differs often in how it *tells* the Esther story – presenting what some have considered an "alternative version"[3] – and one will notice many of these differences as this Greek text presents/deals with moral issues.

There has been some discussion concerning the variances in ethical material between the two books, and it is likely that many would still follow the sentiment of A.E. Morris, more than fifty years ago, that the LXX book of Esther fills in the gaps left by the MT in order to achieve a more "religious tone."[4] But it is doubtful that a modern appraisal such as this one has taken into account the depth and complexity of the LXX Esther narrative; as we shall see, moral matters might not be explained so simply. Moreover, for many ancient readers – beginning with the ones assumed by the colophon of the book (F.11)[5] – such comparative inquiries would not have entered the mind, for the LXX was likely their only Esther text.

---

1   "The LXX translator both translated and interpreted the Hebrew text. The LXX translator of the book of Esther introduced *new dimensions* to the narrative and to this degree *transformed* it into his own narrative" (De Troyer, *The End of the Alpha Text of Esther,* 398 (*emphasis added*)).

2   Dorothy notes that the LXX (which he calls the o′ Text) holds close grammatically to its Hebrew *Vorlage* in this particular instance (*The Books of Esther,* 59). Generally speaking, this *Vorlage* appears to be the MT. This assumption is held even more strongly by De Troyer (*The End of the Alpha Text of Esther,* 398).

3   Harrelson, "Textual and Translation Problems," 205.

4   A.E. Morris, "The Purpose of the Book of Esther," *ExpT* 42 (1930-31), 125. See also the comments of Bar-Ilan in this regard, especially concerning the transformation of the character of Esther (*Some Jewish Women in Antiquity,* 7).

5   On the colophon of the LXX, see the following works: B. Jacob, "Das Buch Esther bei den LXX," *ZAW* 10 (1890), esp. 278-79; E.J. Bickerman, "The Colophon of the Greek Book of Esther," *JBL* 63 (1944), 339-62.

Like the preceding chapter, we shall proceed exegetically. With great care given to context, we hope to make strides in apprehending the moral character of the Esther story as the LXX tells it.

3.1 Astin

3.1.1 Refusal to appear when summoned (1.10-12)

Although the story line of the LXX Astin account holds relatively tightly to its Semitic predecessor, there are some interesting differences. The grandiosity of the belongings and court of the king are portrayed equally impressively, as are the descriptions of the two banquets. The first, which is 180 days in duration and termed a "marriage-feast" [γάμος] (1.5), is given for the friends, remaining nations, and Persian and Median nobles, and the leaders of the satraps [τοῖς φίλοις καὶ τοῖς λοιποῖς ἔθνεσιν καὶ τοῖς Περσῶν καὶ Μήδων ἐνδόξοις καὶ τοῖς ἄρχουσιν τῶν σατραπῶν] (1.3). The subsequent and smaller festive gathering[6] lasts only six days and seeks to provide entertainment for the (leaders of?) nations who were found in the city [τοῖς ἔθνεσιν τοῖς εὑρεθεῖσιν εἰς τὴν πόλιν] (1.5). Although a clear and complete understanding of the above guest lists eludes us, our main objective in mentioning these banquets is to set the scene and point out an interesting feature in the description of the second one that touches (perhaps only lightly) upon the portion of the Astin narrative that will be highlighted here.

The opening words of 1.10 cause us to ponder the motive (or mistake) of the Greek author as he wrote the following words: "Now, on the seventh day" [ἐν δὲ τῇ ἡμέρᾳ τῇ ἑβδόμῃ]. Interestingly, 1.5 describes the second banquet as lasting only six days [ἡμέρας ἕξ]. What then are we to make of this *seventh* day that is related in 1.10? Concerning 1.5, subsequent Greek and Latin manuscripts and the paraphrase of Josephus[7] appear to correct what they must have considered to be an error toward the more logical and unifying reading of seven days.[8] Yet in regard to the numbers ἕξ and ἑβδόμῃ, a scribal copying error does not on the face of it afford itself as the obvious explanation for the textual divergences. Nevertheless, an attempt to make narrative sense of the seventh day of a six-day banquet does not prove fruitful

---

6   The word chosen to describe this gathering is πότον, likely describing a drinking feast.
7   Josephus, *Ant.,* 11.187.
8   See Hanhart for the specific text-critical details. Also of note, the later mss. and versions utilised a form of the numeric synonym ἑπτά when they corrected six to seven (*Esther,* 136).

either; a satisfying textual rationalisation does not provide itself.[9] In the end this chronological difficulty provides little hindrance for our particular focus. Its existence does, however, sharpen our awareness of the possibilities of inconsistencies in the LXX Esther text.

We are left, then, to proceed in our investigation of the moral character of Queen Astin in the present text. On this puzzling seventh day the text reports that the king is pleasant or glad [ἡδέως] (1.10a). The reason for the good mood of the king is not explicitly stated, although consonant with the consummation of the second banquet, we might assume that his merriment has something to do with the wine and drinking mentioned in 1.7. Whatever the case, he instructs the seven eunuchs who served him[10] to bring in the queen (1.10-11a). When Astin is brought in, the king intends to make her queen [βασιλεύειν αὐτὴν], placing the diadem on her in order to display her beauty for all to see (1.11b). But his intentions are never realised because Astin does not give ear to him [καὶ οὐκ εἰσήκουσεν αὐτοῦ Αστιν], thus refusing to accompany the eunuchs back to the banquet (1.12a). This both grieves [ἐλυπήθη] and angers [ὠργίσθη] the king (1.12b).

To be sure, a discernible reason for the refusal of the queen is not stated in the narrative. However, it appears that Queen Astin actually *said* something in addition to the loud statement of her physical unwillingness to appear at the banquet. According to the narrator, her *words* (whatever they might have been) provide the concrete (yet unknown) reasons for her downfall. Although the reader is not privy to the content of Astin's speech, it is clear that both the king and the courtiers would use her words of refusal against her – both personally and politically (1.13, 17).[11] Perhaps Queen Astin had uttered a simple 'No' to the attendants of the king. Or maybe she had delivered a powerful speech that explained her reason(s) for denying His Majesty. Beyond what the text relates (or does not, in this case) we are not able firmly to discern.

---

9   Moore decides to smooth over the difficulty by translating ἡμέρας ἓξ in 1.5 as a "week long," somewhat alleviating the (con)textual tension concerning the odd appearance of the seventh day in 1.10 (*Daniel, Esther and Jeremiah: The Additions*, 182). In a more recent treatment of this difficulty, Dorothy, when noting the six-day duration of the banquet, solves the problem in this way: "6 days (+ 1)." Dorothy appears to take the six-day duration as nothing more than a mistake and adds one day to correct the problem (*The Books of Esther*, 61).

10   Interestingly, one of these seven eunuchs is named Αμαν. This is the exact spelling of the Αμαν who is the antagonist of the story (cf. 3.1). That these two are the same person is not unlikely since Αμαν Αμαδάθου seems to have been promoted from a lower office (perhaps a serving eunuch) to a higher one (vizier) later in the narrative. If the Αμαν of both 1.10 and 3.1f. are the same character, however, nothing significant to the plot-line is added by this early appearance.

11   Day, *Three Faces of a Queen*, 211.

What we *are* able to see is that the king had sought to show off his beautiful queen in all of her splendour, emphasising her royalty as well.[12] But even knowing this, it cannot be established if or how the intent of the king factors into her reasoning to decline the royal summons. Did she refuse because her husband appeared intoxicated? Did she decline so that she would not appear as his beauty trophy? Might there have been other reasons? These are questions without clear answers. We can do no better than point to the inconclusive ponderings of § 2.1.1 concerning the moral character of the queen, for a satisfying moral assessment of her refusal here is not at all forthcoming. Nevertheless, though ambiguity surrounds her decision(s), the inaction and subsequent deposing of Astin makes way for one who *would* act in personal crisis, and whose motivations would be more easily discerned.

3.2 Esther

3.2.1 Concealment of Jewishness (2.10, 20)

On the face of the LXX Esther story, little is concealed. Stated more specifically: when we encounter the LXX narrative, we find ourselves privy to the content of certain characters' dreams, inner thoughts and prayers as the plot of the narrative unfolds. This is, no doubt, the intention of the author of the story. Yet the tendency towards disclosure (or exposure) does not necessarily make for a bad story. To be sure, Haman's is not the only soul that is laid bare in this text (cf. § 2.4).

Concerning Esther's successful concealment of her race [γένος] (2.10a) and homeland[13] [πατρίδα] (2.10a, 20a), the narrative presents different pictures. That they differ does not necessarily imply that they are inconsistent – they could, in the end, turn out to be complementary. In the initial clauses of both 2.10 and 2.20, the message given, though not in identical fashion, is nevertheless clear: Esther keeps the knowledge of her homeland (and race) to herself. This act of concealment is undertaken by Esther in obedience to her cousin, Mardochaios, whose leadership she is seen to respect both before and after she rises to the throne. Again, although one verse does not quote the

---

12 Day, *Three Faces of a Queen,* 211.
13 Day provides the translation "ancestry" here and submits that the combination of γένος and πατρίδα in 2.10 "suggests concern with a political country as well as an ethnic group" (*Three Faces of a Queen,* 33, 38). It could be, however, that with the use only of πατρίδα in 2.20a, that the terms employed in 2.10 are more closely related and able to be summarised in the term πατρίδα in 2.20a.

other, the reason given for her concealing (in)actions is the same: ὁ γὰρ Μαρδοχαῖος ἐνετείλατο αὐτῇ μὴ ἀπαγγεῖλαι (2.10b); and, οὕτως γὰρ ἐνετείλατο αὐτῇ Μαρδοχαῖος (2.20bα). Yet whereas 2.10b leaves the issue at the command of cousin Mardochaios – "for Mardochaios commanded her not to announce [her origins]," the adverbial, mediating clause of 2.20bα looks forward to further information and elaboration on the matter – "for in this manner Mardochaios commanded her." This clause flows naturally into 2.20bβ, in which the manner of Mardochaios's command is filled out: φοβεῖσθαι τὸν θεὸν καὶ ποιεῖν τὰ προστάγματα αὐτοῦ, καθὼς ἦν μετ᾽ αὐτοῦ. Simply elucidated, Esther is to fear God and do his [i.e., God's] commandments just as she did when she was with him [i.e., Mardochaios].[14] The outcome of this disambiguated enjoinder is reported in 2.20c in the following way: καὶ Εσθηρ οὐ μετήλλαξεν τὴν ἀγωγὴν αὐτῆς.

The probable ramifications of the resultant behaviour of the queen, however, are difficult to harmonise with the comportment of purposeful concealment initially proposed. Bickerman has anticipated our concerns here: "The whole Purim story hinges on Esther's keeping her origin secret."[15] Precisely. If the queen does not alter her manner of life – a reality that 2.20c asserts and one to which C.25b-29 adamantly testifies – are readers seriously to believe that Esther can possibly conceal her true colours in the midst of this? Bickerman, for one, does not, and claims that this difficulty "renders the whole plot absurd."[16] But let us not abandon ship just yet. If the queen does indeed fear God and do his commandments just as she has done when she was living under the roof of Mardochaios (as C.25b-29 puts forth), she must do so with the utmost skill and in deepest secrecy – a secrecy that even evades the notice of Aman.

We should recall that in A.17, Aman sets out to hurt both Mardochaios *and* his people as a result of the spoiled initial genocide plot. Why Aman seeks to harm the people of Mardochaios in addition, and whether and/or how he knows of their identity are not details that the narrative provides. Yet *if* Aman is indeed knowledgeable about the people of Mardochaios, we should think that he would also know exactly who Queen Esther is and whence she comes (cf. 2.11). Given all of this, the success of the ability of

---

14 While acknowledging the comments of Day concerning the ambiguities presented by the 3ms pronoun (αὐτοῦ), it would seem more likely in this particular context that the rendering submitted above makes better sense. However, in the case of the initial αὐτοῦ, I would grant that it might have been difficult for Esther to separate her submission to Mardochaios from her obedience to God (*Three Faces of a Queen*, 40, 199).

15 Bickerman, *Four Strange Books of the Bible*, 226.

16 Bickerman, *Four Strange Books of the Bible*, 226.

Esther to conceal her identity *seems* highly unlikely. Yet this concealment is just what the story purports – an incredible feat. In the end, the story gives no reason for readers to believe that she does not conceal her origins (and without deception). Just how well or carefully she performs this task, however, is debatable, though it is not a live question of the narrative. In the end, what might appear absurd to the reader is not necessarily problematic in the plot.

3.2.2 Apprehension about transgressing the law (4.11)

Being a Jewess under the cover of the Persian throne must have been a precarious position indeed given the nature and tone of the recently published genocidal edict of Aman (section B), the newly elevated vizier of the king (3.1). In view of the slanderously propagandised reputation of the Jews concerning civil laws (cf. § 3.5.1), it is no wonder that Queen Esther should be apprehensive about legal matters, especially as they directly concern the king. These things should be kept in mind when considering the remarkable charge of Mardochaios to the queen in 4.8, and her circumspect response in 4.11.

As we recognised in § 2.2.3, the edict of Aman against the Jews has had a marked effect on the entire empire. To be sure, the objects of his contempt have displayed their grief in a most serious way. The image of Mardochaios in sackcloth and ashes crying out 'Injustice!' at the top of his lungs (4.1; § 3.3.4), coupled with the loud crying [κραυγη], lamentation[17] [κοπετος], and great grief [πένθος μέγα] on the part of Jews throughout the kingdom (4.3), speaks for itself. Yet even the city of Sousa is confounded[18] [ἐταράσσετο] at the news (3.15). This brings us to examine the reaction of Esther: in light of all this, would she assume the posture of a condemned Jew or the Persian queen?

---

17 LS equates κοπετὸς with κομμός and gives idea that it is not mild, but rather despairing lamentation that is pictured in the use of this term. It could possibly have been that there is striking and beating of breasts involved (443). At the least, we must recognise the seriousness and force of the reaction of the Jews to the publication of the decree of Aman.

18 The exact sense of the verb ταράσσω is difficult to pin down in this case. In a physical sense, it can be used to relate the notion of stirring up or troubling. With an emotional or mental slant, it can denote the state of being troubled in the mind, confounded, agitated and disturbed (LS, 792). It is most likely that this second, emotional/mental, sense governs the use of the middle voice form of the verb employed here. Although it is remotely possible that the Sousians have reacted in some physical fashion to the news, the narrative does not attest to this. Even if they have stirred themselves up in a physical manner, it would have been as a result of the prior mental confusion that has occurred directly from the publication of the edict.

It would be difficult to believe that Esther is oblivious to what is going on in the greater empire. And according to 4.4a, it is unlikely that she is completely detached from outside matters. Because it is related that the maids and eunuchs of the queen enter and report[19] [ἀνήγγειλαν] to her, perhaps Esther has sent them out before this to inquire concerning all the commotion that must have engulfed the city. On hearing what has happened, she too is confounded[20] [ἐταράχθη], although it is difficult to know how extensively the news affects her,[21] or what exactly perplexes her. Whatever is told to her, however, affects the queen seriously enough that she in turn desires that Mardochaios be dressed and his sackcloth be taken away (4.4b).[22] The royal initiative enjoys no success (4.4c). Esther then intensifies her efforts as she actually seeks through her eunuch, Achrathai, to learn "exactness" [τὸ ἀκριβές] from her cousin (4.5b). Whereas before she had been inexplicably confounded, knowing an undisclosed amount of information, now the queen apparently desires to find out full disclosure. That is exactly what she receives in 4.7-8a, and then some.

Using Achrathai as a mouthpiece, Mardochaios relates to Esther just what has been done by Aman in order to procure the destruction of their common race (4.7). He even includes a copy of the document, perhaps in order to accentuate the reality of what he considers to be their shared plight (4.8a). Mardochaios then arrives at the heart of the matter. On his behalf Achrathai is instructed

ἐντείλασθαι αὐτῇ εἰσελθούσῃ παραιτήσασθαι τὸν βασιλέα καὶ ἀξιῶσαι αὐτὸν περὶ τοῦ λαοῦ μνησθεῖσα ἡμερῶν ταπεινώσεώς σου ὡς ἐτράφης ἐν χειρί μου, διότι Αμαν ὁ δευτερεύων τῷ βασιλεῖ ἐλάλησεν καθ᾽ ἡμῶν εἰς θάνατον·

---

19 Lit: "to carry back tidings of, report" (LS, 53).

20 As with the use of ταράσσω in 3.15, the sense here is likely restricted to the effect of emotional/mental trouble and confusion on the queen. This reaction does not necessitate a physical manifestation however (LS, 792). As noted in the preceding chapter (§ 2.2.3), Moore suggests rendering the verb ἐταράχθη as "perplexed," giving the sense of a nonphysical reaction (*Esther*, 48).

21 With the employment of the hithpalpel verb תתחלחל in the MT, the severity of the queen's reaction, though figuratively expressed, is quite obvious – Esther shows deep distress (§ 2.2.3). The LXX, however, does not appear to put forth so stark a message with the use of ἐταράχθη.

22 Lit: καὶ ἀπέστειλεν στολίσαι τὸν Μαρδοχαῖον καὶ ἀφελέσθαι αὐτοῦ τὸν σάκκον. It is difficult to tell if Esther has sent orders *to the effect* that Mardochaios be clothed and his sackcloth taken away (so Dorothy, *The Books of Esther*, 106-7), or if we are to understand that Esther has sent [clothes] *in order* to clothe Mardochaios making his sackcloth unnecessary, hence the need to take it away (so Day, *Three Faces of a Queen*, 46). Contextually, it is more likely that Esther has sent *her servants* (already known in the context and the *embodiment* of her orders) to Mardochaios rather than sending him *clothes* (not known in the context and not a necessary addition in order to make sense of the clause).

ἐπικάλεσαι τὸν κύριον, καὶ λάλησον τῷ βασιλεῖ περὶ ἡμῶν καὶ ῥῦσαι ἡμᾶς ἐκ θανάτου.

to command her to go [in order] to beg the king and petition him concerning the people, being mindful of the days of your low estate as you were reared by my hand, since Aman – the second to the king – spoke against us for death. Call upon the Lord, and talk to the king concerning us and deliver us from death[23] (4.8b-c).

With this, Esther is faced with a dilemma: will she identify with the her people – taking on their burden, calling on their Lord – and use her Persian standing to win the king over to their cause so that they might be delivered? Or might she attempt to blend into her Persian surroundings – abandoning her people – and leave the Jews in the way of impending desolation? To be sure, the queen is in a privileged enough position to have such a choice, and she is not long with her answer (through Achrathai):

Τὰ ἔθνη πάντα τῆς βασιλείας γινώσκει ὅτι πᾶς ἄνθρωπος ἢ γυνή, ὃς εἰσελεύσεται πρὸς τὸν βασιλέα εἰς τὴν αὐλὴν τὴν ἐσωτέραν ἄκλητος, οὐκ ἔστιν αὐτῷ σωτηρία· πλὴν ᾧ ἐκτείνει ὁ βασιλεὺς τὴν χρυσῆν ῥάβδον, οὗτος σωθήσεται. κἀγὼ οὐ κέκλημαι εἰσελθεῖν πρὸς τὸν βασιλέα, εἰσὶν αὗται ἡμέραι τριάκοντα.

---

23 *Pace* Day, it is not *necessarily* the case that in both the AT and LXX the grammatical structure of this final clause stresses "Esther's action of delivering the people over her actions of calling upon God and speaking to the king" (*Three Faces of a Queen*, 53-4). Day contends that in the AT, ἐπικαλεσαμένη and λάλησον are participles which are acting "in a circumstantial manner" in the service of the following active imperative – ῥῦσαι. Her point is this: "As Esther calls upon God and speaks to the king, these two actions [ἐπικαλεσαμένη and λάλησον] will be necessary to meet the objective of what is specified by the finite verb [ῥῦσαι], that is, to save the people" (53). Concerning the LXX, she claims that her syntactical point still stands even though the infinitive ἐπικάλεσαι has replaced the initial participle ἐπικαλεσαμένη. There is, however, another grammatical option, providing a different translation in *both* versions, that would cause us to view the final enjoinder of Mardochaios in a different light. We shall return to the thoughts of Day concerning the AT in due course (§ 4.2). For now, as pertains to the LXX, λάλησον could be parsed *either* as a neuter nominative singular future active participle (so Day, I am assuming) *or* a 2nd singular aorist active imperative (as I have translated). Also, ἐπικάλεσαι could be taken *either* as an aorist active infinitive (so Day) *or* a 2nd singular aorist middle imperative (as I have translated). With these parsing decisions available, it does not appear necessary *grammatically* to conclude that the call of Mardochaios for Esther to deliver is being stressed over his summons for her to call upon the Lord and talk to the king about the situation of the Jews. Given the theological tone of the story and the fact that Esther does not appear to be a particularly strong character at this particular juncture, it is more likely that Mardochaios stresses all three actions equally, with imperatival force, as I have chosen to render it above. Mardochaios realises the need for the Lord in this situation, urges Esther to talk to the king, and is beginning his process of persuasion, culminating in 4.14, with parental leverage and a challenge for Esther to deliver her people from death.

All the nations of the kingdom know that any man or woman[24] who shall go into the king – into the inner court – uncalled, there is no deliverance for that one, except [for the one] to whom the king extends the golden rod – this one shall be saved. And I have not been called to go into the king; it is these thirty days (4.11).

Esther appears to have found some measure of comfort within the palace walls, and it is not clear at this point whether she really counts herself among those Jews who are in danger of the genocidal edict of Aman. She would surely not wish to identify herself with a 'subversive' group of people (cf. section B) by means of a possibly unnecessary and certainly unlawful action. It appears as if the resulting tone of 4.11, stemming from her convenient commitment to decrees of the king, is one of apprehension as she ponders the call of Mardochaios to civil disobedience. At this point, the Jewish queen seems somewhat jaded about her Persian standing and safety. Mardochaios's process of persuasion, however, is only just beginning.

3.2.3 Apprehension not totally reversed (4.16)

Possibly perceiving the sense of comfort Esther might have felt in the palace, Mardochaios seeks to counter any such notion as he assures his cousin that she ought not convince herself of any special ethnic immunity accompanying her privileged position in the Persian court (4.13). As he begins his persuasive efforts, little time is spent on subtlety; Mardochaios drives straight to issues of life and death, for he considers it to be the same for all Jews. Diplomacy quickly shifts into brinkmanship as Mardochaios comes to the bottom line, warning Esther:

ἐὰν παρακούσῃς ἐν τούτῳ τῷ καιρῷ, ἄλλοθεν βοήθεια καὶ σκέπη ἔσται τοῖς Ἰουδαίος, σὺ δὲ καὶ ὁ οἶκος τοῦ πατρός σου ἀπολεῖσθε·

If you should fail to listen[25] at this time, from another place help and protection will be to the Jews, but you and the house of your father will be destroyed (4.14a).

---

24 Admittedly, the phrase ἄνθρωπος ἢ γυνή is not the normal way to express "man or woman." One would have expected ἀνήρ in place of ἄνθρωπος (usually denoting "human being") if the idea of "man or woman" was the one intended here. Since an odd construction exists, we must leave open the possibility of other ideas in rendering it. For example, πᾶς ἄνθρωπος ἢ γυνή could have been used here to relay the following thought: "any person or (even) woman." Thus, Esther could have been highlighting her (lower) status as a woman in her explanation to Mardochaios. In short, her message could have been that anyone, especially a woman (!), who enters into the king unsummoned will die if not for the golden rod. (I should note that Prof. A.G. Auld brought this issue to my attention.)

25 The correct sense of παρακούσῃς – "to hear carelessly, take no heed to" (LS, 598) – is captured in the translation of Day, which I have followed (*Three Faces of a Queen*, 50).

Familial leverage (cf. 4.8) has turned into ultimatum as Day observes:
"Esther's decision lies within the realm of obedience to Mardochaios. He
warns her not to fail to pay attention to the commands and arguments he has
presented [ἐὰν παρακούσῃς]."²⁶ The picture Mardochaios paints is quite
bleak. Although the mood of his communication seems conditional, the
reader gathers that there are no *real* choices to be made. Yet Esther would, in
time, have to choose. And it appears that if she ignores his commission, her
entire family would suffer dire consequences. Nevertheless, and this assurance appears to be guaranteed, the Jewish people will receive their rescue
ἄλλοθεν. Here the sense of indestructibility governs the Jewish mindset (at
least Mardochaios's).²⁷ As Achrathai comes to the end of Mardochaios's
message (and ropes), her Majesty hears this parting challenge: καὶ τίς οἶδεν
εἰ εἰς τὸν καιρὸν τοῦτον ἐβασίλευσας; (4.14b). Who knows? Perhaps
Queen Esther would take this opportunity to put a defining mark on what has
been to this point a charmed reign?

Push has come to shove. Although months of time stand between the present and the time when the edict of genocide would be acted upon, we might
get the impression that in the midst of the narrative tension nail-biting sec-
onds are all that remain. What will the reply of Esther be? Through (the tire-
less) Achrathai, the queen sends one last message to her cousin:

Βαδίσας ἐκκλησίασον τοὺς Ιουδαίους τοὺς ἐν Σούσοις καὶ νηστεύσατε ἐπ'
ἐμοὶ καὶ μὴ φάγητε μηδὲ πίητε ἐπὶ ἡμέρας τρεῖς νύκτα καὶ ἡμέραν· κἀγὼ δὲ
καὶ αἱ ἅβραι μου ἀσιτήσομεν, καὶ τότε εἰσελεύσομαι πρὸς τὸν βασιλέα παρὰ
τὸν νόμον, ἐὰν καὶ ἀπολέσθαι με ᾖ.

After going, hold an assembly of the Jews in Sousa and fast for me – neither eat nor
drink for three days, night and day; and I and my maids shall abstain from food, and
then I shall go in to the king against the law, although it might be that I perish²⁸
(4.16).

26　Day, *Three Faces of a Queen*, 56. Note that ἐὰν παρακούσῃς is a conditional clause in
　　which the aorist subjunctive is utilised. This usage "appears in the great majority of
　　cases, both in general conditions and in those referring to something impending" (F.
　　Blass and A. Debrunner, *A Greek Grammar of the New Testament and Other Early
　　Christian Literature* (trans. and rev. by R.W. Funk; Chicago: The University of Chicago
　　Press, 1961), § 373. Cf. N. Turner, *Grammar of New Testament Greek* (vol. III – Syn-
　　tax; Edinburgh: T & T Clark, 1963), 114.
27　Day, *Three Faces of a Queen*, 56.
28　The dependent clause, ἐὰν καὶ ἀπολέσθαι με ᾖ, is a difficult one to render. Gram-
　　matically, the combination of ἐὰν καί is usually understood concessively and translated
　　"although" (Blass and Debrunner, *A Greek Grammar*, § 374). However, since the sub-
　　junctive ᾖ is present and sets the mood of the clause, it is doubtful that the whole clause
　　should be understood concessively. Therefore, a conditional tone is supplied in the

According to her statement Esther appears not to be without hope, although it
is clearly only a glimmer. The very fact that she calls the Jewish community
in Sousa to a fast, in which she and her maids will participate, coupled with
the conditional nature of the final clause – ἐὰν καὶ ἀπολέσθαι με ᾖ – gives
us the impression that she does not believe all is lost.[29] Martyrdom is not necessarily the only prospect.[30] At this point we gather that the Jewess is placing
all her faith in a graceful reception when she enters before the Persian king.
Yet a brave queen is not pictured here. Great violence[31] is looming for both
the Jews collectively and their new leader (cf. 4.17) particularly because of
the royal decree. As sections C and D dramatically record, this impending
peril strikes tremendous fear into the heart of Esther, but not utter despair.

3.2.4 Imprecatory petitions (C.22c, 24)

Instead of shrinking away in solipsistic retreat, Esther falls humbly to her
knees.[32] Rather than gathering power and courage from within, she focuses
on a greater power from without as she beseeches κυρίου θεοῦ Ισραηλ
(C.14a).[33] Without question, the queen is still suffering internally [ἐν ἀγῶνι

---

above translation even though the word "although" is retained (Turner, *Grammar* (vol.
III – Syntax), 321).

29 I would agree with the point Day makes concerning the sense of optimism that Esther
    might have had in 4.11 has receded significantly by 4.16 (*Three Faces of a Queen*, 198).
    However, instead of being optimistic in 4.11 about her chances at the prospect of going
    before the king, I would suggest that Esther is likely more optimistic in 4.11 concerning
    the possibility that she might avert the Jewish problem altogether living within the pal-
    ace walls. This optimism is short-lived, though, and by 4.13 it begins to abate. And at
    the end of her speech in 4.16, the queen appears quite pessimistic about her upcoming
    encounter with the king. Pessimistic, but not hopeless.

30 *Pace* Dorothy that the declaration of Esther is one of "self-sacrifice" (*The Books of
    Esther*, 109). Remember that the golden rod is the loophole in the royal anti-
    encroachment statute (4.11).

31 In the span of ten verses a form of the verb ἀπόλλυμι – "to destroy utterly; to perish
    utterly" (LS, 101-2) – is employed four times (4.7, 8, 14, 16). Whether it is used to de-
    scribe the fate of the Jews as a result of the decree of Aman (4.7 – ἀπολέσῃ; 4.8 –
    ἀπολέσθαι), warn of the threat to Esther and her family (4.14 – ἀπολεῖσθε), or relate the
    danger that stared down at the queen (4.16 – ἀπολέσθαι), the gravity of the Jewish
    situation is most likely enhanced in the mind of the Greek reader (Day, *Three Faces of a
    Queen*, 58).

32 One aspect of this can be seen quite descriptively in how Esther prepares her outward
    appearance to come before the Lord (C.13).

33 Boyd-Taylor suggests that within Greek novels, prayers "depict figural consciousness,"
    giving the author "a chance to present a self-disclosure of character" as well as often
    creating "a certain impression of piety" ("Esther's Great Adventure," 111). These fea-

θανάτου κατειλημμένη] (C.12) – an actuality that even shows in her external appearance (C.13). Yet she realises the fact that she is alone, even alienated, and has no help save in her God (C.14b-c, 25).[34] Thus, she begins her
prayer: "My Lord our king, *you* are [the] only one" [Κύριέ μου ὁ βασιλεὺς
ἡμῶν, σὺ εἶ μόνος] (C.14b). The message here, although expressed awk-
wardly,[35] appears to have a double significance: Esther is not only asseverat-
ing her newly resolved affinity with her people [ὁ βασιλεὺς ἡμῶν], but she
is also recognising the spiritual reality that her allegiance is to her heavenly
king no matter what awaits her in the upcoming encounter with her earthly
king. Indeed, Esther's ancestral solidarity within the story of Israel receives a
further (and more concrete) witness in C.16,[36] while the attestation of her true
monarchical loyalty takes clearer shape as she prays on (see C.21-30). By
now it is clear that the queen has decided to identify fundamentally with her
kin rather than her crown; determined to be counted among her people, she
seeks refuge in the Lord, God of Israel.

Upon this foundation, we are better able both to understand the intimacy
Esther feels as she prays to the Lord, and apprehend the impassioned fervour
in which she frames her requests. Acknowledging the sovereignty of God as
the one holding the sceptre [τὸ σκῆπτρόν], Esther implores her Lord never
to give it over "to those who are not"[37] [τοῖς μὴ οὖσιν; i.e., heathen gods],
and not to let them [i.e., the nations (cf. C.21)] laugh at our falling [τῇ
πτώσει ἡμῶν] (C.22a). It is likely that the prayer of the queen is simultaneously directed at two levels: the heavenly and the earthly. As she pleads with
God not to relinquish his power τοῖς μὴ οὖσιν, Esther also addresses im-

tures certainly can be seen both in the prayer of Esther and of Mordecai (§ 3.3.3), and
both in the LXX and the AT (see chapter 4 below).
34 See Day's concise discussion of Esther's realisation of her "aloneness" and how that
affects her prayer – "She can only rely on God" (*Three Faces of a Queen*, 78, 83).
35 Kottsieper, *Zusätze zu Ester*, 178.
36 Moore, *Daniel, Esther, and Jeremiah: The Additions*, 210-11; Day, *Three Faces of a
Queen*, 70, 78.
37 *Pace* Day (*Three Faces of a Queen*, 72), μὴ οὖσιν is a plural construction and *can* refer
to those among the nations (C.21) who stand ready to laugh at the current plight of the
Jews and whose purposes Esther will pray are turned back against them (C.22). Another
suggestion for μὴ οὖσιν is that they are "non-existent" gods (i.e., "heathen" gods – no
gods at all in comparison with the God of Israel) to whom the Lord is not to surrender
his heavenly sceptre (cf. Wisd 13.10-19; 14.13; 1 Cor. 8.10) (Moore, *Daniel, Esther,
and Jeremiah: The Additions*, 211; Fox, *Redaction*, 56). Interestingly, the AT in this instance reads τοῖς μισοῦσί σε ἐχθροῖς, "to the enemies hating you," which either purposely understands the earthly notion or misinterprets the heavenly, intended scope. In
the LXX, nevertheless, both horizontal *and* vertical realms could have been in view –
the writer might have understood the nations to have been guided by heathen gods, pic-
turing the battle to be taking place both above (i.e., God v. gods) and below (i.e., Jews v.
nations).

mediate concerns 'on the ground' as the nations, led ultimately by these heathen gods, stand poised to scoff at the predicament in which the Jews find
themselves. She continues:

...ἀλλὰ στρέψον τὴν βουλὴν αὐτῶν ἐπ' αὐτούς, τὸν δὲ ἀρξάμενον ἐφ' ἡμᾶς
παραδειγμάτισον.

...but turn back their counsel upon themselves, and make an example of the one who
began against us (C.22b).

The one who "began against" the Jews, in the context of the story, likely refers to the person who had devised the plan for the demise of the Jews, i.e.,
Aman.[38] He should suffer along with those among the nations who would plot
against the people of God. Even more specifically, Esther desires that when
she does in fact enter before her earthly king, the Lord would

μετάθες τὴν καρδίαν αὐτοῦ εἰς μῖσος τοῦ πολεμοῦντος ἡμᾶς εἰς συντέλειαν
αὐτοῦ καὶ τῶν ὁμονοούντων αὐτῷ·

transform his [i.e., the king's] heart to hatred of the one hostile to us, for [the] end of
him and those who are in agreement with him (C.24b).

Thus, Esther seeks that her husband be made an agent for God, as the scope
of her imprecatory petitions ranges from Aman to any persons in the empire
who fall in line with his genocidal intentions. Ironically, at this point in the
story the king himself might be counted among this number (cf. § 3.6.3). We
might add also that implicitly included in these ranks are the heathen gods
who lie behind (dwell above) both the planner and those who will carry the
plan out.

How one views the nature of the queen's imprecatory desires will depend
on how the context of their utterance is understood. In this case, Esther is
certainly, though somewhat ambiguously, calling on God to act retributively
(preemptively?) on behalf of his chosen and endangered people[39] – a mode of
prayer certainly not foreign to the mindset and literature of the Old Testament.[40] What she is definitely *not* doing in this instance, however, is resolving to take vengeance and retribution into her own hands.

---

38 Dorothy, *The Books of Esther*, 118; Moore, *Daniel, Esther, and Jeremiah: The Addi-
    tions*, 212.
39 This request, of course, is alongside the primary and overall petition that the troubled
    Jews be saved (Day, *Three Faces of a Queen*, 82).
40 See Kottsieper, *Zusätze zu Ester*, 174. Kottsieper cites such text as Pss 7.13-17; 9.16f.;
    35.4-8; 40.15 as displaying this same motive.

3.2.5 Appearing as a pious Jewess (C.25b-29)

In the section above, we observed and began to explore the conscientious quest of Esther to identify with her people and their God as she becomes acutely aware of the potential danger of her isolation within the palace walls (C.14). That realisation and resolving drives her to a prayer of adoration and desperate petition. Yet included in the midst of this is a discernible "protestation of innocence,"[41] much like what we notice in a portion of the prayer of Mardochaios as he explains before God his reasons for not bowing before Aman (C.5-7; § 3.3.3).[42] It is in this appeal that we most notably witness the pious portrait of Esther.

The queen commences her defence by making the following confession: πάντων γνῶσιν ἔχεις (C.25b).[43] As she acknowledges her Lord's knowledge of all things, Esther continues to avow her humble condition – a condition that appears to place entire dependence on God. Included in this emotional posture is the hope that God is actually as close to her as she believes and now needs. This hope governs the tone of the remaining prayer, save her final petitions (C.30),[44] and is boldly put on the line in the four "asseverations"[45] of Esther. The first two of these concerns can be grouped together for reasons that will become apparent. The queen asseverates the following:

καὶ οἶδας ὅτι ἐμίσησα δόξαν ἀνόμων καὶ βδελύσσομαι κοίτην ἀπεριτμήτων καὶ παντὸς ἀλλοτρίου. σὺ οἶδας τὴν ἀγάγκην μου, ὅτι βδελύσσομαι τὸ σημεῖον τῆς ὑπερηφανίας μου, ὅ ἐστιν ἐπὶ τῆς κεφαλῆς μου ἐν ἡμέραις ὀπτασίας μου· βδελύσσομαι αὐτὸ ὡς ῥάκος καταμηνίων καὶ οὐ φορῶ αὐτὸ ἐν ἡμέραις ἡσυχίας μου.

You know that I hate(d) [the] honour of lawless ones and loathe [the] marriage-bed of [the] uncircumcised[46] and everything foreign. You know my necessity, that I loathe

---

41 Dorothy, *The Books of Esther,* 119. Kottsieper terms it "eine Selbstrechtfertigung" (*Zusätze zu Ester,* 175).
42 For further comment and comparison of the two prayers, see Levenson, *Esther,* 86; and Day, *Three Faces of a Queen,* 79-82.
43 According to Bar-Ilan, reference to the omniscience of God is component of many post-biblical prayers of remembrance (*Some Jewish Women of Antiquity,* 98). This observations can also be applied to the similar confession of Esther in her AT prayer (§ 4.2.4).
44 ὁ θεὸς ὁ ἰσχύων ἐπὶ πάντας, εἰσάκουσον φωνὴν ἀπηλπισμένων καὶ ῥῦσαι ἡμᾶς ἐκ χειρὸς τῶν πονηρευσομένων καὶ ῥῦσαί με ἐκ τοῦ φόβου μου (C.30). At the end of her prayer matters are still not resolved, and the queen remains fearful.
45 Dorothy, *The Books of Esther,* 119-20.
46 Esther's disdain for the marriage-bed of the uncircumcised is perhaps best understood in light of R. Frye's comments concerning the Hellenistic worldview, in which ethnic identity had been replaced by religious identity ("Minorities in the History of the Near East," in J. Duchesne-Guillemin, et al (eds), *A Green Leaf: Papers in Honour of Professor Jes P. Asmussen (Acta Iranica,* 28; Leiden: E.J. Brill, 1988), 461-71 (cited in Berlin, *Esther,* l-li).

the sign of my arrogance,[47] which is upon my head in days of my appearance; I loathe
it like a menstruous rag and do not wear it in days of my leisure (C.26-27).

It appears that Esther's particular target here is any assumption or suggestion
that she might actually enjoy her luxurious and tempting court lifestyle. Thus,
in hope that God really does know the constraints of her present situation,
Esther makes sure to set the record straight: she abhors the honour of ones
who are lawless (i.e., ones in the court), has no enjoyment in her sexual encounters, and hates (in a manner most graphically described) the royal turban.[48] Dorothy suggests that the attitude of the queen here is "Torah-led," and
serves as a basis for her staunch denials.[49] That Esther would have been intimately familiar with Torah could be deduced from earlier portions of her
prayer (esp. C.16), even though there is no explicit mention here of Jewish
law or regulations. But in her attempt to distance herself from ones and things
lawless, Esther does not necessarily assert that she herself has been lawful. At
this point, we might assume that this attitude of dissenting assimilation is all
in the service of her overall and ongoing concealment efforts.

The second set of asseverations can be coupled as well, for they concern
things not that Esther was unhappy doing, but behaviour that she has conscientiously avoided.

καὶ οὐκ ἔφαγεν ἡ δούλη σου τράπεζαν Αμαν, καὶ οὐκ ἐδόξασα συμπόσιον
βασιλέως οὐδὲ ἔπιον οἶνον σπονδῶν· καὶ οὐκ ηὐφράνθη ἡ δούλη σου ἀφ'
ἡμέρας μεταβολῆς μου μέχρι νῦν πλὴν ἐπὶ σοί, κύριε ὁ θεὸς Αβρααμ.

Your bondwoman has not eaten [at the] table of Aman, and I have not honoured [the]
drinking-party of the king nor drunk wine of libations; your bondwoman has not been
joyous since the day of my removal until now except on account of[50] you, O Lord,
God of Abraham (C.28-29).

In matters of diet, the Persian queen acts as we might expect a 'faithful' Jew
to behave.[51] In the midst of her avoidance, however, one might wonder if a
curious court eyebrow would have been raised. Yet despite her dietary stance
and overall sombre demeanour (C.29), the cover of Esther is surprisingly not
blown. For Day, this highlights the queen's "talent for acting,"[52] but we are

---

47 I.e., "proud position."
48 "Given the Jewish taboos on menstruation (cf. Lev 15:19-24), one can hardly imagine a
   stronger expression of Esther's abhorrence for her royal turban" (Moore, *Daniel, Esther,
   and Jeremiah: The Additions*, 212).
49 Dorothy, *The Books of Esther*, 119.
50 J.H. Thayer suggests the possibility of this metaphorical use which fits the context here
   (*A Greek-English Lexicon of the New Testament* (Edinburgh: T & T Clark, 1901⁴), 233).
51 Cf. the conscientious abstinence of Daniel and his friends in the court of Babylon (Dan
   1.8), and the comportment of Judith in the presence of Holofernes (Jud 12.1-2).
52 Day, *Three Faces of a Queen*, 83.

unsure upon what standard Esther bases her decisions concerning sexual and
dietary regulation: unhappily participating in the one; completely abstaining
from the other. Whereas the concealment endeavour aids us in understanding
the former, it brings confusion to the consideration of the latter.

In terms of the moral character the story *seeks* to project, however, the picture is clear:

> Esther is a pious person. Her character includes a religious dimension. She appears
> accustomed to praying, as she enters readily into a lengthy and articulate prayer. We
> know Esther as one who recognizes the God of Israel, is in a relationship with God,
> and is dependent upon God for guidance and wisdom...She hates sleeping with the
> king. Esther does not eat with the Persians...Esther holds real animosity towards Gen-
> tiles as a whole...[and] views such persons as enemies both of the Jews and of God.[53]

Indeed, this is the prevailing view of the queen from this point in the interpretative history of the story onward.[54] But how are we to understand the behaviour of Esther here in view of Jewish regulations? Are her actions, both dissenting and avoiding, to be reckoned as Torah influenced? Or is Esther
merely living the complex existence of a Jew in a Diaspora court, attempting
to keep separate her "public" and "inner" selves?[55] Needless to say, our suspicions are raised;[56] the moral character submitted here is not necessarily
straightforward.

3.2.6 Tact at the second banquet (7.1-8)

After Mardochaios and Esther finish praying, the fortunes of the Jews begin
to look increasingly bright. The fears of the queen are at last settled as she
successfully negotiates her traumatic encounter before the king (D.1-5.3).
Much (if not most) of the credit for her achievement, however, owes to God
as the heart of the king is changed from anger to gentleness (D.8). This transformation in the king enables Esther to take courage and begin implementing
her strategy for Jewish deliverance (5.4f.). Mardochaios also enjoys a better
lot. With divine superintendence (6.1), the king sees fit finally to reward the
Jew for his loyalty in foiling the assassination plot(s) (§ 3.3.1; 3.3.2). With
this, Mardochaios is now on the ascendancy as Aman poises for a nosedive.

---

53 Day, *Three Faces of a Queen*, 82-83.
54 For a discussion of how the rabbis further developed the piety of Esther, see Bronner,
    "Esther Revisited: An Aggadic Approach," esp. 183-87.
55 Wills employs these terms and raises similar questions concerning Esther as seen in her
    prayer (*The Jewish Novel in the Ancient World*, 123).
56 Along with those of Kottsieper (*Zusätze zu Ester*, 175).

And according to the opinion of the declining vizier's wife, Zosara, all of this was happening because the "living God" is with the Jew, Mardochaios (6.13).

Meanwhile, as she grows in courage and resolve, Esther gains the presence of both the king and Aman at her initial banquet (5.6). There, she requests for them to come yet again the following day to join her at the table (5.8). It is at this second banquet that we encounter the craft and rhetorical skill of the queen.

With the king and Aman present with the queen at her table (7.1), the action begins. Curious as to why they have gathered together to drink for a second consecutive day, the king, perhaps a bit more sensitive at this point (cf. D.8-9), queries his wife: "What is it?" [Τί ἐστιν] (7.2a). This general question is immediately followed by more specific ones pertaining to the request [αἴτημά] and petition [ἀξίωμά] of Esther, as the king assures her that she would not be denied her desires – up to half of his kingdom[57] [καὶ ἔστω σοι ἕως τοῦ ἡμίσους τῆς βασιλείας μου] (7.2b-c). Esther answers in the following words:

Εἰ εὗρον χάριν ἐνώπιον τοῦ βασιλέως, δοθήτω ἡ ψυχὴ τῷ αἰτήματί μου καὶ ὁ λαός μου τῷ ἀξιώματί μου.

If I have found favour before the king, let life[58] be given for my request, my people for my petition (7.3).

The request of the queen – δοθήτω ἡ ψυχη – makes sense in the context of the story and causes her two answers to become one, *twofold* reply. If it is understood in this way, the specific and latter, ὁ λαός μου, qualifies the general and former, ἡ ψυχη; thus, her corporate concern is in the foreground. Given Esther's resolved upon and confessed affinity with her people (cf. C.14, 16, 20-22a), this should not surprise. But it is not as if Esther the individual has vanished from the scene and been totally subsumed in the midst of the Jewish cause, for at the moment, she is their leader and greatest

---

57 Day reasons that the imperative ἔστω "lends forcefulness and assurance to the king's statement of meeting her desires" (*Three Faces of a Queen*, 120-21).

58 Although many later mss. 'correct' ἡ ψυχὴ τῷ αἰτήματί μου to τη ψυχη μου το αιτηματι μου (e.g., *O* – 93), it might not be necessary to understand Esther in this way (see Hanhart on this and other cases [*Esther*, 181]). Day suggests that "she requests only life in general...not necessarily her own, which lends the idea that she is pleading for the lives of all the people whom she mentions next" (*Three Faces of a Queen*, 122). Has the LXX translator/author interpreted his *Vorlage* to be equating Esther with her people here (cf. Fox, *Character and Ideology*, 83)? The question is a difficult one. The translation, "give life for my request," makes sense in its LXX context given Esther's close identification with her people. However, if one chose to understand a μου to be inserted, "give *my* life for my people," the sense of the passage would not be lost.

human hope. For instance, notice the initial portion of 7.4: ἐπράθημεν γὰρ
ἐγώ τε καὶ ὁ λαός μου – "For we were sold, both I and my people." The
Jewess is still exercising her prerogative as Persian queen; it is she who has
gained access to and enjoys a company with the king.

What transpires next is quite remarkable. By stating that her people were
sold [ἐπράθημεν], Esther is probably alluding to the offering of a great sum
of money by Aman to the king so that an unnamed people in the empire
might be destroyed (3.9; informed to Esther in 4.7).[59] Whether or not the
money had ever been deposited in the treasury of the king, however, is unclear. Either way, the cash-for-life *intention* of Aman provides a sufficient
foundation on which Esther can build her case. Her argument continues as
she mentions for or into what specifically her people have been sold, Esther
names three things: destruction [ἀπώλειαν]; plunder [διαρπαγὴν]; and servitude [δουλείαν] (7.4a).[60] All of this information the queen claims she has
overheard [παρήκουσα], though the reader is aware from whom Esther has
received her knowledge (cf. 4.7-8). As her case is now nearly complete,
Esther adds this scathing remark:

οὐ γὰρ ἄξιος ὁ διάβολος τῆς αὐλῆς τοῦ βασιλέως.

for the slanderer is not worthy of the court of the king (7.4b).[61]

---

59 The narrative does not make clear whether or not the silver ever changes hands. In 3.11
    the king made the statement that Aman should keep the silver and treat the nation as he
    wished. Yet in 4.7 Mardochaios related the plight of the Jews to Esther in a way that
    made mention of Aman's *promise* of money in exchange for license to destroy the Jews.
    Whether or not the money is ever deposited into the treasuries of the king, however, ap-
    pears inconsequential in the eyes of the narrative because the argument of Esther in 7.4
    is likely assuming that it has been (or, if not, the *intention* of Aman to exchange cash-
    for-life functions just as if he had made the deposit).
60 The first two of these can be easily referenced in the intentions of Aman (3.7, 9, 13;
    section B). Yet the third, δουλείαν, has no such referent, either explicit or implicit. In
    neither Aman's plotting (3.7f.) nor Mardochaios's relating (4.7-8) is there found any
    mention of or allusion to the Jews being sold into any form of bondage. Furthermore,
    unlike its MT counterpart (7.4), there does not appear to be any rhetorical strategy pre-
    sent in Esther utilisation of the servitude image here. Yet, interestingly, the queen pro-
    ceeds to elaborate on the details of the impending subservience – adults and children
    would be affected (7.4a). In the end, the confusion that δουλείαν brings the reader of the
    LXX might be attributed to a scribal error. Since ולאבד is the third in the MT triad, the
    LXX translator could have mistaken the root אבד for the similarly sounding root עבד,
    denoting servitude. If so, δουλείαν would have been an understandable rendering.
61 It is interesting that, if understood differently, Esther could have also implicitly been
    including herself in this statement. Although the substantive, ὁ διάβολος, is clearly
    masculine and refers to Aman, the queen had just stated that she had overheard her in-
    formation and might have included that fact to give credibility to her argument. Thus, in
    offering that she had actually overheard what she was now presenting, Esther might
    have been bolstering her own case against an accusation of slander. In short, she was

The implications here are potentially lethal and would have definitely captured the curiosity of the king. Esther has gone as far as she possibly could have to designate Aman as the offender without actually mentioning him by name. And in a move of real craft in order to entice the king even more, the queen highlights the court as being the overall entity under threat, not merely a group of people.[62] His Majesty takes the bait and demands to know who is responsible for the matter (7.5). Needless to say, Esther is ready with a response, claiming that Aman is this hostile [ἐχθρός] and evil [πονηρός] person (7.6a). And with the accusation finally made clear, the text relates the vizier's trouble or distress [ἐταράχθη] in the presence of the monarchs – fear is likely characterising his condition (7.6b).[63] (It must be remembered that throughout this whole scene Aman has been present at that same table.) This supposition is substantiated somewhat by the fact that as soon as the king leaves the room for the garden, Aman entreats the queen, "for he saw himself being in bad [circumstances]" [ἑώρα γὰρ ἑαυτὸν ἐν κακοῖς ὄντα] (7.7). His position, however, is not yet as regretful as it would soon be. 7.8 informs us that when the king returns from the garden, he witnesses Aman assuming an unfortunate posture – he has fallen upon the couch of the queen as he beseeches her (7.8a). This spectacle provokes the following royal outcry:

Ὥστε καὶ τὴν γυναῖκα βιάζῃ ἐν τῇ οἰκίᾳ μου;

So even the woman you/he[64] would force in my house (7.8b)?

If he had not come to a conclusion in how to handle the dilemma in the garden, the king surely decides the fate of Aman now as he assesses the current situation unbelievingly. As far as the narrative is concerned, it is the *appear-*

---

putting her own credibility on the line – if judged to be a slanderer, she herself would not be worthy of the court of the king. Though likely not the primary thrust of the passage, this explanation might further elucidate the intricate rhetorical strategies of Esther.

62 Day, *Three Faces of a Queen,* 124.

63 The use of the root ταράσσω here is interesting. Whereas in D.13 it was the heart of Esther that was troubled by fear beholding the glory of the king, now it is the condition of Aman that is troubled before both the king and the queen. With the employment of ἐταράχθη, Esther and Aman have (in one way) traded places (Day, *Three Faces of a Queen,* 127).

64 One could either parse βιάζῃ as the 3rd person present active singular subjunctive of βιάζω (as above), or as the 2nd person present middle singular subjunctive of βιάζομαι. Both options would generally carry the same verbal meaning, but the difference would be in how the king is addressing Aman here. Is he directing his disbelieving accusation primarily to the vizier ("So even the woman *you* would force in my house"), or might the king be addressing the issue in a more indirect manner of speaking or even to others in the room ("So even the woman *he* would force in my house")?

ance of Aman that signals his demise (cf. § 2.2.5; 2.4.4). A realisation of the
dire situation is likely also apparent to Aman as the text relates that upon
hearing this, Aman turns his face away [διετράπη τῷ προσώπῳ] (7.8c).
Aman had taken liberties with the queen,[65] and it has been interpreted in the
worst possible way by her husband. Once she had tactfully set the trap, all
Esther has to do was quietly lounge upon her couch and watch the enemy
self-destruct.

3.2.7 The vengeful queen? (9.13)

Although the textual foundations for asking questions concerning Esther and
vengeance remain steady as they were laid out in § 2.2.6, the contexts of the
two scenes are somewhat different. Thus, the issue must be investigated
freshly. In doing this, we still must be careful not to attribute more or less to
the queen than the text affords in this matter.

In 9.11, the number of those who have been destroyed in Sousa on 13
Adar is related to the king. He then turns to his queen and informs her of the
number of casualties in the capital as a result of the fighting. The reported
number dead at the hand of the Jews in Sousa is 500 men (9.12a). Having this
information, the mind of the king is curious to know the full extent of the
overwhelming victory of the Jews on that day. Thus, almost as if he is won-
dering to himself and not really expecting a precise answer, he inquires of
Esther:

ἐν δὲ τῇ περιχώρῳ πῶς οἴει ἐχρήσαντο;

And in the country round about how do you suppose they [i.e., the Jews] have availed
themselves[66] (9.12b)?

Despite the serious circumstances surrounding them, the royal couple appear
to be having a rather cordial exchange here. Given the closeness of their developed relationship in the LXX,[67] this type of conversation should come as
no great surprise. Receiving no comment from his wife on the matter, the
king presses on to more manageable matters as he queries Esther once again.
This time, however, his question warrants a response. With the formulaic
assurance that she would surely receive her desire, Esther ponders what fur-

---

65 Dorothy, *The Books of Esther,* 176.
66 The rendering of Day seems best to capture the sense of the aorist middle here (*Three
    Faces of a Queen,* 152).
67 See Day, *Three Faces of a Queen,* 184-85. Section D especially highlights the closeness
    of this relationship.

ther she might request (9.12c). Without protocol, and likely with a measure of forcefulness,[68] she replies:

Δοθήτω τοῖς Ἰουδαίοις χρῆσθαι ὡσαύτως τὴν αὔριον, ὥστε τοὺς δέκα υἱοὺς κρεμάσαι Αμαν.

Let it be given to the Jews to use the morrow in such a manner, so as to hang the ten sons of Aman (9.13).

We must admit that the initial part of the request of Esther is difficult to understand. Can we be certain what exactly it is that Esther is petitioning? Is her appeal for the sanctioning of *further* bloodshed on the part of the Jews in the spirit of what occurred on 13 Adar? If so, it seems odd that the sanction is non-specific concerning the location of this further action that the Jews are being authorised to undertake. Not until 9.15 do we learn that the Jews have assembled in Sousa on 14 Adar and have killed 300 men. Important questions remain, however: Has this additional killing been authorised by Esther in 9.13a? or Have the Jews (mis)interpreted their leader to be giving such a sanction? furthermore, Can Queen Esther be held responsible for what happens in Sousa on 14 Adar?

With a particular understanding of 9.13b, Day proposes a slightly different way of interpreting the verse that would serve to weaken any assertion of vengeance on Esther's part in this case. Day argues that because "ὥστε with the infinitive (κρεμάσαι) tends to express result," we should understand that the hanging of the sons of Aman to be the "primary goal" of the Jews.[69] In other words, Esther is strongly requesting that the Jews be able to continue in the spirit of the recent conflict *with the result that* the ten sons of Aman be hanged. The public humiliation of the sons is to be their main objective and action. Together with her handling of 9.13b, the rendering that Day provides for 9.13a – "Have it granted to the Jews to avail themselves in the same manner tomorrow"[70] – leaves the reader to suppose that the further killing in Sousa on 14 Adar is a secondary goal or perhaps even a coincidental result of the wishes of Esther. This, however, does not appear to be a necessary condition of or conclusion from the petition of the queen.

The translation of 9.13 given above – "Let it be given to the Jews to use the morrow in such a manner, so as to hang the ten sons of Aman" – could point to the fact that Esther has but *one* request: to have the sons of Aman

---

68 Day contends that toward the end of the story, and in this instance, the confidence of Esther in the presence of the king increases, even to the extent that she actually commands him (*Three Faces of a Queen*, 183).
69 Day, *Three Faces of a Queen*, 155.
70 Day, *Three Faces of a Queen*, 152.

hanged on 14 Adar. In other words, the queen might never have envisioned the sanction of further bloodshed in the capital or anywhere else. It is possible (even plausible) that the public humiliation of the ten sons of Aman is the *only* thing on her mind as she petitions her husband in this instance. If this interpretation is correct, there are important implications for both Esther and the Jews. Concerning the queen, any charge of vengeance would have to be based solely on her treatment of the sons of Aman who had been killed on 13 Adar according to the decree of that day (9.6-10).[71] Yet, for the Jews, an accusation of gratuitous killing in Sousa on 14 Adar would be a live option (9.15). Given the commonness and acceptance of impaling dead bodies for the purposes of humiliation in the ancient context, coupled with the fact that they were killed 'legally' the day before, it is doubtful that any condemnation could be levelled against Esther for this request. Concerning the Jews, we must await further consideration (§ 3.5.7).

3.3 Mardochaios

3.3.1 Loyalty seeking justice (A.12-13)

Early on in the story the reader is informed that Mardochaios is a Jew [ἄνθρωπος Ἰουδαῖος] from the line of Benjamin, "a great (important)[72] person" [ἄνθρωπος μέγας], and one who is serving in the court of the king [θεραπεύων ἐν τῇ αὐλῇ τοῦ βασιλέως] (A.2b). With these descriptions of ethnic identity, personal prominence and professional position having been given, the reader is already acquainted with Mardochaios even before he acts in the narrative. Furthermore, after A.2, we have likely obtained a sense of the narrator's opinion of Mardochaios as well – feelings that are not necessarily void of moral connotations. The positive and possibly ideal character of Mardochaios is asserted quite early in the narrative.

In the second year of the king's reign, Mardochaios sees a dream [ἐνύπνιον] (A.1). We can only assume that he is sleeping or day-dreaming at the time, and in A.11 we are informed that this is indeed so – "and when Mardochaios awoke" [καὶ διεγερθεὶς Μαρδοχαῖος]. But between A.4 and

---

71 A charge that D.J. Harrington indeed levies solely on account of Esther's treatment of the bodies of the sons of Haman (see ch. 4, "The Additions of Esther," in Harrington's *Invitation to the Apocrypha* (Grand Rapids: Eerdmans, 1999), 51). It is not clear to me that the verdict is so clear-cut. Vengeance might be too strong a word to characterise Esther's impalement of Haman's sons, especially in light of the customs of the day.

72 Levenson, *Esther*, 37.

A.11, this mysterious dream intervenes – a symbolic, allegorical dream[73] that becomes clearer to Mardochaios (and to the reader) as events unfold. It is a dream in which noises [φωναί], uproar [θόρυβος], thundering [βρονταί], earthquake [σεισμός], and confusion [τάραχος] have come upon the earth (A.4b). In the midst of this tumult two great dragons [δύο δράκοντες μεγάλοι] emerge, each ready for conflict (A.5a). By their voices nations are summoned to fight: aligned with one dragon is the nation of the just [δι-καίων ἔθνος]; with the other dragon stands every (other) nation (A.6). As global conflict looms, it is no wonder that such disorder is reigning upon the earth in this dream. Further descriptive nouns sketch the picture of that portentous day: darkness and gloom, oppression and confinement (distress), ill-treatment and great confusion [σκότους καὶ γνόφου, θλῖψις καὶ στενοχωρία, κάκωσις καὶ τάραχος μέγας] (A.7). Facing all of this, the nation of the just becomes fearful and calls out to God as they see death on their horizon (A.8b-9a). But the description that follows their crying out is especially mysterious:

ἀπὸ δὲ τῆς βοῆς αὐτῶν ἐγένετο ὡσανεὶ ἀπὸ μικρᾶς πηγῆς ποταμὸς μέγας, ὕδωρ πολύ· φῶς καὶ ὁ ἥλιος ἀνέτειλεν, καὶ οἱ ταπεινοὶ ὑψώθησαν καὶ κατέφαγον τοὺς ἐνδόξους.

and from their crying arose, as though from a little spring, a great river, much water; light and the sun arose,[74] and the humble were exalted and devoured the eminent (A.9b-10).[75]

Although a clear understanding of the above image is not forthcoming, we do get the sense that one side emerges victorious in the end. But for both Mardochaios and the reader, time will only make clearer the designs of God [τί ὁ θεὸς βεβούλευται ποιῆσαι] and what his dream might fully signify (A.11a). In the meantime, Mardochaios "keeps it all in his heart, wishing to interpret every detail,[76] until night" [εἶχεν αὐτο ἐν τῇ καρδίᾳ καὶ ἐν παντὶ λόγῳ ἤθελεν ἐπιγνῶναι αὐτὸ ἕως τῆς νυκτός] (A.11b).

The amount of time that elapses between the dream of Mardochaios and when he is (again) resting in the court with Gabatha and Tharra – two of the eunuchs who guard the court [τῶν φυλασσόντων τὴν αὐλήν] – is un-

---

73 Wills employs the term "mock-apocalyptic" here, and then proceeds to note how the dream in section A differs from apocalyptic visions of "contemporary Jewish literature" (*The Jewish Novel in the Ancient World,* 116-17).
74 Or, this could be a hendiadys: "the light of the sun arose" (Fox, *Redaction,* 75 n. 75).
75 This translation follows the rendering of Moore (*Daniel, Esther and Jeremiah: The Additions,* 173-74).
76 For the rendering of ἐν παντὶ λόγῳ, see Fox (*Redaction,* 76).

known.[77] While tight temporal succession cannot be assumed between A.11-12, issues of time do not elicit elaboration on the part of the author. Here it seems to be the case that *what* happens is more important than precisely *when* events take place. As Mardochaios rests there, the narrative goes on to inform the reader that the Jew not only overhears the calculations [λογισμους] of Gabatha and Tharra, he also investigates their anxious thoughts [τὰς μερίμας αὐτῶν ἐξηραύνησεν] and learns of their intention to assassinate the king (A.13a). With this information discovered, Mardochaios informs His Majesty of the plot of the conspirators (A.13b).

There are at least two points of interest concerning the moral character of Mardochaios in this scene. First, the narrator appears to place emphasis on the fact that Mardochaios makes a significant effort to investigate the conspiring of the two court guards. The Jew could have played it safe when he overheard their assassination talk, hoping that the plot would have either failed or have been uncovered by someone else. Being a foreigner in the court, this course of action might have been the smarter and less risky one, for it is unknown at this point in the narrative how much influence Mardochaios actually has in the government of the king. Instead, he shows much bravery as he seeks to learn of the guile of Gabatha and Tharra.

The second, and not dissimilar, point of interest proceeds from the first. After Mardochaios learns about the plot of regicide there is still work to be done so that the two eunuchs would not succeed. Someone in high authority with power to act against the conspiracy should be notified. With no (apparent) sign of hesitation or deliberation the narrator tells us that Mardochaios informs the king concerning them [καὶ ὑπέδειξεν τῷ βασιλεῖ περὶ αὐτῶν] (A.13b). That the Jew has direct access to the king is quite extraordinary, for we get no impression that he proceeds through any intermediary; it is as if he approaches the king himself in order to warn His Majesty. This likelihood does not resonate well with the prohibition (chronologically later) that only summoned ones are allowed to enter into the presence of the king (cf. 4.11) Yet the text does not envision this difficulty at all. Instead, it em-

---

77 Most scholars suppose that there is less than 24 hours between the dream of Mardochaios and his resting in the court (Moore, *Daniel, Esther and Jeremiah: The Additions,* 177-78; Fox, *Redaction,* 76; Levenson, *Esther,* 41). Concerning this time gap, Dorothy suggests that the final words of A.11 (τῆς νυκτός) and the verb ἡσύχασεν that follows them in A.12 "probably intend to compress the action into a single day-night sequence" (*The Books of Esther,* 51). Even so, it is not at all clear that the verb ἡσύχασεν implies the sleeping that one would do at night. LS gives the following general suggestions for the verb: "to be still, keep quiet, be at rest." However, in the aorist stem, the verb has a causal sense – "to make still, lay to rest" (355). It could be the case that Mardochaios was simply resting in the court at some later, unspecified time. Whatever the case, the temporal relationship between A.11-12 is neither explicitly stated nor easily perceived.

phasises the loyalty and courage of Mardochaios the Jew in the foreign court
as it progresses with a description of the interrogation, confession and leading
away [ἀπήχθησαν] of the eunuchs (A.14), the interesting double recording
of the prior events (A.15), and the establishment of a position within the
court for Mardochaios and the reward of gifts (A.16).

Despite all of this success, however, the reader becomes aware that all
does not bode well for Mardochaios within the palace walls. A certain Ἀμαν
Ἀμαδάθου Βουγαῖος – one who is honourable before the king [ἔνδοξος
ἐνώπιον τοῦ βασιλέως] – has observed what has transpired and intends to
do harm to Mardochaios and his people on account of the two eunuchs of the
king [ὑπὲρ τῶν δύο εὐνούχων τοῦ βασιλέως] (A.17). Because of his
loyalty to the king, and possibly as a result of his new-found court status, the
lives of Mardochaios and the Jews would not be easy ones in their adopted
land. As we begin to gather and shall continue to see, the one whom the author here calls Βουγαῖος will stand at the heart of Jewish distress and pain.

3.3.2 A joint policing operation (2.21-23)

As similar as the aforementioned conspiracy to assassinate the king is to the
one that will be discussed presently, their notable differences warrant some
measure of comment even if their general purposes appear to be akin – "to
augment Mordecai's value to the king."[78] Consider the words of Dorothy
concerning the two regicide texts:

> In o′ this second plot by high-placed eunuchs appears at first blush to be a doublet of
> A 12-14…Closer inspection, however, shows that, in its final form, o′ wants the
> reader to understand this [i.e., 2.21-23] as a second and separate episode of Mardo-
> chaios saving the king's life.[79]

It is this final form, which includes both regicide accounts, that will engage
our attention here. And for our immediate purposes, we shall concentrate on
the second account of conspired regicide with a view to an ongoing assessment of the moral character of Mardochaios.

---

78 Fox, *Redaction*, 60 n. 62.

79 Dorothy, *The Books of Esther*, 60. Not everyone, to be sure, would follow these
    observations this far. For example, note Kottsieper's detailed grappling with the
    presence of both accounts in the LXX. In the end, Kottsieper concludes the presence of
    a "Doppelung" in the LXX, but does not offer any thoughts beyond an
    acknowledgement of the presence of "Widersprüche" therein – *Widersprüche*,
    incidentally, that Kottsieper believes the AT smoothes out with its single telling of the
    conspiracy account (*Verschwörungserzälung*) (*Zusätze zu Ester*, 145-48).

Taking a closer look at the narrative, one notices somewhat of an awkward transition between 2.20 and 2.21 – only the general location in the palace complex links the two verses. The story proceeds from intimate description of the concealment plan of Mardochaios and Esther (2.20) to a description of how two eunuchs, the chief bodyguards [ἀρχισωματοφύλακες] of the king, were distressed [ἐλυπήθησαν] at the promotion [προήχθη] of Mardochaios (2.21a). Although all is not entirely clear, it is likely that the promotion which is distressing the chief bodyguards is the commendation Mardochaios received in A.16.[80] Yet the prominence of his court rank is not outstanding – Mardochaios does not appear, on the face of things, to be a threat – so the reason for the bodyguards' grieving is unknown.

In an interesting twist, the eunuch bodyguards seek to rid the court not of the *object* of their torment, but the *source* of it – they endeavour to kill the king himself (2.21b)! But in a symbolic progression from darkness to light, the secret matter of the eunuchs becomes clear[81] [ἐδηλώθη] to Mardochaios, who in turn, shows Esther[82] [ἐσήμανεν Εσθηρ], who then declares[83] [ἐνεφάνισεν] the plot to the king (2.22). With justice having been done in 2.23a, His Majesty gives orders to commend a memorial for the good-favour [εὐνοίας] of Mardochaios in the royal library (2.23b).

After viewing 2.21-23 more closely, we affirm confidently the following with Dorothy: "Clearly o´ presents two different regicide plots."[84] When viewed cumulatively the differences between the two narrative accounts argue against the presence of a simple doublet.[85] It appears, literarily, as if the

---

80 A.16: καὶ ἐπέταξεν ὁ βασιλεὺς Μαρδοχαίῳ θεραπεύειν ἐν τῇ αὐλῇ καὶ ἔδωκεν αὐτῷ δόματα περὶ τούτων ["and the king appointed Mardochaios to serve in the court and he gave him gifts for these things (i.e., his saving deeds)"]. We are aware from A.2 that Mardochaios serves in the court of the king (notice that this is repeated in 2.19, likely to explain his proximity and access to Esther). A.16 appears not to promote the Jew further in the court hierarchy, but rather to narrate how Mardochaios achieves the court standing described in A.2. To be clear, it does not appear as if Mardochaios is promoted from a lesser official in the court to a greater one. Thus, it seems as if it is merely the appointment of the Jew to serve in the court that occasions the distress of the chief bodyguards (*pace* Dorothy, who does not see any promotion in section A (*The Books of Esther*, 60)). However, one might fairly say that Mardochaios was 'promoted' from one status to another, even if it was from subject to court employee.
81 Lit: "was clear." I am taking ἐδηλώθη as intransitive and rendering it in its second sense, "to be clear, plain" (LS, 182).
82 I.e., he informs Esther, makes it known to her.
83 I.e., she brings the matter to light.
84 Dorothy, *The Books of Esther*, 60.
85 Dorothy notes the differences between the regicide plots of A.12-14 and 2.21-23 (*The Books of Esther*, 60):
   • A.12 names Gabatha and Tharra; no names are given for the eunuchs in 2.21-23.

narrator seeks to *accent* the point of the conscientious initiative and involvement of Mardochaios within his present setting and his loyalty to his present (earthly) ruler. This much is clear in both cases. Although in this second case he proceeds carefully through a conduit (i.e., Esther, now queen) to inform the king of the danger, Mardochaios takes an obvious risk as he acts faithfully in the court. Thus, his value to the king has now been *doubly* stressed in the story. The stability of the kingdom has been greatly aided by loyal Jews – Mardochaios, and to a lesser extent, Esther.

3.3.3 Refusal to bow before Aman (3.1-4; C.5-7)

The civic value of Mardochaios having been observed, we now turn our attention to an obedience of a different kind. We shall observe that in the face of courtly obligation and pressure, the *religious* convictions and loyalties of Mardochaios appear to transcend his more mundane allegiances and duties. This will serve to complicate our assessment of his moral character.

The sudden elevation of Aman is an inexplicable development that follows upon the account of the failed assassination attempt of the eunuchs (2.21-23).[86] But whereas the newly promoted Aman is called הָאֲגָגִי in the MT, here he is described in the following manner: Αμαν Αμαδάθου *Βουγαῖον* (3.1). To be sure, "Aman, the son of Amadatha" is a recognised name if one is familiar with the Greek story, but the etymology of the epithet "Bougaion" is far from clear. R.J. Littman suggests that this word can be derived from a combination of the noun βοῦς ("bull") and the verb γαίω ("to exult"), carrying the meaning, "bully, braggart or monster."[87] This would go along well with the LS entry for the word, ὁ βουγάϊος, which is defined as "a great bully or braggart."[88] If these guides are accurate, in its present usage the word

---

- The eunuchs are τῶν φυλασσόντων τὴν αὐλὴν in A.12; ἀρχισωματοφύλακες in 2.21.
- No known motive is known for the plot of the eunuchs in A.12-14; the 'promotion' of Mardochaios serves as the reason for the conspiracy of the eunuchs against the throne in 2.21.
- Mardochaios informs the king of the plot in A.13; Esther informs the king of the plot after Mardochaios makes her aware of it in 2.22.
- Mardochaios receives a position in the court and rewards for his deeds in A.16; no reward mentioned in 2.23.

86 In the LXX narrative, of course, we are referring here to the second account of attempted regicide.

87 R.J. Littman, "The Religious Policy of Xerxes and the *Book of Esther*," *JQR* 65 (1975), 151. See further Kottsieper, *Zusätze zu Ester*, 145-46.

88 LS, 154.

would seem to be being used adjectivally – i.e., Aman, son of Amadatha, *[a]
bully*. However, there might be further connections associated with this uncertain appellation.

Aside from the explanation of J. Lewy which derives from connections
with the Babylonian Marduk-Ishtar mythology,[89] and the preference of Clines
to read a variant of the name,[90] few scholars have ventured deeply into a discussion of this curious appellation. However, in a recent study Jobes undertakes a thorough survey of the patronymic[91] and has proposed that there
might be a word play between βουγαῖος and a certain Persian general named
βαγώσης, whose story is noted both by Josephus and Diodorus Siculus.[92]
Apparently, this general was a friend neither of the Jews nor of the established political order in his day. Indeed, his hands were heavy upon the Jews
and lethal for the current Persian king, Artaxerxes III, whom Bagoses assas-
sinated in a *coup d'état* (338 B.C.E.). Thus, Bagoses, the 'bully' of Jews and
assassinator of royalty, might well have been symbolically personified in the
name βουγαῖος, which is then appropriately applied in a pejorative fashion to
Aman.[93]

With this connection tentatively established,[94] one must recall that in the
wider narrative Aman appears to be somehow connected with the initial assassination attempt on the king in A.17. There, too, he is called Αμαν
Αμαδάθου βουγαῖος, and the perceptive reader might have discerned the
implicit (but still ambiguous) connections at that early point.[95] Even though it

---

89 J. Lewy, "The Feast of the 14th Day of Adar," *HUCA* 14 (1939), 134-35. K.H. Jobes
    critiques the proposal of Lewy by noting that it "does not satisfactorily explain the
    manuscript evidence, because the name "Bougaios" occurs in what is clearly a Greek
    version of the Jewish *biblical form* of the Esther story, and not of some earlier literary
    stage where Babylonian mythology was prominent (if such a stage ever existed in the
    development of the book of Esther)" ("How an Assassination Changed the Greek Text
    of Esther," *ZAW* 110 (1998), 76 (*emphasis original*)).
90 Clines, *The Esther Scroll,* 197 n. 7. His preferred variant, γωγαιον, is only found in ms.
    93. However, he believes this to be the original reading and an interpretation of the
    MT's הָאֲגָגִי in connection with the name Gog found in Ez 38-39.
91 Note that Jobes' propositions and conclusions centre on the AT version of the story.
    However, the research that she has done concerning this particular discussion applies
    also to the LXX material in focus here.
92 Jobes notes that in his *Antiquities,* Josephus utilises the spelling βαγώσης, but Diodorus
    Siculus refers to the name as βαγώας (a variant in Josephus) (*The Alpha-Text of Esther,*
    126; "How an Assassination Changed the Greek Text of Esther," 76).
93 Jobes, *The Alpha-Text of Esther,* 126. Kottsieper describes it as "Verballhornung"
    (*Zusätze zu Ester,* 146). Cf. De Troyer, *The End of the Alpha Text of Esther,* 382-83.
94 De Troyer questions Jobes' suggestion, especially the lack of connection between
    Josephus' telling of the Esther story and the narrative surrounding Bagoas (*The End of
    the Esther Text of Esther,* 400). This, among other factors, leads De Troyer to propose
    an alternative historical context for the AT story (400-3).
95 This ambiguity begins to dissipate, however, with section E (§ 3.4.5).

does not carry along with it the ethnic connotations of הָאֲגָגִי, βουγαῖος seems similarly to be a term of reproach in Jewish ears. Therefore, as we read the narrative and come to 3.1 where Αμαν Αμαδάθου Βουγαῖον is enigmatically elevated, the suspicions possibly sparked in A.17 now begin to be kindled, and will soon grow into alarming flames.

According to the orders of the king, all in the court were to do obeisance [προσεκύνουν] to Aman (3.2a). Even though in the NT and in extrabiblical Greek the implications of προσκυνέω extend from "worship" to "simple appreciation,"[96] in the LXX, προσκυνεῖν most commonly renders הִשְׁתַּחֲוָה with the connotation of the act of reverent or submissive prostration.[97] This is likely the situation in 3.2b as we are informed that Mardochaios did not do obeisance to him [ὁ δὲ Μαρδοχαῖος οὐ προσεκύνει αὐτῷ] – Mardochaios refuses to prostrate himself formally before his court superior. Unfortunately for the reader, no accompanying reason for this behaviour is given.

Yet as the story proceeds, and we witness the persistent questioning of those in the court concerning his unwillingness to uphold the civil obligation (3.3-4a), Mardochaios provides an obscure clue. As soon as Aman is told of the resistance of Mardochaios, we are informed that Mardochaios has shown them that he is a Jew [καὶ ὑπέδειξεν αὐτοῖς ὁ Μαρδοχαῖος ὅτι Ιουδαῖός ἐστιν] (3.4c). Because the ethnic connections and context that gave rise to our suggestions in § 2.3.2 are not nearly as visible in the LXX narrative, other approaches must be taken. Without too much effort, though, one can discern another possibility in understanding why it is significant that Mardochaios has disclosed his Jewishness at this point. Of course, the fact that he is Jewish must come to be known for the plot of the story to advance, but more specifically to the immediate context, there appears to be an important *religious* situation in view. This religious facet of Mardochaios's Jewishness appears within the intimacy of his prayer life (C.5-7).

Though it is logically placed in the wake of the fully hatched plan of genocide proposed by Aman, the prayer of Mardochaios in section C serves to illuminate our focus in this particular episode. The present form of the story allows the reader to reflect back upon the events that have come before when section C is read, but we believe it is appropriate here to look ahead at this point in our study so as to approach a fuller apprehension of the significance of Mardochaios's refusal to bow down to Aman. In section C he recounts

---

96 H. Balz and G. Schneider (eds), *Exegetical Dictionary of the New Testament* (Grand Rapids: Eerdmans, 1993), 3:174.
97 Fox, *Character and Ideology*, 277.

counts events that have occurred prior to his prayer, and it seems reasonable
to allow his retrospection to help inform our present investigation.

C.5-7 contains the middle section of the prayer of Mardochaios, providing
us with a commentary, more or less, on his decision not to do obeisance to
Aman (3.2-4). With this information the reader of this Greek text obtains
special insight into his restless soul. Pictured here, the character who has
been somewhat reserved until now becomes quite emotionally forthcoming in
the privacy of his prayer life. Mardochaios prays:

...σὺ οἶδας, κύριε, ὅτι οὐκ ἐν ὕβρει οὐδέ ἐν ὑπερηφανίᾳ οὐδὲ ἐν φιλοδοξίᾳ
ἐποίησα τοῦτο, τὸ μὴ προσκυνεῖν τὸν ὑπερήφανον Αμαν.

...you know, O Lord, that [it was] neither in insolence nor in arrogance nor in
vainglory [that] I did this, not to do obeisance to the arrogant Aman (C.5).

Here, in the first part of his prayer, Mardochaios protests his innocence[98]
while seeking "to parry the charge that it was his pride alone that brought the
calamitous circumstances upon his people."[99] With such an opening, the
needed information left "tantalizingly unspecified" in chapter three has now
been supplied.[100] The reader is now beginning to realise the fuller story.

The content of verses six and seven provides the substance of what Mardochaios meant when he told the servants that he would not do obeisance to
Aman because of his Jewishness. Prefacing his reasons by the fact that he
actually "would have been well pleased to kiss[101] the soles of his [Aman's]
feet for the safety of Israel"[102] [ηὐδόκουν φιλεῖν πέλματα ποδῶν αὐτοῦ
πρὸς σωτηρίαν Ισραηλ] (C.6), Mardochaios humbly confesses in verse
seven that he has not bowed to Aman because he will never put the honour of
another in a place above the honour of God.[103] By these strong words it be-

---

98   Moore, *Daniel, Esther and Jeremiah: The Additions,* 204. See also Dorothy, *The Books
     of Esther,* 115-16.
99   Levenson, *Esther,* 84.
100 Levenson, *Esther,* 84.
101 This present infinitive form gives us the impression that Mardochaios continues to feel
     this way; his commitment to his people is unyielding, as we have seen.
102 Dorothy appears to link the kissing of feet in this context with an act of worship (*The
     Books of Esther,* 116). However, Kottsieper (following Ryssel) suggests the likelihood
     that this would have been no more than an act of "self-humiliation" (*Selbstdemütigung*)
     on the part of Mordecai, something much less serious than prostration (*Zusätze zu Ester,*
     163 n. 167).
103 The LXX literally reads: ἀλλὰ ἐποίησα τοῦτο ἵνα μὴ θῶ δόξαν ἀνθρώπου
     ὑπεράνω δόξης θεοῦ, καὶ οὐ προσκυνήσω οὐδένα πλὴν σοῦ τοῦ κυρίου μου καὶ
     οὐ ποιήσω αὐτὰ ἐν ὑπερηφανίᾳ "but I did this in order that I might not set [the] glory
     of man above [the] glory of God, and I shall not do obeisance [(to) anyone] – not at all –
     except you my Lord, and I shall not do these things in arrogance" (C.7). Wills notes the
     parallels with the "Jewish martyr accounts" of 2 Macc 6-7 that could be drawn here.

comes evident that the unwillingness of Mardochaios to bow before Aman stems from a deep *religious* commitment – his loyalty to God must have been at stake in such a matter.[104] However, it is not certain that Mardochaios withholds obeisance from humans altogether – perhaps only in extraordinary cases like this one. To extrapolate somewhat, for the praying Mardochaios it might be that the act of προσκυνέω to Aman means (or implies) committing idolatry, giving misplaced worship.[105] If this is the case, such devotion and resistance would have been honourable and encouraging in the eyes of ancient Jewish readers.[106] To be sure, this understanding builds upon the more formal, physical sense of προσκυνέω appearing in the context of 3.2-4. His theological interpretation of this physical act is plain to see, even if it is not fully understood. Nevertheless, the moral and religious convictions of Mardochaios are far from subtle in C.5-7 as they drive his decisions concerning whether or not to follow this court decree. The faithful Jew appears to have broken the civil law on religious grounds; clearly, the highest loyalty of Mardochaios is to his *heavenly* king.

3.3.4 A cry of injustice (4.1)

This does not imply, however, that Mardochaios is some kind of religiously impassioned renegade, recklessly neglecting civil order in the name of divine principle. It is clear that the Jew is indeed discerning and not necessarily careless in the battles he chooses. The next two episodes will testify to this. We join the story now with Aman having initiated his genocidal plan against the Jews and having gained regal authority for it through both the verbal consent of the king (3.11) and the giving of his ring to seal the official letter (3.10, 12-14; section B). This threat has troubled [ἐταράσσετο] the city of

---

Therein, he points out that "Jews are given opportunities to save other Jews by refuse to cheat God of the divine glory" (*The Jewish Novel in the Ancient World,* 121).

104 In the context of offering a comparison of the prayers of Esther and Mordecai, Day comments on the relationship the latter has with God. The glory of God is tantamount in the 'theological' understanding of Mordecai (*Three Faces of a Queen,* 79-82). See also Kottsieper concerning Mordecai's cultic obligations possibly in view here (*Zusätze zu Ester,* 163).

105 Bickerman likens the explanation of Mordecai to the one of Callisthenes who refused to do obeisance to Alexander the Great because it was to be done before the gods alone. Bickerman reasons that "[I]n the eyes of a Jew educated in Hellenic manner, Mardochaios now appeared as another Callisthenes. His insolence...is here transformed into a defense of human dignity" (*Four Strange Books of the Bible,* 220-21).

106 Levenson, *Esther,* 84. See also the comments of Kottsieper concerning the Jewish mindset and behaviour during Hasmonean times which might be relevant here (*Zusätze zu Ester,* 164-65).

Sousa (3.15) and gives rise to some remarkable behaviour on the part of
Mardochaios. Upon learning what has been accomplished by Aman, the Jew
divides his garments, puts on sackcloth, and sprinkles ashes upon himself
(4.1a). We might well expect this sort of customary behaviour from a conscientious and religious Jew like Mardochaios (cf. 2.20; section C). Yet this
admission in no way takes his actions for granted or views them as ordinary
in a Persian societal context. For, surely, by his posture Mardochaios be-
speaks his Jewishness and characterises the distress of his people.

But his postural statement, distinctive and powerful though it is, only
marks the beginning in the overall communication of his grief. The narrative
goes on to explain what transpires next:

> καὶ ἐκπηδήσας διὰ τῆς πλατείας τῆς πόλεως ἐβόα φωνῇ μεγάλῃ Αἴρεται
> ἔθνος μηδὲν ἠδικηκός.

> and having leaped out through the street[107] of the city he cried out [with] a loud voice:
> "A nation that has done no wrong is being taken (seized)" (4.1b).

By both his physical response and his verbal anguish, Mardochaios leaves no
doubt in the eyes and ears of onlookers (both ancient and modern) of his ethnic solidarity. He is not a Jew who seeks to blend in quiescently with his Persian surroundings as his world caves in around him. It should be noted that at
this point in the drama Mardochaios is the primary Jewish actor and leader
and his behaviour cannot be considered marginal. It would appear that his
convictions and courage prompt him to exercise freely and publicly both his
mourning customs and his deep-seated anguish as a result of (what he considers) the unfairly appointed fate of his people. In this instance the passion
of the Jew is in clear view.

3.3.5 Refusal to transgress court regulations (4.2)

Yet passion is not his only attribute; principle also characterises the Jewish
hero. As we have seen in § 3.3.1 and 3.3.2, and as we shall witness again
presently, when it comes to most matters of civil obedience, Mardochaios
seeks to do what is proper in the eyes of the kingdom. What we observe in
4.2 does nothing to deter this working supposition.

The sudden motion of the despairing Jew out into the street of Sousa,
when he perceives what has been decreed at the instigation of Aman, appears
to have continued after the desperate cry for his people had gone up. In 4.2a,

---

107 LS, 644.

the narrative explains that he proceeds until he reaches the gate of the king and goes no further [καὶ ἦλθεν ἕως τῆς πύλης τοῦ βασιλέως καὶ ἔστη]. Why does Mardochaios stop here?[108] Why does he not take the case of his people through the gate and into the presence of power? It certainly is not for a lack of passion. Here, the answer appears plain: Mardochaios respects (fears?) the king and seeks to do nothing against the good of his kingdom and its regulations. The civil regulation that is explained by the narrator in 4.2b – "for it was not allowed for him to go into the court wearing[109] sackcloth and ashes" [οὐ γὰρ ἦν ἐξὸν αὐτῷ εἰσελθεῖν εἰς τὴν αὐλὴν σάκκον ἔχοντι καὶ σποδὸν] – clarifies the reason for Mardochaios's halting in 4.2a. Here, again, he is pictured as a loyal subject of the king.

3.4 Aman

3.4.1 Seeds of hatred (A.17)

The figure of Aman emerges at least once, possibly twice, in the early portions of the LXX Esther story. As we mentioned in § 3.1.1, a certain "Aman" is mentioned first among a list of eunuchs who were charged to bring Queen Astin to the banquet. From his position in that sequence, it would not be surprising if this Aman held the highest rank among the servants listed. Furthermore, assuming that the Aman of 1.10 is the Aman of 3.1, the promotion of Aman in chapter three would not appear to arise out of personal and professional obscurity. In other words, if Aman is all the while a prominent eunuch in the royal court (as the above references cumulatively suggest), we are better able to conceive his sudden elevation, even though an exact reason for his rise remains obscure. The connection of the two Amans could be undermined, however, by the information that the latter Aman has a wife, Zosara (cf. 5.10, 14; 6.13). If these references point to only *one* Aman, they do so in the midst of some narrative tension, for eunuchs do not normally have wives.

A second (and firmer) reference to the Aman who plays a most significant part in the Esther story is found chronologically earlier in the narrative. As we have seen at the end of § 3.3.1, Αμαν Αμαδάθου Βουγαῖος emerges onto the scene after the initial assassination attempt on the king had been

---

108 See the relevant footnotes in § 2.3.3 that address some of the questions that arise considering the reasonings of Mardochaios for stopping at the gate of the king here.
109 Lit: "having."

spoiled. Foreshadowing his elevation in 3.1, and likely consonant with any possibility of the same Aman among the eunuchs in 1.10, A.17a communicates that Aman is one honourable before the king [ἔνδοξος ἐνώπιον τοῦ βασιλέως]. His status then established, the narrative proceeds to disclose that because of the role of Mardochaios in the foiled regicide effort of the eunuchs (A.12-15), Aman was seeking to hurt him and his people [καὶ ἐζήτησεν κακοποιῆσαι τὸν Μορδοχαῖον καὶ τὸν λαὸν αὐτοῦ] (A.17b).

On account of this, the reader becomes aware that the seeds of Aman's personal hatred for his court associate have now been planted. Yet the appendage – καὶ τὸν λαὸν αὐτοῦ, even though understandable in the overall context of the story, is difficult to grasp here. Has Aman any reason to despise the entirety of Mardochaios's people? Does he even know who they are at this point of the story? Unless we are to assume that the anger of Aman is so fierce that it is too great to be exacted upon only one man, the first question is likely answered in the negative. Concerning the second, there is no mention or even implication that the race of Mardochaios is known this early in the narrative. It could well be that the author expects his readers to hold the curious mention of people of Mardochaios in check until further clarifying details are provided. Yet the phrase in question might also be the product of an untidy work of redaction in the process of forming the LXX Esther story as we now have it. Whatever the case, we become aware early on in the narrative of Aman's personal roots of hostility towards Mardochaios coupled with his devious intentions concerning the people of Mardochaios.

3.4.2 Concrete plans for genocide (3.5-9)

But it is not until later in the plot that the rancour and initial threat of Aman turn into a palpable danger for Mardochaios and the Jews. The reasons for his scorn in A.17 do not resurface again in the narrative, although one might assume that they continue to exist within him. Yet in chapter three, *further* reasons arise for personal animosity which stem from a conflict regarding court protocol. This individual antipathy then develops into peril on a much wider scale as the entire race of the Jews is now *formally* placed under threat.

As we have witnessed in § 3.3.3, the honouring and uplifting of Αμαν Αμαδάθου Βουγαῖον begins to alter life in the court of the king, especially for Mardochaios. Specifically, he is the only one reported to have refused to do obeisance to his court superior – an inaction that appears to have mostly to do with the fact that Mardochaios is a Jew (3.4c). In addition, § 3.3.3 witnessed our examination of the curious epithet, Βουγαῖον, which has to this point served to describe Αμαν Αμαδάθου. Following the efforts of Jobes, we supposed that there was likely both an anti-Jewish and an anti-establishment overtone in the appellation that has been anachronistically applied to the character of Aman in the Greek texts. However, this particular explanation does not begin to explain why Mardochaios refuses to perform his courtly duty to the new vizier. It is not until later in the progression of the story (C.5-7) that the reader begins to grasp the mindset of Mardochaios concerning his unwillingness to bow – a frame of mind that appears to have religious conviction at its base. At the beginning of chapter three, however, we are only aware that the Jewishness of Mardochaios has *something* to do with his obstinacy in this matter.

The narrative does not pause for too much deep reflection at this point. For Aman, any excuse or rationale behind the refusal of Mardochaios appears inconsequential; in fact, no contemplation of his antagonist's reasoning even enters the narrative picture. Instead, after the palace officials have given Mardochaios ample chance to fall into line with the command of the king (3.4a), the text reports the following: "they indicated to Aman [that] Mardochaios set himself against the words of the king" [καὶ ὑπέδειξαν τῷ Αμαν Μαρδοχαῖον τοῖς τοῦ βασιλέως λόγοις ἀντιτασσόμενον] (3.4b). When Aman had noted [ἐπιγνοὺς] the unyielding posture of his court inferior, he was greatly angered [ἐθυμώθη σφόδρα] and took counsel[110] to destroy utterly [ἐβουλεύσατο ἀφανίσαι] all of the Jews in the kingdom on 14 Adar[111] (3.5-6). The result of this deliberation is a decree[112] [ψήφισμα] made by Aman to slay in one day the race of Mardochaios [ἀπολέσαι ἐν μιᾷ ἡμέρᾳ τὸ γένος Μαρδοχαίου] (3.7).

Whereas in A.17b Aman devises to harm Mardochaios and his people [καὶ ἐζήτησεν κακοποιῆσαι τὸν Μορδοχαῖον καὶ τὸν λαὸν αὐτοῦ],

---

110 With whom Aman "took counsel" is not mentioned.

111 In the text of the subsequent decree (B.6), the date given for the destruction of the people is also given as 14 Adar. In conflict with this date, 8.12, 9.1-2, and E.20 report that the decisive action resulting from this intention and decree happens on *13* Adar. The reason for this inconsistency is not fully known, but Moore suggests that 14 is likely a "copyist's error" which can be understood if one is aware that in several early manuscripts (including the Chester Beatty papyrus) "the easily misread alphabetic equivalent of the number (*iota delta*) was used instead of spelling the number out" (*Daniel, Esther, and Jeremiah: The Additions,* 192-93). For a charted comparison of pogrom dates in MT, LXX, AT, OL and Josephus, see Fox, *Redaction,* 80 n. 84.

112 Technically, ψήφισμα denotes "a proposition carried by vote: esp. a measure passed in the ἐκκλησία" (LS, 901). In this context one can see why this particular word was chosen since Aman has taken counsel in order to occasion this ψήφισμα. Indeed, the influence of sophisticated Greek rhetoric (possibly political thought) is seen in the word choice at this point.

3.7 does not differentiate between Mardochaios individually (the object of Aman's wrath) and the Jews collectively (the people of Mardochaios's race). Further, it is interesting that Aman targets the entirety of Mardochaios's people here even though their identity has not been made explicitly known to him. Clearly, some in the court know that Mardochaios is a Jew – those whom he has shown [ὑπέδειξαν] (3.4b). But if Aman knows the same, the reader is left unaware. We must assume, though, that the vizier has *some* sort of specific knowledge about the people of Mardochaios, for he appears to have definite, discrediting words in mind when he presents his case before the king. Aman adamantly states that a "nation scattered among the nations" [ἔθνος διεσπαρμένον ἐν τοῖς ἔθνεσιν] of the kingdom possesses laws that differ [ἔξαλλοι] from the laws of every other nation (3.8a). Furthermore, he claims that this (unnamed) people disregards[113] the laws of the king [τῶν δὲ νόμων τοῦ βασιλέως παρακούουσιν] (3.8b). Upon all this evidence, Aman wishes to persuade His Majesty that it would not be expedient [συμφέρει] on his part to let them alone [ἐᾶσαι αὐτούς] (3.8c). Then, after the stage has been set, the vizier entreats the king to decree the utter destruction of this (still) unnamed (but obviously known) people (3.9a). To this appeal the king gives his knowing consent (i.e., his ring), and the fate of the Jews is sealed (3.10). Thus, the machination of Aman has fully surfaced after what would appear to have been a long process of premeditation.

3.4.3 Genocide for the good of the kingdom (B.2-7)

The scheme of the vizier, however, is not naïve. Having procured the assent of the king to treat the nation as he wishes [τῷ δὲ ἔθνει χρῶ ὡς βούλει] (3.11b), Aman proceeds to take full advantage of the privileges of his power. At his bidding the court scribes draw up an edict, written in the name of the king, which authorises the utter destruction and plundering of the Jews on one day[114] [ἐν ἡμέρα μιᾷ] in the month of Adar (3.13b). To be sure, the real power behind this decree lies not with the king but with Aman,[115] and its influence would stand or fall not because of its royal seal but with the sway of its rhetoric – the manner in which the edict is persuasively framed, appealing

---

113 In this context, παρακούω likely carries the negative connotation "to take no heed to" although this is not its commonest usage (LS, 598).
114 Interestingly, though the text specifies the duration of the edict's authorisation – ἐν ἡμέρα μιᾳ – and the month of Adar in which it was to come into effect, no mention of the specific day is present even though it was known at this point (cf. 3.7).
115 Wills, *The Jewish Novel in the Ancient World*, 117.

to readers' sense of law and order and seeking to convince them that the vizier has the best interests of the kingdom in mind. Without success in this endeavour the city of Sousa would never have been so troubled (3.15b).

What we encounter in the words of the 'edict of the king' (section B) is nothing short of a masterpiece of rhetorical and political composition.[116] Indeed, its Greek has been characterised as "very eloquent and florid" in its effort to influence.[117] Throughout, it sounds the call for tranquillity, stability, order and peace in the kingdom. It is for this reason, it seems, that the government exists, and it is to the these ends that it will prove itself indefatigable. The leaders in this noble quest are the king, who is characterised by humility, equity [ἐπιεικέστερον], and the utmost gentleness [ἡπιότητος] (B.2), and Aman, the second in command, who exhibits a soundness of mind [ὁ σωφροσύνῃ], is notably unwavering in good-will [ἐν τῇ εὐνοίᾳ ἀπαραλλάκτως], and maintains a steadfast loyalty [βεβαίᾳ πίστει] for the good of the kingdom (B.3). Standing sharply against this utopian picture (and the ones who are seeing to it) is a certain hostile people [δυσμενῆ λαόν], mixed-up within the kingdom, who are ill-disposed to all laws but their own (B.4a). Because of this narrow predilection, they continually dismiss [παραπέμποντας διηνεκῶς] the commands of kings, hence, standing in the way of a stable, unified government over the kingdom (B.4b). Surely, such misanthropic people are true menaces to society (B.5).

With this institutional threat existing, no one, it would seem, could possibly be able to enjoy any peace. Thus, in the service of an undisturbed state of affairs (B.7b), Aman published this "narrativized" royal decree[118] in order to authorise the enemies of this troublesome people to completely destroy them on 14 Adar, showing no mercy and sparing noone, even women and children (B.6b). By this issuance, the "second father" [δευτέρου πατρὸς] of the kingdom (B.6a) has nobly taken it upon himself to ensure peace and well-being in the lives of his 'children'. In light of section B, Aman is portrayed as the undisputed hero of the people; his literary actions have 'saved' them from

---

116 Wills notes that the Greek here is "quite pretentiously and rhetorically composed in perhaps the highest-level Greek in the entire Greek Bible" (*The Jewish Novel in the Ancient World*, 117).

117 Levenson, *Esther*, 75. For detailed comments on the composition, style, syntax and likely origin of section B, see C.A. Moore, "On the Origins of the LXX Additions to the Book of Esther," *JBL* 92 (1973), 384-86; R.A. Martin, "Syntax Criticism of the LXX Additions to the Book of Esther," *JBL* 94 (1975), 65-72; and Jobes, *The Alpha-Text of Esther*, 25-28; 170-71. Further, for comment on the genre of epistolary fiction in the Greek novel in the first centuries C.E. and its significance within the LXX-Esther redaction, see Boyd-Taylor, "Esther's Great Adventure," 110-111.

118 After a lengthy discussion, Dorothy comes to this conclusion concerning the genre of section B (*The Books of Esther*, 102).

disturbance. Yet, reckoned alongside our ongoing assessment of the vizier's moral character, section B has only complicated the matter.

3.4.4 Sinister satisfaction (5.9-14)

So far in the LXX telling of the Esther story it would not be surprising if we found ourselves to some extent confused about the moral character of Aman. In the progression of the narrative the reader has likely been suspicious of his endeavours (A.17), wary of his appellation, Βουγαῖος (A.17; 3.1), and alarmed by his genocidal intentions (A.17?; 3.5-9). Yet as we read on we also come across a carefully composed and brilliantly spun piece of political writing that serves to cast the second in command in a most flattering light. Even though the reader knows that Aman himself is the driving force behind the decree published in the name of the king (3.12), the portrait of his exemplary character painted by the polished, utilitarian rhetoric in section B appears unblemished and perhaps has a balancing effect in an assessment of the moral character of Aman.[119] Yet in all the events that have thus far transpired, his only *emitted* emotions have been negative ones. So far as we can tell, the thoughts and actions of Aman have only been those of jealousy, anger and conniving hate – emotions that differ with the (self)portrait so eloquently described in section B, and ones at odds with the words of Mardochaios weighed against the reputation of his adversary in 4.8b and C.5. How might the emotionally unstable material found in 5.9-14 further inform our ongoing appraisal?

We observe in 5.4-8 that Aman is a privileged invitee to both of the exclusive banquets given by Queen Esther. After the first of these, the narrative expressly indicates that the vizier leaves in an extremely good mood. The text describes him explicitly as being "overjoyed" and "delighted" [ὑπερχαρής, εὐφραινόμενος] (5.9a). But [δὲ] just as soon as Aman catches sight of Mardochaios the Jew his demeanour changes drastically and he becomes extremely angry [ἐθυμώθη σφόδρα] (5.9b). Interestingly, nothing is said or done by Aman as a result of this 180 degree swing of emotion. Neither does the author editorialise upon the emotional state of the vizier at this point. The reader instead accompanies Aman into his house where we receive a rare

---

119 However, it could have the opposite effect. Following J.B. Schildenberger, Moore posits that the pogrom either becomes "more sensible" and "less ruthless" as we become more acquainted with the "kind" and "noble" Haman who drafted it, or it engenders further spite in us as we observe the length of Haman's vainglory (*Daniel, Esther and Jeremiah: The Additions*, 192).

glimpse of his deeper self in the presence of his friends and wife. In the description of the scene it is stated that Aman proudly

ὑπέδειξεν αὐτοῖς τὸν πλοῦτον αὐτοῦ καὶ τὴν δόξαν, ἣν ὁ βασιλεὺς αὐτῷ
περιέθηκεν, καὶ ὡς ἐποίησεν αὐτὸν πρωτεύειν καὶ ἡγεῖσθαι τῆς βασιλείας

showed them his wealth and splendour,[120] that which the king had invested in him,
and how he [i.e., the king] made him to hold the first place and to lead in the kingdom
(5.11).

This, we must assume, is the way that Aman chooses to deal with his anger.
By building himself up in the presence of those who likely already think
highly of him and are quite aware of the privileged responsibilities with
which he has been endowed, the desire of Aman for public importance and
recognition is on full display. Indeed, with a sense of great pride (and a hint
of desperation) he goes on to speak of his prized seat in the presence of royalty at the banquets given by the queen (5.12). Yet in the face of all of these
high honours it is clear that Aman enjoys no satisfaction; there is something
that continually serves to undermine all of his success. For as long as he sees
Mardochaios the Jew in the court [ὅταν ἴδω Μαρδοχαῖον τὸν Ιουδαῖον
ἐν τῇ αὐλῇ] there can be no appeasement for his inner rage (5.13). Aman's
emotional pendulum has swung 180 degrees once again, and it seems that
from the sick feeling of his present despair within he can find no remedy.
Help is to come, however, not from within, but from without. In order to lift
his spirit above its constant source of agitation, his wife and confidants propose a plan that would lift Mardochaios fifty cubits high upon a gallows
(5.14a). Thus, the cause of much emotional self-torture would be hanged, and
the psychological noose that was growing ever tighter around his neck now
sees occasion to be loosened. With the consent of the king the next morning
the scheme would be put into action (5.14a). The thought of all of this serves
to placate and satisfy the vizier (5.14b).
    The enjoyment of his satisfaction, however, is ephemeral. Aman's emo-
tional pendulum swings one last time as the next day he sees his professional
life crumble before his very eyes (6.4b-13). Just at the time that he is on top
of the world hoping to lift Mardochaios high upon the gallows, Aman is cast
down to earth as he is required to elevate his enemy in a different manner –
upon the royal horse. And if this humiliation and disappointment were not
enough, at the occasion of his last remaining source of pride – his place at the
second banquet of Esther – we witness the personal demise of Aman (7.6-
10). Having been craftily exposed as the one hostile [ἐχθρός] to the people of

---

120 I.e., "reputation, honour, glory" (LS, 209).

the queen, the wrath of the king consumes Aman. This anger, though, appears
to be directed mainly (if not exclusively) at Aman's appearance of impropriety on the couch [κλίνην] of Esther, rather than at any genocidal intentions
he harboured against the Jews (cf. § 2.4.4). Nevertheless, despite our perception of the cause of the royal anger at this point, it is Aman's malevolent purpose against the Jews that is *officially* highlighted and remembered throughout the remaining story (cf. 8.7; § 3.4.5).

3.4.5 A final portrait – civil and divine censure (E.2-14, 17-18)

Our task in providing a final portrait of Aman is made more manageable by
two factors: first, despite the glowing and scrupulous (self)portrait of section
B, there is little doubt, even at a casual reading, what kind of man Aman has
been portrayed to be; and second, section E does much of the summarising
work for us.

With the mind and (likely) pen of Mardochaios behind his words (cf. 8.8),
'the king' sets out quite elaborately to champion once again the causes of
peace and an undisturbed existence for all of his subjects (E.8). The attain-
ment and maintenance of these desired ends, however, has been disrupted by
ones who have taken advantage of the generosity of His Majesty, thus threatening others in the kingdom with their power. In his introductory words he
states:

πολλοὶ τῇ πλείστῃ τῶν εὐεργετούντων χρηστότητι πυκνότερον τιμώμενοι
μεῖζον ἐφρόνησαν καὶ οὐ μόνον τοὺς ὑποτεταγμένους ἡμῖν ζητοῦσιν κα-
κοποιεῖν, τόν τε κόρον οὐ δυνάμενοι φέρειν καὶ τοῖς ἑαυτῶν εὐεργέταις
ἐπιχειροῦσιν μηχανᾶσθαι

Many, having been honoured too much by the most abundant kindness of their
benefactors, have become frequently conceited; not only do they seek to maltreat our
subjects, unable to bear such satiety, they also endeavour to contrive against their own
benefactors (E.2-3).

By their arrogance these πολλοὶ have been blinded to and deprived of all
that is good (E.4a). Nevertheless, they would not escape the evil-hating
judgement of the ever-seeing God (E.4b). Even so, civil measures have to be
taken in addition to the looming divine censure – the "undisturbed and peaceful"[121] existence of the empire is dependent upon such action (E.8a).

The primary task in this civil endeavour concerns how to handle Αμαν
Αμαδάθου Μακεδὼν, the man singled out among the offending πολλοὶ

---

121 Following the rendering of Levenson (*Esther*, 111).

(E.10). Given the title, "Macedonian," in this particular instance, the status of Aman as a foreigner most likely is being underlined.[122] Yet the appellation probably signifies more than that. Also implied in the designation is the connection that the vizier has with the eventual conquerors of the Persian Empire in 333 B.C.E. led by Alexander the Great.[123] These suspicions are confirmed in E.14 as Aman is described as an infiltrator in the kingdom and collaborator with the enemy.[124] Much like his earlier epithet, Βουγαῖος, negative connotations are in view here, and especially ones that endanger the stability of the kingdom.[125] What had heretofore been ambiguous concerning Aman is now coming to light; his conspiratorial threat to the king and his subjects is now being fully exposed. And if we once had reasonable doubt concerning the role of Aman in the assassination plot described in section A, the words of the king in E.12 serve to dispel any remaining scepticism:

οὐκ ἐνέγκας δὲ τὴν ὑπερηφανίαν ἐπετήδευσεν τῆς ἀρχῆς στερῆσαι ἡμᾶς καὶ τοῦ πνεύματος

but unable to bear [his] arrogance he [i.e., Aman] undertook to deprive us of sovereignty and spirit (life).

Further, if we had been unclear previously as to the exact reasons for the condemnation of the vizier in 7.8-10, we are informed of the following explicitly in E.13, 18:

τόν τε ἡμέτερον σωτῆρα καὶ διὰ παντὸς εὐεργέτην Μαρδοχαῖον καὶ τὴν ἄμεμπτον τῆς βασιλείας κοινωνὸν Εσθηρ σὺν παντὶ τῷ τούτων ἔθνει πολυπλόκοις μεθόδων παραλογισμοῖς αἰτησάμενος εἰς ἀπώλειαν. ...τὸ αὐτὸν τὸν ταῦτα ἐξεργασάμενον πρὸς ταῖς Σούσων πύλαις ἐσταυρῶσθαι σὺν τῇ πανοικίᾳ, τὴν καταξίαν τοῦ τὰ πάντα ἐπικρατοῦντος θεοῦ διὰ τάχους ἀποδόντος αὐτῷ κρίσιν

through intricate cunning [and] deception he craved for [the] destruction of our saviour and benefactor in all things, Mardochaios, and blameless sharer of the kingdom, Esther, with their entire nation. ...he who plotted these things was hanged with [his] household from the gates of Sousa, a worthy judgement of the all-ruling God speedily repaid upon him.[126]

---

122 See Kottsieper, *Zusätze zu Ester*, 191f.
123 Levenson, *Esther*, 114.
124 Bickerman suggests that Haman's whole plan is traitorous and is enlightened by the epithet Μακεδών. Haman is seeking, by the destruction of the Jewish people, to make the way clearer for a Greek takeover. That is why the damaging charges have been made against them and why it would not be prudent for the king to let them be (*Four Strange Books of the Bible*, 223).
125 Jobes, *The Alpha-Text of Esther*, 127-28.
126 It is obvious that accuracy of the events and precise chronology were not the most important factors for the composer of this section. Moore has pointed to two contradictions that stand out (he has the MT in mind, but for our purposes the contradictions apply to

Thus, final words – both human and divine[127] – concerning Aman have been given, and the entire kingdom is specifically instructed *not* to act upon the genocidal edict previously sent by him (E.17). The Aman of the LXX has turned out to be a complete failure in the final analysis; not even the self-aggrandising efforts of section B can rescue him from the evil legacy with which he will always be associated.

3.5 The Jews

3.5.1 A disparaging portrait (3.8; B.4-5)

Beginning with the indefinite threat that they receive in A.17, the Jews figure somewhat consistently throughout the LXX Esther story. As such, they are never too far removed from the ongoing action. This is especially the case in chapter nine in which they take centre stage and leave the reader with a victorious last impression. Yet in the early portions of the narrative, the images we receive concerning them are not in the least complimentary. Recall, for instance, the accusation from the mouth of Aman in the presence of the king that a nation scattered about in his kingdom possesses and practises laws that differ from those of everyone else in the empire (§ 3.4.2). But it is not the case that these people (here unnamed) merely acknowledge legal plurality, Aman claims that they are paying *no* attention to the laws of the king! This, according to the vizier, constitutes a dangerous state of affairs, and it would not be prudent for His Majesty to let them be (3.8).

Further, in § 3.4.3, we observed an eloquent, though cutting, portrait of a people who are hostile in nature and found to be mixed within the people of the empire. Because of their disposition only to their own laws, the commands of kings are continually shunned and the establishment of a unified government is perpetually being undermined (B.4b). Thus, Aman, acting in the authority of the king and in his words, resolves publicly that the Jews,[128]

---

the LXX as well): 1) Haman was hanged on the gallows outside his house, not from the gates of Susa (cf. 7.9-10); 2) 9.13-14 relates that the sons of Haman were hanged on 14 Adar after being killed on 13 Adar, dates that lay months after the publication of the counter-edict. Moore concludes that the point of the author of section E is that the family of Haman shared in his doom (*Daniel, Esther, and Jeremiah: The Additions*, 236).

127 Cf. De Troyer, *The End of the Alpha Text of Esther*, 385.

128 Although the nation is unnamed in section B, for the reader she has already been named in narrative (3.13). Thus, we all are quite aware of the object of Aman's civilised and proper contempt in this instance.

above all others [μονώτατον], are threateningly in opposition to every
man,[129] antagonistic to the kingdom, and even guilty of "plotting heinous
crimes."[130] With them in the midst of the empire, there can be no peace (B.5).
In fact, we gather that anywhere there are Jews, there is serious danger present. Something must be done (3.9; B.6).

3.5.2 A cry from the community (C.11 [F.6a])

The situation could not have looked worse for the Jewish people at this stage
of the story. They have now been threatened twice (A.17; 3.9), with the second of these threats manifesting itself in a real and grave danger (section B).
In the midst of their woe, however, a solitary, yet discernible, cry can be
heard from the mouths of all Israel [πᾶς Ισραηλ] (C.11a). The presence of
this desperate appeal slightly alters the exclusively passive portrait of the
Jews observed thus far in the story. Although they will still generally allow
their leaders, Mardochaios and Esther, to negotiate and act on their behalf
throughout most of the story, the supplication of the community that we find
in C.11 is significant, especially in light of the summarising interpretation
provided in F.6a.

This cry of Israel is given little investigation in Esther literature.[131] At
most, it is noted as a "closing narrative frame" for the prayer of Mardochaios
found in C.2aβ-10.[132] Yet in a portion of the narrative devoted to fervent
prayer (section C), the prayer of the people seems wholly appropriate, if not
expected. They, too, are concerned about their plight. That every single Israelite [πᾶς Ισραηλ] cried out is likely hyperbolic, yet it is clear that many
more than just Mardochaios and Esther bowed themselves before their God
in these difficult times.[133]

The petition of the community is found between the prayers of Mardochaios (C.2-10) and Esther (C.12-30), and follows the appeal of Mardochaios
to κύριε ὁ θεός, ὁ βασιλεύς, ὁ θεός Αβρααμ not to forsake the portion

---

129 Lit: ἐν ἀντιπαραγωγῇ παντὶ διὰ παντὸς ἀνθρώπῳ. This is noted by Moore to be "a
   military metaphor" with a similar usage in 1 Macc 13.20 (*Daniel, Esther, and Jeremiah:
   The Additions*, 192; see also Kottsieper, *Zusätze zu Ester*, 157). If so, the Jews are not at
   all being portrayed as peaceful, though certainly peculiar, people co-existing in the empire. The remainder of the verse bears this supposition out.
130 Dorothy, *The Books of Esther*, 94; cf. the rendering of Levenson, *Esther*, 74.
131 However, see the recent, though brief, comment of Kottsieper (*Zusätze zu Ester*, 166).
132 Dorothy, *The Books of Esther*, 115, 17.
133 Kottsieper suggests that the corporate crying out was from Jews throughout the empire,
   not just from those in Sousa (*Zusätze zu Ester*, 166).

[μερίδα] which God has redeemed (C.8-9). Then, after Mardochaios had petitioned emotionally on their behalf, it is related that

καὶ πᾶς Ισραηλ ἐκέκραξαν ἐξ ἰσχύος αὐτῶν, ὅτι θάνατος αὐτῶν ἐν ὀφθαλμοῖς αὐτῶν

All Israel cried aloud[134] out of their strength, for their death [was] in their eyes (C.11).

In light of the religious element that pervades some parts of the narrative (such as this one) and makes but a token, yet real, showing in others (e.g., 2.20), the prayerfulness of the Jewish people does not at all surprise the reader of this story; in fact, it might have been anticipated. After all, death stares them squarely in the face (C.11b), and the narrative clearly relates that it is to God that the Jews turn, singularly and collectively, in this time of crisis. In the mind of the author their prayer plays an integral part in their ultimate salvation. F.6a reasons that Israel cried out to God and were saved [βοήσαντες πρὸς τὸν θεὸν καὶ σωθέντες]. This cry likely refers to the prayer that is cried aloud in C.11, and serves to illustrate the cosmic scope of the LXX Esther story. For in the end, God is proved to have been both providential among God's own and victorious in the world (F.6b-9).

3.5.3 A reason for their plight? (C.17-18a)

But moving back into the dramatic plot of the story (yet to be resolved), we encounter the mysterious confession of sin from the mouth of Esther on behalf of the Jews. Its presence will perhaps serve to complicate the moral character of the Jews somewhat. In the midst of her heart-wrenching invocation in C.12-30, the queen, without any palpable foundation, admits that the Jews have sinned [ἡμάρτομεν] before God in that they have given glory to their [i.e., Persian] gods. This, we are to infer, is the reason why God has given them over to their enemies (C.17-18a). To be certain, this is a remarkable confession and twist of plot, but we cannot necessarily be sure as to its motivation. Esther could have been assuming that her community must have done *something* wrong to have ended up in the predicament that now pressed in upon them.[135] However, it appears more likely in the scope of the present

---

134 ἐκέκραξαν appears to be a reduplicated aorist form of κράζω that is found elsewhere in the LXX in similar contexts – Judg 3.15; Ps 21.6; 1 Macc 11.49. Note that other mss. witness to different aorist forms in this instance – εκραξαν 249′ 311; εκεκραξεν (εκραξεν S; εξεκραξεν 108) S V O-A 76 46-64-381-728 108 (Hanhart, *Esther*, 163).
135 Cf. the assumptions of Job's friends. Also, cf. 3 Macc 2.13 – a confession of past general sinfulness occasioned by a particular present suffering.

text that the queen has something specific in mind which, in the grand scheme of things, has occasioned the plight of the Jews – namely, their idolatry [ἀνθ' ὧν ἐδοξάσαμεν τοὺς θεοὺς αὐτῶν] (C.18a).[136] This is the reason that they found themselves in bitter slavery [πικρασμῷ δουλείας] – a situation which they were enduring as their punishment. But now they find their very existence as a nation in jeopardy, and Esther calls upon God to be true to the promises made to God's inheritance (C.20).

3.5.4 A license to use their own laws and customs (8.11a; E.19b)

Being in the dregs of despair, the fortunes of the Jews could only rise; and on the shoulders of their leaders, Esther and Mardochaios, they most certainly do. As the queen fervently prays for herself and the community (C.12-30), musters the courage to enter into the throne-room of the king (4.16), dramatically achieves an audience with His Majesty (section D), crafts her plan at two banquets (5.4-8; 7.1-2), and finally sees to the downfall and death of Aman at the second of these (7.3-10), the hope of the Jews rises incrementally. Similarly, as Mardochaios offers up a prayer for himself and the community (C.1-10), and receives the (overdue) honouring of the king at the hands of Aman (6.11), downcast Jewish faces would have occasion to look up. Literarily speaking, the barometer of Jewish emotion and existence rises and falls with the successes and setbacks of their leaders.

The state in which the Jews find themselves at the beginning of chapter eight is quite positive. There is, however, still work to be done – the genocidal edict of Aman (section B) did not die with its sponsor. Thus, the Jews are officially still in harm's way as 13 Adar dawns. It would seem that something extraordinary is required. That 'something' manifests itself in a counter-edict – requested by the queen (8.5-6), ordered by the king (or perhaps Esther or Mardochaios?) and empowered by the ring of the king (8.7-10) – which grounds Jewish hopes and fosters their prominence within the kingdom (8.15-17). Although the plot development is remarkable enough, there is one particular facet of the 'royal' authorisation that especially stands out.

---

136 Might it have been something further than the previous apostasy against God that had occasioned the exile in the first place? For a discussion of this issue, see Kottsieper, *Zusätze zu Ester*, 173-74.

It is recorded in 8.11a that he/she[137] enjoined [ἐπέταξεν] the Jews "to use"[138] their own laws in every city [χρῆσθαι τοῖς νόμοις αὐτῶν ἐν πάσῃ πόλει] as they help each other and treat their adversaries and attackers as they please. This issue is taken up again in E.19b where it is stated that the Jews are to be free to use their own customs [χρῆσθαι τοῖς ἑαυτῶν νομίμοις] so that they would have every opportunity to be ready to defend themselves when they were attacked (E.20).[139] Even though it is unclear all that is entailed in the enjoinder and permission for the Jews to observe their own laws and customs, what is certain in these instances is that in fact *official* measures have been taken to ensure that the Jews would have every opportunity to be ready for an attack from their enemies. It is especially significant that the very aspects of Jewish life that have alienated them from society and have caused the greatest threat to the kingdom initially (§ 3.4.2; 3.4.3) turn out to be important factors in their ultimate success and victory. The laws and customs which had once condemned them would now would serve to aid the Jews in their fight for survival.

3.5.5 A reversing portrait (E.15-16)

But if it is not enough that the powers that be allow and even charge the Jews to use their own laws, we find in E.15-16 a phenomenal confession in the words of the king, which not only approves of the their laws, but also recognises the place of the God of the Jews in the kingdom. On the heels of his public exposure of Aman, the king makes the following acknowledgement:

---

137 One might assume that the subject of ἐπέταξεν is the king. He has issued the command and assurance of 8.8, appears still to be the subject of ἐνετείλατο in 8.9, and is the prominent figure in 8.10. However, one could make a grammatical and contextual case that Esther or Mardochaios becomes the subject of the relevant verbs beginning with ἐνετείλατο in 8.9. Since the king has charged both of them to "write" and "seal" in 8.8 – γράψατε καὶ ὑμεῖς ἐκ τοῦ ὀνόματός μου ὡς δοκεῖ ὑμῖν καὶ σφραγίσατε τῷ δακτυλίῳ μου – any one of the three characters could reasonably be the subject of the following verbs in the context of the decree writing. For her part, De Troyer submits that "[H]e (= the king) gives "them" a charge" (*The End of the Alpha Text of Esther*, 236).

138 Cf. De Troyer: "act according to" (*The End of the Alpha Text of Esther*, 177).

139 De Troyer makes points out an important distinction between 8.11 and E.19: Whereas in 8.11 permission to act according to their own laws is given *to* the Jews (dative), E.19 communicates the "obligation or command…that the Jews are to be left to live (infinitive with the object in the accusative) according to their own laws." De Troyer maintains that the writer of Section E "clearly noted that the LXX of Esther made a distinction between the addressees, i.e., the Jews, and those being placed under orders, i.e., the archons and the governors of the satraps" (*The End of the Alpha Text of Esther*, 386).

ἡμεῖς δὲ τοὺς ὑπὸ τοῦ τρισαλιτηρίου παραδεδομένους εἰς ἀφανισμὸν Ἰουδαίους εὑρίσκομεν οὐ κακούργους ὄντας, δικαιοτάτοις δὲ πολιτευομένους νόμοις, ὄντας δὲ υἱοὺς τοῦ ὑψίστου μεγίστου ζῶντος θεοῦ, τοῦ κατευθύνοντος ἡμῖν τε καὶ τοῖς προγόνοις ἡμῶν τὴν βασιλείαν ἐν τῇ καλλίστῃ διαθέσει.

But we find that the Jews, who were given over to destruction by the thrice-dyed[140] (i.e., archvillain), are not malefactors, but ones governed by very just laws, and sons of the Most High, the living God,[141] who is keeping the kingdom straight for us as also for our forefathers in the most beautiful arrangement (E.15-16).

This recognition and endorsement seems not only to clear the Jews of any hint of impropriety in the story, but also counts the Persian king among those who confess the Most High, the living God. This latter point should not come as too much of a surprise to us since similar words have been in the mouths of foreign kings concerning the God of Israel.[142] But more importantly for our focus here, the moral character of the Jewish people has been portrayed to be most exemplary.[143] This is a complete reversal from the maligning portrait of § 3.5.1; instead of being characterised by lawlessness and subversiveness, integrity and faithfulness finally describe the υἱοὺς τοῦ ὑψίστου μεγίστου ζῶντος θεοῦ in the LXX book of Esther.

3.5.6 13 Adar (9.1-2, 6-10, 16)

Any discussion of the battle report that describes the actions of the Jews on 13 Adar in the LXX must be prefaced by this perplexing statement from the mouth of the king:

καλῶς οὖν ποιήσετε μὴ προσχρησάμενοι τοῖς ὑπὸ Αμαν Αμαδάθου ἀποστελεῖσιν γράμμασιν

Therefore, you will do well not availing yourselves of the letters sent by Aman, son of Amadatha (E.17).

---

140 Moore comments that this same derogatory epithet was also used of Nicanor in 2 Macc 8.34 & 15.3. Moore uses the term "blackguard" to render the term (*Daniel, Esther, and Jeremiah: The Additions*, 236). We have followed Dorothy and supplied "archvillain" to convey something close to the intended sense of the author (*The Books of Esther*, 184).

141 Following the rendering of Levenson concerning τοῦ ὑψίστου μεγίστου ζῶντος θεοῦ (*Esther*, 112).

142 Levenson cites Ex 9.27; 18.10-11; Num 22-24; 2 Kgs 5.15; and Ezra 1.2; 6.10 (*Esther*, 113-14). Moore adds to this list Isa 45.1-7 and Dan 4.34-37 (*Daniel, Esther, and Jeremiah: The Additions*, 236). Moreover, theological language is especially at home within section E (4b, 18b, & 21), and not out of place in the scope of the entire LXX narrative.

143 Cf. a similar royal exoneration of Jews in 3 Macc 7.6f.

What is the king actually getting at here? This is an important point because of the manner in which this portion of the counter-edict is usually rendered.[144] Is the sense of μὴ προσχρησάμενοι to be understood such that the king is officially *rescinding* the genocidal decree of Aman? Or is he merely *advising* that the edict of Aman be practically disregarded in light of the person he has turned out to be (cf. E.10-14), although its formal power is still in effect? Solid answers might be unattainable, but in the (at times confounding) narrative of LXX Esther, it would not be surprising if the word of the king in this instance (E.17) serves practically to invalidate a decree that is, supposedly, legally inescapable (cf. 8.8b).[145] The relevance of the above investigation should become obvious at this point concerning the material in present focus. For if the edict of Aman has indeed been nullified by the words of the king, the actions of the Jews on 13 Adar become suspicious of being unprompted and offensive. But if the decree of Aman is still in legal force, we are in better stead to understand the occurrence of the battle account, even if a measure of scepticism persists.

In beginning to describe the events on 13 Adar the text merely reports: "the letters arrived that were written by the king" [παρῆν τὰ γράμματα τὰ γραφέντα ὑπὸ τοῦ βασιλέως] (9.1). Presumably the actual letters had arrived much earlier than that day and it is probable that what is being communicated here is the fact that the edict has now become effective. Nevertheless, now that the decree has reached its operative date, the narrative relates simply that on 13 Adar those who opposed the Jews utterly perished [ἀπώλοντο], for no one could even withstand the Jews because they feared them [οὐδεὶς γὰρ ἀντέστη, φοβούμενος αὐτούς] (9.2). Is the text stating that no one even took up arms against the Jews, or is this better understood metaphorically? To rephrase the question: Is this an unprompted Jewish offensive, or is the text communicating that the battle was so one-sided that it is *as if* no one withstood the Jews? If the former, it might be the case that the people of the kingdom actually heeded the order or advice of the king in E.17 and disregarded the edict of Aman. If so, they would not have been anticipating any armed conflict on 13 Adar. However, if the latter, this may be the literary way the author chooses to describe the sense of the overwhelming Jewish triumph in a lopsided, but consensual battle.

---

144 Moore (*Daniel, Esther, and Jeremiah: The Additions*, 233) and Levenson (*Esther*, 112) suggest that the participial clause, μὴ προσχρησάμενοι, is best translated "not to act upon"; Dorothy offers the translation "not executing" (*The Books of Esther*, 184). The senses of these renditions appear to be quite similar.

145 Cf. the thoughts of Bickerman on this question (*Four Strange Books of the Bible*, 227).

Whatever one decides concerning this matter, the testimony of the text is that there are notable casualties as a result of the Jews' part in the conflict: the Jews killed [ἀπέκτειναν] 500 men in Sousa plus the ten sons of Aman (9.6); they utterly destroyed [ἀπώλεσαν] 15,000 of their enemies in the rest of the empire (9.16). If any among these numbers actually organised an effort to attack the Jews, the text takes relating such information for granted.[146] As it stands, one can only *assume* at this point that there has been such an assault.

Additionally, the narrative also reports that the Jews plunder on that day. Since the initial verb, ἀπέκτειναν, applies to the whole of 9.6-10 in one continuous phrase, everything within the phrase is syntactically its object. This observation only sets up our point of interest. The final verb at the end of the four-verse clause, διήρπασαν, would appear to govern all that comes before it (9.10). Thus, the Jews have plundered the property of everyone who has been killed in Sousa that day – the 500 men and the sons of Aman.[147] This detail presents us with conflicting messages in the text in which sometimes the Jews take spoil, and other times they do not (cf. 9.15-16). Even if there is no apparent logic in the Jews not plundering their enemies one day and not taking spoil the next, this is the way the text is, and there is no strong manuscript evidence in the text-critical apparatus that would suggest overwhelmingly to the contrary.[148] An interesting observation though it is, there is little to inform our moral assessment here because in the LXX the Jews are never told that they should or should not take the spoil of their enemies. Therefore, despite the internal disagreement and subsequent readerly confusion on the issue, a moral commendation or reproach might seem presumptuous.

---

146 It appears that E.20 assumes that there will be an attack on the Jews. Later, in the interpretation of A.6, F.5 suggests that τὰ ἔθνη represents those "who assembled to destroy the name of the Jews" [τὰ ἐπισυναχθέντα ἀπολέσαι τὸ ὄνομα τῶν Ἰουδαίων]. Dorothy submits that this assemblage is a gathering of troops (*The Books of Esther*, 218).

147 *Pace* Harrelson that the plundering is only connected with the household of Haman ("Textual and Translation Problems," 202).

148 Fox suggests that "the LXX...undoubtedly lost a negative through copyist error since it has a negative in 9:15, which speaks of 14 Adar, and there would be no point for the Jews to take spoil one day but refrain the next" (*Redaction*, 84). Though the point that Fox makes is logical, one would have thought that this 'error' would have been corrected in the early copies of the manuscript. As it turns out, only Compl (Complutensian Polyglot – 16th century) suggests that οὐ be inserted (Hanhart, *Esther*, 199).

3.5.7 14 Adar (9.15)

In light of the conclusions of § 3.2.7 that suggest the likelihood that Queen
Esther has nothing (directly) to do with the bloodletting actions on 14 Adar,
the moral character of the Jews appears to be suspect. Yet the broader context
of the LXX book of Esther, and the portrait of the religious Jews within it,
might serve to mollify any judgement a reader might levy upon those fighting
on 14 Adar. Despite the unsubstantiated, undermining charges of Aman
against them, the Jews have not been depicted as being beyond reproach (cf.
§ 3.5.3). So even though they are generally portrayed positively in the story,
one must hold out the possibility that they find themselves carried away in
the spirit of the battle and subsequently step over the line in Sousa on 14
Adar, gratuitously killing 300 more men (9.15). Just what prompts them to
act in this way we cannot be sure.

3.6 The King (Ἀρταξέρξης)

3.6.1 Decisive action (A.14)

As we observed in § 3.3.1 the regicidal contrivance of Gabatha and Tharra
ends in failure thanks to Mardochaios, whose loyal efforts are there highlighted. But what we did not dwell upon in that section was the manner in
which the king acts upon receiving the tip given to him. This particular matter is related tersely in the following way:

καὶ ἐξήτασεν ὁ βασιλεὺς τοὺς δύο εὐνούχους, καὶ ὁμολογήσαντες ἀπήχθησαν.

The king interrogated the two eunuchs, and after they had confessed they were led
away (A.14).

In commenting on this portion of the narrative, Dorothy claims that the king
"tortured" the two eunuchs, thus extracting their confessions.[149] If this is so,
the initial impression of the character of the king would be far less than positive in the mind of the reader. Yet the charge of Dorothy should not be taken
without some consideration.[150] He maintains that the verb ἐξήτασεν should

---

149 Dorothy, *The Books of Esther*, 52, 301.
150 Before we even begin, there is a question concerning which verbal root Dorothy sup-
    poses. He appears to deduce ἐξαιτέω as the lexical form of ἐξήτασεν (54). Though they
    are of similar meaning, it is ἐξετάζω, and not ἐξαιτέω, which lies behind the verbal
    form seen here in A.14.

be rendered this strongly when it is considered alongside the other "verbs of investigation" found within its immediate context – ἐξηραύνησεν and ἔμαθεν (A.13).[151] Though we concede that ἐξήτασεν is indeed a stronger verb than both ἐξηραύνησεν and ἔμαθεν, it is unlikely that it should be rendered any more forcefully than we have done in our translation above.[152] To do so, even in the service of dramatic effect or a comparative point, seriously alters the tone of the scene in that the effective power of the king is transformed into nothing less than tyranny. In the mind of Dorothy, a torturing king is the only option in this passage. It is unlikely that the matter is so clear cut, for there is nothing contextually present to suggest that the king actually uses tactics of torture or extracts confessions from the eunuchs. What we receive in the words of A.14 is the distinct sense that when the moment arrives for kingly authority and action, His Majesty willingly and ably steps in and delivers a decisive, though not necessarily abusive, response; the king appears to be in charge of his court to a great extent at this point.

3.6.2 Order in the court (2.23a)

In addition to the conviction shown in § 3.6.1, His Majesty continues to emit a certain sense of control in his surroundings as we progress through the initial banquet scenes and into the infuriating episode of Astin's refusal (§ 3.1.1). Though one might make the argument that the ultimate 'winner' in the confrontation is the deposed queen, if we focus in, we would have to admit that it is the king who takes some measure of initiative in these events. It is he who initiates judicial proceedings against her (1.13), endorses the political plan of Μουχαῖος in order to get rid of her and stabilise the kingdom (1.21), and finally clears his mind of the incident,[153] seemingly satisfied with the

---

151 Note also that Dorothy compares ἐξήτασεν to the milder ἤτασεν of A.14 (AT) in making his case (*The Books of Esther*, 301).
152 LS offers nothing stronger than "*to examine* or *question* a person *closely*" in its entry on ἐξετάζω (273). However, while BAGD offers a similar series of possibilities generally, leaves open a stronger sense when the verb is used as a legal technical term. In this case, the use of ἐξετάζω in judicial questioning has been connected with torture in some authors (275). This is not to say, however, that it must necessarily imply torture in all legal contexts. Thus, the rendering of ἐξήτασεν as "interrogated" appears to relate the strength of the verb fairly in its particular judicial context above.
153 Lit: καὶ οὐκέτι ἐμνήσθη τῆς Αστιν. If what we encounter in the LXX is rendering the Heb. זכר as is witnessed in MT 2.1, the translator clearly understands "remember" in a different way from the Heb. author. With the negative element introduced, the Gr. translator describes a varying thought process in the king – he is moving on with his life, whereas in the MT one gets the impression that the king's life is moved on for him (cf.

verdict he has handed down concerning his former queen (2.1). Thus, we can suggest that in matters of *personal* conflict the king should not be seen as one who is prone to shrink back.

This mentality is witnessed once again in the account of the second assassination attempt in 2.21-23. Recall from § 3.3.2 that two chief bodyguards of the king become disgruntled with the advancement of Mardochaios within the court (2.21a). Thus, likely holding the king responsible as the source of their discontentment, they seek to kill the sovereign (2.21b). The conspiracy, however, is discovered by Mardochaios who then joins forces with Queen Esther so that the matter might be brought before the king (2.22). But unlike other occasions in which those around His Majesty predominantly handle the royal business, the king takes full control of this situation in which his life is threatened. The text specifically relates that *he* examined [ἤτασεν] the two bodyguards and hanged[154] [ἐκρέμασεν] them (2.23a). Here, royal actions are similar to those in the initial depiction of an attempt on his life in A.14, although a few variations should be noted concerning 2.23a: 1) the manner in which the king performed his judicial action is less intense (ἤτασεν v. ἐξήτασεν); 2) no confession is uttered by the accused; and 3) the sentence handed down is more specific (ἐκρέμασεν v. ἀπήχθησαν). What has not changed, however, is the commitment of the king to order in the empire – an end whose means seem to be, most importantly, the protection of the royal throne.[155] Yet this beloved sense of stability would not last for long; a greater threat now looms on the horizon.

3.6.3 A deceived accomplice (3.9-11; E.5-6)

In being so focused on his efforts for self-preservation, the king, on at least one occasion, cannot see the forest for all the trees. Through great political savvy, Aman has submitted before him that an unnamed people in his empire poses a significant threat to his kingdom because they possess laws that differ from all other peoples. But it is likely the fact that these folk actually neglect

---

Harrelson, "Textual and Translation Problems," 201; Dorothy, *The Books of Esther*, 77-78). Interestingly, later Latin (LaJM) and Coptic-Sahidic (Sa) mss. omit οὐκέτι in order to 'correct' the text toward MT and Compl (Hanhart, *Esther*, 142).

154 It is likely that hanging was the sentence that the king decided in this case, not that the king actually carried out the hanging.

155 This regal trait should not come as a surprise given the way Greek writers conventionally portrayed the Persian monarchy: despite despising it, the Greeks "could not but be impressed by its power and opulence" (Berlin, *Esther*, xxxi). This kingly power is seen even more strongly in the roughly parallel episode in the AT (see § 4.6.1).

the laws of the king that causes fear in the throne-room and prompts His Majesty not to let them alone (3.8; § 3.4.2). Thus, when his authority is undermined, and his safety imperilled, the king takes no chances and empowers Aman to treat the nation as he wishes [τῷ δὲ ἔθνει χρῶ ὡς βούλει] (3.11b). The manifestation of this royal sanction is elaborately borne out in B.4-6 – a text in which the machination of Aman, fuelled by the anxiety of the king, takes on its most elegant form.

This floridity has turned repulsive, however, by the time we reach section E. We have seen heretofore the overwhelming sense of betrayal that the king had felt in E.2-3 realising that his generosity had been abused (§ 3.4.5). This impression is so poignant that he even questions the existence of any measure of good in the πολλοί whom he had once trusted (E.4a). His own human verdict aside, however, the king is sure that they would not elude the evil-hating judgement of the all-seeing God (E.4b). Upon that foundation he makes the following disclaimer:

πολλάκις δὲ καὶ πολλοὺς τῶν ἐπ' ἐξουσίαις τεταγμένων τῶν πιστευθέντων χειρίζειν φίλων τὰ πράγματα παραμυθία μετόχους αἱμάτων ἀθῴων καταστήσασα περιέβαλεν συμφοραῖς ἀνηκέστοις τῷ τῆς κακοηθείας ψευδεῖ παραλογισμῷ παραλογισαμένων τὴν τῶν ἐπικρατούντων ἀκέραιον εὐγνωμοσύνην.

Often times, too, the persuasiveness of friends, who have been entrusted with the management of affairs, has made many in authority sharers in innocent blood [and] has involved them in irreparable misfortune; deceiving the unmixed good will of those ruling over them with malicious, false deception (E.5-6).[156]

An exercise in rhetoric though it may be, one suspects that the king has a more pointed focus; the feeling of betrayal that he feels is likely not this generic. What is the actual cause of the "misfortune" to which the king is referring? By whom has His Majesty been deceived? Concerning these questions the king unambiguously submits that Aman – one who has been welcomed among them even though a foreigner, honoured by them, even becoming the second to the king – via his crafty and deceptive ways [πολυπλόκοις μεθόδων παραλογισμοῖς], has sought to destroy the entire Jewish race because he is unable to bear his own arrogance [οὐκ ἐνέγκας δὲ τὴν ὑπερηφανίαν] (E.10-13). As odd as such an admission would sound from the lips of a monarch, the king is admitting to have been "duped," as Moore puts it, "by a trusted adviser and friend."[157] His political strategy is, however,

---

156 I have relied on the rendering of Levenson here (*Esther*, 111).
157 Moore, *Daniel, Esther, and Jeremiah: The Additions*, 235. Kottsieper submits that the sovereign had been incited by way of slander (*Verleumdung*) against innocent ones (*Unschuldige*) in this case (*Zusätze zu Ester*, 190).

to downplay the appearance of complicity in the genocidal plot of Aman. By casting the situation in this manner, perhaps the pledges he has given for action and equity might be taken more seriously (E.8-9). His Majesty has effectively realigned himself in political terms. And, in the end, it would seem that the moral character of the king has benefited from the words he chooses in communicating his decree, the tone he takes in delivering it, and the leadership he shows in the midst of the crisis that is set to affect his entire empire.

3.6.4 A spiritual transformation (D.8)

But can all of this be explained facilely by shifting political winds? The text leaves open the possibility of a religious transformation in the life of the king. While it is beyond doubt, according to Mardochaios's dream interpretation in section F, that God works behind the scenes of the entire drama, section D relates that ὁ θεός enters explicitly into the story at a crucial point. The narrative impact of this divine activity is nothing short of miraculous as it turns a situation of impending Jewish doom into one of ongoing, yet still fragile, hope. Nevertheless, we must admit that the specific, *personal* effects of God's work in the king are more difficult to discern.

All of this takes place amidst the detailed episode of Esther's approach to the king so that she might plead the desperate case of her people (D.1-16). After an intense season of prayer concerning the challenge before her (C.12-30), the queen proceeds to the crossroads of life and death. Although she has adorned herself beautifully, the text suggests that her strength comes from her "all-seeing God and saviour" [τὸν πάντων ἐπόπτην θεὸν καὶ σωτῆρα] (D.2); as she stands before the king, we get the impression that God is near and sustaining. But despite the presence of her Lord with her, the deified and angry appearance of the king overwhelms Esther as she faints and falls forward onto her maid (D.6-7). All of her efforts of inward and outward preparation seem to have come to naught. Yet God has not abandoned her; as human ability falters, divine power miraculously intervenes. The narrative starkly declares that "God changed the spirit of the king to gentleness" [καὶ μετέβαλεν ὁ θεὸς τὸ πνεῦμα τοῦ βασιλέως εἰς πραΰτητα] (D.8a). This "radical,"[158] spiritual transformation manifests itself in physical acts of com-

---

158 In the words of Kottsieper, what God brought about in this instance was a "radikale Wendung" (*Zusätze zu Ester*, 184).

passion and words of comfort as the king rushes to the side of Esther and personally sees to the needs of his ailing queen.[159]

It could be suggested that this is the turning point for Esther and the Jews in the LXX story, for after this scene their fortunes only improve.[160] Though the threat of the genocidal edict of Aman looms for a while longer, there is little reason to fear its implementation because the presence of God remains from now on in the foreground of the story and, more importantly, on the behalf of the Jews. Especially interesting in the remaining portions of the narrative is the fact that to a certain degree it is the king who is in the closest vicinity of most of the occurrences of the name of God in the story from here forward – in many instances the two characters are intriguingly intertwined. For instance, it is the king from whom ὁ κύριος removes sleep in 6.1, and in the counter-edict the words of His Majesty proclaims the name of the "all-seeing," "living," "all-ruling," and "all-powerful" God as if his own (E.4, 16, 18, 21, respectively).[161] We could say that by means of God's intervention, resulting in the king's reflective insomnia, Mardochaios is finally given his just reward for past service in 6.10. Moreover, it is in the name of God that the king endeavours to rule his empire equitably and peacefully for all people (section E). Thus, the king appears to be a man who has been transformed, and one whose moral character has been informed by the spiritual reversal encountered in D.8.

3.6.5 Joint role in the production of the counter-edict? (8.8-11a)

Yet we would not wish to take this point too far; there is no explicit evidence that the king has become anything close to a Jewish 'convert.' He does, however, appear to turn his efforts decidedly in favour of Jewish survival and subsequent prosperity, doing what he can within his power (i.e., the decreed law) to aid them. To be sure, this is not a monarch who only looks within, concerned solely with himself. Yet discerning the extent of his direct involvement in the cause of Esther and Mardochaios presents some difficulty.

---

159 Lit: καὶ ἀγωνιάσας ἀνεπήδησεν ἀπο τοῦ θρόνου αὐτοῦ καὶ ἀνέλαβεν αὐτὴν ἐπι τὰς ἀγκάλας αὐτοῦ, μέχρις οὗ κατέστη, καὶ παρεκάλει αὐτὴν λόλοις εἰρηνικοῖς (D.8b). See the comments of Kottsieper for information concerning the outstanding words of affection that the king uses in this particular instance (*Zusätze zu Ester*, 184).

160 A view initially proffered by W.H. Brownlee who calls it "La l'unique miracle" ("Le Livre grec d'Esther et la royauté divine. Corrections orthodoxes du au livre d'Esther," *RB* 73 (1966), 182 [cited in Moore, *Daniel, Esther, and Jeremiah: The Additions*, 218]).

161 For consistency of presentation, I am following the renderings of Dorothy here (*The Books of Esther*, 181-85).

We suggested above that the tide began to turn for the Jews as a result of divine intervention. As soon as his spirit is turned about, the king seems to assume the role of a vessel through whom God acts in the story. Although it is not at all defined, we would even suggest that after his spiritual reversal the king functions to work *alongside* the Jewish leaders, all as conduits through whom the ultimate purposes of God would be carried out.

The initiative His Majesty takes both to reward Mardochaios (6.10) and to protect the honour of his queen (7.8-10) serves to further the notion, hitherto suggested, that the king is shown to exhibit a measure of control over and leadership within his court (§ 3.6.1; 3.6.2). With the timely contribution of βουγαθαν accelerating the demise of Aman, the king begins to return stability to the throne-room. Yet even though his body no longer is able to harm (7.9b-10), the threat of Aman continues to loom dangerously over the empire.

Seeking to counterbalance this, His Majesty strives further to cut Aman off from the land of the living by handing over to the queen everything that had belonged to him [ὅσα ὑπῆρχεν Αμαν] (8.1a).[162] This ongoing shift in ancillary power is made complete when Mardochaios – now publicly shown to be a relation of Esther – receives the signet-ring from the king and is appointed over all that was Aman's by the queen (8.1b-2). One might anticipate that the king would now fade from the centre stage now that matters were stabilising, leaving Mardochaios and Esther to handle matters from here on. This, as we shall see, was not to be so; his character remains influential in the later stages of the narrative. We observe this state of affairs most noticeably in the text of the counter-edict, in which royal proclamation takes centre stage (section E). Although his voice is obviously preeminent therein, his role in the formation of the document might also be considerable.

In verses three through six we notice that Esther makes another formal approach[163] before the king in hopes of achieving a specific reversal of the Amanic decree that still threatens the Jewish people. What she seeks, however, she does not receive. What Esther instead acquires is a non-specific, open-ended permission from His Majesty: γράψατε καὶ ὑμεῖς ἐκ τοῦ ὀνόματός μου ὡς δοκεῖ ὑμῖν ["you (pl.) write in my name as it seems

---

162 Here, Aman is pejoratively called τῷ διαβόλῳ – "the slanderer, false accuser" (LS, 185; cf. De Troyer, *The End of the Alpha Text of Esther*, 182, who adds "denigrator" and "adversary" to the description). It is interesting, though appropriate, that this comment is found here since it foreshadows the tone and stance that the king assumes in section E, distancing himself from his former vizier.

163 This approach is thought formal because of the appearance of the golden rod (8.4). Yet why Esther would have had to proceed through formal protocol having already achieved a successful audience the king and at this stage in her relationship with him is puzzling.

[good] to you (pl.)"]¹⁶⁴ (8.8a). Just this, we gather, Esther and Mardochaios
plan to do. Yet the narrative continues to assume the language of royal origin
and gives the impression that the king is still making decisions and wielding
some amount of influence in this scene.

A syntactical explanation is not required to accompany the submission that
the king is the speaker in 8.8 and likely the one giving the charge in 8.11a;
contextually, this appears plain enough. In between, however, the subject-
verb decisions are not quite so easily perceived. In 8.9 a measure of doubt
exists concerning who is commanding the various authorities in this instance
– i.e., who is the subject of the verb ἐνετείλατο: Esther? Mardochaios? or
the king?¹⁶⁵ We suspect, for reasons of narrative flow and a lack of explicit
evidence to the contrary, that the king remains the main acting and speaking
figure in the present scene, exercising authority over his governors and rulers.
Unfortunately, the following verse does not necessarily clarify the situation
as it relates that the scripts are written διὰ τοῦ βασιλέως (8.10a) – either *by*
the king, or *through* him (i.e., with his authority)¹⁶⁶ – leaving slightly open
the possibility that Esther and/or Mardochaios hold(s) the initiative in this
case. Even if this is so, it is most likely that the king has not been a mere bystander or rubber-stamp in these proceedings. The writings are then sealed
with his ring [καὶ ἐσφραγίσθη τῷ δακτυλίῳ αὐτοῦ] before they are carried off into the empire (8.10bc). Since Mardochaios now possesses this ring
(8.2), he would have to be involved to some extent in the sealing process,
giving us the impression that the king is not the sole actor or decision-maker
here. Furthermore, from the subject matter of the document produced, it
seems obvious that either one or both of the Jewish leaders would have exercised influence in its creation for they had been just before been authorised to
formulate at their discretion (8.8a). Yet what also appears clear in these
verses is the reality of the joint and active role of the king in the production
of the counter-edict: "In short, whatever Esther and Mordecai do has the approval of the king."¹⁶⁷ At the least, we can say that he has not faded from the
picture; at the most, his part in countermanding the decree of Aman discloses
his committed interest in the welfare of the Jewish people (or at least Esther

---

164 De Troyer's rendering is stated perhaps even more strongly: "You also must write in my
   name as it pleases you" (*The End of the Alpha Text of Esther*, 176).
165 Dorothy, *The Books of Esther*, 160.
166 Cf. De Troyer, *The End of the Alpha Text of Esther*, 234 n. 137.
167 De Troyer, *The End of the Alpha Text of Esther*, 215. De Troyer proceeds to add that
   "[I]t would appear from the very face of his response that from the king's perspective
   the matter has been resolved" (215), underlining the monarch's degree of overall support – support that is underlined further by the king speaking in the first person in the
   LXX rather than the Hebrew third person (215 n. 96).

and Mordecai). The monarch appears to have been personally active in the cause of Jewish survival.

3.6.6 A partner in dealings with enemies (9.14)

This commitment and activity does not appear to be swayed as the story plays out. In fact, the picture that we have been sketching in the immediately preceding sections – one suggesting the 'Jewish' posture of the king – encounters nothing particularly to the contrary in the final portions of the narrative. The casualty report that the king offers in 9.12a – 500 dead in Sousa – and the interesting queries that follow it – ἐν δὲ τῇ περιχώρῳ πῶς οἴει ἐχρήσαντο; τί οὖν ἀξιοῖς ἔτι; – make some sense if the king is clearly on the side of the Jewish people, striving for their benefit. Moreover, the compliance he shows concerning Esther's activity on 14 Adar might have been expected (9.14). Clearly, it is neither a surprise nor seems to be a moral problem to the author that the king should support his Jewish queen – he appears, at heart, to be one of them.

4 Moral Character in the AT

4.0 Introduction

We get the sense as we read the AT Esther story that we have been here before. Indeed, this would be an accurate perception in more than one respect. In its current shape, the AT narrative looks much like the LXX with its initial dream, eloquent letters, pious prayers, dramatic entry scene, culminating theological interpretation and overall cosmic scope. But while it is the case that the two Greek texts have much the same flavour, their differences stand out as well[1] – something that will become particularly evident, although incidentally so, in this study of moral character in the AT.

Yet it is not only the LXX Esther story that the AT narrative brings to mind. The way in which the AT story expresses itself and is often economically related – over against the longer and more cumbersome LXX – resembles the tighter narrative of MT Esther. Narrative flow and editorial care can be seen clearly in many places. But although the AT has been shaped to read like a unit at the final level of the text, or so it would appear, few interpreters, if any, would fail to recognise that lingering textual and logical difficulties remain therein.

Despite the various similarities, it should nevertheless be understood that the AT Esther story is its own. This narrative tells a distinctive tale played out by characters, who, though familiar, are not merely mirror images of those found in either the MT or LXX. This can be especially observed as one investigates issues of moral character in the AT narrative. Let us turn to that focus now as we once again proceed in an exegetical manner.

---

1   "The AT relocates, omits, compensates, fleshes out, etc." (De Troyer, *The End of the Alpha Text of Esther*, 281-82).

4.1 Ouastin

4.1.1 Refusal to appear when summoned (1.9-12)

Like the MT (§ 2.1.1) and LXX (§ 3.1.1), chapter one of the AT begins with
a description of the riches, power and dominion of the king (1.1, 6-8). From
India to Ethiopia, it is reported, 127 lands are subject to him (1.1b). In order
to display this wide-ranging influence and authority, the king puts on a drinking feast [πότον] for his rulers and officials from near and far (1.3). The text
states that the revelries last for 180 days so that "the wealth of the glory of
the king and the honour in which he boasted" [τὸν πλοῦτον τῆς δόξης
τοῦ βασιλέως καὶ τὴν τιμὴν τῆς καυχήσεως αὐτοῦ] could be shown
(1.4). Indeed, the purpose of this gathering is clearly ostentatious.[2]

Interestingly, from the vagueness of the transitional words of 1.1[3] – Καὶ
ἐγένετο μετὰ τοὺς λόγους τούτους – there does not appear to be an obvious connection to section A, which immediately precedes it. Connections,
however, are often subtle. From the information related in 1.5a, we learn that
for the inhabitants of Sousa – from prominent people to commoners[4] – an
additional seven-day drinking-feast is given by the king. Yet in distinction
from the purpose of the initial feast, this second party is to celebrate his (the
king's) deliverance [ἄγων τὰ σωτήρια αὐτοῦ] (1.5b). This, of course, begs
the question: From what or whom had the king been delivered? Perhaps the
kingdom had just been victorious in war and has occasion now to be joyous
in their deliverance as an empire from an enemy. Or, maybe the king himself
had recently been spared from a personal tragedy which marks a reason for
this celebration.

In the present form of the AT, this second suggestion might have some
support. In addition to relating the dream of Mardochaios, section A mentions the deliverance of the king from an assassination plot at the hands of
two of his eunuchs (A.11b-14). Thus, at the seven-day banquet the reason for
the celebration could be the deliverance of the king from that particular attempt of regicide. As the text reads presently, this possible connecting theme
between section A and chapter one is worth pointing out.

---

2   On the boastfulness of the king, see further § 4.6.2.
3   According to Fox, these are the transition words of the redactor who sought to bring
     together section A (he calls it Add A) and chapter one (which he designates the begin-
     ning of the Proto-AT) (*Redaction*, 35). Clines calls texts like this "patches" that have
     been made between the Additions and canonical portions (*The Esther Scroll*, 105).
4   Lit: "from great until small."

During this time of prolonged festivity, it would seem, we learn also that Queen Ouastin gives a great reception [δοχὴν μεγάλην] for all of the women of the court of the king (1.9). Although we are not told just how lengthy or extravagant the party given by the queen is, it is related that at the culmination of the second banquet of the king the presence of Ouastin is sought. On this seventh day of drinking the text reports that His Majesty "was merry" [εὐφρανθῆναι] with wine (1.10a). Whether or not this merry state influences or even occasions his summoning of the queen is not clear. All the narrative tells us is that Ouastin is to come before the army of the king wearing the royal diadem (1.11). Why would the queen be called to do this? Day claims that there is but one reason: "to make clear her royalty and her authoritative status within the kingdom."[5] If this is indeed the intention of the king, the opposite effect is reported to have occurred. What transpires next increases the tension dramatically:

καὶ οὐκ ἠθέλησεν Ουασιν ποιῆσαι τὸ θέλημα τοῦ βασιλέως διὰ χειρὸς τῶν εὐνούχων.

[B]ut Ouastin did not will to do the will of the king through [the] hand of the eunuchs (1.12a).

Instead of being distinguished positively in the presence of the people, the refusal of Ouastin signals her demise as queen. For when the king hears of her unwillingness, he is severely distressed and his wrath burns within him (1.12b).

As a result, a counsel of wise men and legal experts is called together (1.13). These men were to decide both how to deal with Ouastin and how best to spin the embarrassing royal episode to the public. Through the mouth of a certain Βουγαῖος, a statement is given that in effect widens the scope of 'crime' of Ouastin. At the end of the day, it is officially decided that she has wronged all the leaders of the land, and soon everyone in the kingdom will be aware of it (1.16). There is no telling what kind of trouble might result from the report of such defiance! One thing is for sure, however: Ouastin must be replaced by one who is "better" [κρείττονι] than she (1.18). And in 1.20a, we find out just what characteristic will circumscribe this 'better' woman – obedience to the voice of the king.

As is the case with the other two versions we are at a loss to understand just why Ouastin refuses the will of the king at this point, even if his intentions might be more readily determined (cf. § 2.1.1; 3.1.1). Once again a satisfying moral assessment of her (in)action cannot be satisfactorily concluded.

---

5   Day, *Three Faces of a Queen*, 210.

However, in a similar fashion to the events in the other narratives, the downfall of Ouastin sets the stage for the rise of Esther in the story. Yet, in this
story, the condition is that the successor of Ouastin must be obedient, for
with that quality "she will do good to all the kingdoms"[6] [ποιήσει ἀγαθὸν
πάσαις ταῖς βασιλείαις] (1.20b). Only time will tell just how obedient to
the king Esther will be, and how much good she will do to all the kingdoms.

4.2 Esther

4.2.1 Apprehension as the Jews face danger (4.7b-8)

Even though the AT narrative relates the Esther story economically, much
has occurred from the beginning of the narrative until this point. In order to
contextualise the current inquiry concerning Esther and her difficult decision,
we would benefit from being exposed to the relevant and important happenings so far. Recall that after the deposing of Queen Ouastin (1.13-18), an
obedient replacement is required (1.20a). However, and this is an interesting
point, the text communicates that *beauty* is to be an (the?) important trait of
the subsequent queen (2.2), and that she should be one that would please[7] the
king (2.4). Just this Esther would do, and it should be noted, to a great extent
[ἤρεσεν αὐτῷ σφόδρα] (2.9b). The expected manner of queenly obedience
is no longer explicitly emphasised, if even still in the frame. This would seem
to be an ironic shift in expectation as far as the reader is concerned, even
though it is taken in stride in the narrative.

After Esther marries the king (2.18), a crisis of life or death falls upon the
new queen and her people. Given birth in the angry mind of Aman and then
made official *via* the law (consent) of the king, a genocidal plot is put in
place that spells doom for Israel[8] (3.8-19). According to the edict of Aman,

---

6   I am following the rendering and contextual understanding of Day concerning the verb
    ποιήσει who argues against the translation of Clines (*The Esther Scroll*, 221) in this
    case (*Three Faces of a Queen*, 210 n. 1). Another rendering that would make sense in
    the context is suggested by Dorothy, "it will benefit all kingdoms" (*The Books of Esther*,
    71). In other words, the reality of an obedient queen would be beneficial to all. In the
    end, however, Dorothy sides with the understanding of Clines and believes that with an
    obedient wife, the king will do good to all (i.e., he will appear benevolent) (77).
7   Throughout this scene, forms of the verb ἀρέσκω are employed to communicate both
    the expectation of the replacement of Ouastin and the effects that Esther would have
    upon all with whom she would come in contact, including the king (2.4, 8, 9).
8   καὶ καρδίᾳ φαύλῃ ἐλάλει τῷ βασιλεῖ κακὰ περὶ Ισραηλ. Here, the narrator identi-
    fies the people hatred by Aman explicitly for the reader, although we gather that they are
    still anonymous to the king (cf. 3.6).

the Jews should all be killed and "in one day go together to Hades" [ἐν ἡμέρᾳ μιᾷ συνελθότες εἰς τὸν ᾅδην] (3.18b). In the mind of Mardochaios (at least), Queen Esther would not be safe from this threat even within the palace walls (4.10). As news of the genocidal edict spreads, reaction is certain. The city of Sousa is confounded[9] at the happenings [ἐταράσσετο ἐπὶ τοῖς γεγενημένοις], while among the Jews there is "great and bitter grief" [πένθος μέγα καὶ πικρὸν] wherever the news had reached (4.1). In the outer court of the palace complex Mardochaios appears in sackcloth and ashes (4.2). It is from this location that he engages in a monumental mediated dialogue with his cousin, the queen.

It is worth noticing the detail that Mardochaios initiates the exchange by sending one/a eunuch [εὐνοῦχον ἕνα] to the queen (4.3a).[10] Why Mardochaios does this is not stated. Is Esther aware of the disturbance, and upon that knowledge, does she desire a report from her cousin who is on the outside? If so, we would have expected her to send *him* a eunuch in order to inquire concerning the matter. But it is more likely that Mardochaios is attempting to establish the lines of communication with Esther in the manner described. Obviously informed of the appearance and posture of Mardochaios, the queen apparently sends more than one eunuch[11] back to Mardochaios, bearing these terse imperatives: "Take off the sackcloth and bring him in" [Περιέλεσθε τὸν σάκκον καὶ εἰσαγάγετε αὐτόν] (4.3b). Upon hearing these, the narrative communicates that Mardochaios is unwilling [οὐκ ἤθελεν] to submit himself to one or both of these commands (4.4aα).[12] Though we cannot be sure, it is likely that Mardochaios wishes not to remove the outer manifestations of mourning and prefers (or deems it necessary) to continue his dialogue with Esther through intermediaries. It is also possible that he seeks to continue to identify with the grieving Jews of kingdom and not appear to flee to a safe haven within the walls of the palace. His next

---

9   See the relevant footnote on LXX 3.15 (§ 3.2.2) for some thoughts on the understanding of ἐταράσσετο in a similar context. In its usage here, we are explicitly told that the Sousians are aware to some extent of what has transpired. This information, however, does not necessarily clue us in to the specific kind of reaction that they were giving.

10 Day, *Three Faces of a Queen*, 51.

11 By the plural tenses of the verbs in 4.3b and 4.4b, we might deduce this. Why the queen sent more than the one eunuch back to Mardochaios is not known. Jobes concludes that the reply of Mardochaios, beginning with the words Οὕτως ἐρεῖτε αὐτῇ, "makes no sense in the context. The implied plural subject of the verb has no referent...and produces narrative dissonance" (*The Alpha-Text of Esther*, 207). Could there be other reasons for multiple eunuchs? Perhaps it had something to do with the prominence of her office in that she had many servants at her disposal. In short, it might have been royal prerogative. Despite these attempts, however, the difficulty persists.

message hints in this direction even as it seeks primarily to urge Esther towards action for her people:

Μὴ ἀποστρέψῃς τοῦ εἰσελθεῖν πρὸς τὸν βασιλέα καὶ κολακεῦσαι τὸ πρόσωπον αὐτοῦ ὑπὲρ ἐμοῦ καὶ τοῦ λαοῦ μνησθεῖσα ἡμερῶν ταπεινώσεώς σου ὧν ἐτράφης ἐν τῇ χειρί μου, ὅτι Αμαν ὁ δευτερεύων λελάληκε τῷ βασιλεῖ καθ' ἡμῶν εἰς θάνατον. ἐπικαλεσαμένη οὖν τὸν θεὸν λάλησον περὶ ἡμῶν τῷ βασιλεῖ, καὶ ῥῦσαι ἡμᾶς ἐκ θανάτου.

Do not refuse[13] to go in to the king or to flatter him[14] on behalf of me and the people,[15] being mindful of [the] days of your low estate in which you were brought up by my hand; for Aman, the second in command, has spoken to the king against us for death. Therefore, calling upon God, talk to the king concerning us, and deliver us from death[16] (4.4b-5).

---

12 Day points out that the precise reason for the unwillingness of Mardochaios is unclear (*Three Faces of a Queen*, 52).
13 Following the rendering of Clines (*The Esther Scroll*, 227).
14 Lit: "his face."
15 Why Mardochaios has singled himself out among the Jews here is not known. See further § 4.3.4.
16 In a footnote on LXX 4.8c (§ 3.2.2) we noted the rendering and grammatical/syntactical argument of Day concerning the final three verb roots in the clause. In that particular instance, we concluded that Day's point was not overly persuasive. In the AT parallel (4.5), her reasoning stands in better stead grammatically, but still does not fully convince us in view of the overall context. Day argues that the grammatical structure of this final clause – ἐπικαλεσαμένη οὖν τὸν θεὸν λάλησον περὶ ἡμῶν τῷ βασιλεῖ, καὶ ῥῦσαι ἡμᾶς ἐκ θανάτου – stresses "Esther's action of delivering the people over her actions of calling upon God and speaking to the king" (*Three Faces of a Queen*, 53-4). She contends that in the AT, ἐπικαλεσαμένη and λάλησον are participles that are acting "in a circumstantial manner" in the service of the subsequent active imperative, ῥῦσαι. Her point is this: "As Esther calls upon God and speaks to the king, these two actions [ἐπικαλεσαμένη and λάλησον] will be necessary to meet the objective of what is specified by the finite verb [ῥῦσαι], that is, to save the people" (53). There is no mistaking the participial form of ἐπικαλεσαμένη, yet how to render the participial clause is not necessarily straightforward. Should Esther call upon God and *then* proceed into the presence of the king (so Clines, *The Esther Scroll*, 107)? Or is she being exhorted to be prayerful *all the while* she is talking to the king and seeking the deliverance of the Jews? Perhaps it is something different altogether? I admit that I have left my translation above uncommitted in this regard. Concerning the second verbal form, λάλησον, it should be noted that it could be parsed *either* as a neuter nominative singular future active participle (so Day, I am assuming) *or* a 2nd singular aorist active imperative (as I have translated, and deem to be the more likely contextually). Given that the parsing/rendering decisions here are not perspicuous, context plays an even greater part in aiding one's interpretative decisions. Briefly, and grammatically speaking, it does not appear that Mardochaios is stressing Esther's task of delivering over her actions of calling and speaking. In this context, it seems that calling upon God is vitally important, as is talking to His Majesty. And in the mind of Mardochaios they might be circumstantially related to the hope of deliverance, yet not in the manner or to the extent that Day proposes.

With this, the pain (distress) of Israel [τὴν ὀδύνην τοῦ Ἰσραηλ] is related to Esther (4.6).[17]

Now aware of this great difficulty, Esther is faced with a decision: will she risk her life for her kindred? Initially, the queen is reluctant to commit herself as she offers Mardochaios the reminder that everyone knows it is a death wish for anyone to enter in to the king uncalled unless the golden rod is mercifully extended (4.7). Such a gamble is not one that Esther is keen on taking. She informs her cousin that she is out of favour with the king[18] having not been called before him for thirty days (4.8a). Then she offers what appears to be a preliminary refusal[19] in the following unhopeful words:

καὶ πῶς εἰσελεύσομαι νῦν ἄκλητος οὖσα;

and how will I go in now, being uncalled (4.8b)?

It is clear from this message (4.7-8) that the queen is quite apprehensive about going into the presence of the king. Yet one cannot be sure of the main driving force causing this apprehension. Although the civil law does not occupy as prominent a role in the AT as it does in the other two stories, might Esther mainly be hiding behind a convenient commitment to the civil law of the king all the while thinking that she might escape danger in the palace (cf. § 2.2.3; 3.2.2)? Or is this primarily a personal crisis of national identity and commitment for the Persian queen? This latter explanation appears at the moment more likely. In this episode the danger posed to the Jewish people has been stressed (4.4-6), and will continue to be the main negotiating point of Mardochaios as the dialogue continues (4.9). For now, though, Esther appears relatively uncommitted to her people and is definitely apprehensive about doing what she might for her threatened race. To be sure, her present attitude does not reflect too well on her moral character, even if it is difficult to grasp fully.

---

17 Clines (*The Esther Scroll*, 77), Day (*Three Faces of a Queen*, 54) and Dorothy (*The Books of Esther*, 105) suppose that the subject of ἀπήγγειλεν is the intermediating eunuch. This decision, however, likely supposes the existence of only one eunuch who served as intermediary between Mardochaios and Esther. Given the possibility that there were multiple eunuchs going between, it might also be that 4.6 is a narrative summation of the message of Mardochaios to his cousin. Dorothy considers this possibility, but does not adopt it (105). Yet we could understand this statement in the following way: "he [Mardochaios – not personally, but ultimately through intermediaries] made known to her the pain of Israel." This understanding, while getting at the heart of the matter, effectively side-steps the single/multiple eunuch confusion.

18 Following the understanding of Clines (*The Esther Scroll*, 145) and Day here, although she emphasises 4.8b in this deduction (*Three Faces of a Queen*, 55).

19 So designated by Dorothy, *The Books of Esther*, 111.

144 Moral Character in the AT

4.2.2 Reversal of apprehension (4.11)

Issues of national solidarity govern the continuation of this mediated exchange between the two Jews. Esther has marked out her initial stance on the issue (4.8b), perhaps thinking or hoping that the discussion would go no further. Because she does not enjoy any royal privileges at the moment (4.8a), the queen perceives her hands to be tied in the matter. Mardochaios obviously believes otherwise; the initial 'No' related by Esther would not deter his persistence as he sends the following warning back to the queen:

’ Ἐὰν ὑπερίδῃς τὸ ἔθνος σου τοῦ μὴ βοηθῆσαι αὐτοῖς, ἀλλ᾽ ὁ θεὸς ἔσται αὐτοῖς βοηθὸς καὶ σωτηρία, σὺ δὲ καὶ ὁ οἶκος τοῦ πατρός σου ἀπολεῖσθε·

If you neglect your people, not being of help to them, nevertheless God will be to them a help and a deliverance, but you and the house of your father will be destroyed (4.9).

It seems clear that this strong and cautionary message of Mardochaios firmly places issues of ethnic solidarity above all others. Esther should not necessarily act out of obedience to him; instead, she must aid the Jews out of a sense of wider personal responsibility and commitment. Who knows? The queen might even have come to reign in Persia for just this crisis (4.10). Yet, whatever her decision, we get the impression that God would somehow come to the aid of the Jews and deliver them even if Esther disregards their plight. If we are understanding the words of Mardochaios properly, if Esther does indeed act for her people, we could consider her decision to be "national in scope,"[20] for she might thereby save her people. However, if the queen resolves not to help the Jews and does not enter in before the king as an intercessory, we could view her decision to be out of personal fear and/or selfishness, for she and her house would be the only casualties. In other words, according to Mardochaios the Jews *will be saved* either by the agency of Esther or in some other way by God. It is really only the fate of the queen and her family that appears to be ultimately in the balance, or so it seems from the brinkmanship rhetoric employed by Mardochaios.[21] In his view, Esther is "not indispensable"; God will save the Jews even if she will not.[22]

---

20 Day, *Three Faces of a Queen*, 56.
21 In seeking to understand the tact Mardochaios exhibits in this exchange, it is helpful to remember that Mardochaios and Esther are related – he is a member of the family who would apparently be doomed if Esther does not act, even if the rest of the Jews are saved (or so it should go if the narrative logic is followed). The thinking and persuasive techniques of Mardochaios here are not, however, fatalistic. If they were, he would not be making the arguments that he is; too much would be at stake. And although he might believe that God will somehow save the Jewish people from their present travail, he does

It goes without saying that the choice for Esther is not too enticing. On the one hand, if she refuses, death seems to be a certainty. On the other, even if she proceeds into the presence of the king, an uninviting risk looms. What would she decide? Her final reply might be somewhat surprising and unexpected to the reader.

Παραγγείλατε θεραπείαν καὶ δεήθητε τοῦ θεοῦ ἐκτενῶς· κἀγὼ δὲ καὶ τὰ κοράσιά μου ποιήσομεν οὕτως, καὶ εἰσελεύσομαι πρὸς τὸν βασιλέα ἄκλητος, εἰ δέοι καὶ ἀποθανεῖν με.

Announce an assembly[23] and beseech God intensely; and I, also, and my maidens will do so, and I will go in to the king uncalled, if it were necessary for me to die[24] (4.11).

This remarkable climax contains many interesting aspects. The plural imperatives, Παραγγείλατε and δεήθητε, are directed towards the Jews at large, although Mardochaios must obviously relay them. It is as if Esther is addressing the Jews corporately *via* their representative and exhorting them to announce an assembly, and beseech God intensely; in effect, the queen is speaking directly to her people in these words.[25] This is an extraordinary show of national solidarity as Esther now begins to assume the reins of Jewish leadership. Further, as the Jews assemble and pray, Esther and her maidens pledge to do likewise. All of this precedes the dramatic entrance into the presence of the king – an action which Esther has now (wholeheartedly?) resolved to do. But even more noteworthy, it would seem that in her resolving the queen has accepted that she would be proceeding self-sacrificially.[26] Day summarises this last point well: Esther is "not so much concerned with herself or her own survival.... A [the AT] gives the impression that it is a higher good for which Esther finds it proper and needful to give up her own life."[27] Whether out of guilt or as a result of reflection or a sense of loyal conviction, we get the strong impression here that Queen Esther would now go

---

not exhibit a fatalistic attitude in light of his assurance. As can be seen later in his prayer, Mardochaios has faith in the God who has covenanted with his people, but he does not take that covenant for granted. Thus, he prays fervently for deliverance in hope (4.16-17).

22 Dorothy, *The Books of Esther*, 114.
23 Following the rendering of Clines, *The Esther Scroll*, 107. Clines notes that this sequence most resembles LXX Joel 1.14; 2.15 – κηρύξατε θεραπείαν, translating the Heb. עצרה (193 n. 23).
24 For the most part, I am following the rendering of Day in this final phrase (*Three Faces of a Queen*, 50), although I am understanding the optative δέοι in a slightly different manner.
25 See also Day, *Three Faces of a Queen*, 57.
26 Dorothy, *The Books of Esther*, 112.
27 Day, *Three Faces of a Queen*, 57.

forth selflessly for her own,[28] though, we should note, not without some trepidation (4.18a, 29; 5.3b). This is quite a marked change from the apprehension of § 4.2.1.

4.2.3 Imprecatory petitions (4.23b, 25b)

Although they are not carbon copies, the prayer of Esther in the AT is remarkably similar to its counterpart in the LXX (cf. § 3.2.4; 3.2.5). Even with a cursory glance it is obvious that one recasts the other.[29] Though we shall not seek here to offer a close comparison and contrast of the two, previously investigated aspects of the prayer of Esther found in the LXX which are shared with the AT version will certainly aid us in our present endeavours. In the midst of this, we would do well to keep in mind that the context of the AT is its own and warrants particular and measured treatment.

Upon the heels of her dramatic change of affections, we find Esther honouring the commitment to prayer that she had expressed earlier (4.11). As the queen there exhorts the Jewish people to δεήθητε τοῦ θεοῦ ἐκτενῶς, she, too, now beseeches the Lord [ἐδεήθη τοῦ κυρίου] (4.19aα). The picture painted by the narrator is vivid, describing in great detail the extent to which Esther goes in order to humble herself in the sight of God (4.18).[30] In her hour of greatest need and danger, the Jewess seeks refuge in the Lord, her heavenly King, and to her mind the only source of help (4.19aβ-b).

Following the suggestion of Jobes, the prayer of Esther in the AT is all about her hope in the continuity of God's covenant with Israel.[31] Esther begins by recounting how she has heard from the book of her patrimony [πατρικῆς μου βίβλου] of the special redemption of her people, and how God has delivered what he had promised to them – i.e., Israel, an eternal inheritance [Ισραηλ κληρονομίαν αἰώνιον] (4.20). But now Israel, the chosen

---

28 This impression only solidifies. Observe Esther's own speech as she utilises plural pronouns, including herself, when she refers to the Jews (*Three Faces of a Queen*, 73). Day believes that altruism is one of Esther's most noticeable features in the AT (196).
29 Cf. the discussion in § 1.2.2.
30 See the detailed comments of Day (*Three Faces of a Queen*, 68) and Kottsieper (*Zusätze zu Ester*, 177-78) concerning this picture. See further Wills for comments on the theme of female self-abasement in Jewish novels that might shed some light on the preparations of Esther here (*The Jewish Novel in the Ancient World*, 13-14).
31 Jobes, *The Alpha-Text of Esther*, 176-80. Jobes points out many allusions to the covenant in Exodus, and especially, Deuteronomy.

people of God,[32] is in grave danger in the hands of its enemies. On behalf of the people, Esther expresses real and seemingly urgent fears because the enemies of the Jews have covenanted[33]

ἐξᾶραι ὁρισμὸν στόματός σου, ἀφανίσαι κληρονομίαν σου καὶ ἐμφράξαι στόμα αἰνούντων σε καὶ σβέσαι δόξαν οἴκου σου καὶ θυσιαστηρίου σου καὶ ἀνοῖξαι στόματα ἐχθρῶν εἰς ἀρετὰς ματαίων καὶ θαυμασθῆναι βασιλέα σάρκινον εἰς τὸν αἰῶνα.

to shatter [the] decree[34] of your [i.e., God's] mouth – to destroy your inheritance and block up [the] mouth of those who praise you and quench [the] glory of your house and your altar[35] and open the mouths of enemies for excellence of vain things and (for) a mortal king to be idolised forever (4.22).

In the face of this threat Esther pleads with the Lord not to hand over his sceptre [τὸ σκῆπτρόν] "to enemies who hate you" [τοῖς μισοῦσί σε ἐχθροῖς] (4.23aα).

Although the specific identification of enemies is not made, the way that the writer designates them is quite interesting. In 4.21 it is clearly the enemies of the Jews who are in focus. Yet the following verse leaves its form of ἐχθρός [ἐχθρῶν] as a vague reference; we cannot say specifically whose enemies are in view – the Jews', God's, or both? Finally, in 4.23aα, it is the enemies of God who are in view. The context gives us the impression that from 4.21 to 4.23, the enemies are actually common – i.e., the enemies of the Jews *are* the enemies of God, and vice versa. The progression seen here serves further to highlight the covenant relationship that exists between God and Israel – a bond that Esther prays God would defend as she pleads for God not to let the enemies rejoice at the present/future state of difficulty of the people (4.23aβ). Even though Israel has not been faithful (4.21), the queen hopes that the Lord would be jealous for and gracious to the chosen ones.

---

32 Bar-Ilan notes that this emphasis on the chosenness of the Jews in prayers for rescue is not uncommon in post-biblical literature (cf. the prayer of Jael in Pseudo-Philo, 31) (*Some Jewish Women in Antiquity*, 98).

33 Lit: ἐπέθηκαν τὰς χεῖρας αὐτῶν ἐπὶ τὰς χεῖρας τῶν εἰδώλων αὐτῶν. Clines expresses this act by the translation "covenanted" (*The Esther Scroll*, 231). This appears to be a fair rendering of the gist of the Greek phrase and fits well into the context of opposing covenants in the prayer – the covenant of God with Israel and the covenant of the enemies with their idols.

34 Lit: "a marking out by boundaries, limitation" (LS, 568). It appears that the enemies were threatening to abolish that which God had specifically set out and purposed.

35 Even in the midst of Diaspora the AT story looks, it would seem, towards the Jerusalem temple (Jobes, *The Alpha-Text of Esther*, 177). As noted by Kottsieper (although with different emphases) the prayer of Esther concentrates on many of the same themes as does the (model) prayer of Solomon in 1 Kgs 8.46-53 (*Zusätze zu Ester*, 173-74). Chief among these is the invocation for God to remember and be jealous for God's chosen people, those whom God has redeemed.

But the prayer of Esther is not only for the defence of the Jews; she also hopes for destructive actions on the part of God to be levelled against their foes. At this point her prayer takes a decisive turn as she advocates divine offence:

στρέψον τὰς βουλὰς αὐτῶν ἐπ' αὐτούς, τὸν δὲ ἀρξάμενον ἐφ' ἡμᾶς εἰς κακὰ παραδειγμάτισον.

Turn back their plans [i.e., the enemies' plans] upon themselves, and make an example of the one who began against us for evil (4.23b).

With this, Esther is targeting both the head and the body of the Jews' present/impending troubles. She seeks a backfiring of the plans of the enemies (3.18) along with a special punishment for the one who initiated all of the evil against them – i.e., Aman.[36] Yet her hatred for and wishes against Aman broaden as she continues and looks forward to her entrance into the presence of the king:

καὶ μετάστρεψον τὴν καρδίαν αὐτοῦ εἰς μῖσος τοῦ πολεμοῦντος ἡμᾶς εἰς συντέλειαν αὐτοῦ καὶ τῶν ὁμονοούντων αὐτῷ·

And turn his [i.e., the king's] heart around to hatred of the one hostile to us, for [the] end of him and those who are in agreement with him (4.25b).

Thus, Esther seeks that the affections of her husband might be changed so that he would then hate the one hostile to them. The scope of her imprecatory petitions begins with Aman and then branches out to include any persons in the empire who agree with his genocidal intention. Ironically, at this point in the story the king himself should be counted among this number (see § 4.6.3). Again, how one views the nature of the wishes of the queen here will depend on how he or she understands the entire context of the prayer and story. In this case, Esther is clearly petitioning the God of Israel to act retributively (preemptively?) on behalf of the threatened covenant people. Vengeance is to be the Lord's.

4.2.4 Appearing as a pious Jewess (4.25e-28)

Without neglecting the overall corporate scope of her beseeching, Esther focuses now, though just for a moment, on more personal matters. Yet the fact

---

36 Dorothy, *The Books of Esther*, 118; Moore, *Daniel, Esther, and Jeremiah: The Additions*, 212. Day submits that Esther displays a discernible individual animosity towards Aman in the AT (*Three Faces of a Queen*, 189).

that they are personal does not ultimately dissociate them from the larger Jewish situation. Acting as an advocate for her people, the queen feels the need come clean, as it were, laying her soul bare before her Lord. As the representative of the Jews, she does not want to be the cause of further woes by being counterproductive or unclean as an intercessory vessel. Esther believes that what she does/has done personally has relevance in the wider covenant community situation, or at least in the current crisis. Therefore, seeking to justify her behaviour in the Persian court and the purity of the motivations behind how she has (not) lived, Esther continues her prayer.

The queen sets the tone for her moment of personal confession and defence by unequivocally avowing God's knowledge of all things (4.25e). She desires to retain a humble posture as she now enters into quite delicate matters. It is clear from the narrative that the queen herself feels as if she has done well and acted rightly in her privileged office. However, as she is before the Lord, Esther would not want to appear overconfident or argumentative. She therefore often prefaces her remarks by acknowledging the omniscience of God (4.25f, 26a). Initially, Esther seeks to explain the aspects of her present life that she deems to be queenly necessities, thus justifying her participation in them. Though necessary actions (at least in her mind), the queen desires to make it crystal clear how she views the following three duties:

καὶ οἶδας ὅτι βδελύσσομαι κοίτην ἀπεριτμήτου καὶ ἐμίσησα δόξαν ἀνόμου καὶ παντὸς ἀλλογενοῦς. σύ, κύριε, οἶδας τὴν ἀνάγκην μου, ὅτι βδελύσσομαι τὸ σημεῖον τῆς ὑπερηφανίας, ὅ ἐστιν ἐπὶ τῆς κεφαλῆς μου...καὶ βδελύσσομαι αὐτὸ ὡς ῥάκος ἀποκαθημένης.

You know that I loathe [the] marriage-bed of [the] uncircumcised (one) and [that] I hate(d) [the] honour of [the] lawless (one) and all foreigners. You, O Lord, know my necessity, that I loathe the sign of arrogance,[37] which is upon my head...and I loathe it like the rag of one who sits apart (4.25f-26b, d).

The feelings of Esther are clear enough, but what of her consequent actions? We gather that although she loathes sleeping with the king, she has done so nonetheless. Even though she hates the honour she has received from those around her – likely as a result of her formal status as queen – she has done nothing to silence her laudators. Though she despises her royal turban, detesting it in the most graphically descriptive terms, we shall soon see that she still dons it when publicly expected (4.26c).

In focusing in on these deductions, it is not as if fault is necessarily being concluded; we might have expected this kind of behaviour from a outsider attempting to assimilate herself as queen in the Persian court. However, a

---

37 I.e., "proud position."

measure of confusion arises as we learn of other aspects of her court life. A differing message accompanies the explanation of what she has clearly *not done* in her privileged office. The following are her denials:

καὶ οὐ φορῶ αὐτὸ εἰ μὴ ἐν ἡμέρᾳ ὀπτασίας μου...καὶ οὐκ ἔφαγεν ἡ δούλη σου ἐπὶ τῶν τραπεζῶν αὐτῶν ἅμα, καὶ οὐκ ἐδόξασα βασιλέως συμπόσια καὶ οὐκ ἔπιον σπονδῆς οἶνον· καὶ οὐκ εὐφράνθη ἡ δούλη σου ἐφ᾽ ἡμέραις με-ταβολῆς μου εἰ μὴ ἐπὶ σοί, δέσποτα.

I do not wear it [i.e., the turban] except on [a/the] day of my appearance...and your bondwoman has not eaten upon their tables at the same time,[38] and I have not hon-oured the drinking-party of the king and I have not drunk [the] wine of libation; and your bondwoman has not been joyous upon [the] days of my transition except upon[39] you, O Master (4.26c, 27-28).

Mediating between stances of extremely reluctant acquiescence and staunch refusal stands the attitude of Esther towards her royal turban. Although she abhors it and everything associated with it (4.26b, d), we learn here that she does indeed wear it – but only *sometimes*. Esther seems desperate to commu-nicate that only in necessity does she assume the royal symbol, refusing to associate herself with it whenever possible. The same public/private pre-dicament does not face her in gustative matters though. The queen has been careful not to make a dietary mistake (as she would assess it), and has stayed clear of wine at least in circumstances that might be inadvisable or lend to the sacrilegious. Throughout her days in the palace Esther has only had joy in God, her δέσποτα. Aside from these times we would assume that the queen has been miserable internally.

What leads Esther to assume certain behaviour discontentedly on the one hand (4.25f-26) and avoid other actions immovably on the other (4.27-28) is not clearly defined in the text. Upon what standard, if any, does Esther base her everyday behaviour? Should her dissenting and avoiding actions be un-

---

38 The phrase ἐπὶ τῶν τραπεζῶν αὐτῶν ἅμα could also be rendered "upon the tables together with them" (so Clines (with small variances), *The Esther Scroll*, 86, 231; Fox, *Redaction*, 56; Day, *Three Faces of a Queen*, 75; and Dorothy, *The Books of Esther*, 127). Though the referent of the pronoun αὐτῶν is equally ambiguous either way, ac-cording to Day, decisions on how to translate the entire phrase are not without conse-quence. Day contends that "the difference would lie in whether Esther is primarily op-posed to the people themselves or to their tables (and the food on them)" (75). Yet it would seem that the main thrust of her denial would stem from the main verb of the lar-ger phrase – ἔφαγεν. The point is that the queen has neither *eaten* at the same time as, or together with them. In this disavowal we might imply that food is the larger issue. If not eating at the same time as, or together with others, Esther could have had the occasion to request different, *kosher* food to be served to her.

39 Thayer suggests "on account of" as a metaphorical understanding of ἐπὶ. This might help us to better grasp the sense in which the preposition is being used in this instance and context (*A Greek-English Lexicon*, 233).

derstood as guided, however loosely, by Torah observance?[40] Or is the queen merely living the complex and ambiguous existence of a Jew in a Diaspora court, which is clearly not a normal life (§ 3.2.5)? To be sure, although Esther presents herself as being blamelessly pious,[41] the moral character witnessed here is undoubtedly complicated. Perhaps the outworking of Jewish piety in the Persian court is not necessarily as straightforward as one might think, even in the mind of Esther. What exactly is the interplay between the her "public" and "inner" selves?[42] In the midst of attempting to justify both the virtue of her motivations and the propriety of her actions, might Esther have been (re)interpreting Jewish piety in a new, Diaspora context?

4.2.5 Tact at the second banquet (6.23c-7.12a)

As we observe how Esther works out her piety after she emerges from her prayer, notice the manner in which the outward behaviour of the queen corresponds with her inward convictions and commitments. To be sure, inconsistency is not a necessary conclusion; the narrative does not explicitly seek to portray a stark contrast between her private heart and public actions. Yet as we shall see, a measure of tension does exist – an *implicit* tension which serves to complicate an assessment of moral character in Esther.

Upon recalling the ending comments of § 4.2.2, we might remember that the prospect of entering the presence of the king unbidden paralyses Esther with fear and anguish (4.18a, 29; 5.3b). The reality of the situation proves to be even worse as the physical strength of the queen flees from her, leading ultimately to her complete collapse as a result of the fierce gaze of her husband[43] (5.2, 4-6). Nevertheless, as the story intimates, the timely intervention of God changes matters to the benefit of the Jewess (5.7). Soon after, the queen begins to grow in confidence, thus able to initiate her efforts for Jewish deliverance. She would still face difficulties and occasions for fear, but the same God who has changed the spirit of the king – turning his anger [θυμὸν] into gentleness [πραότητα] – remains close to Esther, upholding her in many times of need.

---

40 So Dorothy, *The Books of Esther*, 119.
41 Day, *Three Faces of a Queen*, 82-83.
42 These are the terms Wills utilises as he tries to come to terms with the praying Esther (*The Jewish Novel in the Ancient World*, 123).
43 Lit: ἐνέβλεψεν αὐτῇ ὡς ταῦρος ἐν ἀκμῇ θυμοῦ αὐτοῦ (5.5b).

After the queen has been assured and comforted by her transformed hus-band[44] and his entourage, she embarks on her quest to attain a better lot for the Jews. In a quickly narrated progression of events, the vizier, Aman, and the king are invited to join Esther at her table on the following day (5.14). To her wishes they both oblige (5.16). At the initial gathering when the king wishes to know the desire of his queen, Esther begins her tactics of stalling, proposing that the three of them get together in the same manner on the fol-lowing day (5.18). To this invitation the king unemotionally assents; but the text relates that Aman marvelled [ἐθαύμασεν] at his good fortune and (ap-parent) rise in prominence (5.20b). His greatest moment, however, marks the beginning of his downfall. Following the account of the professional debacle of Aman (6.7-13), which culminates in the honouring of Mardochaios (6.14-19), we encounter the continuation of the banquet designs of Esther. In the midst of being rebuked by his wife, Aman is whisked away to sit at the table of the queen once more (6.23a). Having gone through so much recent disap-pointment and humiliation,[45] the royal summons serves to lift his mood (6.23b) – but only for a moment.

The suspenseful stage has now been set. Let us now proceed to examine the way in which Esther brings about the demise of Aman – a vital step in her efforts to save her people. With the three of them again together in a relaxed setting (though superficially so), it is the king who breaks the ice with these discerning questions:

Τί ἐστιν ὁ κίνδυνος καὶ τί τὸ αἴτημά σου;

What is the danger, and what [is] your request (7.1b)?

The tension in the room is now pungent, and must have showed in the ap-pearance of her majesty somehow. Esther struggles in reply to the queries of the king[46] because of the presence of "the opponent"[47] [ὁ ἀντίδικος] there with them (7.2b). It appears as if she is to a great extent debilitated by the

---

44 Once appearing as a bull to her (5.5), the king now comforted his wife with brotherly care (5.8). It is certainly not a necessary condition that a Persian king would display this kind of affection to a wife.

45 6.13 relates the feelings of Aman dramatically: ὡς δὲ ἔγνω Αμαν ὅτι οὐκ ἦν αὐτὸς ὁ δοξαζόμενος, ἀλλ᾿ ὅτι Μαρδοχαῖος, συνετρίβη ἡ καρδία αὐτοῦ σφόδρα, καὶ μετέβαλε τὸ πνεῦμα αὐτοῦ ἐν ἐκλύσει.

46 The narrative creates a gripping picture: καὶ ἠγωνίασεν Εσθηρ ἐν τῷ ἀπαγγέλλειν (7.2a).

47 ἐχθρός is the more common word used pejoratively of Aman by Esther. The connota-tion here is of a legal proceeding. Together with the words κρίσις and ἀγωνίζομαι, Day envisions the presence of ὁ ἀντίδικος to be contributing to the creation of a courtroom scene (*Three Faces of a Queen*, 121-22).

increasingly uncomfortable situation. However, just at that moment, a measure of courage is given to her as she prayerfully remembers God (7.2c).[48] As was the case previously (5.6-7), God changes the course of events from despair to hope. But this time it was Esther who receives a divine work of inner transformation. Now, more confident, the queen steadies herself to answer the questions of the king in reverse order.

Εἰ δοκεῖ τῷ βασιλεῖ, καὶ ἀγαθὴ ἡ κρίσις ἐν καρδίᾳ αὐτοῦ, δοθήτω ὁ λαός μου τῷ αἰτήματί μου καὶ τὸ ἔθνος τῆς ψυχῆς μου. ἐπράθημεν γὰρ ἐγὼ καὶ ὁ λαός μου εἰς δούλωσιν, καὶ τὰ νήπια αὐτῶν εἰς διαρπαγήν, καὶ οὐκ ἤθελον ἀπαγγεῖλαι, ἵνα μὴ λυπήσω τὸν κύριόν μου· ἐγένετο γὰρ μεταπεσεῖν τὸν ἄνθρωπον τὸν κακοποιήσαντα ἡμᾶς.

If it seems (right) to the king, and [if] the decision is good in his heart, let my people be given for my request – even the nation of my life.[49] For we have been sold, I and my people, into bondage, and their little children for plunder; but I did not wish to report [it], lest I should grieve my lord; for it has happened that the person who did evil to us has undergone change[50] (7.3-4).

The response of Esther brings about two important results. Although we cannot conclude finally concerning the exact intentions of the queen, the effects of her words can be clearly seen. First, although Esther explicitly states that she did not wish to inform her husband of this matter – so as not to burden him with it – we realise that the opposite has occurred. With the uttering of her disclaimer the queen ends up achieving the result she had (supposedly) wanted to avoid – that is, the infuriation of the king [καὶ ἐθυμώθη ὁ βασιλεὺς] (7.5a). As a result the angry monarch goes on the offensive – an outcome that leads nicely into a discussion of the second result as the king demands to know answers.

Τίς ἐστιν οὗτος, ὃς ἐτόλμησε ταπεινῶσαι τὸ σημεῖον τῆς βασιλείας μου ὥστε παρελθεῖν τὸν φόβον σου;

Who is this, who has dared to disparage the sign of my kingdom so as to disregard the fear of you (7.5b)?

By this enraged question we can tell that Esther has succeeded in identifying herself with her people. In 7.3 Esther answers the king by stating her sole request: δοθήτω ὁ λαός μου τῷ αἰτήματί μου καὶ τὸ ἔθνος τῆς

48 Cf. Neh 2.4.
49 I am following the rendering decisions of Day here (*Three Faces of a Queen*, 122). The above translation makes the best sense of the Greek, grammatically, syntactically and contextually.
50 Dorothy interprets that in this context, undergoing change (he calls it "reversal") is a way of communicating that Aman has been shown to be a villain (*The Books of Esther*, 174).

ψυχῆς μου. In other words, as Day points out, we get the impression that the queen "finds her identity, her very life, in her people."[51] The king does nothing to dissuade this notion as he takes offence at the disrespect of the queenly office.[52] Just at the time when the king could have divorced personal and ethnic matters from the realm of public and kingdom interest, he chooses to stand by his wife and, subsequently, her people (the two appear to be one package even though the king appears primarily to be concerned with Esther). All along the queen has endeared herself to her husband in a strong way; now she has effectively secured his agency in her fight to save her threatened race.

With the king on her side, Esther pursues the end of Aman once and for all. In her attempts to pacify her husband by offering to postpone furthering the matter until the following day, she might know that His Majesty is wound up too tightly to drop the discussion cold (7.6). His anger persists as he demands to know the identity of the arrogant offender (7.7). Seeing that the patience of the king is at its end,[53] Esther senses that this is right time to press forward – she could not waste her moment (cf. 4.10). Therefore, drawing on the sense of confidence she has previously received (7.2c), the queen takes the ultimate risk and exclaims:

Αμαν ὁ φίλος σου ὁ ψευδὴς οὑτοσί, ὁ πονηρὸς ἄνθρωπος οὗτος.

Aman, your friend, [is] this deceiver, this evil person (7.8)!

If the stage had not been perfectly set, the revelation of Esther could have caused her disaster. After all, she is accusing the second in command in his own presence, thereby putting the king in a very difficult situation.[54] His Majesty becomes furious, and the queen must have realised that her husband

---

51 Day, *Three Faces of a Queen*, 122, 181. Dorothy offers the above understanding as well. However, he also leaves open the possibility for "plurisignation" in this case: "with the genitive/ablative form it is possible to think of verbs of buying a selling used with the genitive and of an elliptical (ἀντὶ) τῆς ψυχῆς μοῦ [sic], meaning, 'in exchange for': Esther is willing to sacrifice her life for her people" (*The Books of Esther*, 174). Indeed, Esther has resolved to give her life for her own (4.11), but we must recognise that the matter as she has presented it at this time is the prospect of enslavement. Life and death for the Jews, at least in the present scene, is not at issue. Therefore, it still seems best to remain with the grammatical, syntactical and contextual decisions that lie behind our rendering of 7.3.
52 See also Day, *Three Faces of a Queen*, 131.
53 The narrative relates the seriousness of the moment in these words: καὶ ὤμοσεν ὁ βασιλεὺς τοῦ ἀπαγγεῖλαι αὐτὴν αὐτῷ (7.7a).
54 Clines suggests that because Esther named Aman as the friend of the king, it was then more difficult for him to decide quickly, and in her favour (*The Esther Scroll*, 146). In other words, as the queen closely associated His Majesty with the accused, the king was given little room to manoeuvre.

would react to this disclosure. But in what manner? Would he turn against her and side with his friend? Or might he continue to commit himself to his wife (and her people)? The verdict, as it were, is not immediate.

The narrative communicates that the already enraged monarch becomes even more furious as he takes some time to himself (7.9).[55] Aman, not surprisingly, sees the writing on the wall and is troubled [ἐταράχθη] (7.10a). This emotional state leads him to take desperate measures as he falls down at the feet of the queen as she reclines upon the bed (7.10b). It is interesting to note that the author uses the word κοίτην when designating the place where Esther is reclining. This choice, over against the more general term for bed, κλίνη, occasions the possibility of a sexual overture being present here, for the κοίτη is a marriage-bed – a place for conjugal relations.[56] Though one cannot be conclusive, we have reason to wonder whether the queen might have enticed Aman into a scandalous position. At the least, it appears that Esther is not dissuading the vizier from digging a deeper hole for himself. The story, however, does not oblige our curiosity. When the king returns, it is only related that he perceives the posture of his vizier (rightly or wrongly) in the worst possible way, saying in disbelief:

Οὐκ ἱκανόν σοι ἡ ἁμαρτία τῆς βασιλείας, ἀλλὰ καὶ τὴν γυναῖκά μου ἐκβιάζῃ ἐνώπιόν μου; ἀπαχθήτω Αμαν καὶ μὴ ζήτω.

Is the transgression[57] of (against) the kingdom not enough for you, moreover you would also force my wife before me? Let Aman be led away and let him not live (7.11b-d).

Carelessness regarding both the empire and his appearance with the queen leads to the demise of Aman [καὶ οὕτως ἀπήγετο] (7.12a). Because of the culpable nature of his posture, it is not known whether his crime against the kingdom would have incurred the highest penalty. Yet when coupled with what the king perceives upon re-entering the room to be an extremely personal offence, Aman has no hope of surviving. Indeed, the vizier has effectively signed his own death warrant when he decides to approach the reclining queen. For her part, as far as we can tell for sure, Esther only has to lounge there.

The character of Esther encountered in this section displays God-given courage and resourceful human ingenuity.[58] In 4.25bα she prays that God

---

55 ἔκθυμος δὲ γενόμενος ὁ βασιλεὺς καὶ πλησθεὶς ὀργῆς ἀνεπήδησε καὶ ἦν περιπατῶν (7.9).

56 Day, *Three Faces of a Queen*, 128-29.

57 Because the king had previously expressed his disgust concerning this matter (7.5b), it is most likely that ἁμαρτία is being used here in its ethical sense.

would turn the heart of the king around to hate the one hostile to the Jews. This eventually comes to pass, although not without great suspense and drama. Yet it is interesting to note that the issue at the crux of the matter here is enslavement (7.4a). Though it might seem as if the situation is much graver,[59] Esther has, with good result and with great care, managed to enrage the king to do away with her ἀντίδικος over the prospect (not even the reality!) of Jewish bondage. Divine providence and human skill have come together effectively for the Jewish queen and her people. Even though some tension exists in the midst of that union, there appears to be no ultimate contrariety between them.

4.2.6 The vengeful queen (7.18-21, 46a)

With Aman out of the way,[60] the Jews are left relatively free to change the course of events in the kingdom into their favour. Concerning Esther, this opportunity brings out a more violent side, as we shall observe. Once Aman and his designs are shown to be antithetical to the kingdom, the allegiance of the king swings drastically in favour of the Jews and Jewish causes (§ 4.6.5). But even though Mardochaios becomes the new vizier (7.17),[61] it is Esther who appears to take the reins of power at the moment, especially in matters of life and death.

In view of the fact that 7.18 is one of the major textual points at which the AT narrative comes under discussion concerning its composition history and redaction,[62] we shall continue to focus upon the text that we have before us in

---

58 Day summarises the matter in this way: "Esther's courage is inseparably linked with her piety, for it is only because she first prays to God that she is emboldened in this situation" (*Three Faces of a Queen*, 130).

59 This could be deduced from the heightened states of emotion that govern the scene.

60 The narrative makes the demise of Aman clear. In 7.11d, the king has made it plain that Aman should not live [μὴ ζήτω]. This is followed by the narrator's note in 7.12a that he was led away [οὕτως ἀπήγετο], likely to await execution. The manner of his death is explained in 7.12b-d as Agathas informed the king of the plot of Aman to hang Mardochaios on a stake. The plan of the one condemned was then turned against him as it was pronounced that Aman himself should be hung upon it [Κρεμασθήτω ἐπ᾽ αὐτῷ] (7.13b). This decision was then consummated by the signet ring formality, by which the end of the life of Aman was sealed [καὶ ἐσφραγίσθη ἐν αὐτῷ ὁ βίος αὐτοῦ] (7.13d).

61 "Here it is clearly stated that the affairs of the empire have been placed in the hands of Mordecai" (De Troyer, *The End of the Alpha Text of Esther*, 300).

62 Here is a surface sampling of the discussion: Torrey claims that 7.18-21 serves as a "transitional patch," which sets up the ending of the story taken from the LXX version ("The Older Book of Esther," 16); in a later study entitled, "The *A*-text of the Greek Versions of the Book of Esther," it is H.J. Cook who first suggests that after the corresponding AT equivalent to MT 8.5 (i.e., 7.16) the direction and character of the AT plot

the Göttingen edition, leaving aside hypothetical texts and arguments for the most part. We must admit, however, that from this point in the text forward reading and understanding the Göttingen text is not without its difficulties.[63]

With two Jews in positions of official power, the time is ripe for decisive action. After Mardochaios asks His Majesty for the revocation of the letter of Aman and receives much more (7.16b-17), it is Esther who takes centre stage in a commanding manner, saying:

Δός μοι κολάσαι τοὺς ἐχθρούς μου φόνῳ.

Give me my enemies to punish by slaughter (7.18b).

As pointed (and to the point) as her imperative is,[64] it does leave at least one major gap in understanding: who precisely are *Esther's* enemies? We might assume that these are those enemies of whom she speaks in her prayer – i.e., the enemies of God and the Jews (cf. § 4.2.3).[65] If so, however, we would have expected her to have labelled them as '*our* enemies'. As we continue, the ambiguity remains concerning the particular objects of her wrath. If we take Esther to be the subject of the verb ἐπάταξε in 7.20,[66] only the fact of her vengefulness is clearly perceivable – "and she struck the enemies in great number" [καὶ ἐπάταξε τοὺς ἐχθροὺς εἰς πλῆθος]. Who her enemies are and in which part of the kingdom they are slaughtered is not made clear.

---

changes quite noticeably from what he believed to be its Hebrew predecessor (in the mind of Cook, a recension of the MT) (*ZAW* 81 (1969), 369-76); more recently, Clines, following Torrey and adapting Cook, claims that the original AT narrative ended, though to his mind unsatisfactorily, at 7.17 (8.17 by his versification) (*The Esther Scroll*, ch. 7, esp. 78f.); in response, Fox engages the views of Clines on the original ending of the AT, submitting that Clines' dissatisfaction with 7.17 as the original ending point of the AT could be appeased if 7.18-21 and 33-38 (he numbers these sections viii 18-21 and viii 33-38) were included in the original AT story (*Redaction*, 38). Fox offers considerable argumentation for his views in pages that follow (39-42); for a good discussion of both Clines and Fox concerning this matter, see Jobes, *The Alpha-Text of Esther*, 202-21. For her own unique conclusions about the AT, continue on in the work of Jobes (223-32).

63 Fox lists and discusses a collection of "rough spots" noticed in the redacted AT version (basically, what we find in the Göttingen edition), all of which are found post 7.18 (*Redaction*, 90-92).

64 Cf. De Troyer, *The End of the Alpha Text of Esther*, 302. She goes on to state that "[T]he addition of *with death* gives the punishment something of the character of an 'act of vengeance'" (303 (*emphasis original*)).

65 De Troyer's position is similar here (*The End of the Alpha Text of Esther*, 303).

66 Although the matter is not completely straightforward, since Esther is the subject in 7.18 and continues to direct the action in the following verse, it is most likely that she is the subject of ἐπάταξε in 7.20. Even though it is the case that the king is closest antecedent to ἐπάταξε in the text (7.19c), the context does not particularly support him striking the enemies of Esther at this point. Though complicit in the matter, he is not the instigator or director of the vengeance.

The matter is somewhat different as the narrative relates the treatment of the house of Aman. Here we are at least aware who is bearing the brunt of her animosity. Yet, in this case, the queen consults (conspires?) [ἐνέτυχε] with her husband against the children of Aman "in order that they also should die with their father" [ὅπως ἀποθάνωσι καὶ αὐτοὶ μετὰ τοῦ πατρὸς αὐτῶν] (7.19b). Why she decides to solicit the input of the king concerning this deed after she has unilaterally asserted herself in 7.18 is unknown. Nevertheless, the king consents [Γινέσθω] (7.19c) and places matters of killing solely into the hands of his wife – Ἰδοὺ δίδωμί σοι τοῦ κρεμάσαι (7.21c). Whether this permission for hanging concerns the children of Aman only or has in view a larger scope is unclear. The text does, however, make plain that the house of Aman does not survive (7.37, 44).[67]

Finally, towards the end of the story, we encounter the last and possibly most serious mention of belligerence involving the queen. The exact timing of the following incident is not stated. However, whenever it indeed happens, it seems to be a further violent request of the queen that occurs later in the narrative progression. In 7.45 the king queries Esther as to how her people, both near and far, have availed themselves, giving us the impression that previous conflict(s) have occurred. Forgoing an answer, the queen makes the following request:

Δοθήτω τοῖς Ιουδαίοις οὓς ἐὰν θέλωσιν ἀνελεῖν καὶ διαρπάζειν.

Let it be given to the Jews to kill and plunder whomever they should wish (7.46a).

Is Esther here petitioning for a *carte blanche* authorisation to totally devastate the enemy? It appears so. And with the agreement of the king, the text reports that 70,100 men subsequently pay the ultimate price as a direct result of the queen's wish (7.46b-c). Even if 7.46a is merely giving the details of the slaughter left unspecified in 7.20, as Fox suggests, it is still not the case that the latter account is "pointless," as he claims.[68] At the very least, the account serves to bring added clarity. However, if the advice of the king in 7.28 has gone unheeded and the Jews have indeed been attacked by their enemies according to the decree of Aman in the month of Adar, 7.46a could be describing a *further* conflict in addition to that which had already occurred in 7.20. But it is significant to note that there is no mention of any enemy attack in the context of 7.46a that would have provoked Jewish action. Therefore, Esther *could* have been conducting another offensive strike against her ene-

---

67 De Troyer even submits that "the abusive sons of Haman undergo two executions" (*The End of the Alpha Text of Esther*, 309).
68 Fox, *Redaction*, 137 n. 3.

mies here. Given the way in which the narrative presents itself, we cannot be entirely conclusive concerning the extent of the queen's aggressiveness in all of this, although the basic point of her belligerence is beyond question.

A helpful summary concerning the queen and the matter at hand is put forward by Day in the following words:

> Esther's actions of doing justice are by means of violence. She is a much more forceful, destructive, and violent person in the A text than in the other narratives. This character trait only becomes apparent at the end of the story...and it is only directed towards those who are the Jews' adversaries. Esther is the most concerned about punishment of the adversaries, and, in general, carries out their punishment more herself, by the most forceful and destructive means, and towards the most persons. Because of Esther's requests, the greatest number of people are killed throughout the greatest extent of the kingdom.[69]

The moral character displayed by Esther in the AT story is not always exemplary, especially in the closing portions of the narrative.

4.3 Mardochaios

4.3.1 Loyalty seeking justice (A.11-14)

In a manner quite similar to the opening of the LXX story (§ 3.3.1), the initial verses of the AT narrative put forth a positive view of the character of Mardochaios. Though it is less descriptive of the background of Mardochaios and the present situation in Diaspora, the AT, like its Greek counterpart, mentions his lineage [ὁ τοῦ Ἰαείρου τοῦ Σεμεΐου τοῦ Κισαίου τῆς φυλῆς βενιαμιν], his general standing [ἄνθρωπος μέγας] (at least in the eyes of the narrator), and the reason why he has ended up in a foreign land (A.1b-2). Even though a full portrait of the man is not given, we are able to gather the fact or certainty of his importance – a broad, positive, beginning impression in terms of the moral character that the author seeks to communicate.

We should note, however, that this depiction is initial, incomplete, and likely not even the primary objective in the present purposes of the narrative. In the midst of the introductory words concerning Mardochaios, the immedi-

---

69 Day, *Three Faces of a Queen,* 195. De Troyer, concluding generally, states the matter forthrightly: "Esther is...presented by the AT as a bloodthirsty lady!" (*The End of the Alpha Text of Esther,* 315); and further, "it is clear that the person of Esther has taken on some rather bloodthirsty characteristics: she punishes her enemies without mercy" (399).

ate focus is on his dream.[70] The details of this dream (A.3-8), together with their somewhat elucidating interpretation in 7.53-55, serve as beginning and ending frames for the AT drama.[71] Here is a paraphrase of the ἐνύπνιον of Mardochaios. There is "trouble upon the earth" [τάραχος ἐπὶ τῆς γῆς], as the ear could well hear. A noise [φωνὴ], a cry of uproar [κραυγὴ θορύβου], thunderings [βρονταὶ], and earthquake [σεισμὸς] dominate initial sensations (A.3b). Then comes the visual: two dragons [δύο δράκοντες] approach each other, both ready to fight (A.4). And at their noise (i.e., the sound of their cry), everything is troubled [ἐταράσσετο πάντα] (A.5) A day of darkness [σκότους], gloom [γνόφου], and "a confusion of battle" [ταραχὴ πολέμου] is at hand; every nation is ready to engage in war (A.6a-c).

At a general level we are able to grasp the scene so far, even if we cannot fully understand its significance at this point. Unfortunately, in what is left of this dream description, our ability to perceive is dimmed, even as the text emits a ray of light. As the nations poise for conflict the narrative states that "we uttered a loud cry to the Lord because of the sound of their crying" [καὶ ἀνεβοήσαμεν πρὸς κύριον ἀπὸ φωνῆς τῆς κραυγῆς αὐτῶν] (A.6d). *We* cried out? The text abruptly shifts from describing the dream in a third person manner to a first person one without warning, and without an textual antecedent for the verb ἀνεβοήσαμεν. We might assume, then, that the subject "we" represents the narrator's own people – his community.[72] As a direct result of this heavenward appeal, if we are indeed catching the narrative gist, the following result ensues:

καὶ ἐγένετο ἐκ πηγῆς μικρᾶς ὕδωρ πολύ, ποταμὸς μέγας· φῶς, ἥλιος ἀνέτειλε, καὶ οἱ ποταμοὶ ὑψώθησαν καὶ κατέπιον τοὺς ἐνδόξους.

And there was from a little spring much water, a great river; light, sun arose,[73] and the rivers were exalted and swallowed up the eminent (A.7-8).

---

70 Dorothy, *The Books of Esther*, 48-49.
71 Concerning the frame, see Dorothy, *The Books of Esther*, 276-78.
72 Dorothy suggests that this element might connote a cultic use of this text (*The Books of Esther*, 51). Fox identifies 'we' with Israel and offers the following comment on the first person plural occurrence: "The first-person plural seems to retroject an historical event into the dream itself rather than just aligning event with symbol afterwards in the interpretation. The use of 'we' also highlights the contrast between Israel's wise behavior and the martial preparations of the others. We are probably to understand that 'every nation' preparing for war does not include Israel, for there is an implicit contrast between Israel ('we'), who called upon God, and the others, who did not" (*Redaction*, 74).
73 Fox suggests that the nouns φῶς and ἥλιος, with the singular verb, ἀνέτειλε, appear to be "an apposition," showing the two nouns to be one symbol (*Redaction*, 75 n. 75).

To be sure, the meaning and implications of the dream, especially this last part, are obscure to both Mardochaios and the reader. Behind the symbolism, however, he realises that the "Mighty One" [ὁ δυνατος] is preparing to do something, but Mardochaios remains at a loss to understand the deeper significance (A.9). His persistence to apprehend his dream, however, would soon pay off (A.10).

Later in time when Mardochaios is sleeping in the courtyard near two eunuchs of the king, Astaos and Thedeutes, the "verification" [ἐπίκρισις] of his dream becomes clear to him [διασαφηθήσεται αὐτῷ] (A.11).[74] Just what this ἐπίκρισις is and what exactly becomes plain to Mardochaios is unfortunately not so apparent to the reader. We are under the impression from A.11 that the interpretation of his dream no longer escapes him. But only in the last verses of the narrative does Mardochaios offer anything close to a point-by-point explanation of it (cf. 7.53f.). Yet it is at this present time, as he lies close in proximity to Astaos and Thedeutes, that the ἐπίκρισις of the dream becomes obvious to Mardochaios. Though the narrative logic is a bit difficult to follow here, we assume that it is in his overhearing of the words [λόγους] and slanders [διαβολας] of the eunuchs that Mardochaios begins to ascertain the deeper meanings of his dream. The precise connections he makes, however, are not evident to us.[75] What Mardochaios learns as he listens (according to the narrative), is that the king would soon be (if he is not presently) in fatal danger at the hands of Astaos and Thedeutes (A.12). Such significant knowledge induces Mardochaios, already being well-disposed to the king [εὖ δὲ φρονήσας ὁ Μαρδοχαῖος], to report the matter to His Majesty (A.13).

Once the king examines [ἤτασεν] the eunuchs and confirms the veracity of the accusation against them, it is reported that the fate of Astaos and Thedeutes is sealed (A.14). Upon this the court standing of Mardochaios is sure to improve. Indeed, the first step towards this occurs when the king enters a written record of the loyalty of Mardochaios into the royal book so that his deed would be remembered (A.15; cf. 6.1-3). What is more, Mardochaios is charged to serve in the court of the king by conspicuously watching every door [πᾶσαν θύραν ἐπιφανῶς τηρεῖν] (A.16). In other words, he is now officially employed to do just what he had done in the uncovering of the previous regicide plot. But lastly and of most significance in the story, the text relates the final reward Mardochaios receives in this manner:

---

74 Following the rendering decisions of Fox (*Redaction*, 76).

75 Consider the explanation of Fox: "Perhaps the point is that Haman was embittered by the exposure of his subordinates and came into conflict with Mordecai (i 18), and in this conflict Mordecai recognized the two dragon and saw how the dream's portents would be realized." Yet Fox admits that "this possibility is at most hinted at" (*Redaction*, 77).

καὶ ἔδωκεν αὐτῷ περὶ τούτων Αμαν Αμαδάθου Μακεδόνα κατὰ πρόσωπον
τοῦ βασιλέως.

And he [i.e., the king] gave him, for these things, Aman son of Amadatha, a Macedonian, (who served?) before the presence of the king (A.17).

Though it is expressed difficultly, the thrust of A.17 is simply this: as a reward for his loyal act Mardochaios would now have charge over Aman. Why
the king grants this is not stated. Given the recent show of commitment to
His Majesty, the reward of Aman's services might have been a political move
so that the king could keep a close eye on the Macedonian (foreigner) in his
court (cf. § 3.4.5).[76] If so, the suspicions of the king are correct, for Aman
appears to have been involved in some way in the eunuch's assassination try
(A.18b). This explanation, however, proves less likely when it is weighed
against the promotion of Aman in 3.1f. To be sure, in the scope of the entire
story, the decisions of the king are often difficult to understand and harmonise. What we can say, at the very least, is that here we have witnessed Mardochaios and Aman having been brought together at an early point in the
narrative: the former in order to stress his fidelity to the king and his kingdom; the latter in order to introduce his animosity towards both the king and
his kingdom, and Mardochaios and his people[77] [καὶ ἐζήτει ὁ Αμαν κακοποιῆσαι τὸν Μαρδοχαῖον καὶ πάντα τὸν λαὸν αὐτοῦ] (A.18a). The
loyalty of Mardochaios has not served *all* in the court well.

4.3.2 Refusal to bow before Aman (3.1-4; 4.15)

As the story shows, whatever dominion Mardochaios is given over his court
colleague is not permanent. For reasons unknown to the reader (if they actually exist), the king "was strengthening" [ἐμεγάλυνεν] Αμαν Αμαδάθου
Βουγαῖον (3.1αβ). His Majesty then "exalts" [ἐπῆρεν] Aman – elevating his
official position in the court above his peers [καὶ ἔθηκε τὸν θρόνον αὐτοῦ
ὑπεράνω τῶν φίλων αὐτοῦ] (3.1b). While the reader is fully aware of the
darker side of Aman (A.18), the king is obviously not so cognisant. Thus, as
His Majesty lifts the seat of one who has been implicated in the former regicide attempt to the second position in the kingdom (4.4), we sense a disas-

---

76 Kottsieper, *Zusätze zu Ester,* 149.
77 Jobes, *The Alpha-Text of Esther,* 191. Jobes notes that the conflict of Aman with Mar-
    dochaios here is a political matter, not a personal one. Cf. further the develop-
    ment/complication of this hatred in § 4.3.2.

trous scenario emerging (A.18). But just in case a connection is not made in the mind of the reader, the label, Βουγαῖον, attached onto the name of Aman in this instance, might serve to prod the memory.

As we observed in § 3.3.3 this appellation is in no way a flattering one. Indeed, the most thorough research on the matter suggests that the epithet, Βουγαῖον, alludes historically to the anti-Jewish and subversive proclivities of Aman.[78] With the appearance of the label, Μακεδόνα, which follows the name of Aman earlier in the narrative in the context of his vague connection with the failed assassination attempt (A.17), the seditious proclivities of Aman might be suggested. In the end, his deep-seated plot to overthrow the king is finally realised by His Majesty (7.25-26). Yet it is the anti-Jewishness of Aman that appears to be in focus at the present moment as Mardochaios is faced with a difficult decision as a result of the promoting act of the king.

Upon assuming his new and lofty position of power Aman expects all to bow down as they assume the formal posture of prostration upon the ground before him (3.1c).[79] This is the command [πρόσταγμα] of the king and it is reported that all are abiding by it (3.2a). Everyone except his former superior, that is [Μαρδοχαῖος οὐ προσεκύνει αὐτῷ] (3.2b); one notable in the court remains standing. At this point we are not clear as to the reasons for the abstinence of Mardochaios. Court politics have changed once again – reshuffling the order of power – but the decision of Mardochaios to refuse the command of the king in this manner is difficult to understand. Even if Mardochaios has been made to eat sour grapes by being passed over concerning the promotion that Aman had received, this would not seem to be the best manner of protest. Our curiosity at this spectacle is shared by the παῖδες of the king who subsequently question Mardochaios over his unyieldingness:

Τί σὺ παρακούεις τοῦ βασιλέως καὶ οὐ προσκυνεῖς τὸν Αμαν;

Why are you disregarding[80] the king and not prostrating (before) Aman (3.3c)?

The emphasis provided by the personal pronoun, σὺ, combined with the strength of the initial verb, παρακούεις, together serve to communicate the extent to which those in the court were aghast at inaction of Mardochaios. Their inquiring minds would only be satisfied when he informed them that he

---

78 Jobes adequately surveys the issue in two places: *The Alpha-Text of Esther,* 124-28; and "How an Assassination Changed the Greek Text of Esther," 75-78.

79 For discussion on the likelihood that προσκυνεῖν is being communicated in this formal, physical way, see § 3.3.3.

80 Lit: "striking aside" (LS, 598). The picture presented here appears to be that of Mardochaios thrusting aside the royal command, not merely ignoring it passively.

is a Jew (3.4a). Soon after this revelation, Aman is made aware of the 'Mardochaios situation' (3.4b). By the absence of any follow up questions by the παῖδες we might assume that the Jew has adequately explained his behaviour to the court onlookers by disclosing his ethnic identity. And as we witness the furious reaction of Aman, which prompts him to begin (reinvigorate? cf. A.18) his quest to destroy Mardochaios and his people (3.5), we could get the impression that the Jewishness of Mardochaios stands at the heart of the animosity of Aman towards him, and subsequently, his people (§ 4.4.2). These are, at least, possible deductions. Nevertheless, concerning his own reasons for refusing to bow, we are left to wonder at this particular point. Even if it is the case that both the παῖδες and Aman apprehend the full measure of the Jew's admission, the reader is not so privileged.

We must continue on in the story if we are to begin to penetrate into the deeper thoughts of Mardochaios. We encounter this depth along with an explanation of his refusal not to prostrate before Aman in a moving prayer from his own lips (4.12b-17). Since this prayer reflects back on the events of chapter three it seems fair to analyse it at this point, for we are in a way receiving a description of the thought processes of Mardochaios as he was faced with the questions and pressures of that (chapter three) time. In looking at chapter four it is helpful to note that the prayerful words of Mardochaios are given in retrospect because the genocidal edict of Aman against the Jews had been decreed in the meantime (3.5f.). Even in the face of this, Mardochaios remains strong in his religious convictions as he beseeches his Lord (4.12b).

Like the prayer of Esther, which follows (4.18-29), the prayer of Mardochaios bases its hope in the covenant that God has made with God's chosen people. The Lord must not neglect the portion chosen in Abraham and redeemed out of the land of Egypt (4.16-17).[81] Mardochaios pleads for mercy on this basis, knowing that his "almighty Master" [Δέσποτα παντοκράτορ] knows all things including the extent of his/their desperate plight (4.13-14). Whether or not he feels some measure of responsibility for the straits the Jews are now in is not readily apparent. Yet the way in which Mardochaios approaches the Lord in this instance might lead one to posit that he is feeling pressure from within or without surrounding his role in bringing about the impending disaster. The text, however, is not so explicit. It does, nevertheless, exhibit the distinct message in 4.15 concerning his intent to put the record straight about the unyielding stance he took in chapter three.

In the midst of his prayer Mardochaios expresses his heart, saying that it was neither

---

81   Jobes, *The Alpha-Text of Esther*, 176f.

ἐν ὕβρει οὐδὲ ἐν φιλοδοξίᾳ ἐποίησα τοῦ μὴ προσκυνεῖν τὸν ἀπερίτμητον
Αμαν, ἐπεὶ εὐδόκουν φιλῆσαι τὰ πέλματα τῶν ποδῶν αὐτοῦ ἕνεκεν τοῦ Ισ-
ραηλ· ἀλλ᾿ ἐποίησα ἵνα μηδένα προτάξω τῆς δόξης σοῦ, δέσποτα, καὶ
μηδένα προσκυνήσω πλὴν σοῦ τοῦ ἀληθινοῦ καὶ οὐ ποιήσω αὐτὸ ἐν πει-
ρασμῷ.

in insolence nor in vainglory [that] I acted in not doing obeisance to the uncircumcised Aman, since I would have been well pleased to kiss the soles of his [i.e.,
Aman's] feet for the sake of Israel; but I acted in order that I might place no one in
front of your glory, O Master, and I will do obeisance [to] no one except you, the true
One, and I will not do it in (under) trial (4.15).

The message here is stated clearly: Mardochaios' loyalty to God prohibits
him from prostrating himself in front of Aman even under the fiercest pressure. The reasoning behind it, however, is not necessarily easy to follow.
Mardochaios submits that he is not an arrogant man and that he would be
happy to do many things for the sake of his people, even if it means kissing
the feet of Aman. To be sure, the kissing of another's feet is no trivial manner; humble deference would be associated with such an act,[82] and Mardochaios is even prepared to do such a thing to one who is uncircumcised![83] Yet
the Jew staunchly refuses to show his courtly respect and bow before his
(now) court superior claiming that he is reserving that posture only for his
δέσποτα.[84] There are likely deeper issues involved. As in the conclusion of
§ 3.3.3, it is probable that when confronted with the decision whether or not to
uphold the command of the king and prostrate himself before Aman, Mardochaios refuses on *religious* grounds. The implication here is that if Mardochaios bows to Aman he would be giving him honour that is reserved for God
– in some sense, committing idolatry. Although this understanding lies beyond the formal, physical sense of προσκυνέω, it appears to be his theologi-

---

82 Yet one gathers that feet-kissing does not carry the same burden as the act of prostration
    would in this particular context (Kottsieper [following Ryssel], *Zusätze zu Ester*, 163 n.
    167).

83 Later in the narrative, we observe that not only would Mardochaios be pleased to kiss
    the feet of Aman, he would also obey him when commanded to "[T]ake off the sack-
    cloth" [Περιελοῦ τὸν σάκκον] as he mourned the plight of his people (6.15-16). This
    concrete example of what Mardochaios actually *did do* in the presence of Aman, cou-
    pled with his spoken assurance to God of what he was prepared to do for him, serves to
    complicate our understanding of the unwillingness of the Jew to prostrate himself before
    the vizier. We must search out this discrepancy to some satisfying extent (see § 4.3.5).

84 As noted in § 3.3.3, Wills points out possible parallels with the "Jewish martyr ac-
    counts" of 2 Macc 6-7 that could be drawn here. In the 2 Macc text "Jews are given op-
    portunities to save other Jews by refusing to cheat God of the divine glory" (*The Jewish
    Novel in the Ancient World*, 121).

cal interpretation of the crisis he faces.[85] In the end, we can safely say that his jealousy for the glory of God is indisputable, even if every question concerning his behaviour cannot be satisfactorily understood or answered.

4.3.3 Refusal to transgress court regulations (4.2)

By this point in the narrative chronologically, the pent-up fury of Aman against Mardochaios and the Jews – first ignited in section A (17-18) and later fuelled in 3.1-6b – has finally come to a boil (3.6c, 8-9). A vicious and propagandistic vizierial initiative of genocide has been levelled against Jews everywhere (§ 4.4.2) – a plan that even has royal backing (§ 4.6.3). Thus, the future is looking increasingly bleak for Mardochaios and the Jews. When Mardochaios finds out about the decree we notice that his reaction is under control, even as he shows the signs of grief.

As the edict is made public in the capital (3.19) it is reported that the city of Sousa is "confounded" [ἐταράσσετο].[86] And since the narrative goes on to detail the reaction of the Jews throughout the empire to the news – being in "great and bitter grief" [πένθος μέγα καὶ πικρὸν] – we might assume that the difficulty the Sousians have with the decree hints that its effect stretches across ethnic lines. That is to say, Jews do not appear to be the only persons emotionally affected by the plans of Aman. However, the story does not concentrate on the Gentile or even corporate Jewish reaction beyond this. It focuses instead on the particular response of Mardochaios, relating that after he had put on sackcloth and ashes,

ἐξῆλθεν ὡς ἐπὶ τὴν αὐλὴν τὴν ἔξω καὶ ἔστη· οὐ γὰρ ἠδύνατο εἰσελθεῖν εἰς τὰ βασίλεια ἐν σάκκῳ.

he went out as up to the outer court and stood; for he was not able to enter into the palace in sackcloth (4.2bβ-γ).

In his moment of great grief, we distinctly notice the composure of Mardochaios. Even though the impending danger for the Jews has resulted from his inaction in 3.3 (or so we gather), Mardochaios does not resort to desperate measures when the reader might have expected him to. Instead of taking in the law into his own hands, we are told that he follows the official regulations

---

85   Cf. Kottsieper, *Zusätze zu Ester,* 163-65. In the context of the prayer of Mardochaios, Kottsieper holds that prostration before Aman to be "cultic veneration" (*kultische Verehrung*), which was reserved only for God.

86   See the relevant footnote concerning the sense of ἐταράσσετο in § 3.2.2.

by not transgressing court custom. In this instance (and in general, it should be said), the Jew lives within the civil rules of his adopted society.

4.3.4 Instructing Esther (4.4b-c)

As he stands there mourning in the outer court, Mardochaios gathers his thoughts and focuses on what can be done for the people who are now in dire straits. It would seem that Queen Esther is their best human hope, and Mardochaios therefore initiates communications with her (4.3a). She responds to him, wishing her cousin to come into the palace and speak face to face with her (4.3b). However, Mardochaios is not willing to dissociate himself from the rites of mourning[87] and chooses to continue their mediated dialogue as it had begun, though in an escalated and more intense manner. He is seemingly uninterested in protocol at the moment and wishes to arrive straight at the point concerning the situation of the Jews and what he believes to be the queen's upcoming responsibility in the matter. His address to his cousin is a pointed one:

Μὴ ἀποστρέψῃς τοῦ εἰσελθεῖν πρὸς τὸν βασιλέα καὶ κολακεῦσαι τὸ πρόσωπον αὐτοῦ ὑπὲρ ἐμοῦ καὶ τοῦ λαοῦ

Do not refuse[88] to go in to the king or to flatter him[89] in behalf of me and the people (4.4b-c).

Why Mardochaios singles himself out in this instance alongside the Jews as a whole is puzzling. It might be that he is in some way acknowledging responsibility for his inactions in 3.2f. which, in an extraordinary turn of events, have landed the Jews in their present predicament. Nevertheless, to argue this possibility seriously would demand much more contextual evidence than we are given either here or in the entire story. The more pressing question at present concerns how Esther is to approach the king, not on whose behalf she ought to enter into his inner chambers.

Governed by the prohibitive subjunctive, Μὴ ἀποστρέψῃς, Mardochaios sets out what Dorothy calls a "dual prohibition."[90] This circumscribes both what Esther is to do, and in what manner she is to do it. In other words, it is

---

87 Why Mardochaios chooses to remain in sackcloth and ashes outside of the immediate presence of Esther is not known. However, a few suggestions were put forward in the relevant portions of § 4.2.1.

88 Following the rendering of Clines (*The Esther Scroll*, 227).

89 Lit: "his face."

90 Dorothy, *The Books of Esther*, 110.

made clear that the queen must not refuse to enter into the presence of her husband. But also, as she approaches him, Esther must not shrink back from *flattering* the king for the sake of her cousin and her people. What exactly is being expressed here by the use of κολακεῦσαι is difficult to conclude. Is Esther simply to employ inducing rhetorical techniques in her task of persuasion? Or is there something more implied in the command of Mardochaios? At the very least it seems certain that the Jew is demanding a measure of resourcefulness on that part of Esther as she enters into the presence of the king.[91] Thus, we are left to ponder his ambiguous instructions concerning her *modus operandi* before the royal throne.[92]

4.3.5 Obedience to Aman (6.15-16)

With the exception of the prayer of Mardochaios related in 4.12b-17, the narrative turns to focus on Esther and the beginnings of her efforts for her people after the mediated exchange between the outer court and the inner palace. We observe her prayerful preparations (4.18-29) as well as her actual physical entrance into the presence of the king (5.1f.) in the course of the story which follows. Yet with the coming of chapter six, the text takes up the character of Mardochaios once again; he is not simply left in the outer court in mourning garb.

Mardochaios has not wandered far from the scene of the action, for our next encounter of him likely takes place near the palace, if not within it. In the midst of the efforts of Esther, and on the night before Aman plans to approach the king to request permission to kill Mardochaios, the text explicitly

---

91 In a related comment concerning the intelligence Esther shows in the AT, Day contends that Esther is "an independent thinker" in this particular text. In her support of this claim, Day suggests that the queen did not follow what she calls the "suggestion" of Mardochaios for Esther "to flatter the king to get her way." Instead, the clever queen devised "her own ideas of how best to approach him" (Day, *Three Faces of a Queen*, 194). Day appears to have an idea of just what might have been entailed in the (strong) suggestion of Mardochaios to Esther to flatter her husband. But, in her mind, the flattering techniques are never realised because Esther chose to approach the king in the manner that she deemed best. In an alternative explanation, it could be said that the decisions that the queen subsequently took in her time before the king might have been the actual *manifestation* of her flattering (ch. 5; 7.1-12a). This, to be sure, requires a broader understanding of κολακεύω.

92 Cf. the *modus operandi* of Judith as she approaches Holofernes (Jud 10.6-12.20). Nickelsburg asserts that her *m.o.* is clearly deceit ("Stories of Biblical and Early Postbiblical Times," in M.E. Stone (ed.), *Jewish Writings of the Second Temple Period* (CRINT 2.2; Assen/Philadelphia: Van Gorcum/Fortress Press, 1984), 47). We are not given sufficient detail in Esther's case to be able to make such a judgement.

states that ὁ δυνατος caused His Majesty to be wakeful (6.1). Since he is unable to sleep, the king desires some reading to be done for him from the book of memorials [τὸ βιβλίον τῶν μνημοσυνῶν] (6.2). As his readers oblige him, they come upon the account of the regicide attempt which Mardochaios had spoiled (6.3; cf. A.15). The reminder[93] of this close call in past days affects the king as he listens in the still of the night, causing him to focus intensely upon the matter [καὶ ἐπέστησεν ὁ βασιλεὺς τὸν νοῦν σφόδρα] (6.4a). Not remembering (or perhaps misremembering) the former events, His Majesty fears that the faithful Mardochaios has not been rewarded – an oversight on his part that would call royal justice into question (6.4b-d; cf. A.16-17!). But as the court servants ponder just what should now be done for the saviour of the king, the clear recollection of past events seems not to have eluded them – ἐνέκειτο γὰρ φόβος Αμαν ἐν τοῖς σπλάγχνοις αὐτῶν (6.5). With this gut-wrenching description, our impression is that those in the court are becoming increasingly uncomfortable with how the early hours of the night are shaping up. The servants are obviously aware of the animosity between Aman and Mardochaios (3.3-4) – perhaps even from the very beginnings (A.18).[94] The time bomb that they thought might remain buried within the annals is being resurrected by royal enquiries. This, in turn, strikes great fear into them. As they ruminate in trepidation, the text reports also that the king is reflective [καὶ ἐνόησεν ὁ βασιλεύς] (6.6a). Exactly what the king reflects upon, however, is not clear. From the context we cannot be sure that he is thinking about anything more than how to (further) reward Mardochaios for his saving deed.[95] The minds of the court labour until dawn (6.6b).

---

93 The way in which the narrative presents it, it is questionable whether His Majesty remembered the past events at all.

94 Dorothy, *The Books of Esther,* 149.

95 Clines renders the verb ἐνόησεν, "understood," but offers no comment on the contextual implications of that decision (*The Esther Scroll,* 235). Dorothy appears to follow or at least agree with the translation of Clines and realises that this rendering makes for a confusing narrative understanding. If this translation and subsequent connotation is supplied, a serious question arises: just what did the king understand? Dorothy offers some comment concerning the ambiguity. If the king now understands the nature of the plot of Aman against Mardochaios, the servants must have so informed him. However, the narrative does not even hint in this direction. Does God intervene once more and make things clear to the king concerning the dynamics of his court, thus paving the way for the "peripetic reversal" of the fortunes of both Aman and Mardochaios? If so, why does the narrative choose here to keep implicit what it has explicitly sounded throughout the narrative – i.e., that God is playing an active part in the story? A theological explanation appears shallow given the way the text is presented. Dorothy figures that one option or the other is a likely explanation of the vagueness at the point (*The Books of Esther,* 150). However, retreating a bit, it might not be that "understood" is the best way to render the verb ἐνόησεν here. Contextually speaking, the translation above, "reflected," fits better

With the arrival of Aman in the first hours of light, the story begins to move forward once again. His purpose in paying such an early visit to the king centres around the previously adopted plans to have Mardochaios hanged (6.7; § 4.4.5). But before he can make his intentions known the king queries him with the following words:

Τί ποιήσωμεν τῷ ἀνδρὶ τῷ τὸν βασιλέα τιμῶντι, ὃν ὁ βασιλεὺς βούλεται δοξάσαι;

What will we do for the man, the one who honours the king, whom the king wishes to magnify (6.9b-c)?

Supposing that the court has still not determined the proper reward for the heroism of Mardochaios, it seems possible that the king is now giving Aman a chance to offer suggestions.[96] But His Majesty leaves his question unspecific concerning the desired object of his magnifying – a void that is conceitedly filled by Aman in his own thoughts (6.10). Believing that he must be the one in line for further exaltation, the second in command concocts an extravagant string of royal accolades, complete with a royal robe, a royal horse and an exalted procession through the street (6.11). Finally someone has thought of something appropriate; the king instructs Aman to "[R]un quickly" [Ταχὺ δράμε] and carry out what he has suggested. But there is an ironic twist – the honours that Aman has envisioned for himself are to be for Mardochaios (6.12a-c)! This is the will of the king and the vizier should not waste any time in implementing it [καὶ μὴ παραπεσάτω ὁ λόγος σου] (6.12d). To be sure, Aman is totally devastated at his turn of fortunes,[97] but must proceed with the adopted plan of the king (6.13). It is quite ironic that on the very day Aman seeks to hang his enemy, the deflated vizier is on his way in order to show respect [ἐντρεπόμενος] to Mardochaios with the robe and the horse that he had imagined for himself (6.14).

We might assume that crestfallenness soon turns into agitation. Thus, for Mardochaios, the sight of the disgruntled vizier making hasty strides towards

---

and saves us from having to entertain the suppositions of Dorothy. If we posit that the king was merely reflecting simultaneously upon the matter of the reward for Mardochaios with his servants, the story reads well. However, if we incorporate the king's full or even partial understanding of the Aman-Mardochaios problem at this point, we might expect the king to act differently towards Aman in the rest of the episode that he actually does, especially if his has gained knowledge of the involvement of Aman in the regicide plot.

96 This appears to be the case as Josephus tells the Esther story (*Ant.* 11.251-252).

97 The text is quite emotionally descriptive here: ὡς δὲ ἔγνω Αμαν ὅτι οὐκ ἦν αὐτὸς ὁ δοξαζόμενος, ἀλλ᾽ ὅτι Μαρδοχαῖος, συνετρίβη ἡ καρδία αὐτοῦ σφόδρα, καὶ μετέβαλε τὸ πνεῦμα αὐτοῦ ἐν ἐκλύσει (6.13).

him would likely not have been a pleasant experience. The Jew is unaware of all of the recent discussions and happenings of the court. Therefore, when Aman commands him to "[T]ake off the sackcloth!" [Περιελοῦ τὸν σάκκον] (6.15b), his reaction is worth noting:

καὶ ἐταράχθη Μαρδοχαῖος ὡς ἀποθνῇσκων καὶ ἀπεδύσατο μετ' ὀδύνης τὸν σάκκον καὶ ἐνεδύσατο ἱμάτια δόξης.

Mardochaios was troubled[98] as one who is dying and in the midst of distress stripped off the sackcloth and put on garments of glory (6.16).

Though under the weight of obvious mental and emotional agony, it should be highlighted nevertheless that Mardochaios submits himself to the wishes of Aman in this instance. Whereas previously the Jew had fought any show of obedience or submission whatsoever to Aman (3.1-4; 4.15), here Mardochaios obeys his adversary when he encounters him face to face. Why the change in behaviour? Is the pressure to change clothes any greater than it was to prostrate himself?

Perhaps prostrating himself before Aman and following his wishes in this particular instance and manner are two distinct matters for the Jew. The reader might have expected Mardochaios to have defied the vizier once more at this point, especially as he sits there in sackcloth, still mourning the plight of his condemned people. However, and curiously, this is not the case, making our assessment of his moral character more difficult. The end result is, of course, positive for the Jew as he is honoured by Aman (6.18-19) and subsequently replaces the vizier professionally after his death (7.15-17).

4.4 Aman

4.4.1 Seeds of hatred (A.17-18)

Although we have met the character of Aman in the midst of our comments above concerning Esther and Mardochaios, even receiving an abstract of his moral character coincidentally, it would be profitable at this point to focus upon him in a more concentrated manner.

We first encounter Aman in section A in the midst of the details surrounding the account of attempted regicide (A.11-18). Finding Aman here appears

---

98 Following Clines (*The Esther Scroll,* 237), and because of the particular picture given in the context here – Mardochaios appearing as a dying man – the rendering "troubled" seems best to relay the sense of the verb ἐταράχθη.

to be no coincidence. After Mardochaios had successfully defused the assassination plot of Astaos and Thedeutes, the king determines to reward his saviour. In addition to officially recording an account of the event in the book of the king [τῷ βιβλίῳ τοῦ βασιλέως] for remembrance (A.15), the king appoints Mardochaios to serve in the court as a (or the chief?) door watcher or keeper (A.16). The prominence of this new position seems clear enough, even if we cannot really grasp the political intricacies of the court in full detail. Yet it is the final reward of His Majesty to Mardochaios that has the most impact upon the story: Αμαν Αμαδάθου Μακεδόνα is given to Mardochaios – i.e., Mardochaios is now the court superior of Aman.

All of this serves to underline the "importance and value" of Mardochaios to the king and his empire, as Fox suggests.[99] Nevertheless, how are we to understand this seemingly significant development? Perhaps Aman was formerly the head of the palace guard, and in the aftermath of the recent assassination attempt the king intends to replace his inadequate chief protector with Mardochaios – a man who has proved himself to be extremely loyal and effective in guarding him. We might even suppose that the label, Μακεδόνα, is important here.[100] If this scenario (or something like it) is plausible, we would be in better stead to make sense of the following developments. After we learn that Aman is now to follow the orders of Mardochaios, the text discloses this shocking revelation:

καὶ ἐζήτει ὁ Αμαν κακοποιῆσαι τὸν Μαρδοχαῖον καὶ πάντα τὸν λαὸν αὐτοῦ ὑπὲρ τοῦ λελαληκέναι αὐτὸν τῷ βασιλεῖ περὶ τῶν εὐνούχων, διότι ἀνῃρέθησαν.

Aman was seeking to maltreat Mardochaios and all his people because he had spoken to the king in reference to the eunuchs, because they were taken away (A.18).

Although we might have some trouble understanding the way things have developed in this episode, it is plain to see from what the narrative relates that Aman desires to harm Mardochaios because he had thwarted the plans for regicide. What is also implied in A.18 is that Aman is somehow involved in the foiled plot of the eunuchs. Having this information early on in the narrative, we become aware of his personal animosity towards both Mardochaios and the king(dom). However, it is not readily apparent why Aman targets the people of Mardochaios for maltreatment along with him (cf. § 3.4.1). Why are the people of Mardochaios included as accompanying objects

---

99 Fox, *Redaction*, 77-78.
100 See the general discussion of this epithet in § 3.4.5 and 4.3.1. For more specific comments particularly concerning the presence of the label "Makedone" in AT A.17-18, see Kottsieper, *Zusätze zu Ester*, 148-49.

of hostility? Is the wrath of Aman so great that it can only be satisfied in the harming of the entire race of his antagonist? Furthermore, does Aman even know who the people of Mardochaios are at this point? If he does, we are certainly not told so. For now, we shall keep in the back of our minds that the enmity of Aman towards Mardochaios and his people begins early on in the story; we must wait a few more chapters in order to see that hostility mature. At present, the danger resides only in the vengeful thoughts of Aman.

4.4.2 Heightened enmity (3.5-6, 8-9)[101]

It comes as no great surprise to witness the resurfacing of the Aman-Mardochaios conflict which began to develop in the events surrounding the regicide account and in the mind of Aman. This inceptive enmity that Aman felt in A.18 would soon become greatly intensified, more specifically directed, and finally solidified by means of a royal decree that would now threaten Mardochaios and his people with extinction in a real, palpable way.

As we witnessed in § 4.3.2, chapter three begins with the inexplicable rise of Αμαν Αμαδάθου Βουγαῖον to a high place in the court (3.1a). We recognise this figure from his mention in section A, but the new label, Βουγαῖον, had not yet been seen. Nevertheless, this Aman appears to be the same person that we encountered in the beginning of the story, although there he is given the label Μακεδόνα (A.17bα).[102] His lofty promotion brings along with it one notable personal benefit – the prostration of all before the new vizier by royal decree (3.1b). It is quite likely that this show of subservience is treasured by the new vizier, for when it is told to him that someone in the court was neglecting his postural duty, the reaction of Aman is unreserved:

---

101 Without any explanation, the versification proceeds oddly between 3.6 and 3.13. The text appears to be in a logical order as it reads, but one must follow a numeration that is out of normal sequence. Verse eight and nine follow verse six, but verse eleven follows verse nine. Verse eleven then precedes verse ten, which is followed by verse seven. After this, verse thirteen comes, but there is no verse twelve in the sequence. Given alternatively, this odd sequence runs as follows: 6, 8, 9, 11, 10, 7, 13. It should be noted that rearranging text in an order following the 'correct' sequence of numbers would not be quite as satisfying in terms of the narrative. We shall follow the sequence that occurs in the Göttingen edition.
102 Since we have explored the epithets Βουγαῖος and Μακεδόνα heretofore, we shall not re-enter those discussion again at the present time (see § 3.3.3, 3.4.2, 3.4.5, 4.3.1, and 4.3.2).

ὡς δὲ ἤκουσεν Αμαν, ἐθυμώθη τῷ Μαρδοχαίῳ, καὶ ὀργὴ ἐξεκαύθη ἐν
αὐτῷ...καὶ παραζηλώσας ὁ Αμαν καὶ κινηθεὶς ἐν παντὶ τῷ θυμῷ αὐτοῦ
ἐρυθρὸς ἐγένετο ἐκτρέπων αὐτὸν ἐξ ὀφθαλμῶν αὐτοῦ.

But when Aman heard, he was enraged against Mardochaios and anger was kindled
within him...and Aman, provoked to jealously and being stirred up in all his soul, became red, turning him [Mardochaios] aside out of his sight[103] (3.5a-b; 3.6a-b).

On second thought, describing his reaction as "unreserved" grossly under-
states the case – the vizier is clearly repulsed at the noncompliance of Mardochaios. For anyone – especially one who had recently been his superior
(A.17) – to refuse this duty is a serious offence to Aman; one could even say
that it would be unforgivable. Judging by the practical materialisation of the
rage of Aman, Mardochaios and all his people would now suffer fatal consequences as a result. There would be no second chances with Aman; the
παῖδες of the king have given Mardochaios all the time they could (3.3-5).

Yet it is not certain what exactly ignites such wrath in the vizier. When the
report comes to him, Aman likely learns both that Mardochaios is not prostrating himself and that he is refusing on the grounds that he is Jewish
(3.4).[104] Nevertheless, we are not sure as to which of these pieces of information actually causes such a furious recoil, if not both in combination. The text
relates only that Aman hears [ἤκουσεν] (3.5a). While we can safely say that
what he hears is the report given to him, that just brings us back to wonder
what is specifically entailed *in* that report. Let us assume for the moment that
at the very least Aman is informed of the inaction of Mardochaios and of his
race. And although it would strike us as odd if Aman is indifferent concerning the ethnicity of Mardochaios, we must confess the text is ambiguous
about the matter at this point. Does Aman only consider his honour at stake
here? Or is it that his pride is damaged, his prestige somehow threatened, by
the unwillingness of a *Jew*? In what follows we shall begin to receive some
obscure clues.

---

103 Clines renders ἐκτρέπων αὐτὸν ἐξ ὀφθαλμῶν αὐτοῦ "ordering him out of his sight"
(*The Esther Scroll*, 223), while Dorothy interprets the entire phrase to signal the banishment of Mardochaios from Aman's presence (*The Books of Esther*, 86). I am inclined
to think that the translation of Clines catches the gist here, and even that the interpretation of Dorothy carries the Greek to its logical conclusion.

104 Actually the text does not communicate this so specifically. From 3.4, we must assume
that both the unwilling posture *and* the (apparent) reason for the unyieldingness of Mardochaios were included in the report. And concerning the latter it is only by implication
that we can assume that the Jewishness of Mardochaios was the reason behind his refusal to bow. It is, however, most likely that being a Jew somehow prohibited Mardochaios from prostrating before Aman. The question of how that is to be understood is
taken up in § 4.3.2.

After the initial description of how the information of the παῖδες affects Aman – kindling his anger – we learn that he was seeking to destroy Mardochaios and all of his people on one day [καὶ ἐζήτει ἀνελεῖν τὸν Μαρδοχαῖον καὶ πάντα τὸν λαὸν αὐτοῦ ἐν ἡμέρᾳ μιᾷ] (5.5c). The animosity of the vizier has definitely intensified from the feelings we encountered in A.18a. There, Aman was only seeking to maltreat [κακοποιῆσαι] Mardochaios and his people; now, his ill-will has blossomed into a threat directed against the entire Jewish race (if our assumptions about the contents of the report are correct concerning his knowledge about the race of Mardochaios). Yet following the account of how the resentment of Aman is inflamed, so as to turn his colour red, the narrator informs us that "with an evil heart he was speaking bad [things] to the king concerning Israel" [καὶ καρδίᾳ φαύλῃ ἐλάλει τῷ βασιλεῖ κακὰ περὶ Ισραηλ] (3.6c) – a further clue, given by the narrator, that Aman has the Jews in mind. Yet, actually, in the presence of the king Aman is much more tactful: he declaims against "a people scattered abroad in all the kingdoms" [λαὸς διεσπαρμένος ἐν πάσαις ταῖς βασιλείαις] (3.8aα). In his presentation to His Majesty the vizier does not disclose the identity of the Jews but slanders them only as

λαὸς πολέμου καὶ ἀπειθής, ἐξαλλα νόμιμα ἔχων, τοῖς δὲ νομίμοις σου, βασιλεῦ, οὐ προσέχουσι γνωριζόμενοι ἐν πᾶσι τοῖς ἔθνεσι πονηροὶ ὄντες καὶ τὰ προστάγματά σου ἀθετοῦσι πρὸς καθαίρεσιν τῆς δόξης σου.

a people of war and disobedient, having different ways;[105] but your ways,[105] O king, they are not devoted to; they are reckoned among all the nations to be wicked[106] and they are setting aside your commands towards lowering your glory (3.8aβ-c).

Such a picture would certainly have roused a measure of discomfort in the king. On account of this Aman seizes the moment. In an extremely deferential manner he requests that this nation be given to him for destruction [δοθήτω μοι τὸ ἔθνος εἰς ἀπώλειαν] (3.9bα). In exchange, he would pay ten thousand silver talents into the royal treasury (3.9bβ-γ). Surely, Aman has done whatever he could have to make the threat against Mardochaios and the Jews become a reality; their fate is now in the hands of the king (§ 4.6.3).

---

105 Following the rendering of Dorothy concerning νόμιμα and νομίμοις here (*The Books of Esther*, 86). We assume that laws are being spoken of in this instance.
106 I am following the translation of Clines in this phrase (*The Esther Scroll*, 223).

4.4.3 Representing the king, having the edict written (3.16-18)

His Majesty is not particularly interested in the silver of Aman, or so it appears. But concerning the unnamed people, his feelings would become clear enough, even amidst what seems to be an initial mood of detachment: treat them "as is pleasing to you" [ὡς ἄν σοι ἀρεστὸν ᾖ] (3.11bβ).[107] To the ends of Aman the king soon pledges his official means and support as he sanctions his vizier to "[W]rite to all lands" [Γράφε εἰς πάσας τὰς χώρας] concerning the matter that they have discussed (3.10bα). After this exchange, which finds its climax in the instructions of the king that his own ring should seal the genocidal initiative, we are told that Aman goes to his gods in order to learn the precise time when this people should die (3.7a). Lots are cast and the thirteenth day of Adar-Nisan[108] is determined to be the day upon which "to slay all of the Jews, from male until female, and to seize the young for plunder"[109] [φονεύειν πάντας τοὺς Ιουδαίους ἀπὸ ἀρσενικοῦ ἕως θηλυκοῦ καὶ διαρπάζειν τὰ νήπια] (3.7b-c). A published pronouncement detailing the 'royal' determinations then follows in haste (3.13).

Though it is clear that Aman is responsible for the actual mechanics of the written product [ἐπιστολή] that ensues from the oral transaction above,[110] the document is presented in the name of the king. To be sure, His Majesty's own convictions in the matter – however deep or shallow they reached – should not be diminished or skipped over (see § 4.6.3). Yet it must be said that the ideological driving force behind the royal decree is located in the energies of Aman. When the king instructs him to write in 3.10bα, it is not as if mundane scribal responsibilities have now been added to the vizierial job description; Aman is not simply putting the wishes of the king into words. Instead, he is given latitude as the *representative* of the king to deal with what is presented to be an empire-wide problem in the manner which he determines is best – ὡς ἄν σοι ἀρεστὸν ᾖ (3.11bβ). What follows is the product of the combined 'royal' will, however unevenly it might have been weighted.

---

107 For this phrase, I am following the rendering of Jobes (*The Alpha-Text of Esther*, 122).

108 For a helpful discussion on this unclear, and thus, confusing designation, see Fox, *Redaction*, 61 (cf. Clines, *The Esther Scroll*, 190 n. 33). To be sure, one finds it difficult to keep track of matters of dating throughout the AT, especially concerning the day upon which the Jews were to perish (cf. 3.18; 7.38, 47, 59). On this and other AT dating discussions, see Jobes, *The Alpha-Text of Esther, passim*; and Clines, *The Esther Scroll*, 200 n. 42.

109 This appears to be an adequate understanding of the extent of διαρπάζειν (BAGD, 188; LS, 194).

110 Wills, *The Jewish Novel in the Ancient World*, 117.

Unsurprisingly, the genocidal edict that Aman composes serves to place His Majesty, himself, and their decision in the best possible light. Any and all powerful and positive characteristics that could be imagined are attributed to both the king and Aman. Concerning His Majesty, it is averred that sheer wealth and a vast dominion are not among his chief ambitions and concerns. This selfless sovereign is "not presumptuous with the arrogance of authority" [μὴ τῷ θράσει τῆς ἐξουσίας ἐπαιρόμενος] (3.15bα), but rather is "consistently acting equitably and with utmost gentleness" [ἐπιεικέστερον δὲ καὶ μετὰ ἠπιότητος ἀεὶ διεξάγων] towards his subjects (3.15bβ). According to the document, establishing and maintaining peace for all his subjects is the prime goal of the rule of the king (3.15c-e). An (if not *the*) important factor in this equation of εἰρήνη is the role played by his advisors [σύμβουλοι] (3.16a). One particular counsellor among these particularly stands apart because of his sound mind [σωφροσύνη], unwavering good-will [ἐν τῇ εὐνοίᾳ ἀπαραλλάκτως] and steadfast loyalty [βεβαίᾳ πίστει]. This advisor is, of course, Aman, who has now risen to the second place in the kingdom (3.16b).

It is his keen awareness that recognises an ugly blemish that has surfaced on the complexion of the empire: a certain people scattered among them who are characterised by hostility in manner, peculiarity of law and refractoriness in the face of royal legislation (3.16a-e). As long as their presence remains, the kingdom would never hit the prized and noble mark of stability [εὐσταθείας] (3.16f). Seeing that it is this nation alone – in light of their aforementioned character – which is impeding the forward progress of the administration of this monarchy [μοναρχίᾳ] (3.17e), it is commanded that they be

ὁλορίζους ἀπολέσαι σὺν γυναιξὶ καὶ τέκνοις ταῖς τῶν ἐχθρῶν μαχαίραις ἄνευ παντὸς οἴκτου καὶ φειδοῦς τῇ τεσσαρεσκαιδεκάτῃ τοῦ μηνὸς τοῦ δωδεκάτου (οὗτος ὁ μὴν Αδαρ, ὅς ἐστι Δύστρος)

completely destroyed, with women and children, by the swords of enemies without any compassion or sparing on the fourteenth of the twelfth month (this is the month of Adar, which is Dystros) (3.18c-d).

While there is no doubt upon whom the court is casting its contemptuous eye, two details of this decree conflict with previously given information (at least chronologically). In 3.7b we are told that the fateful day would fall on 13 Adar-Nisan. Here it is stated that the scorned people would die on 14 Adar (3.18d). As far as we can tell this discrepancy has no obvious explanation.[111]

---

111 Although Fox does grapple with the inconsistencies (*Redaction*, 80-81).

However, judging by later mentions of the (then) averted pogrom (7.38) and
its celebratory aftermath (7.30, 47, 59) it would appear that 13 Adar has the
majority of the overall narrative support. In addition to this, we wonder why
it is now the case that children [τέκνοις] are included in the number of those
who would be utterly killed by the sword (3.18c). Before, in the explanation
of Aman before the king, τὰ νήπια are only to be plundered [διαρπάζειν]
(3.7cγ)! To add to the confusion, 3.18eβ supplies an almost verbatim rever-
sion back to the initial plans of Aman in 3.7cγ – that τὰ νήπια be carried off
[ἁρπάζειν] for plunder. In short, the planned fate for the youngest Jews is
confused: are they to be plundered or killed? Interestingly, these conflicting
messages are in close proximity within a portion of the text that is believed to
have been composed as a unit. It appears that even in the incorporation of the
letter of Aman into the Greek Esther stories, there are distinctive, if not com-
peting, details circulating. Whatever the reason for the discrepancy, and although they might cause a bit of confusion, these conflicting details do not
deter us from apprehending the overriding concern of the edict: the Jews are
to be slain (3.18eα)

ἵνα οἱ πάλαι δυσμενεῖς καὶ νῦν ἐν ἡμέρᾳ μιᾷ συνελθόντες εἰς τὸν ᾅδην εἰς
τὰ μετέπειτα εὐσταθήσωσιν καὶ μὴ διὰ τέλους παρέχωσιν ἡμῖν πράγματα.

so that those full of ill-will in time gone by and now may on one day go down together into Hades, and afterwards be at rest and may not cause us business[112] forever
(3.18f-g).

At bottom, the message is that the Jews are menaces to society – always have
been, always will be. Only when they "go down together into Hades" can the
kingdom run properly and enjoy peace. Indeed, the royal determinations and
subsequent decree are presented to be in the best interest of the subjects of
the kingdom. Since the good of the empire is paramount, all hindrances need
to be purged. And because it is his initiative to rid the empire of these people,
perhaps Aman would be seen as the hero and protector and preserver of the
empire.

4.4.4 Boasting before family and friends (5.20-22)

Although the posted edict has confounded the Sousians (4.1b), it stands as it
had been prepared. We have some reason to believe that many in the kingdom intend to take its mandate seriously, although information concerning

---

112 I.e., "trouble."

the subsequent conflicts is not presented in the clearest manner (7.44-46). For the moment, though, with the Jews in the midst of bitter grief in light of looming events (4.1c), Aman appears to be at the height of his career; he is feeling as if he is on top of the world. Yet on the heels of her heart-wrenching prayer (4.18-29), Queen Esther is beginning her efforts to turn the tide initiated by the political masterpiece of Aman (5.1f). As a result of divine intervention (5.7), she begins to achieve a measure of success in the presence of the king. And upon her request, His Majesty agrees that he and Aman, his friend, would attend the drinking-feast [πότον] that the queen plans to give for them the following day (5.14). Actually, this reception [δοχήν] turns out to be an extravagant dinner [δεῖπνον πολυτελές] at which her special guests would be well-satisfied (5.16).

Although the king desires his queen to make her intentions known – τί τὸ θέλημά σου; (5.17αβ) – she prolongs the matter until the next day when she would surely answer the his queries in the comfortable setting of yet another δοχή (5.18). Realising that he has again been invited to be in such exclusive company, we learn that Aman marvels [ἐθαύμασεν] at the prospect (5.20b). To be sure, Aman does not keep matters to himself. The narrative proceeds to inform us that he

εἰσῆλθεν εἰς τὸν οἶκον αὐτοῦ καὶ συνήγαγε τοὺς φίλους αὐτοῦ καὶ τοὺς υἱοὺς αὐτοῦ καὶ Ζωσάραν τὴν γυναῖκα αὐτοῦ καὶ ἐκαυχᾶτο λέγων ὡς οὐδένα κέκληκεν ἡ βασίλισσα ἐν ἐπισήμῳ ἡμέρᾳ αὐτῆς εἰ μὴ τὸν βασιλέα καὶ ἐμὲ μόνον· καὶ αὔριον κέκλημαι·

went to his house and called together his friends, his sons and Zosara his wife, and was boasting, saying how the queen has called no one on her splendid day except the king and me alone; and tomorrow I have been called (5.21).

The recent events have obviously delighted Aman to no end, and with this gathering of intimates he has consummated his joy by his vaunting. What possibly could spoil this mood? The answer: continual remembrances of his nemesis, Mardochaios. Seeming to be a pessimist at heart, Aman allows visions of Mardochaios refusing to do obeisance to him to plague his every moment. Now, on his day of greatest privilege, even after he had successfully sentenced Mardochaios and his people to death, the Prime Minister knows no peace of mind. It is the unyieldingness of the Jew *alone* that continually annoys [λυπεῖ] him (5.22).

4.4.5 Adopted plans for personal satisfaction (5.23-24)

Yet it is only Aman who remains plagued by this. Zosara sees things differently and seeks to shift the focus of her husband from pains to possibilities by
pointing out the following: Mardochaios is of Jewish blood; since "the king
has conceded to you to utterly destroy" [συγκεχώρηκε σε ὁ βασιλεὺς
ἀφανίσαι] his whole race (§ 4.6.3), and (since) the gods have provided you
with "a day of destruction for an avenging of them" [εἰς ἐκδίκησιν αὐτῶν
ἡμέραν ὀλέθριον], avail yourself of the opportunity and kill Mardochaios
sooner than later (5.23aβ-f).[113] In other words, seeing that you have every
power on earth and beyond on your side against the Jews, what could possibly prevent you from going ahead and hanging your court adversary upon a
fifty cubit stake sooner than later? Who is going to stop you? With this being
suggested, Zosara subsequently implores Aman not to worry about his problem at the moment; the difficulty has been theoretically resolved (at least in
her own mind). For now, he should go and "make merry" [εὐφραίνου] with
the king (5.23h).[114] He can speak [λαλήσεις] to His Majesty about the 'Mardochaios proposal' first thing in the morning (5.23g).[115] Apparently, the business of killing can wait; at present, pleasure beckons. This advice pleases
[ἤρεσε] Aman and he adopts it (5.24).

Although Zosara might have believed that she has thought of everything –
how to rid Aman of Mardochaios and how to ensure that her husband enjoys
himself – she does not expect God to intervene directly in human events on
that very night. If only she had instructed Aman to proceed directly to His
Majesty concerning the hanging of Mardochaios! But as we have discovered

---

113 I have obviously paraphrased this last portion even more freely than in the beginning. It
literally reads: κοπήτω σοι ξύλον πηχῶν πεντήκοντα, καὶ κείσθω, καὶ κρέμασον
αὐτὸν ἐπὶ τοῦ ξύλον (5.23d-f).

114 Chronologically, the exchange between Aman and Zosara appears to be on the same day
as the first banquet of Esther, but after he had returned home from it (5.21a). Thus, when
she encourages him later to go and enjoy himself with the king (5.23h), this cannot be in
reference to his attendance at either one of Esther's two gatherings. For, the first banquet
of the queen was now in the past (earlier on the present day), and her second one does
not occur until 6.23f., after he had gone to speak to the king in the early part of the morning on the following day (6.6b-7). Just what the occasion was for Aman and the king to
get together again later on the present day is not known.

115 In what Dorothy calls "a delightful ambiguity," the reader is not entirely sure at this
point whether Zosara is advocating that Aman hang Mardochaios now and speak to the
king about what he had done the next morning, or whether she proposed the hanging *in
theory* and instructed him to go and speak to His Majesty about the plan the next morning and get his approval for the idea. Because of the way that the Greek is arranged, one
cannot be sure which is the case (*The Books of Esther*, 144). Later, 6.7 provides the answer as to how Aman took the advice of his wife: Αμαν δὲ ὠρθρίκει λαλῆσαι τῷ
βασιλεῖ, ἵνα κρεμάσῃ τὸν Μαρδοχαῖον.

before (5.7), are seeing presently (6.1) and shall witness once again (7.2), just at the moment in which it looks dire for the Jews God enters the story for their benefit. Here (in 6.1f.) we read that ὁ δυνατός removes [ἀπέστησε] sleep from the king, thus presenting His Majesty with the opportunity to (re)hear the recorded account of the saving deed of Mardochaios, which gives rise to the resolution to reward properly (or further) his loyal courtier. This turn of events leads to a quite humiliating professional moment for Aman – one in which he is made to show Mardochaios signs of respect, leaving him to retreat home with a look of gloom [ἐσκυθρωπωμένος] (6.20a).[116] Things only deteriorate from there as Zosara, now with keen theological insight (or hindsight), together with wise men [οἱ σοφοί] pronounce the following in chastisement:

’Αφ’ ὅτε λαλεῖς περὶ αὐτοῦ κακά, προσπορεύεταί σοι τὰ κακά· ἡσύχαζε, ὅτι
ὁ θεὸς ἐν αὐτοῖς.

From the time you began speaking bad (ill) concerning him, bad (ill)[117] has been coming to you; be quiet, for God [is] in these things[118] (6.22b-c).

With no time for a reaction to this, Aman is whisked away to the second banquet of Esther. On the day when his professional life has taken a turn for the worse (6.7f.), Aman eagerly grasps onto any hope; on the heels of his confidants' portentous stomping upon his personal/political ambitions, Aman is cheered [ἱλαρώθη] that he still has some professional distinction left (6.23) – or so he thinks. As it turns out, not only is the professional prestige of Aman fast fleeting, so also are the minutes of his earthly existence. The events that follow at the second banquet of Esther see the genocidal plot against the Jews skilfully exposed by the (Jewish) queen. In the end, it is evident that the king has switched allegiances, once and for all sealing the fate of Aman.[119] For both his crimes against the kingdom[120] and his appearance of impropriety before the lounging queen upon her κοίτη, Aman is found guilty and condemned (7.11). Everything he has cared about has caved in on top of him in the matter of one day.

---

116 For a more in-depth, though not exhaustive, treatment of this scene, see § 4.3.5.

117 I am understanding τὰ κακά as a substantive, expressed in the collective singular sense (LS, 394).

118 I.e., God is behind τὰ κακά, the neuter antecedent of αὐτοῖς.

119 For a more detailed analysis of the second banquet of Esther, see § 4.2.5.

120 These crimes are elaborated upon in 7.25-27 and serve to exegete the words of the king in 7.11bγ (at least for the purposes of the story).

4.4.6 A final portrait – civil and divine censure (7.23-26, 28, 31b)

In the course of coming to terms with the moral character of Aman in the AT story, the material for the task has been relatively one-sided. Despite the influence of the propagandistic (self)portrait that might have wooed us for a moment (§ 4.4.3), Aman is provided overwhelmingly with a negative legacy. Even his closest allies appear to desert him in his last hours (6.22; 7.11-12). But if there are any lingering doubts concerning the man and/or the nature of his genocidal plot, they are effectively and finally put to rest by the condemnatory words from the 'mouth' of the king.

In the context of the AT, two letters appear to have been written in order to counteract the previously published 'royal' edict inspired by the machination of Aman (§ 4.4.3).[121] The former, and more extensive one, is composed in the name of the king and is addressed to the Persian leaders in his kingdom (7.22-32);[122] – the latter, which (as the narrative reads) briefly reiterates some portions of the first and establishes the celebratory feast, is sent by Mardochaios and is addressed to the Jews in the empire (7.35-38).[123] As the text now stands, the letter of the king serves to highlight the supporting role of His Majesty in the success of the Jews. His shift in allegiance to the cause of the Jews is unmistakable, and is a 'conversion' that is exhibited most eloquently and persuasively in his summarising and elucidating letter (§ 4.6.5). At present, though, we shall only concentrate on his final portrait of Aman found therein.

---

121 In reality, or at least in the way that narrative has proceeded, the conflicts between the Jews and their enemies have already begun (7.18-21). This makes the letter of the king appear out of place or "unnecessary" in the scope of the narrative: "there is no point in having the king only now order his subjects to ignore Haman's demands" (Fox, *Redaction,* 90; cf. Dorothy, *The Books of Esther,* 194). This point of narrative logic is conceded, although the critique of the king concerning Aman still stands as valid. This is the focus of the moment.

122 This point is argued contextually by Dorothy (*The Books of Esther,* 192). See also Jobes, who states that this letter is "formally from the king" (*The Alpha-Text of Esther,* 214).

123 We should be clear here that we are using the terms 'former' and 'latter' to note the sequence in which these two letters appear in the Göttingen AT text. Which one is actually prior to the other is a matter of debate. Moore submits that the material in the letter of the king expanded the earlier material found in the letter of Mardochaios (*Daniel, Esther, and Jeremiah: The Additions,* 165). Dorothy believes that the influence of the *Königsnovelle* ("royal novella") on the AT Esther story "militates against a royal writing being added *later* to an original Mardochaios writing." This influence can be seen in two important ways: 1) The monarch always acts at the critical juncture in the story because he or she is the central character; and 2) In this Esther narrative, the king either writes himself, or authorises others to write (*The Books of Esther,* 178-79). For more information on *Königsnovelle,* and its influence on the overall thesis of Dorothy, see his discussion in *The Books of Esther,* 302-13.

The king takes great pains in preparing the literary noose for his former Prime Minister.[124] After opening his letter with statements praising the extent of his dominion and greeting (7.22), His Majesty proceeds to build a case against Aman, beginning with broad generalisations and then moving to specific attacks. He commences his efforts quite generally by noting how for many [πολλοί], it is often the case that too much honour bestowed upon them can lead to disaster. Many times, pride results directly from privilege, and this conceitedness might translate into danger for the subjects of an empire or even ill [κακὰ] for benefactors themselves (7.23a-c).[125] In fact, innocent blood [ἀθώων αἱμάτων] has been shed and irreparable misfortune [συμφοραῖς ἀνηκέστοις] has been occasioned on account of the misplaced trust of a sovereign in those considered to be friends (7.23g-l). However, no matter how presumptuous, none of these persons – ones who "know nothing of goodness"[126] – would escape the divine judgement of the "just judge who hates evil and who holds sway over all"[127] (7.23d-f). Moreover, there would be civil consequences for this betrayed trust as well.

At this point the rhetoric begins to move towards the more specific as His Majesty seeks to restore in the minds of his subjects any lost confidence. Lately, it has been impressed on the king that he must keep a tighter leash on those administering on his behalf in the empire (7.24a-b). This commitment would entail that he avoid being subject to false accusations [οὐ χρώμενοι ταῖς διαβολαῖς], but rather treat with reasonableness or fairness[128] [ἐπιεικείας] the matters that come before him (7.24d-e). If this is done conscientiously, the kingdom would no doubt be a more peaceful one (7.24c).[129] Upon all of this, our appetites have been whetted for the kill as the king is now primed to expose officially the particular object of his recent disaffection. It turns out that Αμαν Αμαδάθου ὁ Βουγαῖος – the one who has been in close relations [ἐπιξενωθείς] with the king and his court, the man who has been second in the kingdom, the one called "our father" [πατέρα ἡμῶν] – has actually been alien to the Persian spirit [φρονήματος] and "quite devoid of our kindliness"[130] all the while (7.25). But this is not all.

124 Note that in 7.17 the king has effectively given Mardochaios the position of second in command to run the affairs of the kingdom in the place of Aman.
125 For a more literal rendering of these thoughts, see the translation of the almost verbatim parallel of 7.23a-c (LXX E.2-3) in § 3.4.5.
126 Following the rendering of Clines, *The Esther Scroll*, 241.
127 Following Moore's rendering, *Daniel, Esther, and Jeremiah: The Additions*, 232 n. b-b.
128 LS even allows for the connotative understandings of "clemency" and "goodness" here (291).
129 Kottsieper calls 7.24 "ein syntaktisch komplexer Satz," which it undoubtedly is. His rendering of 7.24 agrees with the picture presented here (*Zusätze zu Ester*, 198).

of our kindliness"[130] all the while (7.25). But this is not all. His Majesty goes on to be even more specific and damning in what follows (still speaking of Aman):

> οὐκ ἐνεγκὼν δὲ τὴν ὑπερηφανίαν ἐπετήδευσεν ἡμᾶς τῆς ἀρχῆς καὶ τοῦ πνεύματος μεταστῆσαι, τὸν δὲ ἡμέτερον σωτῆρα διὰ παντὸς Μαρδοχαῖον καὶ τὴν ἄμεμπτον τούτου κοινωνὸν Εσθηρ σὺν τῷ παντὶ τούτων ἔθνει πολυπλόκοις μεθόδοις διαρτησάμενος εἰς ἀπώλειαν.

> but unable to bear [his] arrogance he undertook to dismiss us of sovereignty and spirit (life), and while deceiving towards [the] destruction of our saviour in all things, Mardochaios, and blameless sharer of this, Esther, with the entire nation through intricate cunning (7.26a-c).

Now narrative strings that might have appeared loose at earlier points in the story are being tightened. Despite its dubious and perhaps unrelated uses in 1.16a and 2.8b, the name Βουγαῖος (or a form thereof) is attached to the full identification of Aman as a pejorative label in the following instances: Αμαν Αμαδάθου Βουγαῖον (3.1αβ-γ); Αμαν Αμαδάθου ὁ Βουγαῖος (7.25αβ). But, whereas early on in the story Aman is called Βουγαῖον, now he is referred to as ὁ Βουγαῖος; the note of indefiniteness concerning the character of Aman in 3.1 is being fully exegeted here in the context of 7.25. Both of the aforementioned aspects of the epithet have now been publicly exposed: assassination and anti-Jewish (§ 3.3.3). Aman has sought to dismiss [μεταστῆσαι] the king of his ἀρχή and his πνεῦμα as well as scheming the destruction [ἀπώλειαν] of Mardochaios, Esther and the whole Jewish race.[131] By these (unsuccessful) means, the king surmises, Aman has been orchestrating a wider plot of subversion in order to achieve or accelerate a seizure of the Persian empire by the Macedonians (7.26d-e). (With this connection made finally and explicitly, the reader can better appropriate what likely lies behind Aman's other label, Μακεδόνα.) However, in all of his quests Aman has miserably failed. Even his letters [γράμμασιν] (or at least the authority of them) has been undermined (7.28a-b). For all of his troubles he is ultimately hanged,

> ἀποδεδωκότος αὐτῷ τὴν καταξίαν δίκην τοῦ τὰ πάντα κατοπτεύοντος ἀεὶ κριτοῦ.

> rendering to him the worthy judgement of the ever all spying-out Judge (7.28d).

---

130 Following the rendering of Clines, *The Esther Scroll*, 243.
131 While it is inconclusive whether Aman is *explicitly* anti-Jewish in the course of the narrative, this is the overall impression that the reader is given. In other words, did Aman plot against Mardochaios and the Jews particularly because they were Jewish? Perhaps. Perhaps not. The text is ambiguous on this point (cf. A.18; 3.4-6, 16-18).

Condemnation and penalty, both human and divine, are justified to have been levelled upon Aman in the final analysis. In these ways, his moral character has been pronounced upon him and would continue to be reiterated so as long as the celebratory festival is observed; the certainty of ultimate ruin for schemers such as Aman should always live freshly in Jewish minds (7.31b).[132]

4.5 The Jews

4.5.1 The cries of the people – the opening frame (A.6b)

In approaching the dream of Mardochaios (A.3-8), the sense of hearing appears to be an important component of any reading, for in the description of many aspects of the scene the audible is given high profile.[133] First of all, there is a "sound"[134] [φωνη]; this is followed by a cry of uproar [κραυγὴ θορύβου] that does not appear to be related to the initial and imperspicuous φωνη (A.3bα). As we read on, A.3bβ describes the sound of thunder [βροντταὶ] and earthquake [σεισμος] – phenomena whose associated noises are generally recognisable in nature. One does not get the sense, however, that these generally identifiable sounds are necessarily describing or specifying the more ambiguous φωνη and κραυγὴ θορύβου of the opening phrase; rather, it would seem that they are acting in concert (or cacophony) with them. In the end, what is most clear is that there is "trouble upon the earth" [τάραχος ἐπὶ τῆς γῆς] (A.3bγ). Just how that τάραχος might sound, though, is difficult to specify.

Emerging from this trouble are two dragons engaged in conflict (A.4). Their collective crying [κραυγή] – i.e., the φωνή that is occasioned by their

---

132 For assistance in understanding this difficult bit of text (i.e., 7.30-31), consult Fox, *Redaction*, 69-70.

133 Cf. the effects of the overwhelming visual stimulation of 1.6-7 which highlight the opulence and excess of the court (note the informative discussion of Fox concerning the effects of MT 1.6-7 (*Character and Ideology*, 16-17)). Perhaps in the same way that the reader becomes distinctly aware of the pomposity of the Persian court *visually* through the description of 1.6-7, he or she here becomes distinctly aware of the τάραχος upon the earth *audibly* through the description of A.3-6.

134 Over against ψόθος, which designates an "inarticulate" sound or noise, φωνη is often used to relate sounds or noises that are "articulate" (LS, 877). In this particular context, however, we are not able to easily discern (if at all) from what or whom this φωνη comes. In this instance, the φωνη appears to be inarticulate. Cf. the unclear φωνὴν of the trumpet in 1 Cor 14.8.

coming forth to fight – troubles everything [ἐταράσσετο πάντα] (A.5). No nation on earth would be immune to this ominous darkness and gloom; everyone is making preparation to fight even as the dragons are (A.6a-c). But just at this point, when matters look their worst, the story informs that the Jews[135] sound out a loud cry to their Lord in response to the crying that the dragons have shrieked [καὶ ἀνεβοήσαμεν πρὸς κύριον ἀπὸ φωνῆς τῆς κραυγῆς αὐτῶν] (A.6d). In the face of danger, at least in the dream of Mardochaios, the Jewish people turn towards God.

4.5.2 A maliciously disparaging portrait (3.8, 16-18)

Just as they do in the LXX Esther story, the Jews figure somewhat consistently throughout the course of the AT narrative.[136] Early on they appear as an unnamed group who utter a loud cry to the Lord in the midst of the dream of Mardochaios (A.6b; § 4.5.1), and are included in the initial threat that Aman spoke against Mardochaios (A.18; § 4.4.1). Even at the beginning of the story difficulty is never far from them. But the reader must wait until chapter three to witness initial shades of trouble having developed into a clear, full-scale and official threat. It turns out that in the hands of Aman, or more specifically, by his words, "Israel" has found themselves to be in grave danger (3.6c).

We noticed in § 4.4.2 that upon hearing the report of the unyieldingness of Mardochaios over prostrating himself before him, a furious Aman burns in anger against both the Jew and his people (3.5). But even as disturbed as he is, Aman approaches the king in a tactful way concerning the matter. He calculates against the Jews cunningly, knowing which buttons to push as he brings his plans before His Majesty. Aman represents the Jews as an anonymous group scattered about in all kingdoms who are characterised as warlike, disobedient, wicked, and above all, refractory concerning the royal law. By these unflattering traits they should be seen by the king as an immediate threat to his authority and glory (3.8αβ-c).[137]

Once Aman is given the charge to deal with the 'problem' as he pleases [τῷ δὲ ἔθνει χρῶ ὡς ἄν σοι ἀρεστὸν ᾖ] (3.11b), the accusations only intensify in malice. After reiterating many of the same condemnations seen

---

135 Though the Jews are not explicitly named in this instance, it is most likely that they were indeed the plural subject of ἀνεβοήσαμεν. Cf. § 4.3.1; Dorothy, *The Books of Esther*, 51; and Fox, *Redaction*, 74.

136 For comment on issues of moral character in the Jews of the LXX narrative see § 3.5.

137 For a more detailed treatment of this portion of 3.8 see § 4.4.2.

above, Aman concludes that as long as this hostile people is allowed to remain among them, the government would never reach a state of "peaceful stability"[138] (3.16f) – indeed, the present monarchy could never be managed (3.17e). What is portrayed as a menacing state of affairs gives rise to plans for a serious effort of purging (3.9; 3.18). By nature of their 'reputation' the Jews find themselves in perilous waters.

4.5.3 A reason for their plight? (4.21)

But could it be that the Jews in this particular Diaspora context are not exactly blameless? While they might be 'guilty' of having and abiding by peculiar laws in the eyes of non-Jews, it seems doubtful that they are blameworthy concerning all of the accusations Aman has levelled against them (3.8, 16-18). However, in the midst of the prayer of Esther (4.18-29), we might be surprised by what amounts to be a corporate confession of sin from the lips of the queen – an admission that is not without consequence for both our apprehension of the AT plot and our understanding of issues of the Jews' moral character therein.

After Esther had meticulously prepared herself (4.18) and humbly approached her Lord (4.19-20), we are faced with the following disclosure:

ἡμάρτομεν ἐναντίον σου, καὶ παρέδωκας ἡμᾶς εἰς χεῖρας τῶν ἐχθρῶν ἡμῶν, εἰ ἐδοξάσαμεν τοὺς θεοὺς αὐτῶν·

We sinned[139] against you, and you have given us into [the] hands of our enemies, if we glorified their gods (4.21).

The reader has certainly not been prepared for this. With no background information supplied and no warning given, we encounter this remarkable confession. If we are understanding correctly, it appears that because the Jews have honoured their [i.e., Persian] gods they are given into the hands of their enemies. It appears to be the case that this occasion of idolatry constitutes the particular transgression in focus here.[140] Furthermore, Esther intimates that on

---

138 Dorothy, *The Books of Esther*, 97.
139 Interestingly, ms. 19′ reads ημαρτον in this instance, placing the responsibility of the sinning solely on the shoulders of Esther (Hanhart, *Esther*, 165). While this reading is not supported by any other AT or LXX mss, it does raise the intriguing possibility that readers of mss. 19′ understood the queen alone to be the transgressor, having brought difficulty upon the community thereby. However, the plural subjects and pronouns in the remainder of 4.21 might be weighed against this understanding.
140 In other words, the confession of Esther concerns something further than the previous apostasy against God that had occasioned the exile in the first place. For a discussion of

account of false worship the Jews have been subjected to "bitter slavery" [πικρασμῷ δουλείας] (4.22αγ) – a punishment that they presently are enduring (or so it would seem). But now the picture has drastically deteriorated; the consequences of their wrongdoing look like they would now become fatal. Because of the 'royal' decree (3.14-18), God's inheritance is face to face with a threat of extinction. But the costs of idolatry are too much for them to pay; only the Lord can deliver them in their time of affliction (4.23-24).[141]

4.5.4 The righteous laws of the Jews (7.27, 29)

The laws of the Jews play an important part within the decrees and letters of the AT narrative as it now stands, even though the reader never has occasion to discern to which laws the material is referring (if not all of them). In the mind and hands of Aman, a certain representation of these laws has served as the lynchpin of his political attack against the Jews both before the king (3.8) and in the 'royal' decree that follows on from it (3.16-17). Because their laws are in opposition to those of everyone else, and on account of their carelessness concerning the laws of the king, these people are slated to be killed for the good of the kingdom (§ 4.4.2; 4.4.3). Yet in the latter portions of the story, after the demise of Aman has taken place (7.11f), the king changes allegiances and reverses his perception of the laws of the Jews altogether (see further § 4.6.5).[142] What would have at one time been the cause of their doom would now serve to be a means of their survival and salvation.

In the midst of undercutting the authority of the letters sent by Aman,[143] His Majesty pronounces favourably concerning the Jews and their ways, claiming that they are not evildoers [μὴ ὄντας κακούργους], but rather

---

this issue, see Kottsieper, *Zusätze zu Ester,* 173-74. Even though comments of Kottsieper concern the LXX in the noted pages, I submit that they can also be applied generally to the AT text in focus presently.

141 It is interesting to note the (glaring) lack of any corporate or even personal repentance on the part of Esther and the Jews here. Are we merely to assume it? We have already pointed out that the prayer of the queen shares much in common with the (model) prayer of Solomon in 1 Kgs 8.46-53, but whereas Solomon explicitly includes the conditions of repentance and supplications as part of a future exiled peoples' prayer for forgiveness (8.47), these elements are nowhere to be found in the prayer of Esther. Were the Jews of AT Esther sincerely desiring to return to Lord with all their heart and soul *via* their confession (cf. 1 Kgs 8.48)? Or were they simply hoping for a rescue without requirements?

142 De Troyer states matters quite clearly: "[The king] gives permission for the Jews to be allowed to live undisturbed according to their laws and to defend themselves" *(The End of the Alpha Text of Esther,* 365).

143 It is not surprising here that the king does not taken any responsibility for the initial edict, even though it is clear that he was at least complicit in it (cf. § 4.6.3).

"ones governed by very just laws" [δικαιοτάτοις δὲ πολιτευομένους
νόμοις] (7.27αγ-bα). Furthermore, and in an astonishing admission, the Jews
are recognised by the king as being "sons of the only and true God"
[ὄντας...υἱοὺς τοῦ μόνου θεοῦ καὶ ἀληθινοῦ] – the very God who well-
maintains and directs his empire (7.27bβ-c). This admission marks the recently transformed monarch out to be a monotheist whose (present) devotion
might even have rivalled the best kings of Judah![144]

But more than accrediting justness to the laws of the Jews, the king sanctions their use within his kingdom for the benefit of this people (and likely
that of the empire as well):

> ἐκτεθήτω δὲ τὸ ἀντίγραφον τῆς ἐπιστολῆς ἐν παντὶ τόπῳ χρῆσθαί τε τοὺς
> Ἰουδαίους τοῖς ἑαυτῶν νόμοις καὶ ἐπισχύειν αὐτοῖς, ὅπως τοὺς ἐν καιρῷ
> θλίψεως ἐπιθεμένους ἀμύνωνται.

> Let the copy of the epistle be issued in every place so that the Jews may act in accor-
> dance with their own laws and prevail by them, so that they may defend themselves
> against[145] those who assail (them) in time of affliction (7.29).[146]

According to Fox, the point of the king here is simply this: so that they will
be able to "meet whatever trials lie ahead," the Jews should abide by their
own laws and "be strengthened (or 'prevail') by them."[147] Just what those
trials might be is unspecified, even in light of the looming conflicts.[148] At
present, however, it is fair to say that the moral character of the Jews has
never looked so good.

4.5.5 Bloody conflicts (7.44, 46c)

Any assessment of moral character in the Jews of the AT would be incomplete without an attempt to make some sense out of the tersely supplied details of the killing that occurs late in the narrative. To be sure, the story has

---

144 Cf. Fox, *Redaction*, 87.
145 This might also be rendered "avenge themselves on."
146 For 7.29, I have adopted the translation provided by Fox (*Redaction*, 82-83). Since I am
 following his lead in the interpretation of the particular portion of text, I have deemed it
 worthwhile to provide his rendering.
147 Fox, *Redaction*, 83.
148 Fox submits that "after Esther's intercession in the AT there is no specific "time of
 affliction" lying ahead, not even the danger of one." He goes on to say that "the mention
 of a "time of affliction" sounds like an indefinite reference to whatever tribulation may
 henceforth befall the Jews. The message is that the Jews' obedience to their laws enables them to withstand future dangers" (*Redaction*, 83). In the thinking of Fox, then, we

kept no secrets concerning the feelings of Aman towards the Jews. Ever since A.18 we have gathered that there would be trouble between Aman and Mardochaios – the ramifications of which would also endanger his entire people (§ 4.4.1). This threat then materialises in chapter three as personal hostility develops into plans for genocide (§ 4.4.2; 4.4.3). At this time, the picture looks bleak for the Jews as official documents seal their fate; death seems inevitable. But through the divinely aided intervention and counter measures of Esther before the king, matters change for the Jews (§ 4.2.5). The royal will is swayed over to Jewish causes as the story proceeds, and by the end of the second banquet (7.17), Mardochaios and Esther are firmly in the positions of influence once occupied by the (now) condemned Aman. Tides have certainly changed. But what of the official threat of chapter three? Would the Jews remain in danger even now?

All indications are that they should no longer fear the purge that had been ordered earlier in the 'royal' edict (3.18). The words of 7.28a make it clear that the subjects of the king are advised *not* to heed the letters sent out earlier by Aman. His manifesto has been undermined; he and his policy measures are now out of favour. By the words and tone of the counter-letter of the king we might well gather that the Jewish people are then in the clear. But are they? Have they any lingering threat to fear? Will the royal advice actually be heeded? Might there still be an attack on them by forces continuing to be sympathetic to Aman or persons remaining under his influence? In attempting to deal with these questions we must admit that the text is not particularly helpful.

As noted earlier, the narrative logic of the AT after 7.17 is not at all straightforward.[149] To understate the situation, the details found in this portion of the text tend to be somewhat confusing, as are the matters of chronology. For instance, and as we mentioned above, His Majesty appears to undermine the letters sent by Aman which threaten the Jews with extinction (7.28a). Yet immediately following this, we notice that the king has made provisions for the Jews to defend themselves against future attack (7.29c). Does he have a particular attack in mind (e.g., one stemming from the first edict)? Or is this merely a general, preparatory measure that attempts to protect the Jews and make them ready for *any* future conflict (§ 4.5.4)? We cannot be exactly sure.

What we can say firmly is that the Jews are indeed involved in future conflicts, even though they are not described in the most understandable way.

---

must assume that the words of the king in 7.28a had nullified any plans there had been for an offensive against the Jews.

149 See the relevant comments in § 4.2.6.

From 7.18-21 we learn of the queen's treatment of her enemies, but it is *not* clear whether the Jews are involved in carrying out this slaughter, or whether her personal vendetta has anything to do with the conflicts that are envisioned in the initial 'royal' edict (§ 4.2.6). In 7.44-46 it is clear that the Jews *are* intimately involved in this particular account of killing. Following descriptions of Jewish ascendancy and dominance (7.39-43), it is reported that in Sousa they have slain [ἀπέκτεινον] 700 men, along with six men previously unheard of in the story, and also the ten sons of Aman, whose possessions they have plundered (7.44). And likely acting on their open-ended royal permit to kill and plunder as they wish, it is stated that the Jews have utterly destroyed [ἀπώλεσαν] 70,100 men (7.46c). (It is probable that these killings have taken place throughout the empire.) Yet while Jewish involvement in conflicts is plain, a clear understanding of the contexts of these bloody encounters is not.

It remains a live question whether or not the Jews are actually attacked in the AT, and we must be clear that the narrative does not state explicitly that they are. But can we *infer* that an enemy attack has taken place? The question of the king in 7.45 might provide a clue as His Majesty queries Esther concerning how her people have fared [κέχρηνται]. How have they fared against whom? and in the context of what? Even if we conclude with Clines that the question of the king in this instance is "poorly motivated,"[150] we might still have reason to ask the following question: Does 7.45 (even remotely) suggest that there was an attack against the Jews? Realising this difficulty, we must hold open the possibility that the Jews have been involved in unprovoked slaughter in the wider empire (7.46). If so, the perception of them according to this narrative would certainly be still *more* negatively coloured. However, given the way this portion of the text is presented, approximations are even difficult. Thus, though we might have certain information concerning Jewish actions (e.g., how many people have died by their hands), we are not able to grasp a full understanding of those actions due to difficulties encountered in the narrative logic. In the end, we can say for sure that the Jews are involved in bloody conflicts; comment beyond that proves as difficult as understanding the text itself.

---

150 Clines, *The Esther Scroll,* 82.

4.5.6 The cries of the people – the closing frame (7.58)

The distinct sound of the Jews crying out as a people, encountered initially in
§ 4.5.1, is not heard again until the closing verses of the AT narrative – although one might argue that as Mardochaios and Esther beseech the Lord
they do so in a representative fashion (4.16-17, 21-24, 29a-ba). At the close
of Mardochaios's reflective and somewhat elucidating interpretation of his
earlier dream, and after the Jewish people had been spared from total annihilation, the narrator concludes that God has remembered his people and has
justified his inheritance [καὶ ἐμνήσθη ὁ θεὸς τοῦ λαοῦ αὐτοῦ καὶ
ἐδικαίωσε τὴν κληρονομίαν αὐτοῦ] (7.57). Realising this, all the people
sound out a loud cry [ἀνεβόησε] in a great voice saying: "Blessed are you, O
Lord, who remembered the covenants with our fathers – Amen" [Εὐλογητὸς
εἶ, κύριε, ὁ μνησθεὶς τῶν διαθηκῶν τῶν πρὸς τοὺς πατέρας ἡμῶν·
ἀμήν] (7.58). Thus, framing the AT story are the cries of the Jews – the former for help amidst tumult; the latter in thanksgiving after the storm has
passed. The impression gained from this observance is that through it all, the
Jewish people are not hesitant to approach their God. And in the AT narrative, even in the midst of clear human contributions, it is the Lord who is
reckoned to be their ultimate saviour.

4.6 The King (Ασσυήρος)

4.6.1 An independent judicial decision (A.14)

Although we shall have occasion to be further and more officially introduced
to him (1.1), our first encounter with the king comes in section A, in the
midst of a dangerous situation. After the description of the noise and tumult
in the dream of Mardochaios (A.3-8), we read of the assassination plot of
Astaos and Thedeutes against the king's life (A.12-15). But by virtue of the
fortunate proximity of Mardochaios to the conspiring eunuchs and his atten-
tiveness to the content of their slanderous discussion, this attempt of regicide
is uncovered by him and reported to His Majesty.[151] For matters of later consideration, it is interesting and important at this point to observe the manner
in which the king handles this situation.

---

151 A fuller account of these events can be seen in § 4.3.1.

καὶ ἤτασεν ὁ βασιλεὺς τοὺς δύο εὐνούχους καὶ εὗρε τοὺς λόγους Μαρ-
δοχαίου, καὶ ὁμολογήσαντες οἱ εὐνοῦχοι ἀπήχθησαν.

The king examined the two eunuchs and found the words of Mardochaios [to be true];[152] and after the eunuchs had confessed they were led away (A.14).

Although it might appear to be an issue of little significance at the moment, the actions of the king in this instance should not merely be passed over without comment. It seems plain from the narrative that after receiving the report of Mardochaios, the leading role in the scene is taken by His Majesty: *he* examines those accused of regicide; *he* probes into the words of Mardo-chaios and judges them to be accurate. As the king takes the reins of the judi-cial proceedings, we get the impression that his fact-finding endeavours re-veal overwhelming evidence against the eunuchs. In the face of all this, the accused admit their crime and are subsequently taken away to face execution. In this case, and contrary to the way in which he handles some other impor-tant decisions within the AT story,[153] the king acts in an independent and de-cisive manner. In short, he behaves in the manner we might have expected of a powerful monarch in the ancient world.

4.6.2 Royal boastfulness (1.1-8; 7.50)

There is no doubt that the king has every reason to be a proud man. Given his position in the kingdom and the vast extent of the empire (1.1b), kingly pride would be expected. And it is a description of exactly this that we encounter in the beginning and ending portions of the narrative. Even though the king is introduced as Ασουήρου τοῦ μεγάλου in A.1 in an effort to establish the temporal context of the dream of Mardochaios, we are not properly intro-duced to his character until chapter one. There, Ασουήρου τοῦ βασιλέως τοῦ μεγάλου is in focus as the immensity of his territory is highlighted (1.1b). As we learned in § 4.1.1, two celebratory drinking-feasts are given by His Majesty for different guests and for distinct purposes. It is the first of these that will occupy our attention at present. An initial, 180-day party is given both for the Persian and Median court officials and for his provincial rulers[154]

---

152 That the words "to be true," or something like them, complete the thought here is the consensus of commentators (e.g., Clines, *The Esther Scroll*, 219; Fox, *Redaction*, 60; Dorothy, *The Books of Esther*, 53).
153 I.e., under the heavy if not controlling influence of those around him (e.g., 1.16-21; 3.9-11, 10; 7.12b-13; 7.18-21; 7.45-46).
154 Lit: οἱ ἄρχοντες τῶν χωρῶν.

εἰς τὸ ἐπιδειχθῆναι τὸν πλοῦτον τῆς δόξης τοῦ βασιλέως καὶ τὴν τιμὴν τῆς καυχήσεως αὐτοῦ

so that the wealth of the king's glory and the honour in which he boasted could be exhibited (1.4a).

It appears clear that pride is the motive behind this huge gala. The king has reason to celebrate and be glad for all appears well within the empire at the present time. This being the case, everyone around is to know of his proud position and good fortune. A similar situation exists in the closing portions of the story after much distress has occurred in the kingdom. In the end, when all is again well, the king writes

τὰ τέλη τῆς γῆς καὶ θαλάσσης καὶ τὴν ἰσχὺν αὐτοῦ, πλοῦτόν τε καὶ δόξαν τῆς βασιλείας αὐτοῦ.

the ends of the earth and sea and his power: both wealth and glory of his kingdom (7.50).

As it had begun for the king, it ends for him – that is, well (if not better). And as the king is on top and enjoying good fortunes, he is pleased to make public the fact(s) of his fame.

4.6.3 An accomplice in plans for genocide (3.11-10, 17-18; 5.23b)

Having observed the way in which the king has so effectively handled the judicial proceedings surrounding the thwarted attempt on his life (§ 4.6.1), we might expect him to act similarly in subsequent crisis situations. Our focus at present concerns the role or association of the king in the plot of Aman to rid the kingdom of the Jews. From relevant texts on the matter, we shall observe a cumulative case building against His Majesty.

The initial text of interest is found in chapter three, following the refusing of Mardochaios and the (subsequent) 'burning' of Aman (§ 4.4.2). Even though we cannot pin down every detail and motive involved in this courtier conflict, it is safe to say that *something* about Mardochaios and/or his behaviour has ignited the wrath of Aman. And for reasons that are not wholly clear, this anger then spills over into a genocidal threat on the entire Jewish race as a result. Yet we gather that Aman, by himself, is able only to enact a limited revenge, or at least an unsatisfactory one; indeed, he needs royal authority to empower the full extent of his inimicality. In search of this, the vizier approaches the king and relates to him the 'dangerous situation' which faces the empire (3.8). After hearing such a disturbing account of current and potential (if not inevitable) lawlessness and disruption, we might expect a strong reaction from His Majesty. Yet we must confess that the mood of the king is difficult to discern; he does not appear to react decisively at all. At the moment in which we might expect a royal tirade in reaction to the picture Aman has sketched, all we receive is a seemingly non-committal sanction which generally supports the vengeful plan of his Prime Minister against the Jews: treat them "as is pleasing to you" [ὡς ἄν σοι ἀρεστὸν ᾖ] (3.11bβ).[155] However, as we read on, the commitment level of the king begins to increase as he pledges his ring and official support in the matter (3.10). Even at this point, royal complicity in the genocidal plot is surfacing.

These events beg an important question: What happens to the monarch whose leadership has been characterised by discerning adjudication (§ 4.6.1)? What we encounter here is a king who has unconditionally put his complete trust in the words of his chief advisor with no questions asked. Of course, it is true that monarchs usually surround themselves with trusted advisors and are likely to take their advice on many aspects of kingdom governance; but here we have a situation in which an entire race of people is hanging in the balance, and the king cannot be bothered to investigate the truth of Aman's claims, even half-heartedly. What is more, he does not even seek to know the identity of the maligned people he is condemning! Mardochaios appeared every bit as trustworthy earlier in the narrative as he reported to the king concerning Astaos and Thedeutes (A.13). Why has the king handled this matter differently from that one (A.14)? Is an attempt of regicide viewed differently from a conspiracy to commit genocide?

Whatever the case, by the time we reach the words of the 'royal' letter (3.14-18), His Majesty appears to be completely on board the genocidal express of Aman. The plans for genocide are no longer merely brewing and isolated within the mind of Aman. Now, on account of the advice of Aman – a man here depicted as having the best of all possible human qualities (3.16b) – the pronouns have changed. The text of the letter makes clear that *we* (i.e., the king and his court) understand the danger that these hostile people embody (3.17), and "we have commanded" [προστετάχαμεν], in line with the letters of Aman, that they should suffer the most severe of consequences as a result (3.18).[156] His Majesty still does not know their name, but it is clear at

---

155 As before (§ 4.4.3), I am following the rendering of Jobes here (*The Alpha-Text of Esther*, 122). We should also point out that while the reader is aware of the object of Aman's disaffection, the king is not. For him, the people destined for destruction are nameless, and he seems (carelessly) happy to keep it that way.

156 For a more detailed look at 3.16-18, cf. § 4.4.3.

this point that the doom of the Jews is sure. According to the narrative, his complicity with and energy in the plans for their destruction is plain. Even though the king might not be cited as the main offender against the Jewish people, he can surely be accorded the label, 'accomplice'.

This understanding of the royal role in all of this is corroborated later in the narrative by a third party – the wife of Aman, Zosara. In the midst of try-ing to appease the uneasy mind of her husband – which is constantly irritated by thoughts of Mardochaios and his unyieldingness – she mentions to Aman that the king "has conceded" [συγκεχώρηκέ] to him to utterly destroy the Jews (5.23b). For the vizier, this bit of information is part of a whole string of encouraging comments which are designed to assure him that the 'Mardo-chaios problem' would soon be history (§ 4.4.5). But, coincidentally, the words of Zosara provide support for the reality of the involvement of the king in the plan of Aman – an association from which His Majesty would ulti-mately choose to distance himself (§ 4.6.5).

4.6.4 A spiritual transformation (5.7)

With the king and Aman in concert concerning the fate of the scattered, hos-tile and lawless people, things could not look bleaker for the Jews. While they are deep in mourning, the people are called to assemble and pray for their leader as she self-sacrificially resolves to appeal in person before the king (§ 4.2.2). But before Esther passes through the doors to stand before His Majesty, she, too, pauses to beseech God (4.19-29). Calling to the Lord ap-pears to be the hallmark of the faith of the Jews in the AT story, as we can observe in the prayer of Mardochaios as well (4.13-17). Indeed, from the tumultuous beginnings of the story to its joyful conclusion, the Jews consis-tently cry out to their God (§ 4.5.1; 4.5.6).

Ever since Mardochaios has awakened from his dream, we have been given the sense that God would play a significant role in the AT Esther story.[157] As it turns out, this would certainly be the case, and not merely in a behind-the-scenes or supporting capacity. God appears active and decisive within this narrative, transforming weakness into strength, despair into hope, defeat into victory.

One of the clearest examples of the decisive action of God in the narrative occurs in chapter five – a scene directly following the heart-wrenching

---

157 A.9: καὶ ἀναστὰς Μαρδοχαῖος ἐκ τοῦ ὕπνου αὐτοῦ ἐμερίμνα τί τὸ ἐνύπνιον καὶ τί ὁ δυνατὸς ἑτοιμάζει ποιῆσαι.

prayers of Mardochaios and Esther which, among other things, seek the aid of ὁ κύριος. The queen has done all things possible in order to prepare herself spiritually and physically; now it is time to be faithful to her commitment and enter before the king. Once more she calls upon her "all-knowing and saving God" [τὸν πάντων γνώστην καὶ σωτῆρα θεὸν], and then proceeds delicately towards the imposing doors, behind which she reckons her life might end (5.2a; cf. 4.11d-e). Yet as her prayer intimates, Esther is not without a measure of hope as this difficult challenge faces her; confident, however, she is not, as we learn that her heart is shrinking[158] [ἡ δὲ καρδία αὐτῆς ἀπεστενωμένη] (5.3c). Standing now on the other side of the doors, there is no relief for her fear. The king appears majestic upon his throne – adorned most extravagantly and appearing very fearful (5.4). The text describes vividly what Esther encounters:

καὶ ἄρας τὸ πρόσωπον αὐτοῦ πεπυρωμένον ἐν δόξῃ ἐνέβλεψεν[159] αὐτῇ ὡς ταῦρος ἐν ἀκμῇ θυμοῦ αὐτοῦ

And lifting his face – inflamed in glory – he gazed upon her like a bull in the height of his anger (5.5).

This is her subsequent reaction:

καὶ ἐφοβήθη ἡ βασίλισσα καὶ μετέβαλε τὸ πρόσωπον αὐτῆς ἐν ἐκλύσει καὶ ἐπέκυψεν ἐπὶ τὴν κεφαλὴν τῆς ἄβρας τῆς προπορευομένης.

and the queen was terrified and her face changed with faintness and she bent over upon the head of the maid who went before her (5.6).

With this turn of events, any hopes of success before the king seem to have been dashed. The enervated queen appears as a lamb led to slaughter. Things could not look worse for the Jewish cause at the moment. Will Esther become a martyr? Has ὁ κύριος even heard their prayers?

No and yes. Just at the point at which the queen symbolises a picture of human weakness, ὁ θεός enters the scene and changes the spirit of the king [καὶ μετέβαλεν ὁ θεὸς τὸ πνεῦμα τοῦ βασιλέως], substituting "gentleness" [πραότητα] for his "anger" [θυμὸν] (5.7). This powerful intervention transforms both the moment, and, it might be said, the rest of the story. The affections of the king have been changed. Seeing what was before him now

---

158 The intransitive uses of ἀφίστημι seem to allow this rendering, or something similar (LS, 139).

159 The reading in ms. 319, επεβλεψεν, is to be preferred in this case over against the form that appears in the text, ενεβλεψεν (Hanhart, *Esther*, 169). In my rendering I am translating επεβλεψεν.

quite differently, His Majesty leaps down [κατεπήδησεν] from the throne in
order to comfort his wife with affectionate words.[160] The text makes plain the
point of his distressed nature [ἀγωνιάσας] on account of the condition of
Esther (5.8aα). Indeed, until the queen is stabilised, the king remains troubled
[ἐταράσσετο] (5.12b).

The efforts of His Majesty not only facilitate the immediate recovery of
Esther, they also serve to aid the Jewish cause and eventual success. One
might suppose that the transforming spiritual act of God in the throne-room
has a lasting impact upon the king. Judging by the extraordinary monotheistic
confession and providential acknowledgement of 7.27, this would appear to
be the case. At the very least, the narrative is clear that God chooses to use
the king for God's purposes. For example, it is ὁ δυνατός who takes the
sleep of the king away on the night he is 'reminded' of the saving deed of
Mardochaios (6.1f.). This, of course, precipitates the rise of the Jew and the
fall of Aman.[161] Coupled with the results of the tactful banqueting campaigns
of Esther (§ 4.2.6), the Jews have cause for renewed hope. To be sure, the
workings of God in the πνεῦμα of the king are by no means insignificant; the
moral character of the monarch begins to change as a result of it.

4.6.5 Changed allegiance (7.23-32)

It is not until we come to the text of the letter of the king (7.22-32) that we
are able to see written proof of the changed allegiance of His Majesty.[162] Yet
from the moment God changes his spirit onwards, we gather (though often
implicitly) that the king is being used as a vessel through whom the Jews
would achieve deliverance – and often an active one. Even though Esther,
Mardochaios and the Jews will still play important roles in this quest, the
royal role stands out and appears vital. Thus, and this perhaps will come as a
surprise, a Gentile king will have a key part to play in the cause of Jewish
salvation as he works *alongside* them. All of this, as the dream interpretation
of Mardochaios will later elucidate (7.53-58), takes place under the purview
and providence of God, but it is not the case that the reader is kept in the dark
until the full picture is suddenly brought to light.

---

160 Although written concerning the parallel point in the LXX (D.8), I submit that the comments of Kottsieper concerning the outstanding words of affection that the king used at
   this juncture apply here as well (*Zusätze zu Ester*, 184).
161 For details on the rise of Mardochaios and the fall of Aman, see § 4.3.5 and § 4.4.5.

The remarkable nature of God's intervention in both the royal throne-room (5.7) and bedroom (6.1) needs no further comment, except to surmise that with these extraordinary occurrences comes the sense, at least in the mind of the reader, that God is turning the tide in favour of God's chosen people. Because of the former, Esther is able to begin her successful banqueting campaign; following the latter, we witness the political rise of Mardochaios at the expense of Aman. As a combined result of these things, an end to all of the endeavours of Aman is brought about. Yet the king is not necessarily a bystander: he continues to oblige the wishes of the queen amidst her stalling when he could easily call an end to it all; he is the one who instructs Aman to honour Mardochaios in royal fashion; it is the king who commands that Aman be hanged upon the same "wood" [ξύλον] that he had prepared for his adversary (7.13a). All of this supports the notion that even when he is not the main actor, the king is nonetheless valuable to the narrative progression.

Yet after the death of Aman, the role and significance of His Majesty in the plot increases even more. Often times, he is even the initiator of the action: bestowing all that was Aman's [πάντα τὰ τοῦ Αμαν] to Mardochaios (7.15b); and soon after, entrusting to Mardochaios the concerns of the kingdom (7.17). But it is especially with his letter that the king takes centre stage. Therein, he makes clear what we have been drawing together for some time now: His Majesty officially renounces Aman and his plot and embraces the Jews and their cause. Heretofore, we have looked in some detail concerning how the king distances himself in every way from Aman and people like him *via* masterful political rhetoric (§ 4.4.6). Aman had compromised the stability of the kingdom in more ways than one, suffering a just recompense because of it. To be sure, he would no longer threaten anyone; and at the advice of His Majesty, neither should the influence of his letters (7.28a-b). Once the closest advisor to the king, Aman is now (and in every way) most estranged.

A similar scenario can be seen in the way that the official standing of the Jews shifts in the story. Formerly thought of as ones being inimical to all things lawful, good and peaceful in the kingdom (§ 4.5.2), the Jews are now officially thought of as epitomisers of goodness, and what is more, godliness; the king not only appreciates the good qualities of these subjects, he also acknowledges their God (§ 4.5.4)! His change in allegiance cannot be depicted in any starker fashion. Judging by the way in which the story presents him, one might even suppose that towards the end of narrative he thinks and acts as a Jew.

---

162 De Troyer understands AT 7.22-32 to be "a response on the part of the king to Haman's request," and sees the king as "the main person responsible for the decree" (*The End of the Alpha Text of Esther*, 365).

4.6.6 Complicity in the vengeance of Esther (7.19, 21, 46c)

Whatever else can be said about the difficult and often illogical text from 7.18 onwards, the fact of the complicity of the king in the vengeance of his queen is undeniable.[163] It appears plain that His Majesty has agreed to the request of Esther's slaughter (7.18), as well as to her wishes concerning the house of Aman (7.19a-b).[164] His declaration in 7.19c, "[S]o be it"[165] [Γινέσθω], seems to cover both. In fact, the narrative even suggests that the king assumes a somewhat active stance, though not a leading one, against the sons of Aman.[166] He becomes more active in 7.21:

ἐν δὲ Σούσοις ἀνθωμολογήσατο ὁ βασιλεὺς τῇ βασιλίσσῃ ἀποκτανθῆναι ἄνδρας καὶ εἶπεν Ἰδοὺ δίδωμί σοι τοῦ κρεμάσαι. καὶ ἐγένετο οὕτως.

and in Sousa the king made an agreement with the queen[167] [for] men to be killed and said "Behold, I grant you to hang (men)." And it happened in this way (7.21).

Now it is the king who assumes the leading role as he makes an agreement with the queen; a bystander in these proceedings he surely is not. Although in the wider scope he should not be thought of the initiator and architect of the Jewish acts of violence upon their enemies, His Majesty certainly plays a considerable part therein. Before, he had sanctioned what appeared to be a large scale slaughter (7.19c); now, by virtue of this additional and distinct permission, men in Sousa are at risk of being hanged (7.21).[168]

There is one further text to be viewed before we can close the discussion of the complicity of the king. In 7.44-46 we encounter casualty reports resulting from the conflicts of the Jews with their enemies. At the very least, here, we see the fallout from the intents and permissions of 7.18-21. The report of the bloodshed occurring in Sousa in 7.44 could be reporting and elucidating

---

163 See Day, *Three Faces of a Queen,* 145.
164 For a discussion of the king's agreements with the queen, see De Troyer, *The End of the Alpha Text of Esther,* 312-15.
165 Following the rendering of Clines (*The Esther Scroll,* 241).
166 The posture of the king in this instance looks to be more than just an assenting one: ἐνέτυχε δὲ ἡ βασίλισσα Εσθηρ καὶ κατὰ τῶν τέκνων Αμαν τῷ βασιλεῖ, ὅπως ἀποθάνωσι καὶ αὐτοὶ μετὰ τοῦ πατρὸς αὐτῶν (7.19a-b).
167 Concerning the phrase ἀνθωμολογήσατο ὁ βασιλεὺς τῇ βασιλίσσῃ, I am following the rendering of Fox (*Redaction,* 120).
168 It is interesting to note later in the narrative it is reported that in Sousa the Jews "killed" [ἀπέκτεινον] 700 men, as well as the ten sons of Aman (7.44). The only person related to have been hanged in the capital is Aman (7.28, 37), and even this is a point of narrative contention. He was supposed to have been hanged on the same wood he had erected for Mardochaios, which, according to Agathas, was in his own courtyard (7.12b-d). The problem is that both the king (7.28) and Mardochaios (7.37) later state that Aman was hanged "at the gates of Sousa" [πρὸς ταῖς Σούσων πύλαις].

on the agreed upon plans of 7.21. Similarly, the numbers of the dead (sup-posedly) from the rest of the empire totalling 70,100 might be clarifying the ambiguity of 7.20 – καὶ ἐπάταξε τοὺς ἐχθροὺς εἰς πλῆθος. However, and as we have suggested in § 4.2.6 and even more strongly in § 4.5.5, it is possible that 7.46 describes a conflict different from and in addition to the one seen in 7.20. If so, the scope of the involvement of His Majesty would thereby be expanded. Nevertheless, even if 7.44-46 only reiterates the mate-rial of 7.18-21, evidence for the complicity of the king in the vengeance of Esther is still strong and clearly seen in the narrative of the AT.

Part III
Extrapolations & Adumbrations

5 Assessing Conclusions

5.0 Introduction

In this chapter we shall begin the work of assessing the moral character we have encountered in the three primary Esther texts. To be sure, the following will not provide closure to the many questions and issues of moral character found in the Hebrew and Greek stories of Esther; instead, these assessing and concluding efforts should serve as profitable ways out of the discussion of such matters. Standing on this side of the elucidative explorations of chapters two, three, and four, it appears clear that there is room for suggestions concerning how to approach and come to terms with the moral material in the three texts. Thus, we shall suggest that the concepts of *ambiguity* and *transformation* may aid us in achieving a better grasp on the presentation of moral character in the respective Esther narratives. In realising that these concepts are able to communicate a variety of meanings, we shall strive to be as precise as possible in our specific employment of them.

5.1 Assessing Moral Character in the Hebrew Book of Esther

Walter Brueggemann has stated recently that "the rhetoric of the Old Testament is characteristically *ambiguous and open....* So much is left unsaid, that the reader is left uncertain."[1] As one approaches the Hebrew book of Esther, Brueggemann's point is underlined. For, as David G. Firth has submitted, in the Esther story a "constant air of ambiguity" is found.[2] This "air of ambiguity" and a distinct sense of openness have certainly been encountered as we have investigated moral character in the MT version. And in our efforts to

---

1   W. Brueggemann, *Theology of the Old Testament* (Minneapolis: Fortress Press, 1997), 110 (*emphasis original*).
2   Firth, "The book of Esther: A neglected paradigm for dealing with the state," 20. Although Firth's comment here concerns the entire Hebrew book, his main focus in the essay is on political matters. Although Firth does not specify how he is using the word "ambiguity," it is likely that something like "unclarity" is being communicated. This is the way in which I am interpreting the use of the word.

narrow many of the gaps, we have often found ourselves at a loss to effect – or sometimes even approach – the kind of closure of which Sternberg spoke earlier (§ 2.0). Rather, something like Brueggemann's uncertainty has been our overall interpretative lot. Any moves towards assessing this material must be undertaken with this in mind.

With the possible exception of Haman, the moral complexions of the characters discussed in chapter two above are more complex than one might first suppose. Yet even though the moral character of the Agagite lacks much nuance, it cannot be taken for granted. In a large way, his dark proclivities and brashness occasion many of the difficult situations to which the other characters must react, and in which they must live and/or survive. Herein lies his primary importance to the study of moral character in the Hebrew Esther narrative.[3] It is Haman's cold and calculated hatred of Mordecai and the Jews that leads him (with the help of the king) to orchestrate what he hopes will be their final end (§ 2.4.1). This action brings about the perilous challenge to which the Jews, both individually and collectively, must respond. In addition, it is his insatiable pride that compels him to seek the premature death of Mordecai (§ 2.4.2; 2.4.3). As a result, Haman hastens his own demise, while, at the same time, setting the stage for the rise of Mordecai. Finally, it is the carelessly misperceivable posture of the desperate Agagite that both spells his ultimate doom and accelerates Jewish success (§ 2.4.4).

The perception of Queen Vashti's actions is not quite so clear. The text does not lend itself to an appraisal of her moral character, as the amount and extent of the gaps limit our view. The author simply does not intend to explore the reasons (moral or other) surrounding the refusal of Vashti. Thus, the behaviour of Vashti appears morally ambiguous because the narrative does not make the thoughts of the queen clear, leaving the reader to wonder about the reasons for her snub.

Her character does, however, serve to cast light upon the assessment of moral character for others in the story. Her simple 'No', when faced with an important decision, contrasts drastically with the complex and personally revealing decision-making process that her successor, Esther, undertakes (§ 2.2.3; 2.2.4). In addition, the episode of Vashti's refusal introduces us to the fickle character of the king (§ 2.6.1), which has puzzled us throughout our

---

3   Perhaps for this reason Weisman claims that Haman is "undoubtedly the main character of the plot" (*Political Satire in the Bible,* 152). The character of Haman, in comparison to that of others, is in large part disclosed. Because of this, it impacts the story in the most blatant and striking ways. In this way, Haman could be described as the main character of the plot, or, at least, one of its most important.

study. Indeed, and in many ways, the episode of Vashti's refusal reverberates through the entire narrative.[4]

The picture is only slightly clearer when we look closely at issues of moral character in the conduct of the Jews. We have submitted that the anonymous group of Jews *appears* to be acting in a defensive manner on 13 Adar. While admitting that the account is not entirely clear in all aspects, this interpretation accords best with the sense of the narrative episode in chapter nine (§ 2.5.1). However, it is unmistakable that more questions remain concerning the actions of a smaller assembly of Jews in Susa on the following day (§ 2.5.2). Even though they have been authorised to act by royal order – thus, placing the heaviest moral implications on the shoulders of the queen (§ 2.2.6) – it would seem that the Jews on 14 Adar "have become too much like their enemies for their actions to be above question."[5] While the actions of the Jews in Adar are surely "memorable" (9.28),[6] they might not have been entirely "free of vengeance, brutality, and overkill."[7] Whether they are in the final analysis deemed defensive or otherwise, interpretative difficulties persist on account of a lack of full disclosure in the narrative. Because of this, it is suggested that the actions of the Jews are morally ambiguous at this point; they are certainly not altogether clear on 14 Adar, and it is likely that they are even untidy and might be fairly investigated.

A similar situation faces us as we grapple with the moral character of Esther. Questions surface on account of the depth of her character and the complexity in which the narrative presents her.[8] Before hasty condemnation is levelled against Esther's concealment, somewhat active bedroom comportment, hesitant loyalty, cunning/indirectness, and highly suspect wishes, we must weigh the context(s) very carefully and not merely judge her against

---

4   See Beal for a concise discussion of many other ways in which the Vashti episode echoes throughout the story (*Esther*, 1-2).

5   B. Webb, "Reading Esther as Holy Scripture," *RTR* 52 (1993), 31. See also the comments of Weisman concerning "self-irony" and the Jews in this matter (*Political Satire in the Bible*, 145).

6   W.T. McBride, "Esther Passes: Chiasm, Lex Talio, and Money in the Book of Esther," in J.P. Rosenblatt and J.C. Sitterson (eds), *'Not in Heaven': Coherence and Complexity in Biblical Narrative* (Bloomington: Indiana University Press, 1991), 223.

7   Fox, *Character and Ideology*, 226.

8   Mills notes that "[I]ronically, the more fully that a character is treated, the more ambiguous she or he tends to be come to the reader" (*Biblical Morality*, 243). Although the character of Esther is not as fully developed (or developed in the same way) as those of Abraham and David (the two other subjects of her character study), a measure of ambivalence is present in terms of Queen's merits and flaws, which results in ambiguity (unclarity).

an abstract standard and/or modern ethical criteria.[9] In the end, Esther might well be challenged for some (perhaps untidy) aspects of her behaviour, even if the full extent of many matters is far from simply decided. What is clear, however, is that her moral legacy is neither romantically positive[10] nor only negative.[11] For Esther, "survival…is indeed a complicated matter"[12] – her life and choices are not as straightforward as one might suppose.

So also with respect to the character of Mordecai. Though his potential moral blemishes are fewer, an honest assessment of his motives and actions, even in their broader contexts, is complicated. His initial and unquestionable loyalty to the king(dom) (§ 2.3.1; 2.3.3) seems to strain in tension with the involved ethnic allegiance that plays a part in the Jew's (and the Jews') pain (§ 2.3.2). Moreover, even though his role and responsibility in the formation and wording of the counter-edict has caused some discomfort, understood in its context(s), it appears less condemnatory (§ 2.3.4; 2.3.5).

To be sure, the circumstances in which the Jewish leaders act are far from ideal, and the resultant moral ambiguity or unclarity often prevents us from either a facile character assessment or "any simplistic construal of the 'sha-

---

9   We cannot afford to make the same mistake as many of the rabbis did in their day. In so
     desiring Esther to be the ideal Jewish woman, they attributed to her the traits and moti-
     vations of pious orthodoxy and reinterpreted her behaviour seeing only an exemplary
     manner (see Darr, *Far More Precious than Jewels,* 187). Magonet submits that Esther is
     placed within the realms of power for a special time, and "to judge her behavior in ab-
     stract moral terms is to misunderstand the choices that she has to make" ("The Liberal
     and the Lady," 174). Yet the more this contextual approach nears a criteria of relative
     ethics, the less satisfying it becomes. The comments of Terry C. Muck, writing in the
     General Editor's preface to Karen Jobes' recent commentary on the book of Esther,
     seem most balanced: to see Esther "as ultra-feminist…politician par excellence…or
     even…as moral role model would be to miss badly the real story of the book. Esther was
     at best an inconsistent feminist; her political skills and judgment have been repeatedly
     questioned, and her moral behavior simply will not pass muster when stacked against
     almost any modern moral theory" (K.H. Jobes, *Esther* (NIVAC; Grand Rapids: Zonder-
     van, 1999), 13).
10   For example, note how O.E. Costas presents the character of Esther, seeing her as a
     paradigm for a liberating theology ("The Subversiveness of Faith: Esther as a Paradigm
     for a Liberating Theology," *The Ecumenical Review* 40 (1988), 70). Costas sees Esther
     more positively and more piously than she actually and explicitly is in the narrative. See
     the cautions of G.J. Wenham concerning the search for models in the biblical narrative
     ("The Gap between Law and Ethics in the Bible," *JJS* 48 (1997), 17).
11   Although the point of Bar-Ilan is valid that the reader should not be lured into thinking
     no ill of the queen and the way she conducts herself in the story (NB: Bar-Ilan is mostly
     concerned with the sexual behaviour of Esther at this point), it seems a harsh judgement
     for him to conclude that "Esther cannot serve as role model for any Jewish woman"
     (*Some Jewish Women in Antiquity,* 9).
12   D.N. Fewell, "Introduction: Writing, Reading, and Relating," in *idem* (ed.), *Reading
     Between Texts: Intertextuality and the Hebrew Bible* (Louisville: Westminster/John
     Knox, 1992), 16.

lom' at the end as a reward."[13] We must keep in mind that all of what is
found in the book of Esther concerning the Jewish people is in the context of
dual loyalties in a Diaspora existence.[14] The reality and consequent lifestyle
of community displacement certainly comes into play as one considers how
individuals and people groups must come to terms with living in a foreign
land under extraordinary circumstances.[15] For Mordecai, and to a different
extent, Esther, there is perhaps some sense of "ethical, or religious or ethnic
allegiance"[16] that in the final analysis can be said to supersede all others, but
the picture presented is far from one-sided or cut-and-dried. Indeed, "[T]hey
are not unblemished heroes, and it would not be true to the story to make
them so."[17] Their inner lives are undoubtedly complex.[18] Thus, the book of
Esther presents "an astonishingly adaptive Judaism,"[19] but not one which is
beyond all moral questioning and contemplation.

We have come, finally, to view the moral character of the king. Issues of
morality in his case are best discerned not on the basis of the company he
keeps, but rather on the company who keeps him (and speaks for him).[20] His
passivity (§ 2.6.1; 2.6.2) is as outstanding as his complicity (§ 2.6.3) in the
early portions of the narrative; while, later on, we witness a slightly more
active, though still mercurial monarch (§ 2.6.4; 2.6.5). It is clear that upon
whomever the king's favour rests and with whomever his voice resides, *there*
is power in the kingdom. To be sure, an obvious discrepancy exists between
"the pitiful insignificance of the king's personality and the immense power of
his words;"[21] the adjectives "weak" and "passionate" paradoxically describe

---

13 Webb, "Reading Esther as Holy Scripture," 34. Note the picture offered in 10.3.
14 Concerning how "dual loyalties" enter into the ethical picture of the Scroll, see Green-
    stein, "A Jewish Reading of Esther," 234,37. See also the extended discussion of Berg
    on this subject (*The Book of Esther*, 98-103).
15 See W.L. Humphreys, "A Life-Style for Diaspora: A Study of the Tales of Esther and
    Daniel," *JBL* 92 (1973), 211-23. See further Morgan's discussion of "living faithfully"
    in troubled times (*Between Text & Community*, 116).
16 LaCocque, *The Feminine Unconventional*, 60. See also Berg, *The Book of Esther*, 103.
17 Webb, "Reading Esther as Holy Scripture," 31. See further on this point Fox, *Character
    and Ideology*, 224.
18 See the relevant comments of Tod Linafelt on this matter (*Ruth*, in idem and T.K. Beal,
    Ruth and Esther (Berit Olam; Collegeville, MN: The Liturgical Press, 1999), xiv).
19 LaCocque, *The Feminine Unconventional*, 80. See also the general comments of S.J.D.
    Cohen on the reality of Jewish adaptation in the Diaspora (*From the Maccabees to the
    Mishnah* (Philadelphia: The Westminster Press, 1987), 45).
20 Elaborating on this notion, Clines surmises that "[T]he ambiguity in the role of the Per-
    sian king...corresponds with the ambiguity of the book's stance towards the Persian
    government, which is experienced by the Jews both as threat and as protection – an ex-
    perience consequently inscribed in the book" ("Reading Esther From Left to Right," 36).
    Cf. Mills, *Biblical Morality*, 74-75.
21 LaCocque, *The Feminine Unconventional*, 52.

his disposition.[22] Such authority in certain hands often turns the affairs of kingdoms upside down. While the king is not a morally neutral character, he is presented neither as essentially evil nor wholly good. In short, the king is, for the most part, a governed governor, whose moral character is most often in direct correspondence to whoever is exerting influence on him at any given moment.[23]

It is quite reasonable to conclude that the moral character presented in the MT version of the Esther story is "patchy and incomplete."[24] Because of this, many are content to ignore or forego serious discussion of moral issues (and their ethical implications) that arise in the story. Indeed, it might even be suggested that the ambiguous (whether unclear or untidy) moral character of the book has played a part in its ecclesial[25] and scholarly marginalisation to the "periphery of biblical history and theology."[26] Such an approach is unfortunate. Should we not take seriously the aspects of the story that have led to this marginalisation, ones that do not seem to fit or appear odd, alien or offensive?[27]

As John Barton points out,

> the profundity of much that the Old Testament has to say in the field of ethics is bound up with the fact that it thus allows for the intricacy and untidiness of human life, and presents us with rounded personalities through whose interplay we can see ethical decision-making, and of course ethical failure, in action.[28]

The book of Esther certainly displays such intricacy and moral untidiness as it tells its story through its rounded personalities. Perhaps this is the kind of picture its author had in mind to present. But even though we might understand the position of William Whiston in principle when he states that the

---

22 Paton, *The Book of Esther*, 121.

23 Weisman calls the king "the object, not the subject" in summarising his character (*Political Satire in the Bible*, 149; see also Firth, "The book of Esther: A neglected paradigm for dealing with the state," 20-21). Berlin notes that the king is "a ruler ruled by his advisors" (*Esther*, xx).

24 Vermes employs these terms and discusses the exegetical options in the face of this kind of narrative situation ("Bible and Midrash," 207f.). Cf. Mills' comments on "gaps and silences" when coming to terms with issues of moral vision in biblical narratives *(Biblical Morality*, 91, 93).

25 Bush contends that "the utter lack of use of the book in teaching and preaching emasculates it" as effectively as any overt condemnation ("The Book of Esther," 40).

26 Jobes, *The Alpha-Text of Esther*, 179. For some general comments here, see Berlin, *Esther*, xlv.

27 W. Brueggemann, *Texts Under Negotiation: The Bible and Postmodern Imagination* (Minneapolis: Fortress Press, 1993), 58. See also B.C. Birch, W. Brueggemann, T.E. Fretheim, and D.L. Petersen, *A Theological Introduction to the Old Testament* (Nashville: Abingdon, 1999), 21.

28 J. Barton, *Ethics and the Old Testament* (London: SCM Press Ltd, 1998), 37.

Hebrew Esther story is "so very imperfect," we should not automatically flee for refuge with him to the more religious and "pious" Greek versions.[29] Might it be that the Hebrew story should not be expected to be perfect, or, stated more contextually, "conformed to the moral and spiritual requirements of the Torah?"[30] Perhaps the story of life in a Diaspora context cannot always be so unambiguously pious and/or so explicitly God-focused.

The Hebrew book of Esther tells a tale that is "concerned to show the face of the Jew that is turned toward the world…It is indeed one important aim of the story to display the conflicting loyalties of the Jews in Diaspora."[31] This Esther story "serves well as a window into the concerns of Judaism at the margins of another society."[32] When dealing with issues of moral character this should always be kept in mind, for they are issues conceived in the Diaspora for the Diaspora.[33] Thus, instead of supposing that the Hebrew story of Esther is an example of "another post-exilic failure to become the exemplary, obedient people that God meant for them to be,"[34] we might more reasonably and contextually suggest that the narrative celebrates a deliverance

> that emerges in the midst of life with its apparently normal flux of events. It is about a world in which pagans hold power and the people of God must watch their every step. A world which throws up hard ethical and religious questions and where very imperfect people struggle to come to terms with events which they cannot fully understand or control.[35]

R.K. Harrison seems to have been on the right track when he asserted that the (Hebrew) book of Esther is "unique among the Old Testament Scriptures in the way in which it deals with…moral issues."[36] Perhaps it would even be appropriate to restate (and perhaps broaden) his determination in the following way: the Hebrew Esther story is unique in the way in which it deals *and does not deal* with moral issues, the way in which it often leaves moral matters unaddressed, unresolved, uncertain. The silence surrounding many of the motives and thoughts in the text might strike a reader as strange, for with the exception of Haman, behavioural evaluation – for purposes of either exonera-

---

29 Flavius Josephus, *The Works of Josephus* (trans. W. Whiston; Peabody, MA: Hendrickson, 1987), 305 n. *h*.
30 F.B. Huey, Jr., "Irony as the Key to Understanding Esther," *SJT* 32 (1990), 39.
31 LaCocque, *The Feminine Unconventional*, 60.
32 Laniak, *Shame and Honor*, 173.
33 Concerning the story's Diaspora situation and agenda, see J.D. Levenson, "The Scroll of Esther in Ecumenical Perspective," *JES* 13 (1976), 446-47; and Bush, "The Book of Esther," 44-45. However, cf. Berlin's relevant comments on the burden of Diaspora stories ("Esther and Ancient Storytelling," *JBL* 120 (2001), 7).
34 Huey, "Irony as the Key to Understanding Esther," 39.
35 Webb, "Reading Esther as Holy Scripture," 32.
36 Harrison, *Introduction to the Old Testament*, 1098.

tion or condemnation – is absent.[37] The narrative leaves much of its (im)morality unspoken, not addressed specifically, or implied at best. This (perhaps disquieting) moral ambiguity – whether due to unclarity or untidiness – should, at the very least, be recognised, if not embraced.

5.2 Assessing Moral Character in the Greek Books of Esther

5.2.1 The question of possible historical contexts

As Day points out towards the close of her 1997 study, ventures into a discussion concerning possible historical contexts of the Greek Esther stories have been few. Even when suggestions have been made, they have been made tentatively. Moreover, these suggestions have focused only on particular sections of the Greek texts and not the whole of the narratives, and have always been articulated in a broad manner.[38] But with the shift in Esther scholarship towards focusing on the Greek texts as whole narratives which tell similar, though unique, stories, interchange concerning possible historical contexts which have produced similar, though unique, literary versions has moved forward. This progression can be seen *via* a consideration of recent contributions of Dorothy, Day, and De Troyer on the subject. It should be noted, however, that concentrated research into the historical contexts of the Esther stories has not been the primary focus in the work of these scholars. Each treats the subject as it flows out of her or his literary/textual studies.

Even though both Dorothy and Day respect the Greek texts of Esther as whole narratives, their proposals remain quite general concerning the possible historical contexts surrounding the stories. Interestingly, the two scholars arrive at opposite conclusions on the matter. Towards the end of his thorough study concerning the structure, genre and textual integrity of the books of Esther, Dorothy makes broad suggestions concerning the possible provenance of each Greek story, basing his decisions on the distinct nature of their literary styles. Concerning the LXX, Dorothy submits that the author, using a neutral, unattached style, shapes a narrative which tells the Esther story in a didactic, objective, and historically-oriented manner. On account of this, he surmises that this version was crafted for a community "at some remove from the communities represented in the narrative,"[39] perhaps a "Hellenized dias-

---

37 Jobes, *Esther*, 20.
38 See Day's discussion in *Three Faces of a Queen*, 226f.
39 Dorothy, *The Books of Esther*, 353.

pora audience."[40] The situation is different for the AT, as it focuses its concern on matters ethnic, communal and homiletical.[41] Thus, Dorothy suggests that this text was the product of an "orthodox, less Hellenized community, perhaps in Palestine itself."[42] He explains his supposition by stating that the AT was translated into Greek "so that segments of the Jewish population (in the homeland or in the Diaspora) could not only read it, but appreciate it as their story, their history, their life."[43] For Dorothy, the LXX author remains neutral in his telling of the story, while the author of the AT version "takes it personally."[44]

Day comes to very different conclusions concerning the possible historical contexts of the Greek Esther stories. But although her literary study concentrates primarily on the character of Queen Esther in the three texts and not on matters relating to provenance, date, and authorial intention, Day does respond to the aforementioned proposals of Dorothy with some "tentative suggestions" of her own.[45] She suggests that the LXX presents a story in which the Jews, particularly Queen Esther, have great affinity with their religious community. Its story telling resembles "*heilsgeschichte [sic]*... God continually working throughout time to help the Jews in an ongoing relationship."[46] On account of this, Day suggests that this version of the story may have been shaped by a community of Jews in Palestine itself, or perhaps by one in the Diaspora which held closely to more traditional religious views and conduct.[47] Her view of the context surrounding the AT is also shaped primarily by the text's presentation of Esther, and suggests that this story portrays the queen as having a lesser concern for her people and things traditionally Jewish. Its story telling is "more detached" and "less personal" as represented in the way in which Esther and Mardochaios manage their Jewish and Persian identities. The relationships between Jews and Persians are seen as positive ones as the Jewish leaders work well within their Diaspora context. Thus, Day suggests that the AT provides "a model of how Jews might successfully live with others," and possibly comes from a community of Diaspora Jews which is "more integrated with non-Jews and more Hellenized in thought and behavior."[48]

---

40 Dorothy, *The Books of Esther*, 355. See Day's summaries concerning Dorothy's positions for a fuller treatment (*Three Faces of a Queen*, 227f.).
41 Day, *Three Faces of a Queen*, 227.
42 Dorothy, *The Books of Esther*, 355.
43 Dorothy, *The Books of Esther*, 356.
44 Dorothy, *The Books of Esther*, 356.
45 Day, *Three Faces of a Queen*, 231.
46 Day, *Three Faces of a Queen*, 232 (*emphasis original*).
47 Day, *Three Faces of a Queen*, 232.
48 Day, *Three Faces of a Queen*, 231.

The study of De Troyer concentrates primarily on the ending of the AT Esther story (7.14-41), but investigates the parallel texts in the MT and LXX (8.1-17 in both) in an in-depth manner as well. At the conclusion of her textual studies, De Troyer broadens her scope in order to make a proposal concerning the historical context of the AT that is more specific than the suggestions put forward by either Dorothy or Day. She believes that the AT is a revision of the LXX which was shaped to highlight the role of Mordecai over Esther in the quest for Jewish deliverance. De Troyer proposes that the narrative was written in Rome (ca. 40-41 C.E.) and was adapted to focus on the Jewish hero, Agrippa, who saved his people from Alexandria by convincing Claudius Caesar to allow the Jews to live according to their own laws. This Agrippa (who is Mardochaios in the AT story), later becomes the king of Judah. In the AT adaptation, Aman represents Flaccus, and the king is, of course, Claudius, but there is no speculation on the identity of Esther. In light of her study, De Troyer makes the concluding suggestion that henceforth in Esther studies 'AT' should now stand for 'Agrippa-Text' instead of 'Alpha-Text'.[49] This designation change situates the AT in the midst of other first century C.E. literature, "within the corpus of Jewish literature which emerged from the period of the Roman occupation."[50]

Like the above works, detailed exploration into possible historical contexts of the Greek books of Esther is not the primary objective of the present literary study. In the course of such a study, however, it would not be inappropriate to address relevant features that might shed some light on historical questions. In the texts of LXX and AT Esther, it is possible that the occurrence of the present passive participle πολιτευομένους provides such a reason for pause. Thus, we shall look briefly at πολιτευομένους – a cognate of πολίτευμα, which is a common word and also a significant technical term in the Diaspora[51] – as it appears in parallel accounts of the Greek Esther narratives.

The term *politeuma* has a broad variety of meanings as it is employed variously in the context of the Greek *polis*. For example, *inter alia*, the word can refer to "political action," "civic right," "state," and "government." In its

---

49 De Troyer's hypothesis concerning the historical context of the AT is worked out in chapter six of her *Het einde van de Alpha-tekst van Ester*, with a brief summary on pg. 360. This discussion is translated and updated in De Troyer's *The End of the Alpha Text of Esther*, 400-403. Additionally, a helpful summary of the position is also given in the review of De Troyer's *Het einde van de Alpha-tekst van Ester* by P.J. Williams (*VT* 48 (1998), 566-67).

50 De Troyer, *The End of the Alpha Text of Esther*, 403.

51 G. Lüderitz, "What is the Politeuma?" in J.W. Henten and P.W. van der Horst (eds), *Studies in Early Jewish Epigraphy* (Leiden: E.J. Brill, 1994), 183.

technical sense, *politeuma* has been employed to denote "groups of people with various forms of organisation."[52] Within this latter type, Gert Lüderitz offers a distinction between two categories of *politeumata:* 1) political bodies with an administrative function within the Greek *polis*; or, more broadly, 2) other organised groups, such as "festival associations of women, a cult society, a club of soldiers, associations of citizens from the same city living abroad, and ethnic communities."[53] We should note, however, that instances of *politeuma* in its technical sense are rare and prove difficult to understand in much detail. Such is the case as we seek to grasp the concept as it relates to the Jews in the Diaspora.

There are only three known occurrences of the term *politeuma* with reference to Jews in the Diaspora. One of these is found in the second century B.C.E. *Letter of Aristeas,* and potentially provides information concerning the organisation of the Jewish community in Alexandria.[54] However, since the reference is not entirely clear, it is difficult to determine precise details from this literary source.[55] It is reasonable only to say that this particular *politeuma* appears to be a distinguishable group within the community of Alexandrian Jews,[56] although there is no direct evidence available to corroborate this supposition.[57] The other two instances of *politeuma* are found in inscriptions of honorary degrees from the Diaspora community of Berenice in the Cyrenaica, and date from the first century B.C.E. to the first century C.E. Significantly, Berenice is the only known site in which a "Jewish organisation with the designation 'politeuma' is really attested."[58] Yet, once again, details of this corporation are not forthcoming. Although it is discernible that the group had leaders, managed funds and exercised some governmental functions, scholars are at a loss to explain the legal position and status of the Jewish *politeuma* in this city.[59] Moreover, because the term is not really attested outside of Cyrenaica, and because it does not receive mention in Josephus or other ancient authors, Lüderitz suggests that one might have to come to terms with

---

52 Lüderitz, "What is the Politeuma?" 183.
53 Lüderitz, "What is the Politeuma?" 185, 189.
54 A. Kasher, *The Jews in Hellenistic and Roman Egypt: The Struggle for Equal Rights* (Tübingen: J.C.B. Mohr (Paul Siebeck), 1985), 208-11.
55 J.M. Modrzejewski, *The Jews of Egypt: From Ramses II to Emperor Hadrian* (trans. R. Cornman; Philadelphia: The Jewish Publication Society, 1995), 82-83.
56 J.J. Collins, *Jewish Wisdom in the Hellenistic Age* (OTL; Louisville: Westminster John Knox Press, 1997), 141-42.
57 See Modrzejewski, *The Jews of Egypt,* 82.
58 Lüderitz, "What is the Politeuma?" 210.
59 Collins, *Jewish Wisdom in the Hellenistic Age,* 141. See also Lüderitz, "What is the Politeuma?" 215.

the possibility that the Jewish *politeuma* in the two inscriptions from Berenice is a "local peculiarity of the Jewish diaspora in Cyrenaica."[60]

The present passive participle πολιτευομένους appears in the LXX
(E.15) and AT (7.27) at parallel points and in very similar contexts. In both
cases the word occurs in the midst of a most remarkable confession from the
mouth of a transformed king, who not only approves of the laws of the Jews,
but also recognises the place of their God in the kingdom. Over against the
charge of Aman that the Jews are a scattered, insignificant, and despised people – ones with peculiar laws who disregard the laws of the kingdom (§ 3.4.2;
3.4.3; 4.4.2; 4.4.3), stands the counter sentiment of the king which comes
later in the narratives and holds that the Jews are not the evil doers formerly
described, but rather are "ones governed by very just laws" [δικαιοτάτοις
δὲ πολιτευομένους νόμοις] and children of the "living" (LXX) and "true"
(AT) God who has been instrumental in the past and present success and
maintenance of the kingdom (§ 3.5.5; 4.5.4).

Even though πολιτευομένους is a cognate of πολίτευμα – a term, as we
have seen, which has some significance in the Jewish Diaspora – its occurrence in the Greek texts of Esther provides little to further the discussion of
possible historical contexts on its own. The use of *politeuomenous* in the
Greek Esther narratives could suggest that the communities in which these
texts were translated were familiar with the concept of *politeuma* as a group
which enjoyed some amount of organisation or even self-government in a
Diaspora context. Yet the employment of the present passive participle occurs in a context which focuses primarily on the "very just laws" of the Jews
rather than on the manner in which the people are governing themselves or
the organisation in which this governing is taking place. Thus, while the word
politeuomenous might not have been meaningless to a community responsible for adapting the Esther story to a new, Diaspora context on account of
their possible familiarity with the concept of *politeuma*, it is unlikely that this
participle can provide us with further information concerning how *politeumata* were organised, how they were governed, or the nature of their legal
position in the cities in which they were known to exist.

5.2.2 The transformation of moral character

In our investigation into both the LXX and AT in the course of this study, it
has been impossible to ignore the fact that these Greek versions tell the

---

60   Lüderitz, "What is the Politeuma?" 222.

Esther story differently from the way it is told in the MT. This has been especially noticeable as we have studied issues of moral character in the three
narratives. We shall now delve into such issues further as we seek a better
apprehension of the way in which LXX and AT Esther present/handle moral
material. In so doing, we shall suggest that the moral character of these Greek
books has been *transformed* by efforts of clarification or definition, expansion or amplification, and even alteration.[61]

All Greek biblical translations[62] – whether considered more literal or freer
– interpret their source text to a certain extent in the process. That is to say,
these translations reflect some degree of exegesis as they render their *Vorla-
gen*. While this exegetical activity may in some cases be limited solely to
matters of grammatical identification and semantic interpretation – i.e., "linguistic exegesis" – it may, in others, display a certain amount of contextual
freedom and adjustment, employing elements that "deviate from the literal
sense of a given word, phrase or sentence" – i.e., "contextual exegesis."[63]
Examples of contextual exegesis often can be observed "in the choice of un-
usual equivalents, in the connections made between words, and in the adaptation of Hebrew to Greek diction."[64] Yet even allowing for a certain amount of
conservative clarification, explanation, adjustment and omission that is found
in contextual exegesis, both the 'linguistic' and 'contextual' translation-
exegetical approaches point to a Greek translator who has not wandered too
far from the source text.

But it is sometimes the case that translation-interpretation[65] extends beyond the bounds of the text into the broader context(s) of a given translator.
On account of matters personal, religious, communal, and societal, translators
often reveal more of themselves in the translation process by inserting extra-
neous material "not necessitated by the context."[66] Emanuel Tov describes
three main types of such exegetical translation – *theological exegesis*;
midrash-type exegesis; and *actualizations* – and considers these approaches
"tendentious."[67]

---

61 See Vermes' discussion in his essay, "Bible and Midrash: Early Old Testament Exege-
    sis", 203f.
62 Although most scholarly work in this area concentrates primarily on the study of the
    LXX, our general comments here, in the context of the Greek books of Esther, can apply
    to the AT as well.
63 Tov, "The Septuagint," 173.
64 Tov, "The Septuagint," 174.
65 A term employed by D.W. Gooding to describe the LXX treatment of its MT source in
    the story of Ahab ("Ahab according to the Septuagint," *ZAW* 76 (1964), 277).
66 Tov, "The Septuagint," 176.
67 Tov, "The Septuagint," 176.

Manifestations of 'theological exegesis' appear as translator-interpreters seek to describe "God and His acts, the Messiah, Zion, the exile as well as various religious feelings."[68] Tendencies towards this type of translation-exegesis can be seen throughout the LXX, for example (especially in sections in which the approach is freer), and show themselves in the form of theologically motivated additions, omissions and choices of translation equivalents.[69] A much broader and more complex category is 'midrash-type exegesis'. According to Tov, elements are considered "midrashic" in a given translation when they "deviate from the plain sense" of their *Vorlage* (e.g., the MT) and reflect actual rabbinic sources or resemble such exegesis. These deviating elements serve to "clarify" their content – e.g., *via* additions or rearrangement – but do so usually in a manner less extensive than that which is found in later targumim.[70]

The two translation-exegetical approaches outlined above attest to the desire of Greek translators to address and communicate to their respective readers relevantly. This end can be approached as well by a third approach, which Tov calls 'actualization'. To aid in readers' understanding, translators often made "actualizing changes" in order to conform their texts to an existing situation.[71] To take an example from the texts of the book of Esther, the designation of Haman as 'the Agagite' in the MT version is actualised in the Greek versions as Aman is called "the Bougaion" and "the Macedonian." While the negative connotations that "the Agagite" contains in the Hebrew are in many ways carried over, the labels "Bougaios" and "Macedonian" in the Greek texts have recontextualised, refocused, and perhaps even reinvigorated the negative sentiment. To be sure, actualisations are not simple substitutions; rather, they are intended communications of the general content and desired effects of the parent/source text by the contemporising element in the (new) context of the Greek version(s).

While elements of both 'theological exegesis'[72] and 'actualization'[73] can be seen clearly in the Greek versions of the book of Esther, we shall not seek primarily to investigate these particular instances presently. Instead, our concentration will focus mainly upon instances in the LXX and AT of the book of Esther that appear to share in common one of the features found in Tov's

---

68 Tov, "The Septuagint," 176.
69 E.g., Isa 38.11. See Tov for further examples ("The Septuagint," 177).
70 E.g., Exod 22.19; Isa 65.22. See Tov for further examples ("The Septuagint," 177-78).
71 E.g., Isa 9.11 (Tov, "The Septuagint," 178). See also R. Bloch, "Midrash," (trans. M.H. Callaway), in W.S. Green (ed.), *Approaches to Ancient Judaism: Theory and Practice* (BJS 1; Missoula, MT: Scholars Press, 1978), 46-47.
72 E.g., 4.8e in the LXX and 4.9c in the AT.
73 E.g., 3.1 in both the LXX and AT.

category of 'midrash-type exegesis',[74] although we shall not employ his terminology.

We shall avoid using the label 'midrash-type exegesis' for two reasons. First, Philip S. Alexander has argued that the technical term 'midrash' must be used with precision, and should be limited to describe early rabbinic Bible exegesis. Utilizing the term out of this context tends to be misleading and fosters imprecision because there are both formal and methodological considerations to be taken into account as one considers whether to call something 'midrash' or 'midrashic'.[75] Thus, one cannot merely deport the sense of the technical rabbinic usage of 'midrash' and import it into the rare, pre-rabbinic occurrences of the word in its titular sense. Such anachronistic explanations are flawed, and ignore the manner in which the term has been employed in pre-rabbinic cases.

A few examples from Qumran and 2 Chronicles are helpful at this point. In a recent study, which includes an exploration and analysis of the occurrence of 'midrash' in the Qumran scrolls, Timothy H. Lim submits that the meanings of the word in its titular sense are able to be grouped into four broad categories: communal study; inquiry; communal regulation; and authoritative interpretation.[76] Paying close attention to the contexts of the use of 'midrash', Lim comes to the following conclusion:

> With the possible exception of 4Q249…other instances of 'midrash' in the Qumran scrolls do not refer to a genre of biblical exegesis, but either have a specific referent in the theological preparation of the way in the wilderness (1QS 8.16) or more generally refer to study as an act in which the community participates (1Q 8.26). The term could also refer to an inquiry or investigation (1QS 6.24) or to an instruction and rule based upon the authoritative interpretation of the Torah (4QS^{d,b}; 1QS 5.1; 4QD^{a,e}; and 4Q249).[77]

The word 'midrash', in its titular sense, also appears twice in the late biblical book of 2 Chronicles. Its occurrence in 13.22 [במדרש הנביא עדו], mentioning a source for the Abijah account, refers to "the story of the prophet Iddo," while the use of the word in 24.27 [כתובים על־מדרש ספר המלכים], in the context of the oracles against Joash and his sons, is usually translated as "in

---

74 For more information concerning the identification of midrash-type exegesis in the LXX, and the limitations of such study, see E. Tov, "Midrash-type Exegesis in the LXX of Joshua," *RB* 85 (1978), 50-52.

75 See P.S. Alexander, "Midrash and the Gospels," in C.M. Tuckett (ed.), *Synoptic Studies: The Ampleforth Conferences of 1982 and 1983* (JSNTSup 7; Sheffield: JSOT Press, 1984), 2-11.

76 T.H. Lim, "Midrash Pesher in the Pauline Letters," in S.E. Porter and C.A. Evans (eds), *The Scrolls and the Scriptures: Qumran Fifty Years After* (JSPSup 26; Sheffield: Sheffield Academic Press, 1997), 285-90.

the commentary (meaning the non-specific sense of interpretation) of the book of the Kings."[78] Though it is still a matter of some debate,[79] scholars generally agree that these two uses of 'midrash' by the Chronicler are not "governed" by its technical usage in rabbinic literature.[80]

These examples from Qumran and 2 Chronicles are important for the present study because they show quite clearly that early, pre-rabbinic uses of 'midrash' are not necessarily exegetical forerunners or direct precursors of the technical, rabbinic usage.[81] The word cannot simply serve as a blanket term for early Jewish Bible interpretation. If it is so employed, it becomes too broad to communicate anything on account of the wide variety of distinctive styles that can be seen in early Jewish Bible exegesis. In short, an indiscriminate employment of 'midrash' leaves open too many questions and evacuates the term of "any real meaning."[82] Thus, to avoid generating "more confusion than light,"[83] we shall choose not to employ the term 'midrash', 'midrashic', or even 'midrash-type' when describing the exegetical interpretation we have encountered in our study of the Greek texts of Esther.

The second reason we are choosing not to make use of the term 'midrash-type' is related closely to the first. The category 'midrash-type exegesis', as outlined by Tov, is too broad for our present purposes. He explains that this exegetical approach is seen in a given translation when elements therein "deviate from the plain sense" of their *Vorlage* and reflect actual rabbinic sources or resemble such exegesis.[84] The above discussion described why it is inadvisable to use the technical term 'midrash' when exploring and commenting upon early Jewish Bible interpretation: 'midrash' has specific formal and methodological characteristics which are found in certain rabbinic texts. Yet we are interested in borrowing the initial portion of Tov's explanation. Our study of the Greek Esther texts has concentrated on those portions in which each narrative has deviated from the plain sense of its *Vorlage*. Because of this deviation – seen in various alterations, modifications, clarifications, and amplifications – we submit that the moral character of the LXX and AT texts of Esther has been *transformed*.

---

77 Lim, "Midrash Pesher in the Pauline Letters," 290.
78 Lim, "Midrash Pesher in the Pauline Letters," 284.
79 See H.G.M. Williamson, *1 and 2 Chronicles* (NCB; London: Marshall, Morgan & Scott, 1982), 17-23, 255, 326. For more general information concerning the masculine substantive "midrash" in 2 Chr, see G. Stemberger, *Introduction to the Talmud and Midrash* (trans. M. Bochmuehl; Edinburgh: T & T Clark, 1996²), 234.
80 Lim, "Midrash Pesher in the Pauline Letters," 284 (citing S. Japhet).
81 Employing Lim's terms ("Midrash Pesher in the Pauline Letters," 283, 291).
82 Alexander, "Midrash and the Gospels," 11-12.
83 Alexander, "Midrash and the Gospels," 1.
84 Tov, "The Septuagint," 177.

According to James A. Sanders, those who translated biblical texts into Greek were interested in producing versions that served their respective communities relevantly.[85] Thus, and in accordance with what they considered to be the "spirit" of the Scriptures, translators produced versions that related the Scriptures to their particular age and context in order to show how the text still addressed and exerted its claim upon its present reader(s). In short, in the production of these versions, texts have been "resituated."[86] This task necessarily required adaptation to some extent.[87]

Examples of modification in translation-interpretation have been often recognised by scholars in the study of biblical Greek versions (most often the LXX).[88] For instance, in an article entitled "Ahab according to the Septuagint," D.W. Gooding contrasts the portraits of Ahab in the MT and LXX. Over against the depiction of Ahab as a notorious king in the MT version, the "LXX depicts a not-so-bad-after-all Ahab, more weak than wicked" in its account of that portion of 3 Reigns.[89] Gooding concludes that where the portrayals of Ahab in the LXX and MT differ, that difference "lies solely in the realm of exposition."[90] It is clear to him concerning the Ahab material that the LXX is not translating a Hebrew text distinct from the MT. Rather, through rearrangement and supplementation, the LXX has reworked the account *via* "translation-interpretation."[91] It would appear that the LXX and AT Esther stories have been reworked in similar ways.

In a later and broader study of 3 Reigns, the same author provides further comment concerning the translation-interpretation of the LXX version. He notes that this Greek retelling of the Hebrew text of 1 Kings "abounds" with what he calls "midrashic re-interpretation."[92] Although we are not supportive of Gooding's label, his observations concerning reinterpretation are especially interesting as they concern matters of moral character, particularly in the case of a number of kings in the narrative. Through various interpretative means, it appears clear that the translator-interpreter of 3 Reigns was quite

---

85 J.A. Sanders, "Text and Canon: Context and Method," *JBL* 98 (1979), 13 (cited in Dorothy, *The Books of Esther*, 355).
86 Bruns, "Midrash and Allegory," 634, 637.
87 Sanders, "Text and Canon," 13.
88 See the following works for examples: R.P. Gordon, "The Second Septuagint Account of Jeroboam: History or Midrash?" *VT* 25 (1975), 368-393 (esp. 393); Gooding, "Ahab according to the Septuagint," *passim*, and "Problems of Text and Midrash in the Third Book of Reigns," *Textus* 7 (1969), esp. 20-29; and E. Tov, "Midrash-type Exegesis in the LXX of Joshua," 50-61.
89 Gooding, "Ahab according to the Septuagint," 272.
90 Gooding, "Ahab according to the Septuagint," 278.
91 Gooding, "Ahab according to the Septuagint," 277f.
92 Gooding, "Problems of Text and Midrash in the Third Book of Reigns," 21.

concerned to "whitewash" certain characters – e.g., David, Solomon, Jeroboam, and Ahab – so that they would appear more pious in the Greek version.[93] As we witness in the Greek books of Esther as well, considerations of
explicit piety appear to have been extremely important in the context of many
of the Greek biblical translations.[94]

But the tendency towards such adaptation cannot be confined merely to
Greek translations of Old Testament material. According to Robert H. Gundry, so-called "midrashic flourishes,"[95] "characteristics,"[96] and "elements"[97]
are evident in *some* portions of the Gospel of Matthew. At certain places in
Matthew – e.g., the genealogy and birth narratives – Gundry claims that the
author takes "editorial liberty,"[98] freely revising and supplementing his
sources[99] in order to communicate a particular message relevantly and effectively. Indeed, "Matthew's intent was to tell the story of Jesus with alterations and embellishments suited to the needs of the church and the world at
the time the gospel was written."[100] Through such bending and shaping, Matthew enlivened and contemporised his material.[101] The result, in Gundry's
view, is a transformed version of events which emphasises Matthew's particular concerns.

Since the practice of embroidery and embellishment appears to have been
quite common in the Jewish literature of Matthew's time, the liberties he has
taken in handling the dominical traditions of his sources is analogous to the
liberties Jewish authors of the same era have taken in treating Old Testament
tradition.[102]

---

93 Gooding, "Problems of Text and Midrash in the Third Book of Reigns," 20f.
94 This is also an important feature in Josephus' retellings. See H.W. Attridge, *The Inter-
  pretation of Biblical History in the* Antiquitates Judaicae *of Flavius Josephus* (HDR 7;
  Missoula, MT: Scholars Press, 1976), ch. 4; see also L.H. Feldman, *Studies in Josephus'
  Rewritten Bible* (Leiden: E.J. Brill, 1998), esp. 513-38. Feldman claims that Josephus'
  Esther story "offers an idealized version of the figures of Esther and Mordecai" (513).
95 R.H. Gundry, *Matthew: A Commentary on His Handbook for a Mixed Church under
  Persecution* (Grand Rapids: Eerdmans, 1994[2]), 632. It would seem that Gundry's use of
  the term "midrashic" is a loose, anachronistic one. His observations would be valid even
  if the term were dropped or substituted.
96 Gundry, *Matthew*, 634.
97 Gundry, *Matthew*, 637.
98 Gundry, *Matthew*, xxiii, 628.
99 In this case, "Mark and the further tradition shared with Luke…[are] Matthew's primary
  sources" (Gundry, *Matthew*, 628).
100 Gundry, *Matthew*, 639.
101 Cf. D.J. Harrington, "Birth Narratives in Pseudo-Philo's *Biblical Antiquities* and the
  Gospels," in M.P. Horgan and P.J. Kobelski (eds), *To Touch the Text: Biblical and Related Studies in Honor of Joseph A. Fitzmyer, S.J.* (New York: Crossroad, 1989), 324.
102 Gundry, *Matthew*, xxiv, xx, 628.

The freedom to transform stories can also be seen in the writings of minor Hellenistic Jewish authors. In many of the preserved fragments, adaptive elements can been seen as these writers have appropriated biblical literature, reshaping it in Greek literary modes, primarily in order to glorify Israel's past and laud "its heroes and their achievements," with the (hopeful) result of strengthening "the Jewish self-consciousness" and promoting "the wish to be Jewish and to remain so."[103] In attempting to respond to the "changed political, social, and religious situation of their times," these pioneering Jewish writers exhibit "free and creative ways" to use and even recast the biblical stories.[104]

In his play, *Exagoge,* Ezekiel the Dramatist[105] tells the exodus story based primarily on the LXX text of Exodus 1-15. Even though he follows the Greek relatively closely, "sometimes almost literally," Pieter van der Horst points out that in the course of this retelling there are points of "significant" deviation from the LXX story.[106] These deviations range from minor matters of detail to entire and expansive scenes of non-biblical material.[107]

The work of adaptation can also be seen in the writings of the 'historian' Artapanus. Three fragments of his work survive, which display the biblical figures of Abraham, Joseph and Moses.[108] Artapanus presents these Jewish heroes apologetically, in quite positive lights, and often *via* purposeful "embellishments" as he deviate from the biblical accounts. It is interesting to note that these departures from the biblical text venture much farther afield than those of other Jewish historiographers (e.g., Demetrius[109]), and often are without exact parallels in either contemporary or later Jewish midrashic lit-

---

103 P. van der Horst, "The Interpretation of the Bible by the Minor Hellenistic Jewish Authors," in M.J. Mulder (ed.), *Mikra: Text, Translation, Reading and Interpretation of the Hebrew Bible in Ancient Judaism and Early Christianity* (CRINT 2.1; Assen/Philadelphia: Van Gorcum/Fortress Press, 1988), 543-45.

104 van der Horst, "The Interpretation of the Bible by the Minor Hellenistic Jewish Authors," 545.

105 He is also called 'Ezekiel the Tragedian' according to the way in which Eusebius (*Praeparatio evangelica* 9.28.1) and Clement of Alexandria (*Strom.* 1.23) refer to him – 'Ezekiel, the Poet of Jewish Tragedies'. For further information concerning Ezekiel and his play, ἡ ἐξαγωγή (preserved by Eusebius from Polyhistor's extracts in *Praepar. evang.* 9.28-29), see Nickelsburg, "The Bible Rewritten and Expanded," 125-30.

106 van der Horst, "The Interpretation of the Bible by the Minor Hellenistic Jewish Authors," 521.

107 Nickelsburg, "The Bible Rewritten and Expanded," 126.

108 These are preserved in Eusebius' *Praepar. evang.* 9.18, 9.23, and 9.27, respectively.

109 Although Demetrius does transform biblical stories for his purposes, examples from his writings are considered to be mild ones (see van der Horst, "The Interpretation of the Bible by the Minor Hellenistic Jewish Authors," 530-32). "Compared to other, later Jewish Hellenistic historians (Eupolemus, Artapanus, etc.) Demetrius is remarkably sober in his descriptions of biblical personalities" (532).

erature.[110] Whatever the reasons for his liberal enhancement,[111] it is clear that Artapanus "felt free to embellish and enrich the biblical story drastically with motives that were designed to enhance the prestige of his people and to bolster their ethnic pride."[112]

Tendencies towards modification in relating biblical material for new contexts and circumstances are quite plain in these cases. The freedom to transform stories is certainly not on the margins of some early Jewish biblical translation-interpretation. Thus it comes as no surprise that in many places in the narratives of the Greek Esther stories, we find adaptive tendencies, interpenetrations,[113] and modifying features. For as Geza Vermes relates, ancient versions such as these "are themselves also part of exegetical literature," possessing a "considerable amount of interpretative material."[114] And as the Esther story was related to and in new contexts, transformed moral characters are seen to emerge.

But even though the moral nature of the tales has been changed (often radically), it is debatable whether the so-called "pious trappings" have actually smoothed out the "rough angles" of the narratives as much as some might suppose.[115] While efforts of adaptation and resituation are clearly evident, the apparent striving after moral clarity and specificity has produced mixed results. To be sure, in many places in the Greek Esther stories the transformation of untidy or unclear moral instances hardly provides satisfactory answers to all of the moral questions.[116]

As we come to a summarising analysis of our research in the following two sections, it will be important to keep focus on the LXX and AT as whole narratives. Our ultimate aim is to relate the fruits of our investigation into the moral character found in the two Greek Esther texts studied. But, of course, when dealing with the presence of modifying features in translated and recon-

---

110 van der Horst, "The Interpretation of the Bible by the Minor Hellenistic Jewish Authors," 533.
111 Here van der Horst points to the fact that Artapanus wrote within the "anti-Semitic atmosphere of Ptolemaic Egypt" ("The Interpretation of the Bible by the Minor Hellenistic Jewish Authors," 537).
112 van der Horst, "The Interpretation of the Bible by the Minor Hellenistic Jewish Authors," 537.
113 Beate Ego terms these interpenetrations "aggadic" and submits that they begin in the Greek versions and find their "continuation and elaboration" in the Esther Targums ("Targumization as Theologization: Aggadic Additions in the Targum Sheni of Esther," in D.R.G. Beattie and M.J. McNamara (eds), The Aramaic Bible: Targums in their Historical Context (JSOTSup 166; Sheffield: Sheffield Academic Press, 1994), 354-59).
114 Vermes, "Bible and Midrash," 203. This particular point is also stressed by Stemberger, Introduction, 235.
115 See LaCocque, The Feminine Unconventional, 68-69.

textualised narratives, a source/parent text is always in the back of one's mind. Nevertheless, the occurrences we have come across in our investigation will be presented in the context of relating the moral character of the LXX and AT. It is an apprehension of the transformed moral character of these texts that ultimately concerns us. Thus, we shall not be offering a point-by-point comparison of moral issues between the LXX and MT, AT and MT, or LXX and AT. Our dealings with the parts should be in the service of a better grasp of the whole.

5.2.3 LXX

It should be admitted initially (and this is perhaps the same for both ancient and modern readers) that the moral character of the LXX is difficult to discern because the characters therein are often depicted as moral paradoxes. Narrative gaps are filled for sure, but perhaps often at the expense of an altogether intelligible assessment. This is especially noticeable as adaptive elements and influences enter the frame.

The one exception might be Astin. Few lacunae in her story are filled in by the LXX, leaving us at a loss to suggest much more about her behaviour than we have done above (§ 3.1.1). The same cannot be said, however, for the moral portraits of the other characters.

Alongside her crafty dealings, suspect and hesitant loyalties and shrewd proclivities, stand the obedience, pious prayerfulness, submitting heart, and perceived blamelessness of Esther (E.13). The story unabashedly highlights the last several of these as does subsequent interpretation of the Jewish heroine.[117] Initially, Esther displays an unwavering obedience concerning the charge and challenge to keep her identity private. As we have observed (§ 3.2.1), the narrative creates the distinct impression that she does just this. But of interest here as well is the manner in which the LXX presents Esther's concealment obligation – an obligation having both horizontal and vertical implications. With her duty being also to God, we get the impression that the weight of Esther's concealment burden becomes even greater. Not only is she to keep her identity quiet, she is also to fear God and do the commandments of God in her new court context. Esther's understanding of what is entailed in this broadened obligation appears to be somewhat elucidated in C.25b-29, but the *manner* in which she carries this concealment obedience out (not to men-

---

116 Harrington, *Invitation to the Apocrypha*, 53. Although Harrington's focus is the LXX, his point can legitimately be extended to the AT as well.
117 Bickerman, *Four Strange Books of the Bible*, 186-87.

tion how she pulls it off) seems to be beside the point of the story. Indeed, this modifying element, perhaps introduced for purposes of clarification, has actually complicated the believability of Esther's concealment initiative and has raised questions concerning her manner of life in the seat of Persian power. Even though it is presented as being unproblematic in the course of the story, the moral character of Esther is not at all as clear as one might suppose, and a measure of narrative tension has been introduced at this point. The transformation of the scene has occasioned a certain degree of moral unclarity and perhaps even untidiness.

The challenge of concealing her identity is followed, however, by an even greater charge – the deliverance of her people from destruction. From this task, Queen Esther initially shrinks back, seeming to enjoy her new identity in the Persian court, leaving the outside world outside (§ 3.2.2). But the persistent Mardochaios eventually penetrates Esther's apprehension enough that she, if only with a glimmer of hope, takes it upon herself to act on behalf of her people (§ 3.2.3). As the affections and commitments of the queen have begun to change, so also has our perception of her moral character.

A much more committed and religious portrait follows as we witness the queen on her knees praying to her heavenly king. Esther is presented as being uncompromisingly devout at this point. Her petition is for the help of the Lord, God of Israel, and lacks neither passion nor reserve (§ 3.2.4). The Jewess now appears to rely entirely upon God, presenting herself piously as a vessel for her Lord's work. But in spite of this presentation, the piety which Esther professes is often confusing and ultimately unconvincing (§ 3.2.5) – additional moral ambiguity (unclarity) results from apparent intentions of clarity *via* transformation. A clearer and more realistic picture can be seen in the scene of the second banquet and beyond. We witness a confident and resourceful queen as she now campaigns tactfully for her people, achieving her desired aims while appearing to be beyond moral reproach in the process (§ 3.2.6; 3.2.7). Throughout the course of the narrative, however, the portrait is not so clear.

In the case of Mardochaios, we have noticed that the narrative goes out of its way to stress his civic law abiding commitment on the one hand and his unbending religious loyalties on the other; the two are upheld together, and without explicit narrative friction. Tension exists, though, for the reader, and should not be ignored. The conscientious loyalty of Mardochaios and his value to both king and kingdom are clear throughout the LXX story (§ 3.3.1; 3.3.2; 3.3.5); the moral character he displays in most cases is undeniable and uncomplicated. However, with his refusal to do obeisance before Aman, our assessment has reason to pause (§ 3.3.3). The loyalty of Mardochaios to God, which is related in his prayer (see esp. C.5-7), appears to transcend his existence and allegiances in Sousa and compels him to take some controversial stances (§ 3.3.4). Indeed, these added and clarifying elements which have been introduced into the LXX story are not inconsequential to either the story or our understanding of Mardochaios's moral character. Yet in the end, even though we are given the distinct impression that the successes of Mardochaios are tied directly to the reality that the "living God" is with him (6.13), moral tension remains. A knowledge of this communion does not automatically answer all moral questions or clarify all moral issues in our quest to understand the decision making of Mardochaios. Again, while adaptive features have introduced some clarity to the story, the resultant transformation has occasioned some haziness as well.

Concerning the anonymous group of Jews, a more complicated picture arises. On the one hand, although they are suffering because of their idolatry – a surprising and interesting feature of clarification (§ 3.5.3) – are they really the lawless hordes that Aman so persuasively represents them to be (§ 3.5.1)? On the other hand, are we to assume that the Jews who cry out so desperately and loyally to God for help in their time of need (§ 3.5.2) are also to be considered untainted in their days of victory (§ 3.5.6; 3.5.7)? Though the narrative gives its answers (§ 3.5.5; and often by silence), a perceptive reader is likely to sense some tension in the moral character that is presented overall. Here, as well, transformed portraits of morality are not necessarily clearer portraits of morality.

This same awareness carries over into a consideration of the king. How might he ultimately be characterised in moral terms? Is he a fair and conscientious monarch who is able to run the affairs of the kingdom (§ 3.6.1; 3.6.2), or does he merely shift with the political winds and at the persuasion of influential people (§ 3.6.3; 3.6.5)? We are given both impressions in different places. Furthermore, after his spiritual reversal (§ 3.6.4) – a certain instance in which the story is being adapted to a new situation – to what extent is the king akin to the Jews? How culpable might he be as a partner in their dealings with enemies (§ 3.6.6)? Concerning these questions, the LXX story does not always provide clear-cut answers. As with most of the other characters, the moral character seen in the king is multi-faceted.

Yet, comparatively, the moral character of Aman is most unclouded, though still not perfectly uniform. Despite a glorifying self-portrait in section B (§ 3.4.3), he emits a paranoid hatred for Mardochaios and his people (§ 3.4.1; 3.4.2; 3.4.4), and is branded as a destructive threat both to the Jews and to the kingdom at large. He is, thus, and in the eyes of the narrative, worthy of his demise (§ 3.4.5). Ultimately, and especially in light of Zosara's declaration in 6.13, Aman never has much of a chance. In the end, the rhetorical onslaught of the transformed king overwhelms him (section E).

For the most part, an assessment of moral character in the LXX Esther story has failed to deliver a clear verdict. Although adaptations, interpenetrations, and clarifications have transformed the story markedly, they have not, on the whole, brought about a moral character that lacks ambiguity. It would seem that the presentation and development of the characters have often brought about a sense of overall moral *obscurity* even when the transformative aim might have been to effect moral *clarity*. Efforts of transformation do not necessarily bring about disambiguation. The situation is similar in the AT version.

5.2.4 AT

Just as we found in our investigations in the LXX, it is often the case that issues of moral character perceived in the AT narrative appear paradoxical. That is to say, it is as if many of the characters therein are morally two-faced – giving us a certain impression at one point and a differing (or even opposite) one at another. This, of course, makes for an assessment effort that is full of challenges. Nevertheless, hope is not lost for the task, though it might turn out best to leave some moral tensions as they are – as the story leaves them.

This is not the case, however, as it concerns Ouastin; her (in)actions remain unexplored and unexplained by the narrative. If she is merely to be publicly distinguished in her summoned appearance before the court, why would she have shrunk from this? While suppositions are plenteous, firm explanations elude us; an occasion for moral appraisal hardly presents itself.

At the other end of the assessment spectrum stands Aman. His animosity towards Mardochaios and his people is clear from the very beginning and remains so as the story proceeds (§ 4.4.1; 4.4.2). Alongside this all the while are suspicions concerning the true identity and intentions of Aman, which have been actualised in the distinctive labels Βουγαῖος and Μακεδόνα. The main narrative focus, however, remains the designs he harbours against his enemies – Mardochaios and the Jews. Through propagandistic persuasion, the utter destruction of this people is made out to be in the best interest of the kingdom (§ 4.4.3). Aman's obsessions with the Jew and his own honour, though, are never satiated (§ 4.4.4; 4.4.5), and, in the end, he receives both civil and divine condemnation for his crimes against the kingdom (§ 4.4.6). His despoiled moral character is never in doubt.

This, however, cannot be claimed for the remaining four characters –
Esther, Mardochaios, the Jews, and the king. So far as the Jewess is concerned, we have discerned a mixed portrait. Her apparent selfishness and
early lack of commitment to the Jews (§ 4.2.1) is soon challenged by a persistent Mardochaios and later rectified by a self-sacrificial resolving for the
cause of her people (§ 4.2.2). Adaptive elements figure in prominent places
in the midst of the mediated exchange between the two Jews, and a palpable
acknowledgement of and reliance upon God comes to the surface (4.9, 11).
But even as the (then) queen reveals her deep and pious commitments to God
as she implores her Lord to act decisively on their behalf, her assimilating
behaviour in the Persian court appears dubious (§ 4.2.3; 4.2.4). Instances of
intended clarification introduce an implicit, though undeniable, confusion
into a discernment of Esther's character in the middle portions of the AT
story. Esther at her most pious is also Esther at her most unbelievable. Perhaps this tension is necessary; perhaps it is not really important. Or maybe
the presence of the logical difficulties should point us to Esther's God,
through whom the miraculous delivery of the Jews ultimately comes. Towards the end of the story, vengeance belongs to Esther, but we are left to
ponder the relationship between God's sovereignty and her responsibility. In
short, her 'inner' and 'public' selves seem often to be in moral tension
(§ 4.2.6). But perhaps this negotiation of tension is the model for a Diaspora
existence, or at least the extraordinary ethics for Esther in the Persian court.

It seems that 'loyal' would appropriately sum up the character Mardochaios in the AT. His loyalty to both king and kingdom is made patently
clear, as is his faithfulness to God (§ 4.3.1; 4.3.3). While presented as being
blameless concerning most civil regulations, Mardochaios instructs and ex-
emplifies resourceful and measured living and decision-making within a foreign land and court (§ 4.3.4). But his unyieldingness to Aman remains
somewhat problematic and only partially grasped (§ 4.3.2). The clarifying
explanation of 4.15 does not really put to rest the questions that arise from
3.1-4; in fact, it might have misinterpreted what is actually being required in
the former reference. This, of course, is a serious matter in the course of the
story and is one that warrants some reflection, especially since in another
situation Mardochaios renders unreserved obedience to Aman, and without
elucidating commentary (§ 4.3.5). Yet the AT story leaves this tension between loyalty to God and loyalty to human beings somewhat unresolved.
Perhaps we must leave it there also.

The commitment of the Jews corporately to their God is likewise demon-
strable in the narrative. Even though they look God-ward in times of trouble
(§ 4.5.1), they are not totally blameless in their actions (§ 4.5.3); attempts at

adaptation have not produced a one-sided moral portrait. But it is doubtful that the Jews are actually as nefarious as Aman slanders them to be (§ 4.5.2). Towards the end of the narrative the Jewish people are seen quite positively – their laws are vindicated and their devotion to God is clearly attested (§ 4.5.4). But this perception should be weighed against their part in the armed conflicts, which is questionable at best (§ 4.5.5). Ultimately, the Lord remembers and delivers them (§ 4.5.6), but throughout that deliverance, the Jews often struggle as the people of God. Efforts which seek to modify the moral perception of the AT Jews help bring this struggle to life; but, in so doing, they bring about moral tensions as well.

By the way in which the narrative communicates it, we get a distinct impression of the power and influence of the king (§ 4.6.2). Initially, His Majesty acts decisively and independently (§ 4.6.1). But even though it appears that he is at times swayed by the influence of others as the story proceeds, the text makes sure that his role in matters is not overshadowed. For instance, the acquiescence of the king to and narrative leadership in the plot of Aman is unmistakable; he is persuaded by the passion of his vizier, and for all practical purposes serves in a leadership role against the Jews (at that point still a nameless people) (§ 4.6.3). This is, by far, the king's lowest moral moment. However, in an attempt to alter the theological tone of the narrative, God enters the story and changes it by transforming the affections of its strongest character. The spiritual transformation of the king appears then to affect his subsequent actions positively (§ 4.6.4); he is now allied with the Jews and leads alongside their leaders (§ 4.6.5). This could be seen as his highest moral moment as far as the narrative is concerned. Yet the story does not end on that note. Because of his complicity in the vengeance of Esther, the king should be subject to the same moral criticism that might be levelled against the queen, for his part in the bloodshed is certainly not insignificant (§ 4.6.6).

As with the LXX, certain adaptive and clarifying elements in the AT have transformed the moral character of the story. Yet in the effort to translate the tale relevantly and meaningfully in a new context, not all has been made clear in moral terms.

5.3 Final Conclusions

Our task in this study has been to investigate and describe relevant episodes in the three primary texts of Esther with a view to a better apprehension and negotiation of the moral character therein and thereof. Following the lead of Robert Gordis, the investigation was initiated by questions concerning the reason(s) why readers have historically been so troubled by issues of morality in the Esther story. Those questions have led to similar and further questions as the work has proceeded and broadened, many of which remain (or have been left) unresolved.

Given the way in which moral issues have been handled (or avoided) in many communities, it is clear that some early receivers of this story have been unsettled. The LXX and AT versions of Esther testify to readers who have been disquieted by the complexity of its moral situations. This has presented an occasion for investigation. And even though the results of our exploration have served to underscore the fact that moral character in the narratives is equivocal, this is not necessarily a reason for disappointment and disillusionment. Perhaps some biblical texts are properly understood *only* when their complexities and ambiguities are recognised and embraced. Even after centuries of reading and interpretation, it might be well that some stories remain "unsettling" and ambiguous to certain extents and in certain respects.[118] In our judgement, the story of Esther remains one of these.

Issues of morality are not on the periphery of the books of Esther; neither are they inconsequential in the narrative flow of the three stories. This much was approximated and anticipated in the Introduction, and has been elucidated and evaluated in chapters two, three, and four. This is not to say, however, that these issues are always or even normally presented clearly in the Esther texts we have investigated; as we have seen, complexity and ambiguity characterise many of the moral moments in the stories. This is even the case at points in which moral character has been transformed. Oftentimes, efforts to dispel moral ambiguity have resulted in further uncertainties or have occasioned new complexities; slight or even radical adjustments have not always produced a clearer moral portrait.

In the 'Introduction' to his recent commentary, Timothy Beal makes the following statement concerning the Hebrew Esther story:

> On first reading it appears so simple, so whole, and its meaning so completely self-evident. Yet the closer one gets to this text, the more perplexing it becomes. Questions lead not to answers but to more profound questions, and a certain distance begins to open between reader and text. Rather than becoming more familiar upon further reading, it appears more and more strange, in some sense unknowable, like a letter fragment which arrives to us from a world that is otherwise inaccessible.[119]

Although he is making a general comment about the entire Esther narrative, Beal's observation can be applied particularly to the moral character of the

---

118 See the recent approach of Linafelt to the book of Ruth (*Ruth*, xiii-xiv).
119 Beal, *Esther*, ix.

story as well. For the closer we have come to issues of morality, the more perplexing many of them have become. Indeed, where we might have initially hoped to have seen broadly, we often have been afforded only "glimpses."[120] So also as regards the Greek stories. In different ways, questions concerning the moral character of these narratives have led also to further and more complex inquiries. This is, perhaps, one of the reasons why the Esther story, in each of its distinctive versions, has been and will continue to be so compelling.

---

120 I am employing the helpful image introduced by C.S. Rodd in his recent volume on OT ethics, *Glimpses of a Strange Land* (OTS; Edinburgh: T & T Clark, 2001). Commenting on the study of OT ethics, Rodd states that "[O]ften when we visit a mediaeval castle we climb a spiral staircase to the top of the keep. For most of the time we are surrounded by blank walls, but as we clamber up we pass slit windows through which we obtain glimpses of the countryside that surrounds the castle. The view is narrowly restricted and we often find it difficult to imagine what the whole panorama looks like" (3). Even as we catch glimpses, a certain "uncertainty remains" (4).

Bibliography

Ackroyd, P.R., "Two Hebrew Notes," *ASTI* 5 (1966-67), 82-86.

Adler, J.J., "The Book of Esther: Some Questions and Responses," *JBQ* 19 (1990-91), 186-90.

Aejmelaeus, A., *On the Trail of the Septuagint Translators* (Kampen: Kok Pharos, 1993).

Albright, W.F., "The Lachish Cosmetic Burner and Esther 2:12," in H.N. Bream, R.D. Helm and C.A. Moore (eds), *A Light Unto My Path: Old Testament Studies in Honor of Jacob M. Myers* (Philadelphia: Temple University Press, 1974), 25-32.

Alexander, P.S., "Quid Athenis et Hierosolymis? Rabbinic Midrash and Hermeneutics in the Græco-Roman world," in P.R. Davies and R.T. White (eds), *A Tribute to Geza Vermes: Essays on Jewish and Christian Literature and History* (JSOTSup 100; Sheffield: Sheffield Academic Press, 1990), 101-24.

_____ "Midrash and the Gospels," in C.M. Tuckett (ed.), *Synoptic Studies: The Ampleforth Conferences of 1982 and 1983* (JSNTSup 7; Sheffield: JSOT Press, 1984), 1-18.

Allis, O.T., "The Reward of the King's Favorite (Esther vi.8)," *PTR* 21 (1923), 621-32.

Alter, R., *The Art of Biblical Narrative* (New York: Basic Books, 1981).

Anderson, B.W., "Introduction and Exegesis to Esther," in G.A. Buttrich, *et. al.* (eds), *The Interpreter's Bible* (Nashville: Abingdon Press, 1954), III: 823-74.

_____ "The Place of Esther in the Christian Bible," *JRS* 30 (1950), 32-43.

Andrew, M.E., "Esther, Exodus and Peoples," *ABR* 23 (1975), 25-28.

Attridge, H.W., *The Interpretation of Biblical History in the* Antiquitates Judaicae *of Flavius Josephus* (HDR 7; Missoula, MT: Scholars Press, 1976).

Aus, R.D., *Barabbas and Esther and Other Studies in the Judaic Illumination of Earliest Christianity* (SFSHJ 54; Atlanta: Scholars Press, 1992).

_____ *Water into Wine and the Beheading of John the Baptist: Early Jewish-Christian Interpretation of Esther 1 in John 2.1-11 and Mark 6.17-29* (BJS 150; Atlanta: Scholars Press, 1988).

Bach, A., *Women, Seduction, and Betrayal in Biblical Narrative* (Cambridge: Cambridge University Press, 1997).

_____"Mirror, Mirror in the Text: Reflections on Reading and Rereading," in A. Brenner (ed.), *A Feminist Companion to Esther, Judith and Susanna* (FCB 7; Sheffield: Sheffield Academic Press, 1995), 81-86.

Bacher, W., "The Origin of the Word Haggada (Agada)," *JQR* 4 (1892), 406-29.

Bal, M., "Lots of Writing," *Semeia* 54 (1991), 77-102.

Baldwin, J.C., *Esther* (TOTC; Leicester: Inter-Varsity, 1984).

Bardtke, H., "Neuere Arbeiten zum Estherbuch: Eine kritische Würdigung," *Ex Oriente Lux* 19 (1965-66), 519-49.

_____*Das Buch Esther* (KAT 17/5; Gütersloh: Gütersloher Verlagshaus Gerd Mohn, 1963).

Bar-Efrat, S., *Narrative Art in the Bible* (JSOTSup 70; Sheffield: Almond Press, 1989).

Bar-Ilan, M., *Some Jewish Women in Antiquity* (BJS 317; Atlanta: Scholars Press, 1998).

Barton, J., *Ethics and the Old Testament* (London: SCM Press Ltd, 1998).

_____*Oracles of God: Perceptions of Ancient Prophecy in Israel after the Exile* (London: Darton, Longman & Todd, 1986).

_____"Understanding Old Testament Ethics," *JSOT* 9 (1978), 44-64.

Barucq, A., *Judith, Esther* (La Sainte Bible; Paris: Cerf, 1959[2]).

Bauckham, R., *The Bible in Politics: How to Read the Bible Politically* (Louisville: WJKP, 1987).

Baumgartner, A.I., "The Scroll of Esther," *EncJud* (Jerusalem: Keter Publishing House, Ltd, 1971), 14:1047-1057.

Beal, T.K., *Esther*, in T. Linafelt and *idem, Ruth and Esther* (Berit Olam; Collegeville, MN: The Liturgical Press, 1999).

_____*The Book of Hiding: Gender, Ethnicity, Annihilation, and Esther* (London and New York: Routledge, 1997).

_____"Tracing Esther's Beginnings," in A. Brenner (ed.), *A Feminist Companion to Esther, Judith and Susanna* (FCB 7; Sheffield: Sheffield Academic Press, 1995), 87-110.

_____"Ideology and Intertextuality: Surplus of Meaning and Controlling the Means of Production," in D.N. Fewell (ed.), *Reading Between Texts: Intertextuality and the Hebrew Bible* (Louisville: Westminster Press/John Knox, 1992), 27-39.

Bechtel, C.M., *Esther* (Interpretation; Louisville: John Knox Press, 2002).

Beckwith, R.T., "Formation of the Hebrew Bible," in M.J. Mulder (ed.), *Mikra: Text, Translation, Reading and Interpretation of the Hebrew Bible in Ancient Judaism and Early Christianity* (CRINT 2.1; Assen/Philadelphia: Van Gorcum/Fortress Press, 1988), 39-86.

_____*The Old Testament Canon of the New Testament Church* (London: SPCK, 1985).

Beller, D., "A Theology of the Book of Esther," *ResQ* 39 (1997), 1-15.

Bellis, A.O., *Helpmates, Harlots and Heroes: Women's Stories in the Hebrew Bible* (Louisville: Westminster/John Knox Press, 1994), 206-23.

Ben-Chorin, S., *Kritik des Estherbuches: Eine theologische Streitschrift* (Jerusalem: Salingré & Co., 1938).

Berg, S.B., "After the Exile: God and History in the Books of Chronicles and Esther," in J.L. Crenshaw and S. Sandmel (eds), *The Divine Helmsman: Studies on God's Control on Human Events* (New York: Ktav, 1980), 107-27.

_____*The Book of Esther: Motifs, Themes, and Structure* (SBLDS 44; Missoula, MT: Scholars Press, 1979).

Bergey, R.L., "Post-Exilic Hebrew Linguistic Developments in Esther: A Diachronic Approach," *JETS* 31 (1988), 161-68.

_____"Late Linguistic Features in Esther," *JQR* 75 (1984), 66-78.

_____"The Book of Esther – Its Place in the Linguistic Milieu of Post-exilic Biblical Hebrew Prose: A Study of Late Biblical Hebrew," (Ph.D. Diss., Dropsie College, 1983).

Berlin, A., *Esther* (The JPS Bible Commentary; Philadelphia: The Jewish Publication Society, 2001).

_____"The Book of Esther and Ancient Storytelling," *JBL* 120 (2001), 3-14.

_____*Poetics and Interpretation of Biblical Narrative* (Sheffield: Almond Press, 1983).

Berman, J., "Aggadah and Antisemitism: The Midrashim to Esther 3.8," *Judaism* 38 (1989), 185-96.

Berman, J.A., "*Hadassah bat Abihail:* The Evolution from Object to Subject in the Character of Esther," *JBL* 120 (2001), 647-669.

Berquist, J.L., *Judaism in Persia's Shadow* (Minneapolis: Fortress Press, 1995).

Bickerman, E.J., *Four Strange Books of the Bible: Jonah, Daniel, Koheleth, Esther* (New York: Schocken, 1967).

_____*From Ezra to the Last of the Maccabees: Foundations of Post-Biblical Judaism* (New York: Schocken, 1962).

_____"Notes on the Greek Book of Esther," *PAAJR* 20 (1950), 101-33.

_____"The Colophon of the Greek Book of Esther," *JBL* 63 (1944), 339-62.

Birch, B.C., W. Brueggemann, T.E. Fretheim, and D.L. Petersen, *A Theological Introduction to the Old Testament* (Nashville: Abingdon Press, 1999).

Birch, B.C., *Let Justice Roll Down: The Old Testament, Ethics, and the Christian Life* (Louisville: Westminster/John Knox Press, 1991).

_____ "Old Testament Narrative and Moral Address," in G.M. Tucker, D.L. Petersen and R.R. Wilson (eds), *Canon, Theology and Old Testament Interpretation: Essays in Honor of Brevard S. Childs* (Philadelphia: Fortress Press, 1988), 75-91.

Bloch, R., "Midrash" (trans. M.H. Callaway), in W.S. Green (ed.), *Approaches to Ancient Judaism: Theory and Practice* (BJS 1; Missoula, MT: Scholars Press, 1978), 29-50.

Blumenthal, D.R., "Where God is Not: The Book of Esther and Song of Songs," *Judaism* 44 (1995), 80-92.

Botterweck, G.J., "Die Gattung des Buches Esther in Spektrum neuerer Publikationen," *BibLeb* 5 (1964), 274-92.

Boyd-Taylor, C., "Esther's Great Adventure: Reading the LXX version of the Book of Esther in light of its assimilation to the convention of the Greek romantic novel," *BIOSCS* 30 (1997), 81-113.

Brenner, A., "Looking at Esther through the Looking Glass," in *idem* (ed.), *A Feminist Companion to Esther, Judith and Susanna* (FCB 7; Sheffield: Sheffield Academic Press, 1995), 71-80.

_____ "On the Semantic Field of Humour, Laughter and the Comic in the Old Testament," in Y.T. Radday, and *idem* (eds), *On Humour and the Comic in the Hebrew Bible* (JSOTSup 92; Sheffield: Almond Press, 1990), 39-58.

Briant, P., "Persian Empire," *ABD* (New York: Doubleday, 1992), 5:236-44.

Bright, J., *A History of Israel* (London: SCM Press, Ltd., 1966).

Brighton, L.A., "The Book of Esther – Textual and Canonical Considerations," *CJ* 13 (1987), 200-18.

Brock, S., "To Revise or Not to Revise: Attitudes to Jewish Biblical Translation," in G. J. Brooke and B. Lindars (eds), *Septuagint, Scrolls and Cognate Writings* (SBLSCSS 33; Atlanta: Scholars Press, 1992), 301-38.

Bronner, L.L., "Reclaiming Esther: From Sex Object to Sage," *JBQ* 26 (1998), 3-10.

_____ "Esther Revisited: An Aggadic Approach," in A. Brenner (ed.), *A Feminist Companion to Esther, Judith and Susanna* (FCB 7; Sheffield: Sheffield Academic Press, 1995), 176-197.

_____ *From Eve to Esther: Rabbinic Reconstructions of Biblical Women* (Gender and the Biblical Tradition Series; Louisville: Westminster Press/John Knox, 1994).

Brooke, A.E., N. McLean, and T.H. St. John (eds), "Esther, Judith, Tobit," in *The Old Testament in Greek* (vol. III, pt. 1; Cambridge: Cambridge University Press, 1940).

Broyde, M.J., "Defilement of the Hands, Canonization of the Bible, and the Special Status of Esther, Ecclesiastes, and Song of Songs," *Judaism* 44 (1995), 65-79.

Bruce, W.S., *The Ethics of the Old Testament* (Edinburgh: T & T Clark, 1909^2).

Brueggemann, W., *Theology of the Old Testament* (Minneapolis: Fortress Press, 1997).

_____*Texts Under Negotiation: The Bible and Postmodern Imagination* (Minneapolis: Fortress Press, 1993).

Bruns, G.L., "Midrash and Allegory: The Beginnings of Scriptural Interpretation," in R. Alter and F. Kermode (eds), *The Literary Guide to the Bible* (Cambridge: Harvard University Press, 1987), 625-46.

Bryce, G.E., Review of S.B. Berg, *The Book of Esther: Motifs, Themes and Structure, JBL* 100 (1981), 276-77.

Bush, F.W., "The Book of Esther: *Opus non gratum* in the Christian Canon," *BBR* 8 (1998), 39-54.

_____*Ruth, Esther* (WBC 9; Dallas: Word Books, 1996).

Butting, K., "Esther: A New Interpretation of the Joseph Story in the Fight Against Anti-Semitism and Sexism," in A. Brenner (ed.), *Ruth and Esther: A Feminist Companion to the Bible* (FCB second series 3; Sheffield: Sheffield Academic Press, 1999), 239-48.

Cameron, G., "The Persian Satrapies and Related Matters," *JNES* 32 (1973), 47-56.

Carr, D.M., "Canonization in the Context of Community: An Outline of the Formation of the Tanakh and the Christian Bible," in R.D. Weis and *idem* (eds), *A Gift of God in Due Season: Essays on Scripture and Community in Honor of James A. Sanders* (JSOTSup 225; Sheffield: Sheffield Academic Press, 1996), 22-64.

Carroll, M.P., "Myth, Methodology and Transformation in the Old Testament: The Stories of Esther, Judith, and Susanna," *SR* 12/3 (1983), 301-12.

Cassel, P., *An Explanatory Commentary on Esther* (trans. A. Bernstein; Edinburgh: T & T Clark, 1888).

Cazelles, H., "Note sur la composition du rouleau d'Esther," in H. Gross and F. Mussner, *Lex Tua Veritas: Festschrift für Herbert Junker* (Trier: Paulinus Verlag, 1961), 17-29.

Childs, B.S., *Biblical Theology of the Old and New Testaments: Theological Reflection on the Christian Bible* (Minneapolis: Fortress Press, 1992).

_____*Introduction to the Old Testament as Scripture* (Philadelphia: Fortress Press, 1979).

_____"Midrash and the Old Testament," in J. Reumann (ed.), *Understanding the Sacred Text: Essays in Honor of Morton S. Enslin on the Hebrew Bible and Christian Beginnings* (Valley Forge, PA: Judson Press, 1972), 45-59.

Clements, R.E., "Christian Ethics and the Old Testament," *The Modern Churchman* 26 (1984), 13-26.

Clines, D.J.A., "Mordecai," *ABD* (New York: Doubleday, 1992), 4:902-04.

_____"In Quest of the Historical Mordecai," *VT* 41 (1991), 129-36.

_____"Reading Esther from Left to Right: Contemporary Strategies for Reading a Biblical Text," in D.J.A. Clines, S.E. Fowl and S.E. Porter (eds), *The Bible in Three Dimensions* (JSOTSup 87; Sheffield: JSOT Press, 1990), 31-52.

_____"The Additions to Esther," in J.L. Mays (ed.), *Harper's Bible Commentary* (San Francisco: Harper and Row, 1988), 815-19.

_____*The Esther Scroll: The Story of the Story* (JSOTSup 30; Sheffield: JSOT Press, 1984).

_____*Ezra, Nehemiah, Esther* (NCBC; Grand Rapids: Eerdmans, 1984).

Coats, G.W., "Genres: Why Should They Be Important For Exegesis?," in *idem* (ed.), *Saga, Legend, Tale, Novella, Fable: Narrative Forms in Old Testament Literature* (JSOTSup 35; Sheffield: JSOT Press, 1985), 7-15.

Coats, G.W., and B.O. Long, *Canon and Authority: Essays in Old Testament Religion and Theology* (Philadelphia: Fortress Press, 1977).

Coggins, R.J., "The Origins of the Jewish Diaspora," in R.E. Clements (ed.), *The World of Ancient Israel* (Cambridge: Cambridge University Press, 1989), 163-81.

Cohen, A.D., "'Hu Ha-Goral': The Religious Significance of Esther," *Judaism* 23 (1974), 87-94.

Cohen, J.M., "Vashti – An Unsung Heroine," *JBQ* 24 (1996), 103-106.

Cohen, S.J.D., "'Those Who Say They Are Jews and Are Not': How Do You Know a Jew in Antiquity When You See One?" in *idem* and E.S. Frerichs (eds), *Diasporas in Antiquity* (BJS 288; Atlanta: Scholars Press, 1993), 1-45.

_____"Religion, Ethnicity and 'Hellenism' in the Emergence of Jewish Identity in Maccabean Palestine," in P. Bilde, T. Engberg-Pedersen, L. Hannestad, and J. Zahle (eds) *Religion and Religious Practice in the Seleucid Kingdom* (Studies in Hellenistic Civilization I; Aarhus: Aarhus University Press, 1990), 204-23.

Collins, J.J., *Jewish Wisdom in the Hellenistic Age* (OTL; Louisville: Westminster John Knox Press, 1997).

Cook, H.J., "The A Text of the Greek Versions of the Book of Esther," *ZAW* 81 (1969), 369-76.

Costas, O.E., "The Subversiveness of Faith: Esther as a Paradigm for a Liberating Theology," *The Ecumenical Review* 40 (1988), 66-78.

Craghan, J.F., "Esther, Judith, and Ruth: Paradigms for Human Liberation," *BTB* 12 (1982), 11-19.

_____*Narrative Books: Esther/Judith/Tobit/Jonah/Ruth* (OTM; Wilmington: Michael Glazier, 1981).

Craig, Jr., K.M., *Reading Esther: A Case for the Literary Carnivalesque* (Louisville: Westminster/John Knox, 1995).

Crawford, S.W., Review of J.D. Levenson, *Esther* (*JBL* 118 (1999), 134-36).

Crenshaw, J.L., "Methods in Determining Wisdom Influence upon 'Historical' Literature," *JBL* 88 (1969), 129-42.

Darr, K.P., "More Than Just a Pretty Face: Critical, Rabbinical, and Feminist Perspectives on Esther," in *Far More Precious Than Jewels: Perspectives on Biblical Women* (Gender and the Biblical Tradition Series; Louisville: Westminster Press/John Knox, 1991), 164-202.

Dancy, J.C., *The Shorter Books of the Apocrypha: Tobit, Judith, Rest of Esther, Baruch, Letter of Jeremiah, Additions to Daniel and Prayer of Manasseh* (London: Cambridge University Press, 1972).

Dandamayev, M., "Babylonia in the Persian Age," in W.D. Davies and L. Finkelstein (eds), *The Cambridge History of Judaism* (vol. I: *Introduction – The Persian Period*; Cambridge: Cambridge University Press, 1984), 326-42.

Daube, D., *Esther* (Yarnton, Oxford: The Oxford Centre for Postgraduate Hebrew Studies, 1995).

_____"The Last Chapter of Esther," *JQR* 37 (1946-7), 139-47.

Day, L., "Power, Otherness, and Gender in the Biblical Short Stories," *HBT* 20 (1998), 109-27.

_____*Three Faces of a Queen: Characterization in the Books of Esther* (JSOTSup 186; Sheffield: Sheffield Academic Press, 1995).

De Lagarde, P.A., *Librorum Veteris Testamenti Canonicorum* (Göttingen, 1883).

De Miroschedji, P., "Susa," *ABD* (New York: Doubleday, 1992), 6:242-45.

De Troyer, K., *The End of the Alpha Text of Esther: Translation and Narrative Technique in MT 8:1-17, LXX 8:1-17, and AT 7:14-41* (trans. B. Doyle; revised and updated; SBLSCSS 48; Atlanta: SBL, 2000).

_____*Het einde van de Alpha-tekst van Ester: Vertaal- en verhaaltechniek van MT 8,1-17, LXX 8,1-17 en AT 7,14-41* (Leuven: Uitgeverij Peeters, 1997).

_____"On Crowns and Diadems from Kings, Queens, Horses and Men," in B.A. Taylor (ed.), *IX Congress of the International Organization for Septuagint and Cognate Studies* (SBLSCSS 45; Atlanta: Scholars Press, 1997), 355-67.

_____"An Oriental Beauty Parlour: An Analysis of Esther 2.8-18 in the Hebrew, the Septuagint and the Second Greek Text," in A. Brenner (ed.), *A Feminist Companion to Esther, Judith and Susanna* (FCB 7; Sheffield: Sheffield Academic Press, 1995), 47-70.

Derby, J., "The Paradox in the Book of Esther," *JBQ* 23 (1995), 116-19.

Dommershausen, W., *Ester* (NEB; Würzburg: Echter Verlag, 1995³).

_____*Die Esterrolle: Stil und Ziel einer alttestamentlichen Schrift* (Stuttgart: Katholisches Bibelwerk, 1968).

Dorothy, C.V., *The Books of Esther: Structure, Genre, and Textual Integrity* (JSOTSup 187; Sheffield: Sheffield Academic Press, 1997).

Driver, G.R., "Affirmation by Exclamatory Negation," *JANES* 5 (1973), 107-13.

_____*Aramaic Documents of the 5ᵗʰ Century BC* (Oxford: Clarendon, 1957).

_____"Problems and Solutions," *VT* 4 (1954), 225-45.

Driver, S.R., *Introduction to the Literature of the Old Testament* (Edinburgh: T & T Clark, 1913).

Edelman, D.V., "Kish," *ABD* (New York: Doubleday, 1992), 4:85-87.

Editorial Staff, "Scrolls, The Five," *EncJud* (Jerusalem: Keter, 1971), 14:1058.

Edwards, R.K., "Reply to 'Ahasuerus Is the Villain'," *JBQ* 19 (1990), 33-39.

Ego, B., "Tagumization as Theologization: Aggadic Additions in the Targum Sheni of Esther," in D.R.G. Beattie and M.J. McNamara (eds), *The Aramaic Bible: Targums in Their Historical Context* (JSOTSup 166; Sheffield: JSOT Press, 1994), 354-59.

Ehrlich, A.B., *Ranglossen zur hebräischen Bibel: Textkritisches, Sprachliches, und Sachliches* (vol. XII; Hildesheim: Georg Olms, 1968).

Eichrodt, W., *Theology of the Old Testament* (vol. II; trans. J.A. Baker; Philadelphia: Westminster, 1967).

_____*Man in the Old Testament* (SBT 4; London: SCM Press, 1951).

Eisenmann, R., and M. Wise, "Stories from the Persian Court," in *The Dead Sea Scrolls Uncovered* (Rockport, ME: Element, 1992), 99-103.

Eissfeldt, O., *The Old Testament: An Introduction* (trans. P.R. Ackroyd; Oxford: Basil Blackwell, 1965).

Ellis, E.E., *The Old Testament in Early Christianity: Canon and Interpretation in the light of Modern Research* (WUNT 54; Tübingen: J.C.B. Mohr (Paul Siebeck), 1991).

Enslin, M.S., *The Book of Judith* (Dropsie University Jewish Apocryphal Literature Series VII; Leiden: E.J. Brill, 1972).

Eskenazi, T.C., "Out of the Shadow: Biblical Women in the Post-Exilic Era," *JSOT* 54 (1992), 25-43.

_____*In an Age of Prose: A Literary Approach to Ezra Nehemiah* (SBLMS 36; Atlanta: Scholars Press, 1988).

Feldman, L.H., *Studies in Josephus' Rewritten Bible* (Leiden: E.J. Brill, 1998).

_____"Hellenizations in Josephus' Version of Esther," *Proceedings of the American Philological Society* 101 (1970), 143-70.

Fewell, D.N., "Introduction: Writing, Reading, and Relating," in *idem* (ed.), *Reading Between Texts: Intertextuality and the Hebrew Bible* (Louisville: Westminster/John Knox, 1992), 11-20.

_____"Feminist Reading of the Hebrew Bible: Affirmation, Resistance, and Transformation," *JSOT* 39 (1987), 77-87.

Field F., *Origenis Hexaplorum quae supersunt* (2 vol.; Oxonii: E Typographeo Clarendoniano, 1875).

Finkel, J., "The Author of the Genesis Apocryphon Knew the Book of Esther," in C. Rabin and Y. Yadin (eds), *Essays on the Dead Sea Scrolls in Memory of E.L. Sukenik* (Jerusalem: Hekhal Ha-sefer, 1961), 163-82.

Firth, D.G., "The Book of Esther: A Neglected Paradigm for Dealing with the State," *OT Essays* 10 (1997), 18-26.

Fisch, H., "Esther: Two Tales of One City," in *Poetry with a Purpose* (Bloomington: Indiana University Press, 1988), 8-14.

Fishbane, M., "Inner-Biblical Exegesis," in M. Sæbø (ed.), *Hebrew Bible/Old Testament: The History of its Interpretation* (vol. I, part 1; Göttingen: Vandenhoeck & Ruprecht, 1996), 33-48.

_____*Biblical Interpretation in Ancient Israel* (Oxford: Clarendon Press, 1985).

Flusser, D., "Psalms, Hymns and Prayers," in M.E. Stone (ed.), *Jewish Writings of the Second Temple Period: Apocrypha, Pseudepigrapha, Qumran Sectarian Writings, Philo, Josephus* (CRINT 2.2; Assen/Philadelphia: Van Gorcum/Fortress Press, 1984), 551-77.

Fox, A.W., *The Ethics and Theology of the Old Testament* (London: Lindsey Press, 1918).

Fox, M.V., "The Redaction of the Greek Alpha-Text of Esther," in M. Fishbane and E. Tov (eds), *Sha'arei Talmon: Studies in the Bible, Qumran, and the Ancient Near East Presented to Shemaryahu Talmon* (Winona Lake, IN: Eisenbrauns, 1992), 207-20.

_____*Character and Ideology in the Book of Esther* (Columbia: University of South Carolina Press, 1991).

_____*The Redaction of the Books of Esther* (SBLMS 40; Atlanta: Scholars Press, 1991).

_____"The Religion of the Book of Esther," *Judaism* 39 (1990), 135-47.

_____"The Alpha Text of the Greek Esther," *Textus* 15 (1990), 27-54.

_____"The Structure of the Book of Esther," in A. Rofé and Y. Zakovitch (eds), *Isaac Leo Seeligmann Volume: Essays on the Bible and the Ancient World* (Jerusalem: E. Rubinstein, 1983), 291-303.

Fox, N.S., "In the Spirit of Purim: The Hidden Hand of God," *JBQ* 18 (1990), 183-87.

Fretz, M.R., "Agagite," *ABD* (New York: Doubleday, 1992), 1:89-90.

Frye, R., "Minorities in the History of the Near East," in J. Duchesne-Guillemin, et al (eds), *A Green Leaf: Papers in Honour of Professor Jes P. Asmussen* (*Acta Iranica* 28; Leiden: E.J. Brill, 1988), 461-71.

Fried, L.S., "Towards the *Ur*-Text of Esther," *JSOT* 88 (2000), 49-57.

Friedberg, A.D., "A New Clue in the Dating of the Composition of the Book of Esther," *VT* 50 (2000), 561-65.

Fuchs, E., "'For I Have the Way of Women': Deception, Gender, and Ideology in Biblical Narrative," *Semeia* 42 (1988), 68-83.

_____"Who is Hiding the Truth? Deceptive Women and Biblical Androcentrism," in A.Y. Collins (ed.), *Feminist Perspectives on Biblical Scholarship* (SBL Biblical Scholarship in North America Series 10; Chico, CA: Scholars Press, 1985), 137-44.

_____"Status and Role of Female Heroines in the Biblical Narrative," *MQ* 23 (1982), 149-60.

Fuerst, W.J., *The Books of Ruth, Esther, Ecclesiastes, The Song of Songs, Lamentations: The Five Scrolls* (Cambridge: Cambridge University Press, 1975).

Gafni, I.M., *Land, Center and Diaspora: Jewish Constructs in Late Antiquity* (JSPSup 21; Sheffield: Sheffield Academic Press, 1997).

Gardner, A.E., "The Relationship of the Additions to the Book of Esther to the Maccabean Crisis," *JSJ* 15 (1984), 1-8.

Gaster, T.H., "Esther 1:22," *JBL* 69 (1950), 381.

Gehman, H.S., "Notes in the Persian Words in the Book of Esther," *JBL* 43 (1924), 321-28.

Gendler, M., "The Restoration of Vashti," in E. Koltun (ed.), *The Jewish Woman* (New York: Schocken, 1976), 241-47.

Gerleman, G., *Esther* (BKAT XXI; Neukirchen-Vluyn: Neukirchener Verlag, 1982²).

_____"Studien zu Esther: Stoff – Struktur – Stil – Sinn," *BS* 48 (1966), 1-48.

Gevaryahu. H.M.I., "Esther is a Story of Jewish Defense not a Story of Jewish Revenge," *JBQ* 21 (1993), 3-12.

Ginzberg, L., *Legends of the Jews* (7 vols; Philadelphia: Jewish Publication Society of America, 1913-38).

Gitay, Z., "Esther and the Queen's Throne," in A. Brenner (ed.), *A Feminist Companion to Esther, Judith and Susanna* (FCB 7; Sheffield: Sheffield Academic Press, 1995), 136-48.

Goldman, S., "Esther," in A. Cohen (ed.), *The Five Megilloth* (Hindhead: The Soncino Press, 1946), 192-247.

Goldman, S., "Narrative and Ethical Ironies in Esther," *JSOT* 47 (1990), 14-31.

Gooding, D.W., "Problems of Text and Midrash in the Third Book of Reigns," *Textus* 7 (1969), 1-29.

_____"Ahab According to the Septuagint," *ZAW* 76 (1964), 269-80.

Goodnick, B., "The Book of Esther and its Motifs," *JBQ* 25 (1997), 101-107.

Gordis, R., "Religion, Wisdom, and History in the Book of Esther: A New Solution to an Ancient Crux," *JBL* 100 (1981), 359-88.

_____"Studies in the Esther Narrative," *JBL* 95 (1976), 43-58.

_____*Megillat Esther: The Masoretic Hebrew Text with Introduction, New Translation and Commentary* (New York: Rabbinical Assembly, 1974).

Gordon, R.P., "The Second Septuagint Account of Jeroboam: History or Midrash?," *VT* 25 (1975), 368-93.

Grasham, W.W., "The Theology of the Book of Esther," *ResQ* 16 (1973), 99-111.

Greene, W.B., Jr., "The Ethics of the Old Testament," *PTR* 27 (1929), 153-92; 313-66.

Greenstein, E.L., "A Jewish Reading of Esther," in J. Neusner, B.A. Levine and E.S. Frerichs (eds), *Judaic Perspectives on Ancient Israel* (Philadelphia: Fortress Press, 1987), 225-43.

Grossfeld, B., "מוצא חן בעיני – 'Finding Favor in Someone's Eyes': The Treatment of This Biblical Hebrew Idiom in the Ancient Aramaic Versions," in K.J. Cathcart and M. Maher (eds), *Targumic and Cognate Stud-*

ies: Essays in Honour of Martin McNamara (JSOTSup 230; Sheffield: Sheffield Academic Press, 1996), 52-65.

_____*The Two Targums of Esther* (The Aramaic Bible 18; Edinburgh: T & T Clark, 1991).

_____*The First Targum to Esther* (New York: Sepher-Hermon Press, Inc., 1983).

Gundry, R.H., *Matthew: A Commentary on His Handbook for a Mixed Church under Persecution* (Grand Rapids: Eerdmans, 1994²).

Gunkel, H., "Fundamental Problems of Hebrew Literary History," in *What Remains of the Old Testament* (trans. A.K. Dallas; London: Allen & Unwin, 1927), 57-67.

_____*Esther* (Religionsgeschichtliche Volksbücher für die deutsche christliche Gegenwart, II, 19/20; Tübingen: J.C.B. Mohr, 1916).

Gunn, D.M. and D.N. Fewell, *Narrative in the Hebrew Bible* (Oxford: Oxford University Press, 1993).

Gunn, D.M., "Reading Right: Reliable and Omniscient Narrator, Omniscient God, and Foolproof Composition in the Hebrew Bible," in D.J.A. Clines, S.E. Fowl, and S.E. Porter (eds), *The Bible in Three Dimensions* (JSOTSup 87; Sheffield: Sheffield Academic Press, 1990), 53-64.

Gustafson, J., "The Place of Scripture in Christian Ethics: A Methodological Study," *Interpretation* 24 (1970), 430-55.

Hallo, W.W., "The Concept of Canonicity in Cuneiform and Biblical Literature: A Comparative Appraisal," in *idem*, B.F. Batto, and K.L. Younger, Jr., (eds), *The Biblical Canon in Comparative Perspective* (Ancient Near East Texts and Studies, vol. II; Lampeter: The Edwin Mellen Press, 1991), 1-19.

_____"The First Purim," *BA* 46 (1983), 19-26.

Hambrick-Stowe, C.E., "Ruth the New Abraham, Esther the New Moses," *Christian Century* 100 (1983), 1130-34.

Hanhart, R., "The Translation of the Septuagint in Light of Earlier Tradition and Subsequent Influences," in G.J. Brooke and B. Lindars (eds), *Septuagint, Scrolls and Cognate Writings* (SBLSCSS 33; Atlanta: Scholars Press, 1992), 339-79.

Hanhart, R., (ed.), *Esther* (Septuaginta. Vetus Testamentum Graecum Auctoritate Academiae Scientiarum Gottingensis editum, VIII, 3; Göttingen: Vandenhoeck & Ruprecht, 1983²).

Harrelson, W., "Text and Translation Problems in the Book of Esther," *Perspectives in Religious Studies* 17 (1990), 197-208.

Harrington, D.J., *Introduction to the Apocrypha* (Grand Rapids: Eerdmans, 1999).

———"Birth Narratives in Pseudo-Philo's *Biblical Antiquities* and the Gospels," in M.P. Horgan and P.J. Kobelski (eds), *To Touch the Text: Biblical and Related Studies in Honor of Joseph A. Fitzmyer, S.J.* (New York: Crossroad, 1989), 316-24.

Harris, M., "Purim: The Celebration of Dis-Order," *Judaism* 26 (1977), 161-70.

Harrison, R.K., *Introduction to the Old Testament* (Grand Rapids: Eerdmans, 1969).

Haupt, P., "Critical Notes in Esther," *AJSL* 24 (1907-8), 97-186.

Hays, R.B., *The Moral Vision of the New Testament* (Edinburgh: T & T Clark, 1996).

Heinemann, J., "The Nature of Aggadah," (trans. M. Bregman) in G.H. Hartman and S. Budick (eds), *Midrash and Literature* (New Haven and London: Yale University Press, 1986), 41-55.

Hengel, M., *Judaism and Hellenism: Studies in their Encounter in Palestine During the Early Hellenistic Period* (2 vols; Philadelphia: Fortress Press, 1974).

Herodotus, *The Histories* (trans. A. de Sélincourt; London: Penguin Books, 1996).

Herrmann, W., *Esther im Streit der Meinungen* (Beiträge zur Erforschung des AT und des antiken Judentums; Frankfurt am Main: Peter Lang, 1986).

Herst, R.E., "The Purim Connection," *USQR* 28 (1973), 139-45.

Herzfeld, E., *The Persian Empire: Studies in the Geography and Ethnography of the Ancient Near East* (Wiesbaden: Steiner, 1968).

Hetzler, M., "The Book of Esther – Where Does Fiction Start and History End?" *BibRev* 8 (1992), 25-30,41.

Hoffman, Y., "The Deuteronomistic Concept of the Herem," *ZAW* 111 (1999), 196-210.

Horbury, W., "The Name Mardochaeus in a Ptolemaic Inscription," *VT* 41 (1991), 220-26.

Horn, S.H., "Mordecai, a Historical Problem," *BR* 9 (1964), 14-25.

Hoschander, J., *The Book of Esther in the Light of History* (Philadelphia: Dropsie College, 1923).

Huey, F.B., Jr., "Irony as the Key to Understanding Esther," *SJT* 32 (1990), 36-39.

Humphreys, W.L., "Novella," in G.W. Coats (ed.), *Saga, Legend, Tale, Novella, Fable: Narrative Forms in Old Testament Literature* (JSOTSup 35; Sheffield: JSOT Press, 1985), 82-96.

_____ "The Story of Esther and Mordecai: An Early Jewish Novella," in G.W. Coats (ed.), *Saga, Legend, Tale, Novella, Fable: Narrative Forms in Old Testament Literature* (JSOTSup 35; Sheffield: JSOT Press, 1985), 97-113.

_____ "A Life-Style for Diaspora: A Study of the Tales of Esther and Daniel," *JBL* 92 (1973), 211-23.

Hyman, R.T., "Esther 3.3 – The Question with No Response," *JBQ* 22 (1994), 103-109.

_____ "Who is the Villain?," *JBQ* 20 (1992), 153-58.

_____ "Questions and the Book of Ruth," *HS* 24 (1983), 17-24.

Jackowski, K., "Holy Disobedience in Esther," *Theology Today* 45 (1989), 403-14.

Janzen, W., *Old Testament Ethics: A Paradigmatic Approach* (Louisville: Westminster/John Knox, 1994).

Jobes, K.H., *Esther* (NIVAC; Grand Rapids: Zondervan, 1999).

_____ "How an Assassination Changed the Greek Text of Esther," *ZAW* 110 (1998), 75-78.

_____ "The Alpha-Text of Esther: Its Character and Relationship to the Masoretic Text," in B.A. Taylor (ed.), *IX Congress of the International Organization for Septuagint and Cognate Studies* (SBLSCSS 45; Atlanta: Scholars Press, 1997), 369-79.

_____ *The Alpha-Text of Esther: Its Character and Relationship to the Masoretic Text* (SBLDS 153; Atlanta: Scholars Press, 1996).

Jones, B.W., "The So-Called Appendix to the Book of Esther," *Semitics* 6 (1978), 36-43.

_____ "Two Misconceptions about the Book of Esther," *CBQ* 39 (1977), 171-81.

Josephus, F., *The Works of Josephus* (trans. W. Whiston; Peabody, MA: Hendrickson, 1987).

Kaiser, W.C., Jr., *Toward Old Testament Ethics* (Grand Rapids: Zondervan, 1983).

Kasher, A., *The Jews in Hellenistic and Roman Egypt: The Struggle for Equal Rights* (Tübingen: J. C. B. Mohr (Paul Siebeck), 1985).

Kaufmann, Y., *History of the Religion of Israel* (trans. C.W. Efroymson; New York: Ktav, 1977).

_____ *The Religion of Israel: From its Beginnings to the Babylonian Exile* (trans. M. Greenberg; London: Allen & Unwin, 1960).

Keil, C.F., *Biblical Commentary: The Books of Ezra, Nehemiah, and Esther* (trans. S. Taylor; Edinburgh: T & T Clark, 1873).

Kessler, M., "Inclusio in the Hebrew Bible," *Semitics* 6 (1978), 44-49.

Klaassen, M.J., "Persian/Jew/Jew/Persian: Levels of Irony in the Scroll of Esther," *Direction* 25 (1996), 21-28.

Klein, L.R., "Esther's Lot," *Currents in Research* 5 (1997), 111-45.

_____"Honor and Shame in Esther," in A. Brenner (ed.), *A Feminist Companion to Esther, Judith and Susanna* (FCB 7; Sheffield: Sheffield Academic Press, 1995), 149-75.

Klingbeil, G.A., "רכש and Esther 8,10.14: A Semantic Note," *ZAW* 107 (1995), 301-303.

Knierim, R., "Criticism of Literary Features, Form, Tradition, and Redaction," in D.A. Knight and G.M. Tucker (eds), *The Hebrew Bible and its Modern Interpreters* (Chico, CA: Scholars Press, 1985), 123-65.

Knight, D.A., "Moral Values and Literary Traditions: The Case of the Succession Narrative (2 Samuel 9-20; 1 Kings 1-2)," *Semeia* 34 (1985), 7-23.

_____"Old Testament Ethics," *Christian Century* 99/2 (1982), 55-59.

Koßmann, R., *Die Esthernovelle. Vom Erzählten zur Erzählung. Studien zur Traditions- und Redaktionsgeschichte des Estherbuches* (VTSup 79; Leiden: E.J. Brill, 1999).

Kottsieper, I., *Zusätze zu Ester* in O.H. Steck, R.G. Kratz, and *idem*, *Das Buch Baruch, Der Brief des Jeremia, Zusätze zu Ester und Daniel* (ATDA 5; Göttingen: Vandenhoeck & Ruprecht, 1998), 111-207.

Kriel, J.R., "Esther: The story of a girl or the story of her God?" *ThEv* 19 (1986), 2-14.

Kuhrt, A., "The Cyrus Cylinder and Achaemenid Imperial Policy," *JSOT* 25 (1983), 83-97.

Laniak, T.S., *Shame and Honor in the Book of Esther* (SBLDS 165; Atlanta: Scholars Press, 1998).

LaCocque, A., "The Different Versions of Esther," *BibInt* 7 (1999), 301-22.

_____*The Feminine Unconventional: Four Subversive Figures in Israel's Tradition* (Minneapolis: Fortress Press, 1990).

_____"Haman in the Book of Esther," *HAR* 11 (1987), 207-22.

Larkin, K.J.A., *Ruth and Esther* (OTG; Sheffield: Sheffield Academic Press, 1996).

Lasine, S., "Indeterminacy and the Bible: A Review of Literary and Anthropological Theories and Their Application to Biblical Texts," *Hebrew Studies* 27 (1986), 48-80.

LaSor, W.S., D.A. Hubbard, and F.W. Bush, *Old Testament Survey: The Message, Form and Background of the Old Testament* (Grand Rapids: Eerdmans, 1996²).

Lebram, J.C.H., "Purimfest und Estherbuch," *VT* 22 (1972), 208-22.

Leiman, S.Z. (ed.), *The Canonization of Hebrew Scripture: The Talmudic and Midrashic Evidence* (Hamden, CT: Archon, 1976).

_____*The Canon and Masorah of the Hebrew Bible: An Introductory Reader* (The Library of Biblical Studies; New York: Ktav, 1974).

Lerner, B.D., "No Happy Ending for Esther," *JBQ* 29 (2001), 4-12.

Levenson, J.D., *Esther* (OTL; London: SCM Press Ltd., 1997).

_____"Is there a Counterpart in the Hebrew Bible to New Testament Antisemitism?" *JES* 22 (1985), 242-60.

_____"The Scroll of Esther in Ecumenical Perspective," *JES* 13 (1976), 440-52.

Lewy, J., "Old Assyrian puru'um and purum," *RHA* 5 (1939), 117-24.

_____"The Feast of the Fourteenth Day of Adar," *HUCA* 14 (1939), 127-51.

Lightstone, J.N., *Society, the Sacred, and Scripture in Ancient Judaism* (Studies in Christianity and Judaism 3; Waterloo, Ontario: Wilfred Laurier University Press, 1988).

_____"The Formation of the Biblical Canon in Judaism of Late Antiquity: Prolegomena to a General Reassessment," *SR* 8 (1979), 135-42.

Lim, T.H., "Midrash Pesher in the Pauline Letters," in S.E. Porter and C.A. Evans (eds), *The Scrolls and the Scriptures: Qumran Fifty Years After* (JSPSup 26; Sheffield: Sheffield Academic Press, 1997), 280-92.

Linafelt, T., *Ruth*, in *idem* and T.K. Beal, *Ruth and Esther* (Berit Olam; Collegeville, MN: The Liturgical Press, 1999).

Littman, R.J., "Religious Policy of Xerxes and the Book of Esther," *JQR* 65 (1975), 145-55.

Loader, J.A., *Das Buch Ester* in H.-P. Müller, O. Kaiser, and *idem*, *Das Hohe Lied/Klagelieder/Das Buch Ester* (ATD 16.2; Göttingen: Vandenhoeck & Ruprecht, 1992), 199-280.

_____"Esther as a Novel with Different Levels of Meaning," *ZAW* 90 (1978), 417-21.

Loewenstamm, S.E., "Esther 9:29-32: The Genesis of a Late Addition," *HUCA* 42 (1971), 117-24.

Loretz, O., "šʿr hmlk – 'Das Tor des Königs'," *Die Welt des Orients* 4 (1967), 104-108.

Lüderitz, G., "What is the Politeuma?," in J.W. Henten and P.W. van der Horst (eds), *Studies in Early Jewish Epigraphy* (Leiden: E.J. Brill, 1994), 183-225.

Lunt, H.G., and M. Taube, "The Slavonic Book of Esther: Translation from Hebrew or Evidence for a Lost Greek Text?," *HTR* 87 (1994), 347-62.

McBride, W.T., "Esther Passes: Chiasm, Lex Talio, and Money in the Book of Esther," in J.P. Rosenblatt and J.C. Sitterson, Jr. (eds), *"Not in Heaven": Coherence and Complexity in Biblical Narrative* (Bloomington: Indiana University Press, 1991), 211-23.

McCarthy, C., and W. Riley, "The Book of Esther: Banquet Tables are Turned," chapter in *The Old Testament Short Story: Explorations in Narrative Spirituality* (Wilmington: Michael Glazier, 1986), 84-111.

McLay, T., Review of K.H. Jobes, *The Alpha-Text of Esther: Its Character and Relationship to the Masoretic Text* (*JBL* 118 (1999), 724-26).

McConville, J.G., *Ezra, Nehemiah & Esther* (DSB – OT; Edinburgh: The Saint Andrew Press, 1985).

McDonald, L.M., *The Formation of the Christian Biblical Canon* (Peabody, MA: Hendrickson, 1995).

McKane, W., "A Note on Esther IX and I Samuel XV," *JTS* 12 (1961), 260-61.

Magonet, J., "The Liberal and the Lady: Esther Revisited," *Judaism* 29 (1980), 167-76.

Martin, R.A., "Syntax Criticism of the LXX Additions to the Book of Esther," *JBL* 94 (1975), 65-72.

Mattingly, G., "Amalekite," *ABD* (New York: Doubleday, 1992), 1:169-71.

Mayer, R., "Iranischer Beitrag zu Problemen des Daniel und Estherbuchs," in H. Gross and F. Mussner (eds), *Lex Tua Veritas: Festschrift für Hubert Junker* (Trier: Paulinus Verlag, 1961), 127-35.

Meeks, W.A., *The Moral World of the First Christians* (Philadelphia: Westminster Press, 1986).

Meinhold, A., *Das Buch Esther* (ZB 13; Zürich: Theologischer Verlag, 1983).

_____"Zu Aufbau und Mitte des Estherbuchs," *VT* 33 (1983), 435-45.

_____"Theologische Erwägungen zum Buch Esther," *TZ* 34 (1978), 321-33.

_____"Die Gattung der Josephgeschichte und des Estherbuchs: Diasporanovelle," Part I: *ZAW* 87 (1975), 306-24; Part II: *ZAW* 88 (1976), 72-93.

Middleton, J., "Comments on Robert Wilson," in S. Niditch (ed.), *Text and Tradition: The Hebrew Bible and Folklore* (SBLSS; Atlanta: Scholars Press, 1990), 207-13.

Miles, J.R., *Retroversion and Text Criticism: The Predictability of Syntax in an Ancient Translation from Greek to Ethiopic* (SBLSCS 17; Chico, CA: Scholars Press, 1985).

Milik, J.T., "Les Modeles Arameens du Livre D'Esther dans la Grotte 4 de Qumran," *RQ* 15 (1992), 321-99.

Millard, A.R., "In Praise of Ancient Scribes," *BA* 45 (1982), 143-53.

_____"The Persian Names in Esther and the Reliability of the Hebrew Text," *JBL* 96 (1977), 481-88.

Miller, C.H., "Esther's Levels of Meaning," *ZAW* 92 (1980), 145-48.

Mills, M.E., *Biblical Morality: Moral Perspectives in Old Testament Narratives* (HSCPRT; Aldershot/Burlington/Singapore: Ashgate, 2001).

Mitchell, H.G., *The Ethics of the Old Testament* (Chicago: University of Chicago Press, 1912).

Modrzejewski, J.M., *The Jews of Egypt: From Ramses II to Emperor Hadrian* (trans. R. Cornman; Philadelphia: The Jewish Publication Society, 1995).

Moore, C.A., "Esther Revisited: An Examination of Esther Studies over the Past Decade," in A. Kort and S. Morschauser (eds), *Biblical and Related Studies Presented to Samuel Iwry* (Winona Lake, IN: Eisenbrauns, 1985), 163-72.

_____"Esther Revisited Again: A Further Examination of Certain Esther Studies of the Past Ten Years," *HAR* 7 (1983), 169-86.

_____*Daniel, Esther, and Jeremiah: The Additions* (AB 44; Garden City, NY: Doubleday, 1977).

_____"Archaeology and the Book of Esther," *BA* 38 (1975), 62-79.

_____Review of G. Gerleman, *Esther* (*JBL* 94 (1975), 293-96).

_____"On the Origins of the LXX Additions to the Book of Esther," *JBL* 92 (1973), 382-93.

_____*Esther* (AB 7B; Garden City, NY: Doubleday, 1971).

_____"A Greek Witness to a Different Hebrew Text of Esther," *ZAW* 79 (1967), 351-58.

_____"The Greek Text of Esther," (Ph.D. Diss., Johns Hopkins University, 1965).

Moore, C.A., (ed.), *Studies in the Book of Esther* (New York: Ktav, 1982).

Morgan, D.F., *Between Text and Community: The 'Writings' in Canonical Perspective* (Minneapolis: Fortress Press, 1990).

Morgenstern, M., "Ruth *and the Sense of Self: Midrash and Difference*," *Judaism* 48 (1999), 131-45.

Morris, A.E., "The Purpose of the Book of Esther," *ExpT* 42 (1930-31), 124-28.

Mosala, I.J., "The Implications of the Text of Esther for African Women's Struggle for Liberation in South Africa," *Semeia* 59 (1992), 129-37.

Mowinckel, S. *The Old Testament as Word of God* (trans. R.B. Bjornard; Oxford: Basil Blackwell, 1960).

Murphy, R.E., "Esther," in *Wisdom Literature: Job, Proverbs, Ruth, Canticles, and Esther* (FOTL 13; Grand Rapids: Eerdmans, 1983), 151-170.

Naveh, J., and J.C. Greenfield, "Hebrew and Aramaic in the Persian Period," in W.D. Davies and L. Finkelstein (eds), *The Cambridge History of Judaism* (vol. I: Introduction – The Persian Period; Cambridge: Cambridge University Press, 1984), 115-29.

Neher, A., *The Exile of the Word: From the Silence of the Bible to the Silence of Auschwitz* (Philadelphia: The Jewish Publication Society of America, 1981).

Neusner, J., *Esther Rabbah I: An Analytical Translation* (BJS 182; Atlanta: Scholars Press, 1989).

Nickelsburg, G.W.E., "Stories of Biblical and Early Post-Biblical Times," in M.E. Stone (ed.), *Jewish Writings of the Second Temple Period: Apocrypha, Pseudepigrapha, Qumran Sectarian Writings, Philo, Josephus* (CRINT 2.2; Assen/Philadelphia: Van Gorcum/Fortress Press, 1984), 33-87.

_____"The Bible Rewritten and Expanded," in M.E. Stone (ed.), *Jewish Writings of the Second Temple Period: Apocrypha, Pseudepigrapha, Qumran Sectarian Writings, Philo, Josephus* (CRINT 2.2; Assen/Philadelphia: Van Gorcum/Fortress Press, 1984), 89-156.

_____*Jewish Literature between the Bible and the Mishnah* (Philadelphia: Fortress Press, 1981).

Nickelsburg, G.W.E., and M.E. Stone (eds), *Faith and Piety in Early Judaism: Texts and Documents* (Philadelphia: Fortress Press, 1983).

Niditch, S., "Portrayals of Women in the Hebrew Bible," in J.R. Baskin (ed.), *Jewish Women in Historical Perspective* (Detroit: Wayne State University Press, 1998[2]), 25-45.

_____*Underdogs and Tricksters: A Prelude to Biblical Folklore* (San Francisco: Harper & Row, 1987).

_____"Legends of Wise Heroes and Heroines," in D.A. Knight and G.M. Tucker (eds), *The Hebrew Bible and Its Modern Interpreters* (Chico, CA: Scholars Press, 1985), 445-63.

Olmstead, A.T., *The History of the Persian Empire* (Chicago: University of Chicago Press, 1948).

Omanson, R.L., and P.A. Noss (eds), *A handbook on the book of Esther: the Hebrew and Greek texts* (New York: United Bible Societies, 1997).

Oppenheim, A.L., "On Royal Gardens in Mesopotamia," *JNES* 24 (1965) 328-33.

Paton, L.B., *A Critical and Exegetical Commentary on the Book of Esther* (ICC; Edinburgh: T & T Clark, 1908).

Phelen, J., *Reading People, Reading Plots: Character, Progression, and the Interpretation of Narrative* (Chicago: University of Chicago Press, 1989).

Pfeiffer, R.H., *Introduction to the Old Testament* (London: A & C Black, 1952).

Plutarch, *The Lives of the Noble Grecians and Romans* (vol. 2; trans. J. Dryden; New York: The Modern Library, 1992).

Polish, D.F., "Aspects of Esther: A Phenomenological Exploration of the *Megillah* of Esther and the Origins of Purim," *JSOT* 85 (1999), 85-106.

Polzin, R., *Late Biblical Hebrew: Toward an Historic Typology of Biblical Hebrew Prose* (HSM 12; Missoula, MT: Scholars Press, 1976).

Portnoy, M.A., "Ahasuerus Is the Villain," *JBQ* 18 (1990), 187-89.

Porton, G.G, "Haggadah," in *ABD* (New York: Doubleday, 1992), 3:19-20.

Radday, Y.T., "Chiasm in Joshua, Judges and Others," *Linguistica Biblica* 3 (1973), 6-13.

_____ "Esther with Humour," in *idem* and A. Brenner (eds), *On Humour and the Comic in the Hebrew Bible* (JSOTSup 92; Bible and Literature Series 23; Sheffield: Almond Press, 1990), 295-313.

Re'emi, S.P., "The Faithfulness of God: A Commentary on the Book of Esther," in *Israel Among the Nations: A Commentary on the Books of Nahum, Obadiah, Esther* (ITC; Grand Rapids: Eerdmans, 1985), 103-40.

Ringgren, H., *Das Buch Esther* in *idem* and O. Kaiser, *Das Hohe Lied/ Klagelieder/Das Buch Esther* (ATD 16.2; Göttingen: Vandenhoeck & Ruprecht, 1981), 387-421.

_____ "Esther and Purim," *SEÅ* 20 (1955), 5-24.

Rodd, C.S., *Glimpses of a Strange Land: Studies in Old Testament Ethics* (OTS; Edinburgh: T & T Clark, 2001).

_____ "New Occasions Teach New Duties? 1. The Use of the Old Testament in Christian Ethics," *ExpT* 105 (1994), 100-106.

Rodriguez, A.M., *Esther: A Theological Approach* (Berrien Springs, MI: Andrews University Press, 1995).

Rogerson, J.W., "The Old Testament and Social and Moral Questions," *The Modern Churchman* 25 (1982), 28-35.

Rösel, M., Review of K. De Troyer, *Het einde van de Alpha-tekst Ester: Vertaal- en verhaaltechniek van MT 8,1-17, LXX 8,1-17 en AT 7,14-41* (*ZAW* 111 (1999), 319).

Rosenheim, J., "Fate and Freedom in the Scroll of Esther," *Prooftexts* 12 (1992), 125-49.

Rosenthal, L.A., "Nochmals der Vergleich Ester, Joseph, Daniel," *ZAW* 17 (1897), 125-28.

_____"Die Josephgeschichte mit den Büchern Ester und Daniel verglichen," *ZAW* 15 (1895), 278-84.

Rossow, F.C., "Literary Artistry in the Book of Esther and Its Theological Significance," *CJ* 13 (1987), 220-28.

Rudavsky, D.C., "In Defense of Tradition: Haftarat Zachor in the Light of Purim," *Judaism* 47 (1998), 80-87.

Rudolf, W., "Textkritisches zum Estherbuch," *VT* 4 (1954), 89-90.

Rüger, H.P., "Das Tor des Königs" – der königliche Hof," *Biblica* 50 (1969), 247-50.

Sabua, R., "The Hidden Hand of God," *BibRev* 8 (1992), 31-33.

Sæbø, M., "Reflections on Old Testament Ethics: Its Dual Character and its Modern Application," in *On the Way to Canon: Creative Tradition History in the Old Testament* (JSOTSup 191; Sheffield: Sheffield Academic Press, 1998), 162-81.

Salvesen, A., כֶּתֶר (Esther 1.11, 2.17, 6.8): "Something to Do with a Camel?" *JSS* 44 (1999), 35-46.

Sanders, J.A., "Hebrew Bible *and* Old Testament: Textual Criticism in Service of Biblical Studies," in R. Brooks and J.J. Collins (eds), *Hebrew Bible or Old Testament? Studying the Bible in Judaism and Christianity* (CJAS 5; Notre Dame: University of Notre Dame Press, 1990), 41-68.

_____*From Sacred Story to Sacred Text* (Philadelphia: Fortress Press, 1987).

_____*Canon and Community: A Guide to Canonical Criticism* (Philadelphia: Fortress Press, 1984).

_____"Text and Canon: Concepts and Method," *JBL* 98 (1979), 5-29.

_____*Torah and Canon* (Philadelphia: Fortress Press, 1974²).

Sandmel, S., "The Haggada within Scripture," *JBL* 80 (1961), 105-22.

Sasson, J.M., "Esther," in R. Alter and F. Kermode (eds), *The Literary Guide to the Bible* (Cambridge: Harvard University Press, 1987), 335-42.

Schmitt, A., *Wende des Lebens: Untersuchungen zu einem Situations-Motiv der Bibel* (Berlin: Walter de Gruyter, 1996).

Schneider, B., "Esther Revised According to the Maccabees," *Liber Annuus (Studii Biblici Franciscani)* 8 (1962-3), 190-218.

Schürer, E., *The History of the Jewish People in the Age of Jesus Christ (175 B.C-A.D. 135)* (vol. 2; rev. and ed. by G. Vermes, F. Millar and M. Black; Edinburgh: T & T Clark, 1979).

Segal, E., *The Babylonian Esther Midrash – A Critical Commentary* (3 vols; BJS 291-93; Atlanta: Scholars Press, 1994).

_____"Human Anger and Divine Intervention in Esther," *Prooftexts* 9 (1989), 247-56.

Shea, W., "Esther and History," *AUSS* 14 (1976), 227-46.

Shmeruk, C., "Purim-shpil," *EncJud* (Jerusalem: Keter Publishing House, Ltd., 1971), 13:1396-1404.

Silver, D.J., *The Story of Scripture: From Oral Tradition to the Written Word* (New York: Basic Books, 1990).

Smith, J.M.P., *The Moral Life of the Hebrews* (Chicago: University of Chicago Press, 1923).

Stemberger, G., *Introduction to the Talmud and Midrash* (trans. M Bockmuehl; Edinburgh: T & T Clark, 1996^2).

Sternberg, M., *The Poetics of Biblical Narrative: Ideological Literature and the Drama of Reading* (Bloomington: Indiana University Press, 1985).

Stiehl, R., "Das Buch Esther," *WZKM* 53 (1965), 4-22.

Stone, M.E., and D. Satran, *Emerging Judaism: Studies on the Fourth and Third Centuries BCE* (Philadelphia: Fortress Press, 1989).

Streane, A.W., *The Book of Esther* (Cambridge: Cambridge University Press, 1907).

Streidl, H., "Untersuching zur Syntax und Stilistik des hebräischen Buches Esther," *ZAW* 55 (1937), 73-108.

Swete, H.B., *An Introduction to the Old Testament in Greek* (rev. by R.L. Ottley; Cambridge: Cambridge University Press, 1914^2).

Talmon, S., "Was the Book of Esther Known at Qumran?" *DSD* 2 (1995), 249-67.

_____"'Wisdom' in the Book of Esther," *VT* 13 (1963), 419-55.

Thornton, T., "The Crucifixion of Haman and the Scandal of the Cross," *JTS* 37 (1986), 419-26.

Torrey, C.C., "The Older Book of Esther," *HTR* 37 (1944), 1-40.

Tov, E., *The Text-Critical Use of the Septuagint in Biblical Research* (JBS 8; Jerusalem: Simor Ltd., 1997^2).

_____*Textual Criticism of the Hebrew Bible* (Minneapolis: Fortress Press, 1992).

_____"The Septuagint," in M.J. Mulder (ed.), *Mikra: Text, Translation, Reading and Interpretation of the Hebrew Bible in Ancient Judaism and*

Early Christianity (CRINT 2.1; Assen/Philadelphia: Van Gorcum/Fortress Press, 1988), 161-88.

_____"The 'Lucianic' Text of the Canonical and Apocryphal Sections of Esther: A Rewritten Biblical Book," *Textus* 10 (1982), 1-25.

_____"Midrash-type Exegesis in the LXX of Joshua," *RB* 85 (1978), 50-61.

Tsevat, M., "בתולה," *TDOT*, 2:341-43.

Tucker, G.M., "Esther, The Book of," in B.M. Metzger and M.D. Coogan (eds), *The Oxford Companion to the Bible* (New York: Oxford University Press, 1993), 198-201.

Ulrich, E., "Double Literary Editions of Biblical Narratives and Reflections on Determining the Form to be Translated," in J.L. Crenshaw (ed.), *Perspectives on the Hebrew Bible: Essays in Honor of Walter J. Harrelson* (Macon: Mercer University Press, 1988), 101-16.

_____"Jewish, Christian, and Empirical Perspectives on the Text of Our Scriptures," in R. Brooks and J.J. Collins (eds), *Hebrew Bible or Old Testament? Studying the Bible in Judaism and Christianity* (CJAS 5; Notre Dame: University of Notre Dame Press, 1990), 41-68.

Ungnad, A., "Keilinschriftliche Beiträge zum Buch Ezra und Ester," *ZAW* 58 (1940-1), 240-44.

van der Horst, P.W., "The Interpretation of the Bible by the Minor Hellenistic Jewish Authors," in M.J. Mulder (ed.), *Mikra: Text, Translation, Reading and Interpretation of the Hebrew Bible in Ancient Judaism and Early Christianity* (CRINT 2.1; Assen/Philadelphia: Van Gorcum/Fortress Press, 1988), 519-46.

van Uchelen, N.A., "A Chokmatic Theme in the Book of Esther: A Study in the Structure of the Story," in M. Boertien, *et. al.* (eds), *Verkenningen in een Stroomgebied* (Amsterdam: [publisher not given], 1974), 132-40.

van Wijk-Bos, J.W.H., *Ezra, Nehemiah, and Esther* (Louisville: Westminster/John Knox Press, 1998).

Vermes, G., "Bible and Midrash: Early Old Testament Exegesis," in P.R. Ackroyd and C.F. Evans (eds), *The Cambridge History of the Bible* (vol. 1 – From the Beginnings to Jerome; Cambridge: Cambridge University Press, 1970), 199-231.

Vischer, W., *Esther* (TEH 48; Munich: C. Kaiser, 1937).

Wahl, H.M., "Das Motiv des "Aufstiegs" in der Hofgeschichte. Am Beispiel von Joseph, Esther und Daniel," *ZAW* 112 (2000), 59-64.

_____ "'Jahwe, wo bist Du?' Gott, Glaube und Gemeinde in Esther," *Journal for the Study of Judaism in the Persian, Hellenistic and Roman Period* 31 (2000), 1-22.

Walfish, B.D., *Esther in Medieval Garb: Jewish Interpretation of the Book of Esther in the Middle Ages* (Albany: SUNY Press, 1993).

_____ "The Two Commentaries of Abraham Ibn Ezra on the Book of Esther," *JQR* 79 (1989), 323-43.

Watson, W.G.E., "Aramaic Proto-Esther," in *Dead Sea Scrolls Translated: The Qumran Texts in English* (Leiden: E.J. Brill, 1994), 291-92.

Webb, B., "Reading Esther as Holy Scripture," *RTR* 52 (1993), 23-35.

Wechsler, M.G., "The Purim-Passover Connection: A Reflection of Jewish Exegetical Tradition in the Peshitta Book of Esther," *JBL* 117 (1998), 321-27.

_____ "Shadow and Fulfillment in the Book of Esther," *BibSac* 154 (1997), 275-84.

Wehr, H., "Das Tor des Königs in Buche Esther und verwandte Ausdrücke," *Der Islam* 39 (1964), 247-60.

Weisman, Z., *Political Satire in the Bible* (SBLSS 32; Atlanta: Scholars Press, 1998).

Wenham, G.J., *Story as Torah: Reading the Old Testament Ethically* (OTS: Edinburgh: T & T Clark, 2000).

_____ "*bᵉṯûlāh*, 'A Girl of Marriageable Age'," *VT* 22 (1972), 326-48.

Wernberg-Møller, P., Review of Gillis Gerleman, *Esther* (*JSS* 20 (1975), 241-43).

White, S.A., "Esther," in C.A. Newsom and S.H. Ringe (eds), *The Women's Bible Commentary* (London: SPCK; Louisville: Westminster Press/John Knox, 1992), 124-29.

_____ "Esther: A Feminine Model for Jewish Diaspora," in P.L. Day (ed.), *Gender and Difference in Ancient Israel* (Minneapolis: Fortress Press, 1989), 161-77.

White Crawford, S. "Has *Esther* Been Found at Qumran? *4Qproto-Esther* and the *Esther* Corpus," *RQ* 17 (1996), 307-25.

Wiebe, J.M., "Esther 4.14: Will Relief and Deliverance Arise for the Jews from Another Place?," *CBQ* 53 (1991), 409-15.

Williams, M.H., *The Jews Among the Greeks & Romans: A Diaspora Sourcebook* (London: Duckworth, 1998).

Williams, P.J., Review of K. De Troyer, *Het einde van de Alpha-tekst Ester: Vertaal- en verhaaltechniek van MT 8,1-17, LXX 8,1-17 en AT 7,14-41* (*VT* 48 (1998), 566-67).

Williamson, H.G.M., Review of D.J.A. Clines, *The Esther Scroll* (*JTS* 37 (1986), 146-52).

_____*1 and 2 Chronicles* (NCB; London: Marshall, Morgan & Scott, 1982).

Wills, L.M., *The Jewish Novel in the Ancient World* (Ithaca: Cornell University Press, 1995).

_____*The Jew in the Court of the Foreign King: Ancient Jewish Court Legends* (HDR 26; Minneapolis: Fortress Press, 1990).

Wilson, R.R., "Ethics in Conflict: Sociological Aspects of Ancient Israelite Ethics," in S. Niditch (ed.), *Text and Tradition: The Hebrew Bible and Folklore* (SBLSS; Atlanta: Scholars Press, 1990), 193-205.

_____"Approaches to Old Testament Ethics," in G.M. Tucker, D.L. Petersen and R.R. Wilson (eds) *Canon, Theology and Old Testament Interpretation: Essays in Honor of Brevard S. Childs* (Philadelphia: Fortress Press, 1988), 62-74.

Winter, P., "Qumran and the Book of Esther," *The Jewish Chronicle* (No. 4602; July 5, 1957), 16.

Wolff, H.W., *Anthropology of the Old Testament* (Philadelphia: Fortress Press, 1974).

Wolkstein, D., "Esther's Story," in A. Brenner (ed.), *A Feminist Companion to Esther, Judith and Susanna* (FCB 7; Sheffield: Sheffield Academic Press, 1995), 198-206.

Wright, C.J.H., *Deuteronomy* (NIBC; Peabody, MA: Hendrickson, 1996).

_____*Living as the People of God: The Relevance of Old Testament Ethics* (Leicester: IVP, 1983).

_____"The Ethical Authority of the Old Testament: A Survey of Approaches. Part I' *TynB* 43 (1992), 101-20.

_____"The Ethical Authority of the Old Testament: A Survey of Approaches. Part II' *TynB* 43 (1992), 203-31.

_____"Ethical Decision in the Old Testament," *EJT* 1 (1992), 123-40.

Wright, J.S., "The Historicity of the Book of Esther," in J.B. Payne (ed.), *New Perspectives on the Old Testament* (Waco TX: Word Books, 1970), 37-47.

Würthwein, E., *Die Fünf Megilloth* (HAT 18; Tübingen: Mohr/Siebeck, 1969²).

Wyler, B., "Esther: The Incomplete Emancipation of a Queen," in A. Brenner (ed.), *A Feminist Companion to Esther, Judith and Susanna* (FCB 7; Sheffield: Sheffield Academic Press, 1995), 111-35.

Yahuda, A.S., "The Meaning of the Name Esther," *JRAS* (1946), 174-78.

Yamauchi, E.M., "Mordecai, the Persepolis Tablets, and the Susa Excava-
tions," *VT* 42 (1992), 272-75.
_____"The Archaeological Background of Esther," *BibSac* 137 (1980), 99-
117.
Young, E.J., *An Introduction to the Old Testament* (rev. ed.; London: Tyndale
Press, 1960).

Zadok, R., "Notes on Esther," *ZAW* 98 (1986), 105-10.
_____"On the Historical Background of Esther," *BN* 24 (1984), 18-23.
_____*The Jews in Babylonia During the Chaldean and Achaemenian Periods
According to the Babylonian Sources* (Studies in the History of the Jewish
People and the Land of Israel Monograph Series 3; Haifa: University of
Haifa, 1976).
Zeitlin, S., "The Books of Esther and Judith: A Parallel," introduction to M.S.
Enslin, *The Book of Judith* (Dropsie University Jewish Apocryphal Litera-
ture Series VII; Leiden: E.J. Brill, 1972), 1-37.
_____*An Historical Study of the Canonization of the Hebrew Scriptures*
(Philadelphia: The Jewish Publication Society of America, 1933).
Zonana, J., "Feminist Providence: Esther, Vashti, and the Duty of Disobedi-
ence in Nineteenth-Century Hermeneutics," in J.C. Hawley (ed.), *Through
a Glass Darkly: Essays in the Religious Imagination* (New York: Fordham
University Press, 1996), 228-49.

Index of Authors

Index of Authors

Index of Biblical Texts